Funded by a State Legislature Grant
Senator Suzi Oppenheimer

Bloom's Modern Critical Views

Bloom's Modern Critical Views

JAMES JOYCE
New Edition

Edited and with an introduction by
Harold Bloom
Sterling Professor of the Humanities
Yale University

BLOOM'S
LITERARY CRITICISM
An imprint of Infobase Publishing

Bloom's Modern Critical Views: James Joyce, New Edition

Copyright © 2009 by Infobase Publishing

Introduction © 2009 by Harold Bloom

Bloom's Literary Criticism
An imprint of Infobase Publishing
132 West 31st Street
New York NY 10001

Library of Congress Cataloging-in-Publication Data

James Joyce / edited and with an introduction by Harold Bloom. —New ed.
    p. cm. — (Bloom's modern critical views)
  Includes bibliographical references and index.
  ISBN 978-1-60413-396-7
  1. Joyce, James, 1882–1941—Criticism and interpretation. 2. Ireland—In literature.
I. Bloom, Harold. II. Title. III. Series.

  PR6019.O9Z63353 2009
  823'.912—dc22

                          2008041691

Contributing Editor: Pamela Loos
Cover designed by Takeshi Takahashi
Printed in the United States of America
Bang EJB 10 9 8 7 6 5 4 3 2 1

Contents

Editor's Note

My introduction centers on my namesake, the immortal Bloom, hero of *Ulysses*, but dwells also on Joyce's other surrogate, Stephen, the lesser of the two sublimities.

Derek Attridge begins this collection of critical essays by astutely reminding us that all words in imaginative literature share in the dangers that *Finnegans Wake* dares so remorselessly.

A marvelous scholar-critic in the Emersonian tradition, Richard Poirier, accurately distinguishes Joyce and T.S. Eliot in their very different visions of the sublime Walter Pater, a critic whom I love with permanent passion, as did James Joyce but not that ingrate, the abominable Eliot, who owed Pater too much for Anglo-Catholic comfort.

The Portrait of the Artist, in Weldon Thornton's exegesis, is an authentic bildungsroman, with that genre's characteristically benign irony of author toward surrogate-protagonist.

"The Dead," the crown of *Dubliners*, Joyce's superb volume of short stories, is read by David Leon Higdon as a discourse in how women both wound and heal.

Shakespeare, with whom Joyce's agon was perpetual and profound, appears through Klaus Reichert's lens as James Joyce's literary father, his precursor in styles and in the creation of character.

Roy K. Gottfried returns us to the *Portrait*, to confront there something of the essence of Irish humor, after which Margaret McBride sensitively reflects on Joyce's quest for immortality in *Ulysses*.

Heroism's resurrection from Homer to Joyce is the focus of Keri Elizabeth Ames, while Jennifer Margaret Fraser devotes herself to the complex intertextual relation of Dante and Joyce.

Neil Murphy finds the influence of *Dubliners* in the early stories of John Banville, my own favorite among contemporary Irish writers of prose fiction.

The darker side of *Ulysses* is brilliantly related to Joyce's drama, *Exiles*, by Vicki Mahaffey, after which this volume concludes with a deeply informed account of *Finnegans Wake* by Margot Norris.

HAROLD BLOOM

Introduction

The fragmentary *Stephen Hero* can be judged to present a more sympathetic Stephen Daedalus (as it is spelled there) than the Stephen Dedalus of *A Portrait* and *Ulysses*. Young Daedalus has more of Joyce's own humor and more capacity for Paterian aesthetic ecstasy than Dedalus will manifest. And yet critics are accurate in seeing Stephen in *A Portrait* as a considerable advance in representation upon *Stephen Hero*. The protagonist of *A Portrait* is naturalistically persuasive, a considerable improvement upon David Copperfield, Dickens's mixed portrait of the novelist as a young man. When Stephen Dedalus appears again in *Ulysses*, he necessarily loses the naturalistic and symbolist center to Poldy. But then, Leopold Bloom is one of a double handful of novelistic personages who possess something like Shakespearean inwardness and complexity of spirit.

Joyce's scholars, with rare exceptions, undervalue Walter Pater, which seems to me foolish and misleading. Stephen in *A Portrait* is Paterian in the best sense: his epiphanies give evidence of the power of the artist over a universe of death. Harry Levin finds Stephen's gift to be the attachment of "literary associations with sense impressions of the moment," which is to follow Pater's project. Hugh Kenner, the High Modernist critic, savaged Stephen as "indigestably Byronic." I don't wish to argue digestions, but Shelley and Pater are far closer to Stephen than was George Gordon, Lord Byron. An ironic reading of *A Portrait* leaves one in the position of Wallace Stevens's Mrs. Alfred Uruguay, who has wiped away moonlight like mud. Stephen is the positive culmination of Pater's vision of the aesthetic consciousness heroically sustaining itself against the flux of sensations. T. S. Eliot (who disliked

1

Pater) is not the author of *A Portrait of the Artist as a Young Man*, though you could not know this by reading some of Joyce's critics. Derek Attridge, in my view, gets Joyce right when he sees him fundamentally as a great naturalistic writer, with realism outweighing the symbolist component. Yet that is precisely the importance of Walter Pater, as much a master of reality-testing as was Sigmund Freud (who admired Pater). Stephen's epiphanies are borrowed from Pater's privileged moments, which are Hamletian bursts of radiance against the darkening background of entropic death-drive. Stephen's heroism in *A Portrait* is precisely Paterian: we have a moment, and then our place knows us no more. The Gospel of Pater teaches perception and sensation, in the predicate that there is nothing more. What is there, in *Ulysses* and *Finnegans Wake*, that transcends perception and sensation? Eliot and Kenner tried to baptize Joyce's imagination, but that, as William Empson emphasized, is to create a mockery of Joyce's lifelong rejection of Roman Catholicism and its "hangman God."

To read *A Portrait* accurately, you need to accept Stephen as a Paterian hero of consciousness, akin to Oscar Wilde or to Pater's own Sebastian Van Storck in his *Imaginary Portraits*. The artist perceives for us, and expands our sensations because, as Nietzsche observed of Hamlet, he thinks not too much but too well. We possess art, according to Pater as to Nietzsche, lest we perish of the truth. Stephen is heroic in *A Portrait* because he intends to go into exile, lest he die of Irish truth. If, in *Ulysses*, Stephen is less persuasive, it is because he has not yet departed into Joyce's permanent exile.

The advent of the twenty-first century clarifies even more precisely that Proust and Joyce, Kafka and Beckett, were the inescapably narrative writers of the twentieth century, compared to whom even such figures as Mann, Lawrence, and Faulkner are secondary. If you regard Freud as a narrative master, he might rival Joyce and Proust, but he was most himself as a moral essayist, more akin to Montaigne and Emerson. Stephen matters in the way the unnamed "Marcel" matters in Proust's vast saga: these are heroes in search of lost time. Pater was an authority on lost time, as was Freud.

When we encounter Stephen again in *Ulysses*, we are saddened because of the waning of his energy. Joyce seems almost content to lose his earlier self to time, while finding himself again in Poldy's curiosity and humane universalism. *Ulysses* might indeed be called *A Portrait of the Artist as a Middle-aged Man*. Poldy seems to me even more of a triumph of representation than much of our criticism acknowledges. Is there a literary character in his century who is his equal? Proust's consciousness is so vast that his narrator cannot grow into it until the closing pages, but Poldy is altogether there from the start. It is too late to quarrel with Joyce's paradigm of *Ulysses*, but Poldy, though an exile and endlessly shrewd, is never cunning or sly. As Joyce was an admirable personage, so indeed is his Poldy: he is morally and imaginatively superior to everyone else in the book. There is more than a bit of the artist in him: he incarnates not only kindness and goodness, but high art's vision of reality.

So strong and complex is Poldy's personality that Stephen's fades in contrast. Anthony Burgess based his portrait of Shakespeare, in *Nothing Like the Sun*, on both Stephen Dedalus and Leopold Bloom, but more on Bloom, though Burgess's Shakespeare, another lover of peace and abhorrer of violence, exists in a time and place that Poldy could not have sustained. The largest mistake one could make about Poldy is to consider him ordinary. My experience of "ordinary" men and women is that they are likely to be quite ruthless. Poldy is just the opposite: he is a figure of capable compassion, a wise man, who goes forth each day in the Chaucerian realization that constantly he must keep appointments that he never made.

What chance has Stephen to distract the reader's interest from so large, so superb a being? Poldy has Shakespearean comedy in his soul; poor Stephen keeps playing an inadequate performance as Hamlet. *A Portrait* is a beautiful and permanent book, but *Ulysses* belongs to the cosmos of the greatest literary art: Chaucer, Shakespeare, Cervantes, Tolstoy, Proust. We give up Stephen because he has been superseded by Leopold Bloom, who touches one of the limits of art.

DEREK ATTRIDGE

Unpacking the Portmanteau; or, Who's Afraid of Finnegans Wake?

THE PLEASURES OF THE PUN

One aspect of Shakespeare's writing Samuel Johnson, for all his admiration of the dramatist, could not stomach: its use of puns. This blind spot of Johnson's is well known, but it is worth paying attention to the apparently extravagant terms he employs in the famous passage from the Preface to Shakespeare:

> A quibble is to Shakespeare, what luminous vapours are to the traveller; he follows it at all adventures, it is sure to lead him out of his way, and sure to engulf him in the mire. It has some malignant power over his mind, and its fascinations are irresistible. Whatever be the dignity or profundity of his disquisition, whether he be enlarging knowledge or exalting affection, whether he be amusing attention with incidents or enchaining it in suspense, let but a quibble spring up before him, and he leaves his work unfinished. A quibble is the golden apple for which he will always turn aside from his career, or stoop from his elevation. A quibble, poor and barren as it is, gave him such delight, that he was content to purchase it, by the sacrifice of reason, propriety and truth. A quibble was to

From *Peculiar Language: Literature as Difference from the Renaissance to James Joyce.* © 1988, 2004 by Derek Attridge.

him the fatal Cleopatra for which he lost the world, and was
content to lose it. (74)

Though Johnson's grandiose metaphors may seem exaggerated, the attitude
they reflect is not one that the intervening centuries have entirely expunged.[1]
The pun remains an embarrassment to be excluded from "serious" discourse,
a linguistic anomaly to be controlled by relegation to the realms of the
infantile, the jocular, the literary. It survives, tenaciously, as freak or accident,
hindering what is taken to be the primary function of language: the clean
transmission of a preexisting, self-sufficient, unequivocal meaning. It is a
characteristic mode of the dream, the witticism, the slip of the tongue: those
irruptions of the disorderly world of childhood pleasures and unconscious
desires into the clear, linear processes of practical and rational thought, those
challenges to what Johnson precisely articulates as the domain of "reason,
propriety and truth." The pun represents a trick of art, imposing duplicity
and self-consciousness upon the singleness and simplicity of nature.

The pun has this power because it undermines the basis on which our
assumptions about the communicative efficacy of language rest: in Saussure's
terms, that for each signifier there is an inseparable signified, the two
mutually interdependent like two sides of a sheet of paper.[2] To the extent
that a language, natural or artificial, fails to match single signifiers to single
signifieds, it is held to fail as language. The possibility of the pun is a mark of
our fallen condition—our language, it seems, like every other aspect of our
existence, is touched with imperfection. But the possibility of the pun is not,
of course, the pun itself, merely the presence of ambiguity in language. And
linguistic theory has learned to handle ambiguity—indeed, ambiguity plays
a crucial part in the argument for a distinction between deep and surface
structures which is central to transformational-generative syntactic theory.
The same surface structure may have two distinct meanings—"The shooting
of the hunters was terrible," "Visiting relatives can be tedious"—and it
follows that each meaning must be derived from a different "kernel sentence"
or correspond to a different "deep structure." Notice, however, that the same
valorizing assumptions haunt the linguist's various metaphors: the single,
unambiguous meaning is awarded the complimentary adjectives "kernel"
or "deep," whereas ambiguity is associated with the husk, the superficial
outside—duplicitous appearance and not monosemous reality.

In spite of its untoward tendency to polysemy, language works well
enough, we are told, because it always operates in a disambiguating context.
We are able to choose one of several potential meanings for a word or sentence
because we are guided by the immediate verbal surroundings, the nature
of the speech act in which the words are uttered and perceived, the social
and historical setting, and so on. As speakers we construct our sentences in

such a way as to eradicate possible ambiguities, and as hearers we assume single meanings in the sentences we interpret. The pun, however, is not just an ambiguity that has crept into an utterance unawares, to embarrass or amuse before being dismissed; it is ambiguity unashamed of itself, and this characteristic is what makes it more than just an inconvenience. The context of a pun, instead of being designed to suppress latent ambiguity, is deliberately constructed to *enforce* ambiguity, to render impossible the choice between meanings, to leave the reader or hearer endlessly oscillating in semantic space.

Pope's reference to Cambridge University in the Fourth Book of the *Dunciad* furnishes a well-known example for discussion:

> Where Bentley late tempestuous wont to sport
> In troubled waters, but now sleeps in Port. (lines 201–2)

In most of our encounters with the word *port* the context in which it occurs (verbal and pragmatic) suppresses large areas of its potential signification. Pope's achievement in this couplet is to leave unsuppressed two apparently incompatible fields of meaning—*port* as in "harbor" and *port* as in "wine"—by inventing a context in which both are simultaneously acceptable. The noble conception of the tempest-tossed bark at last lying peacefully in harbor is radically undercut by the unseemly image of the great scholar reduced to drunken slumber by nightly overindulgence, and the movement between these two is as inescapable as it is perpetual. Bentley's slumber is thus rendered risible by the use of a trope associated with heroic endeavor. At the same time, however, something of that heroism rubs off on Bentley's adventures with the bottle.

Pope's lines do not release all the meanings associated with the word *port*, of course; there is little likelihood of a reader bringing into play the idea of "external deportment, carriage, or bearing" or "the left-hand side of a ship." The semantic movement initiated by Pope's couplet, though never-ending, is strictly controlled: the angel of reason dancing on a pun. If we should encounter the word *port* in a severely impoverished context—it appears on a scrap pushed under the door, for instance, or is uttered in an otherwise silent dream—the range of meaning widens, and the pleasure we take in the word's ambiguity disappears. No longer is language's potential for semantic expansion hinted at but simultaneously kept at bay; it has become threatening and confusing. Remove even more of the context, and the expansion accelerates rapidly—imagine the word being encountered by someone who knows no English, or no Indo-European language, or no human language. Eventually its meaning becomes infinite and, at exactly the same moment, disappears.

It is not surprising, therefore, that the pun is marginalized in our most common uses of language. Outside the licensed domains of literature and jokes, and the uncontrollable manifestations of parapraxes and dreams, the possibilities of meaning in any given use of a word are stringently limited by context. The more that context bears down upon the word, the less the word will quiver with signification, until we reach a fully determining context under whose pressure the word will lie inert, pinned down, proffering its single meaning. But at this point something else will have happened: the word will have become completely redundant. The context will now allow only one meaning to be perceived in the gap that it occupies, and anything—or nothing at all—can be interpreted as providing that meaning. In the terms of information theory, the more predictable is a given item in a message, the less information it carries, and so the totally predictable word conveys, in itself, absolutely nothing. What we have, then, is a continuum from the totally powerless item, devoid of meaning because already completely specified by its surroundings, to the infinitely powerful item, devoid of meaning because completely *un*specified. Meaning resides between the two. What we call the pun is one stage along the way, what we call "single meaning" is another.[3] Exclude the pun, and you exclude the process on which all language rests, the process whereby context constrains but does not wholly constrain the possibilities of meaning.

We can approach the pun from another direction, from which we can again see it as a phenomenon that is part and parcel of the normal procedures of language. The semantic fields of *port* in the sense of wine and of *port* in the sense of harbor have no evident synchronic connection. One's understanding of each normally remains uncolored by one's understanding of the other, because of the constraining effect of context already discussed. The two words usually function quite differently, and it is an arbitrary quirk of the specific language system of English which associates them at all. Yet what Pope has done is to invent a context in which that arbitrary link comes to seem motivated: taking the language as he finds it, he has succeeded in shifting the world into a pattern in which harbors and wine are superimposed. The material envelope of the sign—its phonemes and graphemes—has been allowed to take the initiative and has brought about a coalescence of otherwise distinct fields of reference. This dominance of the signifier, of course, goes against all the rules. Phonemes and graphemes should be servants, not masters, and the mere coincidence of outward similarity should have no bearing on the meanings within. If this were not the case, language would never get off the ground—we would expect all words beginning with the same letter to be semantically related, for instance, or assume that historical or dialectal changes in pronunciation must entail changes in meaning.

The insubordination revealed by the pun is, of course, a feature of all poetic language. The independence of meaning from its material representation required by the linguistic system is challenged by *every* use in poetry of sound or appearance to make connections or to establish contrasts—every effect of rhyme, rhythm, visual patterning, alliteration, or assonance—and the pun is only a particularly extreme case of such articulation at the level of the signifier, relying as it does on *complete* coincidence of sound between two words. Once we generalize the pun in this way, we realize that its mode of operation is not, in the end, peculiar to poetry. For if other manifestations of language completely excluded this mode of establishing relationships of meaning, the only linguistic connections and contrasts with any significance would be those already given (but how?) by extralinguistic reality. Meanings would have to relate to meanings by their own nature, and signifiers would be left to form innocent patterns, mere diagrams of froth on the surface of a profound and unplumbable sea. Such a theory not only disqualifies the characteristic mode of poetry, of popular wisdom and humor, of any discourse that uses the verbal schemes of rhetoric (and what discourse does not?); it also ignores the perfectly normal syntactic and morphemic function of patterning at the level of the signifier. It is not mere chance that there is a similarity of sound between "books" and "cats" or between "looked" and "hoped," and the oppositions single/plural and present/past are not experiential givens that preexist the linguistic patterns which produce them. More generally, to the extent that language is held to affect or determine the subject's perception and categorization of the world, patterning in the signifier must have semantic force, because language has no medium in which to operate other than the patterns of sonic and visual substance. Clearly, there *is* meaning in the coincidences of the signifier, and an absolute separation between the functions of signifier and signified is impossible.[4] Once again the pun turns out to be not an aberration of language but a direct reflection of its "normal" working.

I have suggested two approaches to the pun, both of which reveal it as a product of language's necessary mode of operation: as one signifier with two possible signifieds, which in a particular context are simultaneously activated, and as two identical signifiers, which in a particular context are made to coalesce. Each approach associates the pun with a feature especially characteristic of literary language. The first is polysemy, the second the semantic use of purely formal similarities, and the pun combines these features in a way that heightens the power of both. But it does so at some cost. The effect has to be created by a carefully constructed linguistic envelope (Pope needs fourteen words to prepare us for a bisemous reading of *port*), and it is limited to exact correspondence of sound. Other kinds of polysemy (a word with one primary meaning and several secondary associations, for example) and other kinds of assonance (rhyme, alliteration, etc.) are much more readily available in the language and need no such elaborate scaffolding in order to work. By the same token, however, they are much weaker: the reader can more easily ignore or subdue them, dismissing secondary associations as "irrelevant" or allowing rhyme words to lie side by side without mutual interference, as if chastely separated by a chivalric sword.

Banished from utilitarian discourse, then, the pun finds a home in the literary tradition as long as it is well-behaved, limiting its field of operation in terms of genres (preferably nonserious writing), frequency (punning too often is a sign of immaturity), and the range of its multiple meanings (preferably only two, both clearly defined by the context). But what if there were a way of combining the power of the pun with the ready availability of those weaker effects of polysemy and patterning, of bringing into the foreground those otherwise dismissable associations, and of coupling together in a simultaneous experience those meanings which lie separate in such verbal echoes as rhyme and assonance? And what if the operation of this device could be signaled independently of context and in a completely inescapable way? If this fusion were to be achieved, the processes of exclusion which operate already on the pun would be put into action with redoubled energy, because the new device would expose even more thoroughly the myths of a monosemous language and a preexisting structure of meaning, and it would put even more strongly in question the belief in language's transparency, stability, and rationality. The spirit of Dr. Johnson would prove to be still very much alive, and the new device, together with the text and author employing it, would meet with the same hostility that in the eighteenth century greeted Shakespeare's use of puns. Johnson's denunciation needs very little rewriting to bring it up to date: "A portmanteau word, poor and barren as it is, gave Joyce such delight that he was content to purchase it by the sacrifice of reason, propriety and truth. A portmanteau word was to him the fatal Issy for which he lost the world, and was content to lose it."

THE POWER OF THE PORTMANTEAU

Published responses to *Finnegans Wake* afford examples of this hostility in profusion. That the last major work of one of the language's most admired and influential writers—the product of some sixteen painful years' labor— has remained on the margins of the literary tradition is an extraordinary but well-established fact. That the phenomenon is so evident does not mean that it requires no explanation; on the contrary, if we could properly account for it, we might throw light on the processes of reading and evaluation which determine the shape of the literary canon. Those who find little appeal in Joyce's earlier writing are unlikely to have a good word to say for the *Wake*, but what is more remarkable is that many of those who have written admirably about Joyce's other works testify to difficulties with his last book. Sometimes, as a result, an introductory text that one might expect to offer encouragement to the new reader in tackling Joyce's most ambitious work can have the opposite effect. Thus John Gross asks, in his volume on Joyce in the widely selling Modern Masters series, "What was Joyce's object in devising so outlandish a style?—always assuming, that is, that the entire book isn't best regarded as a hoax?" And he sums up his position as follows: "In the end the *Wake* seems to me a dazzling failure, the aberration of a great man. Viewed as a whole, I don't believe it is nearly worth the effort which it demands" (*Joyce*, 79, 89). S.L. Goldberg says of *Finnegans Wake* in another introductory book on Joyce's entire output: "The work itself seems to me an artistic failure; and despite the enthusiastic assertions of its admirers, the questions it prompts the ordinary reader to ask remain, I believe, still the most important—questions concerned less with its verbal "meaning" or its machinery than with its value: why Joyce ever undertook it, why it seems so laborious and, more particularly, so unrewarding to read through" (*Joyce*, 103).[5] And A. Walton Litz, in his study *The Art of James Joyce*, comments that "at one and the same time the *Wake* is too abstract and too concrete. Paradoxically, it displays a detailed point-by-point fidelity to Joyce's early experiences without reflecting—as do *Portrait* and *Ulysses*—a full sense of the reality of those experiences. The result is an infinitely rich texture combined with a tedium of basic thought. That sense of 'felt life' which Henry James considered the essence of literary form infuses Joyce's artifice by fits and starts" (124). Litz goes on to use the same word as the other two critics, referring to "this failure I find in the *Wake*." Yet it is clear from his valuable discussion of Joyce's writing of the *Wake* that Litz's reservations do not arise from any lack of sympathy, sensitivity, or effort; he seems almost unwilling to reach the conclusion he feels he has to. In his later introductory book on Joyce one hears the same tone:

> I have spoken earlier of the triumphs and limitations of *Finnegans Wake*, which force me to conclude that it is a partial failure. Any set of standards that will account for the essential greatness of *Ulysses* must, I feel, find a certain sterility in *Finnegans Wake*. Even the comic spirit which, much more than the elaborate structural patterns, gives the *Wake* its unity, seems to me ultimately self-defeating. In *Ulysses*, parody and satire have direction because they serve a moral vision; but in *Finnegans Wake* they turn upon themselves and destroy their own foundations. (*James Joyce*, 118)

The many readers who find the *Wake* a source of great pleasure, the many teachers and students who find it a delight to discuss in a small class (once initial prejudices are overcome), will regret that comments like these, sincere though they are, put obstacles in the way of others who might find in the work pleasures similar to their own. But our present task is to ask what about Joyce's last book is so resistant to the efforts of many well-disposed and well-qualified readers to find enjoyment in it. There can be no doubt that a major reason for this negative reaction is the work's intensive use of the portmanteau word, which is what makes the style "outlandish," demands "effort" from the reader, renders the work "laborious" and "unrewarding," inhibits the communication of "felt life." The portmanteau word is a monster, a word that is not a word, that is not authorized by any dictionary, that holds out the worrying prospect of books which, instead of comfortingly recycling the words we know, possess the freedom endlessly to invent new ones. We have learned to accept novels without firm plots or consistent characters, novels that blend historical periods or submerge the authorial presence, even novels that pun and rhyme; but sixty years after it first started appearing, the novel—if it can still be called a novel—that makes the portmanteau word a cornerstone of its method remains a troublesome presence in the institution of literature.[6]

My argument so far suggests an explanation that goes beyond discomfort with the unusual and dislike of the difficult, understandable though these reactions are. The portmanteau word challenges two myths on which most assumptions about the efficacy of language rest. Like the pun, it denies that single words must have, on any given occasion, single meanings; and like the various devices of assonance and rhyme, it denies that the manifold patterns of similarity which occur at the level of the signifier are innocent of meaning. It does so with the pun's simultaneity of operation but more flagrantly and with less warning. There is no escape from its insistence that meaning is an *effect* of language, not a presence within or behind it, and that the effect is unstable and uncontrollable. Notice, too, that whereas the pun can easily be contained by being treated as the index of an imperfect language, allowing ambiguity where it should insist on univocity, the conclusion is harder to escape that the portmanteau can be nothing other than a defining feature of language itself, because the portmanteau derives from the fact that the same segments (letters, phonemes, syllables) can be combined in different ways to encode different meanings. A language in which portmanteau formations were impossible would be a language in which every signified was matched with a unique and unanalyzable signifier—that is, not a language at all.[7]

Not surprisingly, therefore, the portmanteau word has had a history of exclusion much more severe than that of the pun. Outside the language of dreams, parapraxes, and jokes, it has existed chiefly in the form of malapropism and nonsense verse—the language of the uneducated, the child, the idiot. (The very term "portmanteau word" comes from a children's story, *Alice Through the Looking-Glass*, and not a work of theory or criticism.)[8] And the literary establishment has often relegated *Finnegans Wake* to the same border area. How else can it avoid the claim made by the text that the portmanteau word, far from being a sport, an eccentricity, a mistake, is a revelation of the processes upon which all language relies? How else can it exclude the possibility that the same relation obtains between *Finnegans Wake* and the tradition of the novel, that what appears to be a limiting case or a parody, a parasite on the healthy body of literature, is at the same time central and implicated in the way the most "normal" text operates? It is the familiar logic of the Derridean supplement or *pharmakon* I have already discussed in relation to Puttenham's writing: the "artifice" to be excluded from the category of "natural" literature (with its "felt life" and "full sense of reality") which nevertheless reveals the artificial character of literature itself.[9] In the *Wake*'s deconstruction of the oppositional structures of the literary tradition, the portmanteau word proves to be a powerful tool, but its very power has rendered it ineffective. (This is not, of course, to argue that those who find the *Wake* hard going are party to a conspiracy dedicated to the preservation of a metaphysical conception of language; we can never be fully conscious of the reasons for our preferences, and to attempt to explain the acceptance or rejection of a literary text is not to award praise or lay blame.)

To demonstrate the operation of the portmanteau and to explore the reasons why, for all their superficial similarity, the portmanteau and the pun are very different kinds of linguistic deviation, a specific example is needed. The following passage was chosen at random, and the points I make about it could be made about any page of *Finnegans Wake*.

> And stand up tall! Straight. I want to see you looking fine for me. With your brandnew big green belt and all. Blooming in the very lotust and second to nill, Budd! When you're in the buckly shuit Rosensharonals near did for you. Fiftyseven and three, cosh, with the bulge. Proudpurse Alby with his pooraroon Eireen, they'll. Pride, comfytousness, enevy! You make me think of a wonderdecker I once. Or somebalt that sailder, the man megallant, with the bangled ears. Or an earl was he, at Lucan? Or, no, it's the Iren duke's I mean. Or somebrey erse from the Dark Countries. Come and let us! We always said we'd. And go abroad. (620.1)[10]

At the risk of seeming to posit the very things I have said the text undermines—themes, plot, characters—let me tender a bald and provisional statement of some of the threads that can be traced through the passage, in order to establish an initial orientation. The predominant "voice" in this part of the text—its closing pages—is what Joyce designated by △, the shifting cluster of attributes and energies often associated with the initials ALP and the role of wife and mother. The addressee is primarily the group of characteristics indicated by ⊓, the male counterpart frequently manifested as the letters HCE. Two of the prominent narrative strands involving this couple in the closing pages are a walk around Dublin in the early morning and a sexual act, and both are fused with the movement of the river Liffey flowing through Dublin into the sea. Contradictory tones and modes of address are blended, in particular the eager admiration of a young girl for her energetic lover and the disappointment of the aging wife with her now impotent husband. Here ALP is asking HCE to don his new, expensive clothes and go out with her on a jaunt, but she is also inviting him to demonstrate his naked sexual potency. (At first, the words are also those of a mother to her young son; they echo, too, a letter of Joyce's to Nora on 7 September 1909: "I want you to look your best for me when I come. Have you any nice clothes now?" [*Letters*, 2:251].) At the same time what we hear is the river addressing the city of Dublin (reversed in "nill, Rudd"), with its green belt and modern comforts. The relationship is also reminiscent of that between Molly and Leopold Bloom in *Ulysses*. "Blooming in the very lotust" points to the earlier novel, especially the "Lotus-Eaters" chapter; Sinbad the Sailor ("somebalt that sailder") is also associated with Bloom as he goes to bed in "Ithaca"; and Molly's own closing chapter has something in common with ALP's final monologue. It includes, too, the exploitative relationship of England and Ireland ("Proudpurse Alby with his pooraroon Eireen": perfidious Albion and poor Eire or Erin). The passage enunciates a series of ALP's sexual memories, all of which turn out to be memories of HCE in one or other of his guises: as sailor (Sinbad, Magellan, and Vanderdecken, the captain of the *Flying Dutchman*); as military figure (the man with the bandolier, the duke of Wellington, and the earl of Lucan—whether the hero of the Williamite wars or the Lord Lucan who fought at Balaclava); and as the stranger (the man with earrings, the man from the Dark Countries) who is also an Irishman (not only Wellington but Lucan as a village on the Liffey, "Iren" as Ireland, and "erse" as Irish). That the exploits of these figures are partly sexual (or excretory, for the two are not kept distinct in the *Wake*) emerges from the "gallant" of "megallant," "erse" understood as "arse," and another echo of *Ulysses*, this time of Bloom's pamphlet advertising the "Wonderworker," "the world's greatest remedy for rectal complaints" (17.1820).[11] Once phallic suggestions begin to surface, they can be discovered at every turn: a few examples would be "stand up," "straight," "I want to see you" (an instance of the familiar synecdoche discussed in the previous chapter), *bod* (pronounced *bud*) as Gaelic for "penis," "cosh" (a thick stick), "bulge," the "wonderdecker" again (*decken* in German is to copulate), the stiffness of iron, and the Wellington monument. And the evident ellipses (reminiscent of those in the "Eumaeus" episode of *Ulysses*) can easily be read as sexual modesty: "a wonderdecker I once . . . ," "the Iren Duke's . . . ," "Come and let us . . . ," "We always said we'd. . . ." I have provided only an initial indication of some of the meanings at work here, and one could follow other motifs through the passage: flowers, sins (several of the seven deadly ones are here), tailoring and sailing (the two often go together in the *Wake*), and battles. All of these are associated in one way or another with sex.[12]

Let us focus now on one word from the passage, "shuit." To call it a word is of course misleading—it is precisely because it is *not* a word recognized as belonging to the English language that it functions as it does, preventing the immediate move from material signifier to conceptual signified. Unlike the pun, which exists only if the context brings it into being, the portmanteau refuses, *by itself*, any single meaning, and in reading we therefore have to nudge it toward other signifiers whose meanings might prove appropriate. Let us, first of all, ignore the larger context of the whole book and concentrate—as we would for a pun—on the guidance provided by the immediate context. We seem to be invited to take "shuit" as an item of clothing, one that can have the adjective "buckly"—with buckles—applied to it. Three lexical items offer themselves as appropriate: *suit, shirt, shoes.* The first two would account for the portmanteau without any unexplained residue, but "buckly" seems to point in particular to *shoes*, partly by way of the nursery rhyme "One, two, buckle my shoe." A writer employing orthodox devices of patterning at the level of the signifier might construct a sentence in which the separate words *suit, shirt,* and *shoes* all occur in such a way as to make the reader conscious of the sound-connections between them, thus creating what I called earlier a nonce-constellation, but it would be a rather feeble, easily ignored, device. "Shuit" works more powerfully because it insists on a productive act of reading, because its effects are simultaneous, and because the result is an expansion of meaning much more extensive than that effected by the pun. The pun, as we saw in the example by Pope, carries a powerful charge of satisfaction: the specter of a potentially unruly and ultimately infinite language is raised only to be exorcised, the writer and reader are still firmly in control, and the language has been made to seem even *more* orderly and appropriate than we had realized, because an apparently arbitrary coincidence in its system has been shown to be capable of semantic justification. But "shuit" and its kind are more disturbing. The portmanteau has the effect of a *failed* pun—the patterns of language have been shown to be partially appropriate but with a residue of difference where the pun found only happy similarity. And though the context makes it clear that the passage is about clothing and thereby seems to set limits to the word's possible meanings, one cannot escape the feeling that the process, once started, may be unstoppable. In the case of Pope's couplet the dictionary (or our internal lexicon) tells us the accredited meanings of "port," and we can acknowledge at once that the context excludes all those meanings besides "harbor" and "wine." But no reference book or mental register exists to tell us all the possible signifiers that are or could be associated in sound with "shuit," and we have learned no method of interpretation to tell us how to go about finding those signifiers or deciding at what point the connection becomes too slight to be relevant. Certainly other signifiers sound like "shuit," and if similarities of sound can have semantic implications, how do we know where to draw the boundary?

The answer to this question may seem straightforward: like the pun, the portmanteau will contain as much as the verbal context permits it to contain and no more. But the answer brings us to a fundamental point about the *Wake*, because the context *itself* is made up of puns and portmanteaux. So far I have spoken as if the context were a given, firm structure of meaning which has one neatly defined hole in it, but this notion is of course pure interpretative fiction. The text is a web of shifting meanings, and every new interpretation of one item recreates afresh the context for all the other items. Having found *suit* in "shuit," for example, one can reinterpret the previous word to yield the phrase *birthday suit*, as a colloquial expression for "nakedness," nicely epitomizing the fusion of the states of being clothed and unclothed which the passage implies—one more example of the denial of the logic of opposites which starts to characterize this text with its very title. Thus a "contextual circle" is created whereby plurality of meaning in one item increases the available meanings of other items, which in turn increase the possibilities of meaning in the original item. The longer and denser the text, the more often the circle will revolve, and the greater will be the proliferation of meanings. It is important to note, however, that the network of signification remains *systematic*: the familiar accusation that "there is no way of denying the relevance . . . of any meaning any commentator cares to find," to quote Goldberg again (*Joyce*, 111), is without substance. In a text as long and as densely worked as *Finnegans Wake*, however, the systematic networks of meaning could probably provide contexts for most of the associations that individual words might evoke—though an individual reader could not be expected to grasp them all. This sense of a spiraling increase in potential meaning is one of the grounds on which the *Wake* is left unread, but is this not an indication of the way *all* texts operate? Every item in a text functions simultaneously as a sign whose meaning is limited (but not wholly limited) by its context and as a context limiting (but not wholly limiting) the meaning of other signs. There is no escape from this circle, no privileged item that yields its meaning apart from the system in which it is perceived and which can act as a contextless context or transcendental fixing-point to anchor the whole text. The enormous difference between *Finnegans Wake* and other literary works is, perhaps, a difference in degree, not in kind.

The next word, "Rosensharonals," provides another example of the operation of contexts in the *Wake*. As an individual item it immediately suggests "Rose of Sharon," a flower (identified with crocus, narcissus, and others) to go with bloom, lotus, and bud and to enhance further the springlike vitality of the male or his sexual organ. It gives us a reference to the Song of Solomon (itself a sexual invitation), reinforcing the text's insistence that apparently "natural" human emotions are cultural products: love and sexual desire in this passage are caught up not only with the Hebraic tradition but also with Buddhism (both in the lotus and in "Budd"), with *Billy Budd* (a story whose concerns are highly relevant), with *Sinbad the Sailor* (as a tale from the *Arabian Nights* or as a pantomime), and with popular songs (*Eileen Aroon*—"Eileen my darling"—and phrases from "I will give you the keys to heaven"). (I suspect there may also be a song called "The Man with the Bandolier," though I have not been able to trace it; in fact the text problematizes that very urge to "verify" what offers itself as an "allusion.")[13] The sense of new beginnings is also heightened by a suggestion of Rosh Hashanah, the Jewish New Year. In the context of clothing, however, the name sounds more like that of the Jewish tailor who made the garment in question: "the buckly shuit Rosensharonals near did for you," bringing to mind the story of Kersse the tailor and the Norwegian captain from earlier in the book (311–32), a story that involves a suit with a bulge in it, apparently made necessary by a hunchback. But once we move to the context of the whole work, another story, from the same earlier chapter (337–55), comes into prominence: the tale of Buckley and the Russian general, which appears in the text at many points and in many guises. Buckley is a common Irish soldier in the Crimean War who comes upon a Russian general with his pants down, in the act of defecating, and either does or does not shoot at him. The story interweaves with other stories of encounters involving exposure and/or voyeurism, such as the much-discussed event in Phoenix Park involving HCE, two girls, and three soldiers. It has to do with the attack by the younger generation on the older, and the older generation's fall from power before the younger, the drunkenness of Noah and the drugging of Finn MacCool by his young bride being other versions. (It is typical of the *Wake's* method that an indecent anecdote which Joyce heard from his father is accorded the same status as religious myth and epic narrative.) So in the middle of a passage of praise for the virility of HCE comes a reminder of his loss of control, and "near did for you" becomes a reference not to tailoring but to an attempt at, or a resisted temptation to, murder. And our portmanteau *shuit* unpacks itself further, yielding both *shoot* and *shit*.[14]

PARIAH AND PARADIGM

My aim is not to demonstrate the plurality of meaning in Joyce's portmanteaux; that is easily done. It is to focus on the workings of a typical portmanteau to show both how crucial they are to the method of *Finnegans Wake* and how they help make the book conceivable as a central, rather than a peripheral, literary text. The portmanteau shatters any illusion that the systems of difference in language are fixed and sharply drawn, reminding us that signifiers are perpetually dissolving into one another: in the never-ending diachronic development of language; in the blurred edges between languages, dialects, registers, idiolects; in the interchange between speech and writing; in errors and misunderstandings, unfortunate or fruitful; in riddles, jokes, games, and dreams. *Finnegans Wake* insists that the strict boundaries and discrete elements in a linguist's "grammar of competence" are a neoplatonic illusion.

But the portmanteau problematizes even the most stable signifier by showing how its relations to other signifiers can be productive; we find that we can quite easily relate *suit* to *shirt* just as we do in fact relate *suit* to *suits* or *suited*. Instead of saying that in learning a language we learn to ascribe meaning to a few of the many patterns of sound we perceive, it may be as true to say that we learn *not* to ascribe meaning to most of those connections (Freud takes this view in his book on jokes)[15]—until we are allowed to do so again to a certain degree in rhetoric and poetry, and with almost complete abandon in *Finnegans Wake*. The result, of course, is that as we read the *Wake* we test for their possible associations not only the obvious portmanteaux but every apparently normal word as well. The phrase "bangled ears" does not present itself as a portmanteau, and in most texts it would be read as a somewhat odd, but semantically specific, conjunction of adjective and noun. But the context of the *Wake*'s portmanteau style encourages us, as I have suggested, to hear it also as "bandolier," to combine the attributes of the savage or stranger with those of the soldier. Even the most normal and innocent word will invite such treatment. As Jean-Paul Martin has said of *Finnegans Wake*, "the portmanteau word, but also every word, every fragment of a word or of an utterance, marks the interlacing of sinuous and diverse chains of associations which cross codes and languages" ("La condensation," 189). Another theoretical distinction becomes blurred, that between synchronic and diachronic dimensions, because a pertinent meaning may be retrievable from the history of a word. "Erse," for instance, offers both a Middle English word for "arse" and an early Scottish word for "Irish." Here, too, the *Wake* heightens a process that operates in all language, in spite of the Saussurean enterprise of methodically separating synchrony and diachrony.

The implications of the portmanteau word, or rather the portmanteau text, go further, however. The portmanteau undermines the notion of authorial intention, for instance, in a way quite foreign to the traditional pun. The pun in fact strengthens the illusion of intention as a presence within the text: part of the satisfaction to be found in Pope's pun on *port* is the feeling of certainty, once the pun is grasped, that it was intended by its witty and resourceful author. The careful construction of context to allow both meanings equal force and to exclude all other meanings is not something that happens by accident, we feel, and this feeling makes the pun acceptable in certain literary environments because there is no danger that the coincidence thus exposed will enable language to wrest control from its users. But the portmanteau word, though its initial effect is often similar, has a habit of refusing to rest with that comforting sensation of "I see what the author meant." To find *shirt* and *suit* in *shuit*, and nothing else, might yield a satisfying response of that kind: "clearly what Joyce is doing is fusing those words into one," we say to ourselves. But when we note the claims for *shoes*, *shoot*, and *shit* as well, we begin to lose hold on our sense of an embodied intention. If those five are to be found, why not more? The polyglot character of the text, for instance, opens up further prospects. If French ears hear *chute*, one can hardly deny the relevance of the notion of a fall (or of the Fall) to the story of Buckley and the Russian general or to the temptation of HCE in the park.[16] And why should any particular number of associations, in any particular number of languages, correspond to the author's intention? Joyce has set in motion a process over which he has no final control—a source of disquiet for many readers. Litz, for example, complains that "in reading it one does not feel that sense of 'inevitability' or 'rightness' which is the sign of a controlled narrative structure" (*The Art of James Joyce*, 62). Others are more willing to accept the vast scale of what the multilingual portmanteau opens up. In "Finnegans, Wake!" Jean Paris observes that "once it is established, it must by its own movement extend itself to the totality of living and dead languages. And here indeed is the irony of the portmanteau style: the enthroning of a principle of chance which, prolonging the intentions of the author, in so far as they are perceptible, comes little by little to substitute for them, to function like a delirious mechanism, accumulating allusions, parodying analogies, and finally atomizing the Book" (60–61).[17] But *every* text, not just this one, is ultimately beyond the control of its author, *every* text reveals the systems of meaning of which Derrida speaks in his consideration of the word *pharmakon* in Plato's *Phaedrus*: "But the system here is not, simply, that of the intentions of an author who goes by the name of Plato.

The system is not primarily that of what someone *meant-to-say* [*un vouloir-dire*]. Finely regulated communications are established, through the play of language, among diverse functions of the word and within it, among diverse strata or regions of culture" (*Dissemination*, 95).

Similarly, the portmanteau word leaves few of the conventional assumptions about narrative intact: *récit* cannot be separated from *histoire* when it surfaces in the texture of the words themselves. When, for instance, the story of Buckley and the Russian general is woven, by the portmanteau method, into a statement about new clothing, it is impossible to talk in terms of the narration of a supposedly prior event. Rather, there is a process of fusion which enforces the realization that *all* stories are textual effects. Characters, too, are never *behind* the text in *Finnegans Wake* but *in* it; ALP, HCE, Buckley, and the Russian general have their being in portmanteau words, in acrostics, in shapes on the page—though this, too, is only a reinforcement of the status of all fictional characters. Finally, consider the traditional analysis of metaphor and allegory as a relation between a "literal," "superficial" meaning and a "figurative," "deep," "true" meaning. The portmanteau word, and *Finnegans Wake* as a whole, refuses to establish such a hierarchical opposition, for anything that appears to be a metaphor is capable of reversal, the tenor becoming the vehicle, and vice versa. In the quoted passage we might be tempted to say that a literal invitation to go for a walk can be metaphorically interpreted as an invitation to sexual activity. At the level of the word one might say that "lotust" is read literally as *latest*, a reference to fashion, but that the deeper meaning is *lotus*, with its implication of sensual enjoyment. But the only reason for saying that the "deeper" meaning is the sexual one is our own preconception as to what counts as deep and what as superficial. All metaphor, we are made to realize by this text, is potentially unstable, kept in position by the hierarchies we bring to bear upon it, not by its inner, inherent division into literal and figurative domains. I consider in the following chapter further consequences of the *Wake*'s destabilizing of conventional categories and hierarchies.

The fears provoked by *Finnegans Wake*'s portmanteau style are understandable and inevitable, because the consequences of accepting it extend to all our reading. Every word in every text is, after all, a portmanteau of sorts, a combination of sounds that echo through the entire language and through every other language and back through the history of speech. *Finnegans Wake* makes us aware that we, as readers, control this explosion, allowing only those connections to be effected which will give us the kinds of meaning we recognize—stories, voices, characters, metaphors, images, beginnings, developments, ends, morals, truths. We do not, of course, control it as a matter of choice. We are subject to the various grids that make literature and language possible at all—rules, habits, conventions, and all the boundaries that legitimate and exclude in order to produce meanings and values, themselves rooted in the ideology of our place and time. Hence our feeling of security in reading Pope's couplet, for we share both the language and the joke. Nevertheless, to obtain a glimpse of the infinite possibility of meaning kept at bay by those grids, to gain a sense that the boundaries upon which our use of language depends are set up under specific historical conditions, is to be made aware of a universe more open to reinterpretation and change than the one we are usually conscious of inhabiting. For many of its readers *Finnegans Wake* makes that glimpse an experience of exhilaration and opportunity, and as a result the book comes to occupy an important place in their reading; but for many others it can be only a discouraging glimpse of limitless instability.[18] So the book is treated as a freak, an unaccountable anomaly that merely travesties the cultural traditions we cherish, and its function as supplement and *pharmakon*, supererogatory but necessary, dangerous but remedial, is thereby prolonged.

When the *Wake* is welcomed, however, it is often by means of a gesture that simultaneously incapacitates it, either by placing it in a sealed-off category (the impenetrable and inexpressible world of the dream) or by subjecting it to the same interpretative mechanisms that are applied to all literary texts, as if it were no different: the elucidation of an "intention" (aided by draft material and biography), the analysis of "characters," the tracing of "plot," the elaboration of "themes," the tracking down of "allusions," the identification of "autobiographical references," in sum, the whole panoply of modern professional criticism. The outright repudiation of the Joycean portmanteau, though it may one day seem as quaint an attitude as Johnson's rejection of the Shakespearean quibble, is perhaps preferable to this industrious program of normalization and domestication. Johnson's passionate lament for his flawed idol involves a fuller understanding of the implications of the pun than many an untroubled celebration of textual indeterminacy, and to be afraid of *Finnegans Wake* is at least to acknowledge, even if unconsciously, the power and magnitude of the claims it makes.

NOTES

1. In the opening pages of *Shakespeare's Wordplay*, M.M. Mahood discusses the antagonism toward the pun which originated in the seventeenth-century demand for communicative efficiency, noting that Johnson, for all his hostility, had a sharper ear for Shakespeare's puns than his nineteenth-century successors. Sylvan Barnet, in "Coleridge on Puns," observes that despite Coleridge's disagreement with Johnson over Shakespeare's word-play, and his own penchant for punning, his approval of the practice is strictly circumscribed. Thus Coleridge several times claims there are no puns in *Macbeth* (making it necessary to argue that the porter's equivocations are by another hand), and in the *Philosophical Lectures* he endorses the view that the minds of young pupils should be guarded

against the deceptive force of puns. For some valuable comments on the threat so often perceived in the pun, see Richard Rand, "Geraldine," 298–99 and n. 16.

2. Many possible taxonomies are applicable to the range of effects we call "the pun"; I am concerned only with the general phenomenon of homonymy in language and its exploitation in literature. See the suggestions by James Brown in "Eight Types of Puns" and L.G. Heller in "Toward a General Typology of the Pun." Both these writers regard the pun as representing a fundamental property of literary language.

3. The attempt to use polysemy as a defining characteristic of literature—it is one of the criteria suggested by Ronald Carter and Walter Nash in their interesting essay "Language and Literariness," for instance—needs careful qualification. Certain cultural traditions undoubtedly valorize certain kinds of polysemy in the texts they deem literary, which may or may not include both the polysemy produced by an extremely rich context (Shakespeare, Dickens) or by a relatively impoverished one (William Carlos Williams, John Ashbery), but the extremes (*Finnegans Wake*, Dada) tend to be viewed with understandable suspicion.

4. The operation of "folk etymology," which is a significant factor in the diachronic changes in any language, depends on the assumption in the minds of speakers that coincidences of sound are not accidental—an assumption not unreasonably derived from the patterning of morphology and the process of analogical change (see chapter 4 above). Mitsou Ronat usefully relates the portmanteau word to folk etymology in "L'hypotexticale."

5. Goldberg's phrase "read *through*" suggests one reason for the problems he has with the *Wake*.

6. In *Adultery in the Novel*, Tony Tanner comments that "puns and ambiguities are to common language what adultery and perversion are to 'chaste' (i.e., socially orthodox) sexual relations. They both bring together entities (meanings/people) that have 'conventionally' been differentiated and kept apart; and they bring them together in deviant ways, bypassing the orthodox rules governing communications and relationships. (A pun is like an adulterous bed in which two meanings that should be separate are coupled together.) It is hardly an accident that *Finnegans Wake*, which arguably demonstrates the dissolution of bourgeois society, is almost one continuous pun (the connection with sexual perversion being quite clear to Joyce)" (53). As I have tried to show, the pun can constitute a thoroughly respectable coupling, which is why the *Wake* is not, *pace* Tanner, essentially a punning text. Tanner's remark is more appropriate to the promiscuous liaisons of words and meanings in the portmanteau.

7. The portmanteau exploits to the full the language's potential for what in chapter 5 I called "nonce-constellations": groups of words with similar sounds which create the impression of a particular appropriateness between those sounds and the dominant semantic content of the group. In the portmanteau the words in question are presented not as a sequence but as a combined unit. Dwight Bolinger's discussions of sound and sense in *Forms of English*, referred to in that chapter, are highly relevant to the language of *Finnegans Wake*.

8. A text such as Francis Huxley's *The Raven and the Writing Desk*, which treats Carroll's portmanteaux with the comic brilliance they deserve, is equally likely to be overlooked by the literary establishment.

9. See ". . . That Dangerous Supplement. . . ," in *Of Grammatology*, 141–64, and "Plato's Pharmacy," in *Dissemination*, 61–171.

10. References to *Finnegans Wake* are to the standard Faber/Viking edition of 1939 and indicate page number and line number on that page. Where a quotation is of more than one

line, only the first line number is given. In commenting on this passage I have made use of several of the standard reference books on *Finnegans Wake*, and I gratefully acknowledge the labors of their authors.

11. See *Ulysses* 11.1224, 15.3274 and 18.716 for further references to this invention, which "claims to afford a noiseless inoffensive vent."

12. Needless to say, the relation between shifts and indeterminacy in the language and intimations of sexual desire is not fortuitous. See the discussion of the "Sirens" and "Eumaeus" episodes of *Ulysses* in chapter 6 above.

13. Charles Peake has suggested to me a possible reference to the once-popular song "The Bandolero" (private communication). The word "bandolier" is also associated with Leopold Bloom: he is recalled as a school pupil in "Oxen of the Sun," "his booksatchel on him bandolierwise" (14.1047); and in "Circe" he appears with *"fieldglasses in bandolier"* (15.538). The French word "bander," to have an erection, is perhaps in the background.

14. Horne Tooke would have found these multiple associations unsurprising. For him they would have revealed the historical processes of the language—see my summary of his etymological account of the word *shit* in chapter 4, p. 102 above.

15. Freud refers to a group of jokes ("play upon words") that make "the (acoustic) word-presentation itself take the place of its significance as given by its relations to thing-presentations" and observes, "It may really be suspected that in doing so we are bringing about a great relief in psychical work and that when we make serious use of words we are obliged to hold ourselves back with a certain effort from this comfortable procedure" (*Jokes*, 167–68). See also my comments on linguistic motivation in chapter 5 above, p. 141.

16. For a discussion of the effects of Joyce's coalescing of languages which focuses on a single (and apparently simple) portmanteau from the *Wake*, see Derrida, "Two Words for Joyce."

17. See also the discussion by Jean Paris of the portmanteau word in "L'agonie du signe."

18. Someone who was able to go further than most in reading a wide range of literature against the grain of established codes, prefiguring the strategies required by *Finnegans Wake*, was Saussure; but he too took fright at the infinite possibilities he opened up, as Jean Starobinski documents in *Words upon Words*. Starobinski's comments have an obvious relevance to the anxieties and pleasures of reading *Finnegans Wake*: "If this approach [the theory of hypograms] had been further developed, it would soon have become a quagmire. Wave upon wave of possible names would have taken shape beneath his alert and disciplined eye. Is this the vertigo of error? It is also the discovery of the simple truth that language is an infinite resource, and that behind each phrase lies hidden the multiple clamor from which it has detached itself to appear before us in its isolated individuality" (122).

RICHARD POIRIER

The Pater of Joyce and Eliot

According to its author, Frank Kermode, the 'main topic' of *Romantic Image* (1957) has to do with that "esthetic image" explained in Thomist language by Stephen Daedalus in the *Portrait of the Artist as a Young Man* and he almost immediately indicates that St Thomas shares the honours with Walter Pater. Stephen's description of 'epiphany', he remarks, is 'the Joycean equivalent of Pater's "vision"' (Kermode 1957: 1–2). The 'Joyce industry', as Kermode calls it five years later in the title essay of *Puzzles and Epiphanies* (1962: 87), has yet to venture much beyond this merely initial point in the argument of *Romantic Image*, and even when critics refer now and again to Stephen as a Paterian artist, there are seldom any explanations—short of a few references to his theories of 'luminous stasis'—of what it more pertinently means to call him one. As Kermode goes on to suggest, the connections between Pater and Joyce, discoveries of which depend necessarily on a more intense reading than Pater normally receives, are intricate and substantial. They constitute one of the vital links between the 'nineties' and the literary modernism of the first two decades of this century, a conjunction which Eliot was determined to suppress. Eliot's trashing of Pater, combined with his attempted appropriation of Joyce in '*Ulysses*, Order, and Myth' (Eliot 1975), were part of an effort to make Pater and the poets whom Yeats called 'the tragic generation' seem merely eccentric and, in any event, outside the

From *Addressing Frank Kermode: Essays in Criticism and Interpretation*, edited by Margaret Tudeau-Clayton and Martin Warner. © 1991 by Richard Poirier.

main English tradition. From the beginning, Kermode has brilliantly, and against a determined critical consensus, set out to remedy this situation.

In doing so he draws attention to neglected and essential aspects of Pater which are at work in modernist literature. A bit later in the opening chapter of *Romantic Image*, for example, he comments on how 'to our great benefit, Pater in *The Renaissance* and *Marius the Epicurean* and James in "The Art of Fiction" and in his practice, insisted on the moral value of what is highly organised and profoundly apprehended, in life and in art' (Kermode 1957: 11–12). He is suggesting that Pater's impingement on modernism, as it might be represented by Joyce, included his tough awareness of the cost of arriving at or trying to hold onto ecstatic moments and, especially, of finding the right words to represent them. Pater is concerned, that is, as much with the formal disciplines required if one is to achieve intensifications of experience as he is with the intensifications themselves. This, I take it, is what Kermode has in mind when he says that for Pater art 'is the only true morality' (1957: 20).

So conceived, Pater becomes a figure of much greater consequence to Joyce and Eliot than he is usually thought to be, and thus to any revaluation of literary modernism. With a few distinguished exceptions,[1] however, critics tend to ignore or trivialise the role of Pater in these equations, and it is given only a casual nod in the best books on Pater himself, like Wolfgang Iser's estimable *Walter Pater: The Aesthetic Moment* (1960; trans. 1987). Indeed, Pater is a provocative example of how a writer, even when fortunate enough to find a critic sensitive to the historical ramifications of his work, can still be denied the place he has earned in 'the tradition' if to put him there means that the tradition has to be reconstituted.

This is as much the fate of Pater with respect to Joyce, Eliot, and the modernism associated with them, as it is the fate of Emerson and William James with respect to twentieth-century American poets like Frost and Stevens, both of whom are still being disfigured by interpretations slavishly geared to the standard modernist and post-modernist lines of succession. Lines of succession are, to be sure, altered now and then, and there are always disagreements among its fiduciaries, but these seem designed actually to prevent the proper investitures of prodigals like Emerson and Pater. To give them their due would badly disrupt the chronologies and periodisations in which the various modernisms, including 'paleo' and 'post', briskly succeed one another. About such chronologies and periodisations Kermode was as sceptical in the mid-sixties, with the opening section of *Continuities* called 'The Modern', as he is now in the late eighties, with the chapter called 'Canon and Period' in *History and Value*.

Revisions in favour of Pater and Emerson would mean, among other things, that Eliot's version of modernism would be seen as you must, as in the Conclusion of Pater's *The Renaissance* (1984: 60), 'burn always with this hard gemlike flame'. And those who most yearn for that kind of success are always in danger of merely spontaneous combustions. To concentrate on 'burning' is to know how quickly you can burn up; it is to come to the stark realisation that you can be consumed wholly within biological life, to face extinction without memorial. It is, with Pater, to become obsessed with the absoluteness of death.

When referring to Pater's sense of a necessary discipline, I have in mind the particular form of it which he calls '*ascêsis*'. The word and its variants can be found in almost everything he writes. In the Preface to *The Renaissance*, for example, he speaks of 'the charm of *ascêsis*, of the austere and serious girding of the loins of youth' (Pater 1984: 20), and in his essay 'Style' he defines its literary manifestations as 'self-restraint and renunciation' (108). Pater is famous for recommending the maximum degree of intensity in response to experience; yet you will notice his equal insistence on nearly the reverse. That is, in order to produce and sustain this intensity there is need for a high degree of calculated self-curtailment. The position is fraught with difficulty, even contradiction. On the one hand, considerable individual self-trust is required by the desire to maximise the intensity of a feeling; on the other, this intensity depends on self-erasure, so that there will be a minimum of obstruction to the ceaseless changes and accelerations of pure temporality. As Iser notes, 'it is only through the onward movement that our inner world can be enriched with the precious momentary impressions of experience that come and swiftly go. The transitoriness of these moments makes us increasingly conscious of the shortness of our lives' (Iser 1987: 30).

Pater's total commitment to art as an activity is understandable when, as he argues in *The Renaissance*, 'art comes to you proposing frankly to give nothing but the highest quality to your moments as they pass, and simply for those moments' sake' (Pater 1984: 62). Art does not redeem the time or offer any kind of redemption. Instead, as he writes of the school of Giorgione, it gives us the illusion of 'exquisite pauses in time, in which, arrested thus, we seem to be spectators of all the fullness of existence, and which are like some consummate extract or quintessence of life' (Pater 1986: 165). The vocabulary—'exquisite' and 'consummate extract'—is not meant idly or to characterise merely the feelings of the observer. It points rather to artistic performance or, as he says earlier in the same sentence, to the 'admirable tact' by which the artist separates 'ideal instants' from a 'feverish, tumultuously coloured world'. This requires a kind of impersonality which Eliot, never one to credit his predecessors, sets up as an artistic ideal. The artist as a person achieves only such immortality as is vouchsafed anyone else; beyond that he or she can continue to exist only in those performative functions in the work which can afterward be located, as traces of presence, only by particularly responsive readers. It is hoped that these traces will 'arrest' us, as they might the artist, within the passage of obliterating time. The poetry and essays of Stevens are suffused with this sort of Paterian (and Whitmanian) yearning for a life after death in the poems left behind.

But we are here concerned with the Pater found in Joyce. It is found partly in the shared expectation that through the design of a work of art the artist might hope to claim a measure of immortality. This becomes in the writings of both of them a design more specifically of the older artist upon any younger versions of himself. The older artist desires, that is, to cleanse and recompose himself as a young man, and in the process to attenuate the linkages of the later self to an earlier version which by hindsight seems always to have been doomed. In this Pater and Joyce are especially alike. In his late autobiographical story 'The Child in the House', Pater speaks, for example, of 'a certain design he had in view, the noting namely, of some things in the story of the spirit—in that process of brain building by which we are, each one of us, what we are' (Pater 1984: 1). It is made clear that the 'design' is actually being fulfilled in the very writing of the story and therefore in our reading of the story. The writer is here reconstituting and recomposing his younger self in the person of Florian, and the word 'house' refers to more than a place of residence. It refers also to the mind and physical being of this younger self and to the physical being of the older one in whom the child still lives. The narrator is, as a writer, fulfilling the Socratic function described in *Plato and Platonism*: 'to flash light into the house within, its many chambers, its memories and associations, upon its inscribed and pictured walls' (quoted in Iser 1987: 25). The child in the house is, then, two different persons: first, it is the child in its own mind, which is already to some extent written upon by his surroundings, including the physical house which helps mediate all his impressions; and second, it is the child who, at the later time of the story and its composition, still exists in the mind of the writer, the older artist. The writer, unlike any version of the child, is aware of multiple mediations of all the experience that is now held in his, the writer's, mind, and with this awareness comes a recognition of the limitations on freedom of experience. This recognition is something that the child as child, in any of its manifestations, could not have known about, or known only vaguely and intermittently.

In Pater, no less than in Joyce of *A Portrait*, the projected 'design' of the older artist is not, then, merely an imposition on experience; rather it partakes of, participates in, above all repeats those 'designs' or inscriptions which shaped the younger version and, at least to some extent, still therefore persist in the older one. The authorial 'design' is not intended merely to disclose the disorderly contents of a younger self and to give it shape as a *bildungsroman*. Quite the reverse. The older artist now sees that all experience, even as it comes to the mind of the infant child, was already 'designed' or mediated; the superiority of the older artist to the younger one is simply his capacity now to recognise that this was the case, to see patterns which were not visible to the younger self who felt very often in the presence merely of confusions or disorderliness. The older artist knows that experience is always and forever mediated by the forms of language by which it is brought to consciousness, and this includes even the language he is now using.

By virtue of this recognition Pater can be said to discover for himself, and for Joyce, an essential component of modernism attributed by criticism more exclusively to Joyce alone. From the outset, *A Portrait*, no less than 'A Child in the House', shows that experience is mediated by writing, and this long before the writing done later on by the older artist. Within the first 300 words of *A Portrait* the experience of the artist as an infant is filtered to him through various media: the opening lines are a story of a 'moo cow' being told to him by his father; he then hears a song and tries to sing it; he is made to dance while his mother plays the piano; he is introduced to the symbolic colours on the brushes of Dante's press; he is intimidated with nursery rhyme words which will recur in his later experiences at college—'Apologise, / Pull out his eyes'. And still within this compass he is moved from games at home to games at school, to the playgrounds of Clongowes. There, as throughout the rest of this novel and, with some notable exceptions, *Ulysses*, he tries to keep out of the games others play while pretending to be in them. It is here, in the form of emotional trauma, that his theory of aesthetic detachment begins to take shape, and not in any later readings of aesthetic theory. 'He kept', as Joyce says, 'on the fringe of his line' (Joyce 1957: 8).

Interpreters have frequently pointed out that the terms which at this juncture impress themselves on the boy's mind help determine the language by which Joyce represents Stephen's subsequent experience. Thus, 'cold', associated with wetting the bed and guilt, becomes connected with the water of the Clongowes ditch and, later, the sea, the flow of matter into which he falls. Analysis has recorded these repetitions many times over. Words are shown thereby to be less the instruments of liberation that he takes them to be, than a source of entrapment in past experience; and continually, as the novel progresses, words frustrate his declarations of intensity and of freedom. Recall his ecstatic walk by the sea in chapter 4 where his Icarian vision is accompanied by the cries of children at play, 'O, Cripes, I'm drownded!' (169), referring back to the boys at Clongowes who shouldered him into the slime of the ditch. So, too, with respect to Stephen's aesthetic theories in the next chapter; these are often read as if Joyce subscribes to them, as if intellectual-philosophical talk is somehow free of the slippages and ironic pressures at work everywhere else in the language of the book. In fact it doesn't matter whether or by how much Joyce *might* subscribe to any of

Stephen's theories, because what the structure of the book puts into question is the degree to which Stephen's articulation of them can ever be less than embarrassing. Joseph Buttigieg is one of the critics who is especially perceptive about Stephen's theorising in his recent *A Portrait of the Artist in a Different Perspective*, no affront intended by him to Hugh Kenner's laudable essay of 1948, 'The *Portrait* in Perspective'. Stephen's articulation of theory, his wording of it—not to be confused with the same theories worded differently—is a confused mishmash of Pater and Aquinas wherein his terms carry destructive connotations from earlier and, by him, suppressed moments in the story. The patterns of the book require that the reader recall what the young artist is anxious to forget.

Citations of repetition in *A Portrait* are by now so familiar as to have become rather stale. I mention them only as easy examples of the technique by which Joyce shows, despite Stephen's declarations, that it is impossible with respect to any object to 'see that it is that thing which it is and no other thing' (Joyce 1957: 213). There can be no virgin womb of the imagination, because the imagination only knows itself thanks to the words that have already possessed and fertilised it. The implications for language are made embarrassingly evident to Stephen well before *Ulysses*, as when he tries to compose his vilanelle near the end of *A Portrait*, just after his announcement about the virgin womb. The phrases that prosaically intrude upon his poetic fashioning have nothing to do with virgins. Just after the third stanza of the poem as later completed, he lapses into compositional ruminations: 'Smoke went up from the whole earth, the vapoury oceans, smoke of her praise. The earth was like a swinging swaying censer, a ball of incense, an ellipsoidal ball' (218). Any attentive reader will recall that only a few pages back the phrase 'ellipsoidal balls' played a part in the 'rude humour' of Moynihan during a lecture in mathematics. When the professor, quoting from a poem by W. S. Gilbert—Stephen has yet to learn that everything is a quotation—refers to 'elliptical billiard balls', Moynihan 'leaned down towards Stephen's ear and murmured "What price ellipsoidal balls! Chase me, ladies, I'm in the cavalry!"' (192). Even though Stephen will eventually complete the poem, the frustrations of his efforts at this point, and in immediate proximity to his theorising about the imagination, is an encapsulated illustration of how, by these quietly managed repetitions, Joyce denies Stephen the exercise of power over language which he too easily proposes to exert.

Stephen's recommendations of detachment and withdrawal in the interest of artistic gestation result less from intellectual rigour than from compulsions, the repetition compulsion so to speak, made evident as early as Clongowes. He is compelled to separate himself from the games others play and, especially, from what he calls, at another point, 'the sordid tide of life' (98), a tide, he says, that moves within as well as without him. Joyce's images of tides and streams is everywhere anticipated in Pater, often in phrases that catch his curious revulsion from the flow he also desires, as when, in the 'Conclusion' to *The Renaissance*, he speaks of 'the delicious recoil from the flood of water in summer heat' (Pater 1984: 55). The same image of tides, flows, and floods is conspicuous in Emerson and in William James, in writers, that is, who exult in the stream of consciousness but who, for that reason, discover within this image there is a movement inevitably and irresistibly towards oblivion.

One fails to do any sort of justice either to Pater or to Joyce by asking simply if Stephen is a failed Paterian, or if *A Portrait* is in part a fictional substantiation of Eliot's criticism of Pater. The essential question is whether or not there can ever be such a thing as a successful Paterian, one who is not depressed and defeated by his own perception of the role of art and of the artist. The question, as I want to argue, was asked first and most starkly by Pater himself, and Joyce's portrait of Stephen is to be read, I think, less as a critique of Pater than as an assimilation and deep understanding of him. Eliot adopts Joyce's reading of Pater for his own uses only by refusing to understand it.

The 'Conclusion' to *The Renaissance* written in 1868 was withdrawn by Pater from the second edition and then, when restored to the third edition, revised in the hope of making its skepticism less subject to attack. There is no escaping even now its powerful denial of fixed principles and its tough-minded willingness to let the idea of the self become unfixed and floating. It is an alarmingly vivid account of solipsism and its dangers, these being a total transfer of objects into the impressions one has of them, a divestment of the 'solidity with which language invests them' (Pater 1984: 59). The passage, which concludes with the image of the 'continual vanishing away, that strange, perpetual weaving and unweaving of ourselves', looks toward one of *The Imaginary Portraits*, which will be considered presently, named 'Sebastian Van Storck' and beyond that to the portrait of Stephen Daedalus, especially his fragmentation into the self-cancelling assemblage of allusions and sentiments which characterise his language in the first three chapters of *Ulysses*. Here, also, Pater anticipates the image of the 'tide' within as well as without, though he never calls it 'sordid':

> Or if we begin with the inward world of thought and feeling, the whirlpool is still more rapid, the flame more eager and devouring. There it is no longer the gradual darkening of the eye and the fading of the colour from the wall,—movements of the shore-side, where the water flows down indeed, though in apparent rest—but the race of the mid-stream, a drift of momentary acts of sight and passion and thought. At first sight experience seems

to bury us under a flood of external objects, pressing upon us with a sharp and importunate reality, calling us out of ourselves in a thousand forms of action. But when reflexion begins to play upon those objects they are dissipated under its influence; the cohesive force seems suspended like some trick of magic; each object is loosed into a group of impressions—colour, odour, texture—in the mind of the observer. And if we continue to dwell in thought on this world, not of objects in the solidity with which language invests them, but of impressions, unstable, flickering, inconsistent, which burn and are extinguished with our consciousness of them, it contracts still further: the whole scope of observation is dwarfed into the narrow chamber of the individual mind. Experience, already reduced to a group of impressions, is ringed round for each one of us by that thick wall of personality through which no real voice has ever pierced on its way to us, or from us to that which we can only conjecture to be without. Every one of those impressions is the impression of the individual in his isolation, each mind keeping as a solitary prisoner its own dream of a world. Analysis goes a step further still, and assures us that those impressions of the individual mind to which, for each one of us, experience dwindles down, are in perpetual flight; that each of them is limited by time, and that as time is infinitely divisible, each of them is infinitely divisible also; all that is actual in it being a single moment, gone while we try to apprehend it, of which it may ever be more truly said that it has ceased to be than that it is. To such a tremulous wisp constantly re-forging itself on the stream, to a single sharp impression, with a sense in it, a relic more or less fleeting, of such moments gone by, what is real in our life fines itself down. It is with this movement, with the passage and dissolution of impressions, images, sensations, that analysis leaves off—that continual vanishing away, that strange, perpetual, weaving and unweaving of ourselves. (Pater 1984: 59–60)

Stephen Daedalus, 'weaver of the wind' as he calls himself in the opening chapter of *Ulysses*, sounds, in the account I am giving of him, as if he were entirely a function of language. He is of course also a novelistic character sufficiently portrayed so that he can be imagined independently of the words only by virtue of which he exists. And yet for Joyce he principally is, to recall Henry James' phrase, a compositional resource. That is, he is 'used' within a larger inquiry into the way language, under certain cultural conditions, tends to dissolve the objects, including the selves, to which it is supposed to give solidity. This may happen in any work of literature, but it happens in *A Portrait* by repeated design, as in Stephen's efforts at poetic or theoretic composition.

Joyce's portrait of Stephen is most significantly Paterian, then, not when Stephen is mouthing familiar Paterian phrases or when these are used to describe him ('A soft liquid joy like the noise of many waters flowed over his memory and he felt in his heart the soft peace of silent spaces of fading tenuous sky above the waters . . . ' (Joyce 1957: 225).) He is most significantly Paterian when he comes to grief, and it is grief which Pater himself has already compellingly described. I have argued elsewhere that Eliot's essay of 1930 entitled 'Arnold and Pater' is mostly owed, though Eliot never mentions it, to Joyce's *Portrait* and the opening three chapters of *Ulysses* (Poirier 1987: 6–9); it now seems to me that Eliot was only able to find there what he most wanted to use and that he left behind all the best of it. He took only so much of Pater as served the polemical-religious purpose of the moment. The spectre of tides, of things being made to flow into one another, was especially disturbing to Eliot, so that when he describes this process as it occurs culturally, and in a movement generated, so he supposes, by Arnold and Pater—'Religion becomes morals, Religion becomes art'—it is with obvious misgivings. 'The total effect of Arnold's philosophy', he writes, 'is to set up Culture in the place of Religion, and to leave Religion to be laid waste by the anarchy of feeling. And Culture is a term which each man not only may interpret as he pleases, but must indeed interpret as he can. So the gospel of Pater follows naturally upon the prophecy of Arnold' (Eliot 1978: 387).

Eliot is quite likely being instructed here by the kinds of appropriation of religion into art instigated by Stephen throughout the last sections of *A Portrait*, and which are made no less abundantly by Marius and by Pater's Florian in 'The Child in the House'. Stephen, while telling Cranly that he does not believe in the Eucharist and admitting that he fears it may indeed be 'the body and blood of the son of God' (239, 243), is simultaneously anxious, for purposes of art, to hold on to the form and vocabulary of transubstantiation. Similarly, he wishes to take the place of a young priest, whom he observes with a young woman, not only in her regard but in the confessional: 'To him she would unveil her soul's shy nakedness, to one who was but schooled in the discharging of a formal rite, rather than to him, a priest of the eternal imagination, transmuting the daily bread of experience into the radiant body of ever-living life' (221). Surely it took no great critical effort, nor does it constitute any but the most elementary reading of Pater, to remark as Eliot does that *Marius the Epicurean* is a document of that moment in history when 'Religion became morals, religion became art, religion became science or philosophy' (Eliot 1978: 393), or for that matter when religion became sex and politics.

A difference between Eliot and Joyce in their reading of Pater (which *A Portrait* and *Ulysses* can be taken in part to be) is that Joyce attributes a pathos to Stephen's Paterian position and refuses ever wholly to dissociate himself from it. He seems to recognise, as Eliot cannot afford to do, that Pater was fully aware of the risks, deprivations, and loss of selfhood that might follow along, with an exhilarating sense of liberation, from his aesthetics. This is the aspect of Pater which Eliot represses while, as Louis Menand (1987) and Perry Meisel (1987) have shown, he remains heavily indebted to him, even in phraseology, for his idea of impersonality. He is equally indebted, I would add, for other notions, like the suspect claim that in the modern age the poet must perforce become more 'difficult' and allusive than he had hitherto been obliged to be. It seems equally obvious, too, that in Eliot's poems, early and late, there is at work something like Pater's *'ascêsis'*, an expressed yearning for a principle of order that can account for a riot of disturbing because uncontrollable impressions. As an inferable presence in Joyce's work, Pater is understandably less impressive than is the Pater inferable from *Marius* or from the *Renaissance*, but he is never the cardboard and patronised figure of Eliot's essay. 'I have spoken of the book as of some importance', Eliot pompously remarks of *Marius*. 'I do not mean that its importance is due to any influence it may have exerted. I do not believe that Pater, in this book, has influenced a single first-rate mind of a later generation' (Eliot 1978: 392). Such a remark requires no comment, especially given the self-protective evasiveness of the phrase 'this book', as if *Marius* were somehow, from a writer of monotonous consistency of tone and substance, importantly different from any of his other writings. When Eliot goes on to remark that Pater's 'view of art, as expressed in *The Renaissance*, impressed itself upon a number of writers in the "nineties", and propagated some confusion between life and art which is not wholly irresponsible for some untidy lives' (ibid.), it only reminds us that Pater's own life was tidy to a degree almost pitiable, and that his writing, even as it preaches ecstasy and stimulation, managed, especially in *Marius*, to bear the marks of continuously suppressed, controlled, sedated passion. His stories in particular are full of the most elaborate mediations in the telling, with multiple buffers between the writer, especially when he characterises himself within the story, and any earlier version of himself.

As I see it, Pater's writing is most interesting, and also most important to Joyce, when it exhibits contradictory impulses: an acute need for exercises of control and discipline, along with an equally acute impatience with anything that might get in the way of the flow of sensation and impression. Pater's efforts to work within this contradiction help make him a seminal figure in the modernist situation as it is sometimes and, I think, most persuasively described. That situation is one in which the illusion has at last been given up that the self can be satisfactorily understood by an appeal to various forms of external authority. While this to some may represent a loss it represents to others a considerable gain. It makes people freer than they have ever known themselves to be, releasing them to the play of desire, speculation and sensation. It encourages them, otherwise unassisted, to enter what William James would later call, after Emerson, the stream of consciousness.

But even those who take this as an opportunity admit to a number of perplexities. First, if you do not already have a confident sense of self how then do you choose to attend to some sensations or experiences and not to all of them at once? Second, if you do let all of experience come at you indiscriminately, how do you keep from unravelling altogether? We noted awhile back that in his 'Conclusion' to *The Renaissance* Pater speaks of the self as a constant process of weaving and unweaving. This occasions yet another question. How do you get control of the pattern of weaving and unweaving so that it, too, is an experience and not merely an accident? Here, the answer would appear to be an anticipation of Hemingway or the James of 'The Moral Equivalent of War'. In the absence of religious faith and the devotional exercises that can go with it, you turn to more personal exercises like James' mountain climbing or the connoisseurship of Hemingway or you imagine, as did Gertrude Stein long before Mailer, an analogy between conducting a war and your own composition of a work. Pater's taste for the martial arts in his stories is, in that regard, only incidentally homoerotic.

His ideal of discipline seems mostly to be located, as to a degree it is also for these others—as it is everywhere for Joyce—in literary technique, in an idea of style as described in his essay on that subject in *Appreciations*. This raises yet another question. If discipline or self-curtailment or *ascêsis* is to be exercised in style, then to what end? If you do not have a soul to save then, without a soul, what instructs you to bother with efforts to compose the self, if only momentarily, within the flow of sensations? Perhaps the answer, as already mentioned, is that only by exerting some degree of control can you increase the intensity of such moments, cramming each of them with a maximum amount of felt intensity. But why *write* in order to do this? Why not stand on your head? It appears that writing, in the absence of God or soul, is the one form of discipline that might, again, offer some prospect of immortality, an arrest to the otherwise uninterrupted flow toward death. Style offers Pater the best way known to him by which to create structures that can, at least for the duration of the writing and reading, substitute for anything more permanent.

I am trying to describe a dilemma at the heart of Pater's philosophy of art and his own efforts to deal with this dilemma. The discipline of style serves a double purpose, one of which seems to frustrate the other. On the one hand the discipline is necessary to ensure that any given moment is exploited to the fullest, whether it be a moment of perception or of writing;

on the other, because this discipline involves a degree of self-curtailment, of impersonality in the service of style, it thereby threatens to dissolve the very subjectivity which he wishes to enhance, to unweave or shatter the participating self. Pater does not evade this difficulty, and his efforts to cope with it are partly responsible for some of the murkiness of his writing. He tends abruptly to enter words or phrases of qualification into an argument that is heading another way, and to do so in subordinate parts of his sentences, as if to hide them from anyone but himself; or he will make assertions which cannot be reconciled with positions he famously adheres to, as in the last paragraph of 'Style' where, he says, the distinction between great art and good art depends 'not on form but on matter'. At his best, however, he is impressively scrupulous about the negative and self-defeating possibilities in his own philosophy of art. In evidence there is, notably, 'Sebastian Van Storck', a story included in *Imaginary Portraits* of 1887 and published the year before in *Macmillans*.

It is a powerful and disturbing work, unique on a number of counts. First, it is the only one of the *Imaginary Portraits* with a fictional rather than an historical or mythological hero, and though it does contain historical figures, including various Dutch painters of the seventeenth century and a cameo appearance by Spinoza, it is clear that in this instance Pater wants a form loose enough to allow a lot of personal intrusions and ruminations. He manages to bring into the story, as if for inspection and testing, ideas less critically elaborated in both the previously published *Marius* and *The Renaissance*. Second, it is for Pater unusually bleak, as compared, say, to the later 'The Child in the House'. And third, while the Pater of 'The Child in the House' echoes throughout the Joyce of *A Portrait*, especially at points where Stephen is enthusiastically anticipating his artistic emergence, 'Sebastian' anticipates the defeated Stephen and, more important still, the crises which, in Joyce's book, are shown to lurk just beneath the exuberant rhetoric of the Paterian artist. Sebastian is not as 'Paterian', in the popular understanding of that term, as Marius or as Florian, either when Florian is a child or when he is the older narrator of his story; for that matter he is not as Paterian, again in the popular sense, as is Stephen at the end of Chapter 4, 'singing wildly to the sea, crying to greet the advent of the life that had cried to him' (170). Sebastian more nearly resembles the Stephen after Chapter 4, the increasingly detached, prideful, and theoretical intellectual of Chapter 5, a young man obsessed with the sea and, nearly, a hater of his kind in the first three chapters of *Ulysses*.

Sebastian, that is, prefigures Stephen's destiny in an aggravated form and his metaphorical fall into the sea of matter. Before even introducing him, Pater depicts a situation bound by the same parameters that will encompass Stephen's: a stifling domesticity, art, and the sea. That's

Holland for you, and Ireland too. 'The Dutch had just begun to see', Pater remarks, 'what a picture their country was' (Pater 1984: 67)—art informing them about their lives and their landscape. From the very first line, which refers to a winter scene by Adrian van Velde, to the end, where it is revealed that Sebastian has destroyed the one portrait done of him (by Isaac van Ostade), Dutch art and artists are evoked at every turn. And at every turn they are put in contrast to the other constant element in the determination of Dutch landscape, namely 'the sea which Sebastian so much loved' (70). Sebastian has already tired of art and turned away from those domestic refinements which Stephen assiduously tries to recover, if only for a time, after the collapse of family fortunes. 'The arts were a matter he could but just tolerate. Why add, by a forced and artificial production, to the monotonous tide of competing, fleeting experience?' (68) He prefers a quite different 'tide', the obliterating sea which will reduce everything to a *tabula rasa*, an 'empty place.' (69) Pater writes that 'In his passion for *Schwindsucht*—we haven't the word—he found it pleasant to think of the resistless element which left one hardly a foot-space amidst the yielding sand' (71). *Schwindsucht* can refer both to consumption—the artist's disease of the nineteenth century—and to renunciation and self-curtailment. In either case it raises the spectre of a gradual refinement of self out of existence, a grotesque extension of Stephen's idea of a God-like impersonality. And he is like Stephen, too, when, in relation to family and especially his mother, it is said that

> All his singularities appeared to be summed up in his refusal to take his place in the life-sized family group (*très distingué et très soigné*, remarks a modern critic of the work) painted about this time. His mother expostulated with him on the matter:—she must feel, a little icily, the emptiness of hope, and something more than the due measure of cold in things for a woman of her age, in the presence of a son who desired but to fade out of the world like a breath—and she suggested filial duty. 'Good mother', he answered, 'there are duties toward the intellect also, which women can but rarely understand.' (74)

Like Stephen, Sebastian is a theoretician of detachment, with a taste for authorities, and while he cites Spinoza and not Aquinas, it is to much the same effect as Stephen's Thomism. '"Things that might have nothing in common with each other cannot be understood, or explained by means of each other"' (77), he copies into his notebook. These notebooks are a version of Stephen's self-absorbed diary, with which *A Portrait* concludes. Even more to the point, Sebastian's theories are, like Stephen's, forced into embarrassing and sometimes invalidating proximity to the recordings of daily experience. Speaking of the notebooks, Pater observes that

> The volume was indeed a kind of treatise to be:—a hard, systematic, well-concatenated train of thought, still implicated in the circumstances of a journal. Freed from the accidents of that particular literary form with its unavoidable details of place and occasion, the theoretic strain would have been found mathematically continuous. The already so wary Sebastian might perhaps never have taken in hand, or succeeded in, this detachment of his thoughts; every one of which, beginning with himself, as the peculiar and intimate apprehension of this or that particular day and hour, seemed still to protest against such disturbance, as if reluctant to part from those accidental associations of the personal history which prompted it, and so become a purely intellectual abstraction. (76–7)

Sebastian dies in a flood when a dyke gives way, apparently while he is attempting, in an uncharacteristic gesture of human solidarity, to rescue a child. Because he loved the sea, as Stephen does not, he might have welcomed his fate within it, a possibility Stephen finds loathsome. There are, that is, differences. And yet the language which accounts for the relationship of each of them to the sea, the conceptual framework in each case, is markedly similar to the other. Recall, for instance, Stephen's disappointment in Chapter 2:

> How foolish his aim had been! He had tried to build a break-water of order and elegance against the sordid tide of life without him and to dam up, by rules of conduct and active interests and new filial relations, the powerful recurrence of the tide within him. Useless. From without as from within the water had flowed over his barriers: their tides began once more to jostle fiercely above the crumbled mole. (Joyce 1957: 98)

Sebastian's resolve, when he goes to the sea for the last time, had already been phrased similarly by Pater:

> Here he could make 'equation' between himself and what was not himself, and set things in order, in preparation towards such deliberate and final change in his manner of living as circumstances so clearly necessitated. (Pater 1984: 82)

Sebastian's desire for order is intimately connected to a desired escape from the stuff of life which does not submit to order, and it is given expression earlier in the story in terms as unmistakably Icarian as Stephen's. We are told that he 'enjoyed the sense of things seen from a distance, carrying us, as on wide wings of space itself, far out of one's actual surroundings' (68).

In sum, Joyce and Pater jointly recognise the perils of excess, either of self-release into the materials at hand or of self-curtailment in coping with them. They embody the opposition defined by Pater between classicists and romanticists, 'between', as he remarks in the 'Postscript' to *Appreciations*, 'the adherents in the culture of beauty, of the principles of liberty, and authority, respectively—of strength, and order or what the Greeks called [orderly behaviour]' (210). It is mostly thanks to the misleadings of Eliot, who all the while surreptitiously uses Pater's own standards, that criticism persists in putting Joyce and Pater into simple antithetical postures. In both Pater and Joyce, when it comes to the uses of language, this fear of excess means, in Pater's words, from 'Style'—and in Joyce's notorious practice—that 'the literary artist is of necessity a scholar'. And for what reason? Because 'the material with which he works'—it can be language and only language—'is no more a creation of his own than the sculptor's marble' (107). The writer is required to know everything about the past association of words, all of their accumulated meanings and usages, if he is to use any of them with tact and propriety. Only then can he, in Eliot's apposite phrase, 'dis-locate if necessary, language into his meaning'. Pater's essay on 'Style' sounds again and again like a source for Eliot's 'The Metaphysical Poets' of 1921, notably when Eliot explains why 'poets in our civilization as it exists at present, must be *difficult* . . . more and more comprehensive, more allusive, more indirect . . . ' (Eliot 1978: 248) Pater had written in 1888:

> That imaginative prose should be the special and opportune art of the modern world results from two important facts about the latter: first, the chaotic variety and complexity of its interests, making the intellectual issue, the really master currents of the present time incalculable—a condition of mind little susceptible to the restraint proper to verse form, so that the most characteristic verse of the nineteenth century has been lawless verse; and secondly, an all-pervading naturalism, a curiosity about everything whatever as it really is, involving a certain humility of attitude, cognate to what must, after all, be the less ambitious form of literature. (1984: 106)

Not to labour the point, Eliot's argument in '*Ulysses*, Order, and Myth', to the effect that Joyce is 'classical in tendency' is but a version of Pater's claim that the writer must be a scholar if he is to deal properly with the incalculable resonances of language. To be 'classical in tendency', Eliot says, is not superficially to protect yourself by turning away from 'nine tenths of the material which lies at hand'. Rather, it is to do 'the best one can with it' (Eliot 1975: 176–7). Again, what else is this if not a fulfillment of Pater's suggestion in the 'Postscript' to *Appreciations* that classicism and romanticism are 'tendencies really at work at all times in art, moulding it, with the balance sometimes a little on one side sometimes a little on the other' (Pater 1984: 212)? And the balance is needed, he says later, because the problem for literary art 'just now' (meaning 1876) is

> to induce order upon the contorted, proportionless accumulation of our knowledge and experience, our science and history, our hopes and disillusions, and, in effecting this, to do consciously what has been done hitherto for the most part too unconsciously . . . (220)

This says all that Eliot will say in '*Ulysses*, Order, and Myth' about the necessity of Joyce's method, as a way of 'controlling, of ordering, of giving shape and significance to the immense panorama of futility and anarchy which is contemporary history.' And Pater says it, besides, without the accompanying operatics about the horrors of contemporary life and without the elevation of so called 'mythic method'—what else is Milton's?—to a 'scientific discovery' of such magnitude as to make the novel a form 'which will no longer serve' (Eliot 1975: 176–7). It is Eliot, at last, who clearly no longer serves as dependable guide to Pater or Joyce or, for that matter, to literary modernism.[2]

Notes

1. In addition to Kermode, the exceptions would include Graham Hough, *The Last Romantics* (1949); Harold Bloom, *Selected Writings of Walter Pater* (1984: 'Introduction'); Louis Menand, *Discovering Modernism* (1987); Perry Meisel, *The Myth of the Modern* (1987); Carolyn Williams, *The Transfigured World: Walter Pater's Aesthetic Historicism* (1989).

2. A version of this essay first appeared in the *James Joyce Quarterly* 26, 1, Fall 1988.

WELDON THORNTON

The Structures

We turn now to Joyce's novel, illustrating the distance between Stephen's
modernist view of the world and of his psyche, and Joyce's fuller and richer
antimodernist perspective. This chapter explains how indistinguishable the
structures of the novel are from those of Stephen's psyche, and focuses on
certain structural features that reveal how deep into Stephen's mind the
Cartesian subject/object dichotomy has penetrated.

Joyce's *Portrait* depicts the development of Stephen Dedalus from early
childhood to his more or less self-confident late-adolescent flight from Dublin
in pursuit of his calling as an artist. Stephen is a typical *Bildungsroman* hero-
sensitive, intelligent, continually trying to discover what life holds for him.
Every experience is for him a potential gateway to life's meaning, a possible
revelation of "the end he had been born to serve" (*P*, p. 169). He is typical also
in that his development is a true *Bildung*, a process of individuation arising
both from distinctive, innate traits of his psyche and from the influences of
his milieu.

In the face of structuralist and poststructuralist claims that the individual
is no more than a nexus of cultural patterns and structures—"a locus where
various signifying systems intersect" in Sylvio Gaggi's apt characterization
of this view—I must emphasize how *Portrait* testifies repeatedly to the
distinctiveness of Stephen's "individuating rhythm," to how different he

From *The Antimodernism of Joyce's* Portrait of the Artist as a Young Man. © 1994 by Syracuse
University Press.

is from others in his cohort who have been subject to very similar cultural forces.[1] I agree with H. M. Daleski and Stanislaus Joyce that Stephen's development involves the realization of potentialities inherent in his psyche, rather than simply a response to his environment. Daleski says "in *A Portrait of the Artist*, unlike *Mansfield Park* or *The History of Henry Esmond*, for instance, it is not so much the child's circumstances as his consciousness that determines the sort of adult he becomes and colors his whole personality. The child's consciousness is the 'embryo' of character that Joyce starts with and then sets into dynamic relation with circumstance" (*Unities*, p. 175). Daleski goes on to quote Stanislaus' remark that when Joyce set to work on the novel, "the idea he had in mind was that a man's character, like his body, develops from an embryo with constant traits. The accentuation of those traits, their reactions to hereditary influences and environment, were the main psychological lines he intended to follow, and, in fact, the purpose of the novel as originally planned" (*MBK*, p. 17).[2] Stanislaus' specification of both "hereditary influences and environment" as factors the embryo of character *reacts to* shows that he does not identify the psyche with either of these contributory influences.

Baruch Hochman's fine essay "Joyce's *Portrait* as Portrait" (*The Literary Review* 22 [Fall 1978]: 25–55) also addresses these issues. Emphasizing Stephen's development throughout the novel, Hochman points out that "Joyce does not render a merely passive process. Stephen, to be sure, does incorporate elements of his environment. . . . But the internalization is not passive. It is an appropriation, a taking and a making his own" (p. 30). Hochman stresses as well the self-identity that persists throughout the novel, saying "*Portrait* renders the disparate 'Stephens' of the successive moments of his experience. Yet it renders the same Stephen, who is identical with himself even as he undergoes the sea-change of biological, emotional, sociological and intellectual development" (p. 27). He also speaks intelligently to the complex question of the relationships between self and culture, pointing to a paradox that the novel keeps before us:

> One of the novel's governing themes is the primacy of culture—of all the words and images and ideas in which man is so entangled, that his "nature" cannot be discerned in its bare primordiality. Yet there is an important sense in which the thesis reverses itself. It can be said, if I am right about the priorities governing this novel, that the entire mass of cultural material has no vibrancy, hardly any meaning, except in Stephen as constituted: from his muscles and his guts, as we are asked to envision them, up through his rational and imaginative faculties. What animates culture and its images is, if not perceivable "nature," then knowable personality. (p. 51)

In the preceding chapter I proposed that the structures of the *Bildungsroman* reflect the *Bildung*, the development, of its protagonist. Essentially this same point about *Portrait*—that its structure is a function of Stephen's development—has been made by a number of critics; Thomas F. Staley, in a review of studies of the novel's structure, points out that "all of the studies agree that the central structural principle in the novel is informed and even controlled by Stephen's own spiritual growth and development."[3] This means that virtually every study of Stephen's psychological development simultaneously involves claims about structural elements, structural patterns, in the novel. While some of the patterns critics have proposed seem contrived or imposed, most of them are plausible: the number and variety of patterns that have been brought to light both testify to Joyce's genius and suggest how large an array of structural elements can enter into the "individuating rhythm" of one individual's psyche.[4]

I would make two general points about the novel's structures. First, so fully is this characteristic of the *Bildungsroman* realized in *Portrait* that it is questionable whether we can discover any feature of the book's structure that is not simultaneously a feature of Stephen's psyche. Certainly every motif (or complex) that we trace through the novel (e.g., birds, hands, rose, cow, red/green) is not simply a strand in an aesthetic fabric, but a component of the young man's gestating psyche, and analogously, each of the various structural patterns that we detect in the novel is simultaneously an aspect of Stephen's individuating rhythm.[5]

The second point is that virtually all such structural/psychic patterns exist as subconscious elements of Stephen's psyche, since Stephen is not consciously imposing—or even aware of—these patterns. That is, when we trace these patterns and motifs we render explicit something that necessarily exists implicitly in Stephen's psyche. Thus any such analysis of structural patterns inherently refutes the *tabula rasa* image of the mind and the Enlightenment ideal of total self-awareness.[6] The subconscious nature of the patterns is more likely to be insisted on in Freudian or avant garde psychoanalytical readings of the novel—which suggests an "antimodernist" conception of the psyche in such readings—but it is equally the case with all readings that propose underlying structures or patterns within Stephen's development.[7] Compared to the extensive subconscious dynamics of his psyche revealed by these studies of structural patterns, the degree of self-awareness and conscious control of his psyche that Stephen can achieve is relatively small, though not trivial.

While every structural pattern within Stephen's psyche thus involves implicit elements, the pattern or rhythm that I wish to focus on here is very deeply implicit. This pattern derives from his having internalized the Cartesian dichotomy between *res extensa* and *res cogitans*, and is reflected in his construing his experience as oscillating between poles that can best be described as inner/outer, subjective/objective, private/public. This implicit orientation on Stephen's part results in an underlying oscillatory pattern that manifests itself through successive chapters of the novel—and to a lesser extent among episodes within the chapters—and that undergirds most of the other structural patterns described by earlier critics.

* * *

Joyce's *Portrait* dramatizes Stephen's struggle to discover some principle by which to live. In each of the first four chapters Stephen responds to some call, some impulsion, which seems to manifest the life-principle that he is seeking. Consequently, each chapter involves a pattern of rising action or intensification, ending in a climactic scene that dramatically exemplifies his current sense of what is most real and most compelling in his experience. In the first chapter, this climactic scene is his appeal to Father Conmee; in the second, his visit to the prostitute; in the third, his confession to the priest; in the fourth his vision of the wading girl. Each of these scenes epitomizes for Stephen some newly-realized sense of what is most real in his experience and consequently of how he is to approach life. The fifth chapter significantly modifies the pattern of the first four, for two reasons. First, Stephen's discovery of his artistic calling at the end of chapter IV is valid, so that no more must he undergo dramatic rediscoveries of his life-course. Secondly, simultaneously with his discovering his calling as an artist, Stephen asserts a qualitatively greater degree of self-awareness and self-determination— this is what he construes his soul's "aris[ing] from the grave of boyhood" (p. 170) to involve—and this new attitude toward himself is the basis of a significant shift in his demeanor, and consequently in our attitude toward him, in chapter V. In this final chapter Stephen faces the less dramatic but more complex problem of coming to understand what his artistic calling involves—a problem that he has not solved by the end of the novel.

Let me briefly label the life-approaches that Stephen pursues in the first four chapters, offer a generalization about them, and then elaborate. In chapter I, Stephen undertakes a social approach to life; in chapter II this social approach collapses and is replaced by the *sensuous* approach; in chapter III this proves unsubstantial, and Stephen engages in a *religious* approach to life; in chapter IV, he finds the religious approach to life unacceptable, sees his true calling as that of artist, and embarks on the *aesthetic* approach to life.

My generalization about these successive life-approaches derives from my earlier observation that the *Bildungsroman* often depicts the protagonist involved in an oscillatory movement between poles of experience. Stephen exemplifies several types of oscillation, but the most fundamental is between modes of experience he construes as inner or subjective, and those he senses as outer or objective, thus reflecting his implicit division of his experience into outer and inner. That is, in chapter I Stephen's social life-response is to forces that he senses as coming from *without* him. In contrast, the approach that he assumes in chapter II, is a response to forces that he feels to come from *within* him. And as the schema indicates, there is a regular oscillation back to *outer* orientation in chapter III, and once again to *inner* orientation in chapter IV. But while this dichotomization of reality into subject and object, private and public, reveals how deeply into Stephen's psyche the Cartesian split has penetrated, Joyce by various means shows this dichotomization to be simplistic and un-veridical. It is by no means always easy for Stephen to construe his experience in these terms, since all human experience implicitly involves a fusion of "inner" and "outer." But this pattern of oscillation is necessary to Joyce's dramatization of the coming of age of an intelligent young man in a modernist, post-Cartesian intellectual milieu.[8] Nor is it accidental or trivial that Stephen's artistic calling (in chapter IV) comes to him on an inward (i.e., subjectivist) phase of his orientation. As we shall see, this reflects his innate predisposition toward an inner-oriented, symbolist view of art, and it consequently sets the terms of his reading of his problem of artistic identity and the relationship of the artist to society in chapter V.

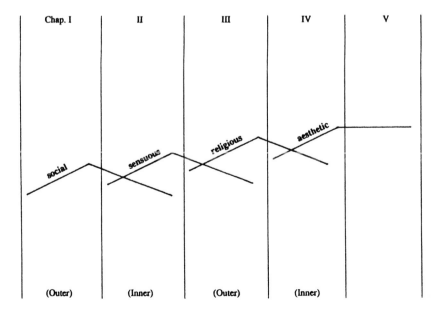

Figure. A structural pattern in Joyce's *Portrait of the Artist*.

The pattern I have just outlined is represented in the accompanying Figure. The schema shows that each of the first four chapters involves the surfacing of a distinctive approach to life on Stephen's part—an approach that is suggested by the rising line for each of the chapters and is epitomized by a climactic event just prior to the end of each chapter.[9] The descending lines in chapters II, III, and IV represent the subsequent collapse of the life-approach or orientation climaxed in the preceding chapter. Chapters II, III, and IV, then, have a chiastic structure, since they involve both the erosion of the preceding approach, and the emergence of a new one, accompanied by an enantiodromic swing between the Cartesian inner/outer poles.[10] Each of the successive climactic peaks is higher than the preceding one, to indicate that for Stephen each successive view of life supersedes what he now regards as an insufficient or mistaken earlier view. That is, in chapter IV, he does not see his aesthetic calling as simply one other possible alternative, but as more profound and fundamental than the preceding life-orientations, which he feels he is now transcending. Each of these middle chapters, then, involves the falling away of one approach to life, accompanied by the coming into being of a "more comprehensive" view. As the diagram suggests, the climax of chapter IV is the true climax of the novel—the highest peak—in the sense that the calling that Stephen discovers there is his true calling: he is by his nature intended to be an artist, not a priest (chapter III), nor a devotee of sensuous experience (chapter II), nor one of "the fellows" (chapter I).

The agenda of chapter V is quite different from that of the earlier chapters: Stephen is intended to be an artist, and so there are no more roller-coaster rises and falls of life-orientation; what remains is the tougher and less dramatic problem of Stephen's coming to understand what an artistic vocation requires of him. But as I have suggested, the terms in which he construes his artistic calling are established by his having come to his artistic vision on an inward swing of his psyche, reflecting his commitment to the symbolist, aestheticist conception of the artist. While this view is challenged by several experiences in chapter V it is not replaced by any new counter vision, leaving Stephen still entrammeled in a subjectivist view of art and the artist at the end of the novel. And while the Stephen that we see in *Ulysses* has been forcibly reoriented toward the material world by the trauma of his mother's death, and he has begun to cultivate a more realistic view of art (epitomized by his Parable of the Plums that stands in such contrast to his villanelle in *Portrait of the Artist*), he has not yet achieved the reconciliation of these presumed opposites that will enable his emergence as an artist.

Let me now clarify how Stephen's various life-approaches in the first four chapters of the novel manifest an oscillation between Cartesian poles. Once he gets beyond his infancy (pp. 7–8), Stephen's life-approach in chapter I is essentially social—i.e., it is a reaction to public, "objective" demands that he experiences as coming from *outside* himself. The primary forces impinging on Stephen during the Clongowes experience are from the society of his school, and during the Christmas dinner scene the young boy is subjected to forces arising from the public elements of politics, religion, and family. Though he does already have a distinctive, characterizable psyche quite different from that of his fellows at Clongowes, Stephen does not yet have any clear sense of his own self, and so he is continually buffeted by various influences and demands from a variety of directions—all sensed by him as arising from somewhere beyond or outside him. Perhaps the most constant note of this chapter is Stephen's puzzlement as to what is going on around him, and how to respond to it. This is epitomized by the questions put to him by Wells about whether he kisses his mother before bed; Stephen finds that either answer is wrong, and finds himself ridiculed by "the other fellows." His bafflement is manifested on a deeper and more traumatic scale by the terrible argument at the Christmas dinner table, and finally by the pandybatting. When he is pandybatted by Father Dolan for something that seems thrust upon him for no fault of his own, he is puzzled and disturbed over what the appropriate response to this injustice should be. Finally, at the urging of the other boys, he decides to pursue the regular social-hierarchical channels available to him, and to take his complaint to the rector. A passage late in chapter I shows how strongly Stephen's coming to this decision is influenced by the importunities of his (older) fellow students:

> —I wouldn't stand it, Fleming repeated, from Baldyhead or any other Baldyhead. It's a stinking mean low trick, that's what it is. I'd go straight up to the rector and tell him about it after dinner.
> —Yes, do. Yes, do, said Cecil Thunder.
> —Yes, do. Yes, go up and tell the rector on him, Dedalus, said Nasty Roche, because he said that he'd come in tomorrow again to pandy you.
> —Yes, yes. Tell the rector, all said.
> And there were some fellows out of second of grammar listening and one of them said:
> —The senate and the Roman people declared that Dedalus had been wrongly punished.

*　*　*

Yes, he would do what the fellows had told him. He would go up and tell the rector that he had been wrongly punished. A thing like that had been done before by somebody in history, by some great person whose head was in the books of history. And the rector would declare that he had been wrongly punished because the senate and the Roman people always declared that the men who did that had been wrongly punished. (pp. 52–53)

This passage suggests how fully Stephen's response to this crisis is socially formed and generated, and it involves a verbal motif that epitomizes the social nature of the forces at work on Stephen—the motif of "the fellows." This apparently bland, general term occurs frequently and at important intervals in this chapter. For example, section I.iv (pp. 40–59) opens with "The fellows," and over the next two pages, six paragraphs have the phrase either as their opening words or in their first sentence, and the last paragraph of the chapter begins with the phrase.[11] Young Stephen's punishment and even his crime have been pressed upon him from without—he feels no real sense of guilt—and now he pursues the socially-instituted mode of appeal because his schoolmates urge it upon him ("Yes, he would do what the fellows had told him"—p. 53.21), and because there is a public pattern for it in history (the senate and the Roman people—pp. 53.10, 53.26, 54.9), which seems to Stephen to involve a reality far more substantial than his fledgling soul. As a result of this urging by his peers, Stephen, in fear and trembling, makes his way through the corridors of the school to Father Conmee's office and tells him of the injustice. The rector listens sympathetically to the trembling boy, tells him that he will look into the incident, and Stephen returns to the playing fields, to be cheered and acclaimed by "the fellows" (pp. 58.16, 58.20, 58.28, and 59.18)—the social reward for his social act.

In his response to this early crisis, Stephen is pursuing a social approach to life and its problems, both in the sense that the actions he takes are strongly influenced by his school mates, and in that he is responding through the channels that the society of his school makes available to him, rather than through wiles of his own devising. Though his fledgling psyche has not yet fully developed the categories of inner and outer, both the source of the crisis and the means of solution are presented as basically *external* to the boy, brought to bear upon him from the outside.

In chapter II (as in every subsequent chapter) there is a marked increase in Stephen's self-awareness, and given his post-Cartesian orientation, he inevitably experiences his self, his psyche, as existing "within" him. Consequently this chapter is marked by more explicit reading on Stephen's part of his experience in terms of inner and outer than was chapter I. Appropriately, John Blades says that "whereas in Chapter I his progress was often the result of his response to *external* stimuli, here it is usually the result of both maturation and obscure *internal* promptings" (*James Joyce: "A Portrait of the Artist,"* p. 33; my emphasis). As a part of his larger individuation process, two important complementary developments occur in this chapter. The first is the gradual but clear erosion of Stephen's attempts to live his life as a social creature, to maintain that unity with the community (including the familial community) that characterized the end of chapter I and the opening of chapter II. The other is his growing awareness of sensuality and sexuality, which he construes as arising *within* him. The public world of relationships with family and friends comes to seem to him less real, less substantial, and the inner world of imagination, especially of sensual and sexual imagination, elaborates itself more fully and more forcibly to him. These two processes are experienced by Stephen as antithetical, and his susceptibility to inner influences is no doubt enhanced and given impetus by his withdrawal from those outer forces that have been so baffling and so hurtful to him in his earlier phase.

Each chapter opens with a carry-over of the life approach that emerged so dramatically in the preceding one, and so here we find Stephen still pursuing, in his relationship with Uncle Charles and with the old trainer Mike Flynn, though passively and perfunctorily, the social role that he had taken on. But we are told that Stephen "often glanced with mistrust" at the trainer's face, and, somewhat surprisingly, that he "respect[ed], though he did not share" his Uncle Charles' piety (pp. 61, 62). During this same period we are told that "his evenings were his own," and that they were spent in his poring over *The Count of Monte Cristo*. When Stephen comes to have a vague sense of his father's financial troubles—doubtless reminiscent for him of the threats he encountered at Clongowes—his response is to brood upon the image of Mercedes, and we are told that "sometimes a fever gathered within him and led him to rove alone in the evening along the quiet avenue" (p. 64). This is the first use in the novel of *within*, a word that occurs frequently as Stephen develops a fuller sense of a world "within" himself. Soon we are told of Stephen's growing sense that "he was different from others," and as a result, "he did not want to play. He wanted to meet in the *real* world the unsubstantial image which his soul so constantly beheld" (p. 65; my emphasis). This passage reveals his growing disdain for the society of his fellows, and the phrasing of the last sentence shows both that the inner world of his imagination (or his soul) is growing in authority for Stephen, and that he is coming to make a distinction between that interior realm and what he still regards as the "real world"—i.e., the public world. His experiences among his fellows and his teachers at Belvedere show Stephen to be much less susceptible to their appeals and accusations than when he was at Clongowes: His trip to Cork with his father only increases his alienation from his family and intensifies his sense of how utterly different he is from every one else, feeling that "an abyss of fortune or of temperament sundered him from [his father and his cronies]" (p. 95).

The crisis of this chapter occurs when Stephen wins the essay prize money and spends it in one last futile attempt to re-cement his familial relations. The erosion of his social ties and the triumph of sensuosity are clearly indicated in several paragraphs late in this chapter, paragraphs that show Stephen's sense of being under the influence of forces that he experiences as "external" and "internal," and the triumph in this phase of his life of the latter:

> How foolish his aim had been! He had tried to build a breakwater of order and elegance against the sordid tide of life *without him* and to dam up, by rules of conduct and active interests and new filial relations, the powerful recurrence of the tides *within him*. Useless. From *without* as from *within* the water had flowed over his barriers: their tides began once more to jostle fiercely above the crumbled mole.
>
> He saw clearly too his own futile isolation. He had not gone one step nearer the lives he had sought to approach nor bridged the restless shame and rancour that divided him from mother and brother and sister. He felt that he was hardly of the one blood with them but stood to them rather in the mystical kinship of fosterage, fosterchild and fosterbrother.
>
> He burned to appease the fierce longings of his heart before which everything else was idle and alien. He cared little that he was in mortal sin, that his life had grown to be a tissue of subterfuge and falsehood. Beside the savage desire *within him* to realize the enormities which he brooded on nothing was sacred. He bore cynically with the shameful details of his secret riots in which he exulted to defile with patience whatever image had attracted his eyes. By day and by night he moved among distorted images of the *outer world*. A figure that had seemed to him by day demure and innocent came towards him by night through the winding darkness of sleep, her face transfigured by a lecherous cunning, her eyes bright with brutish joy. Only the morning pained him with its dim memory of dark orgiastic riot, its keen and humiliating sense of transgression. (pp. 98–99; my emphasis)

While the experience that this passage describes obviously involves so subtle a blending of "inner" and "outer" elements that it is hard to discriminate them, it nevertheless shows that Stephen is construing his experience more and more in such dichotomous terms. The words that I have emphasized show explicitly Stephen's emerging sense of inner and outer, at the same time that other words or metaphors in this passage testify to the inner/outer distinction more subtly. Note the uses here of the images of *heart* and of *blood*, which are felt by Stephen to be inner, and the association of the public world with day and the private world with night.

But while this passage reveals Stephen's inclination to construe his experience in inner/outer terms, it simultaneously invokes more implicit elements of his experience that resist such reading. The term *image*, for example, used twice in this passage, is particularly interesting (and problematic) in terms of Stephen's attempts to distinguish his experiences into inner and outer, since every "image" necessarily involves an interface between subject and object, inner and outer. Probably in this inner-oriented phase of his life, Stephen regards images as something that spring up from within him, owing little or nothing to his public experience of the "outer world"; but we can see even in this passage that Stephen's images inevitably involve an inextricable blend of public and private aspects of his experience. This chapter ends with Stephen rejecting the call of family and society and, driven by lust and lured by the images his mind elaborates, winding his way through the streets of Dublin to his meeting with the prostitute, certain that, in giving himself over to what he feels rising within him, he is responding to the most real powers of life.

Chapter III also has a chiastic structure, depicting the falling away of Stephen's sensuous approach to life, and the rise of the religious approach. The chapter begins with a carryover of Stephen's sensuous phase—"stuff it into you, his belly counseled him" (p. 102)—but it quickly appears that this will be short-lived.[12] Reared and influenced by the Catholic Church— more precisely, by the Jesuits—as he has been, Stephen's sensuous/sensual experiences have always had the taint and the attraction of sin, and now that sense of sin comes to the fore. Under the searing effect of the retreat sermons, Stephen feels that in indulging his sensuality he has been building his life on shifting sands, and he must now turn to the firm rock of the Church. He sees that religion is the only true foundation upon which to build one's life. No doubt this decision is enforced by the sermons' being delivered by Father Arnall; we are explicitly told "the figure of his old master, so strangely rearisen, brought back to Stephen's mind his life at Clongowes.... His soul, as these memories came back to him, became again a child's soul" (pp. 108–109). The idea of Stephen as a vulnerable child is also played upon by the preacher's repeatedly addressing his hearers as "my dear little brothers in Christ," or as "my dear (little) boys." (The priest to whom he confesses also repeatedly calls him "my child.")

The effect of this on Stephen is shown in several ways. One is the sentimental little scene that Stephen imagines between himself and Emma in which both of them are seen as "children that had erred" (p. 116);

another is the great access of fellow-feeling that Stephen has: "at last he had understood: and human life lay around him, a plain of peace whereon antlike men laboured in brotherhood, their dead sleeping under quiet mounds. The elbow of his companion touched him and his heart was touched . . . ," and a bit later, "in utter abjection of spirit he craved forgiveness mutely of the boyish hearts about him" (p. 126). This motif of social companionship is reiterated after Stephen's confession when he feels the beauty, of living "a life of peace and virtue and forbearance with others" and we are told "the boys were all there, kneeling in their places. He knelt among them, happy and shy. . . . He knelt before the altar with his classmates, holding the altar cloth with them over a living rail of hands" (pp. 145–146).[13] Once again the chapter ends dramatically with an act that expresses Stephen's complete acceptance of his new-found religious way of life. Once again trembling with emotion, the boy makes his way through a labyrinth of streets (in order to avoid making his confession at his college), and the chapter ends in the dramatic scene of his pouring out his sins to the old priest.

In terms of the schema proposed above, this chapter involves a swing back on Stephen's part from influences that he experiences as subjective and private, to influences that are public and "social." This may seem an inappropriate characterization of something so emotionally powerful, so intense and personal, as the religious experiences that he undergoes in this chapter. But we are dealing here not with a Protestant fundamentalist or "inner light" tradition in which religious experience is construed as inherently personal, but with Irish Roman Catholicism, in which the institutional element is very strong, as are the ties between the church and other social institutions. To a large extent for Stephen (and for Joyce) religion is a public, social, "external" force, one that, especially in a Jesuit college, inescapably seeks one out and obtrudes itself upon one. Furthermore, there is textual evidence of various sorts that Stephen regards what he is responding to in this phase of his life as an outer (i.e., social) rather than an inner demand. There is, of course a sense in which the images and ideas of the Church get into Stephen's soul so fully that they do become integral to his self, and this is one device by which Joyce makes us realize the impossibility of categorizing modes of experience or influence into inner and outer.[14] But the demands of religion, the possibility of a religious vocation, come to Stephen primarily as external influences. It seems doubtful whether, left entirely to himself and without the pressures of his mentors, Stephen would seriously have considered a vocation in the priesthood, or even have developed on his own so deeply troubling a conviction of his own sin. It is the skillful, subtle voice of the preacher that reawakens his childhood feelings of vulnerability and guilt and sends him wandering once more through the labyrinth of Dublin's streets, again trembling with emotion, this time in search of a priest to confess to.

Chapter IV begins, as have the preceding ones, with a temporary continuation of the way of life dramatically expressed in the climax of the preceding chapter. Stephen has given himself over to the religious life as completely as possible—has laid his life out in devotional areas, etc. But once again the chapter depicts a falling away of one influence—the religious—and its replacement by another—the aesthetic—which Stephen once more presumes to be more substantial, more real, than the life-approach that he is turning his back upon. By this time, the reader may have sensed the pattern of the roller-coaster-like rise and fall of feelings that this young boy has already three times experienced, and so perhaps anticipates another such jaunt. We should not, then, be surprised to find that Stephen's religious approach to life soon begins to dissolve. What rises to take its place again involves a pendulum swing from the external to the internal, for Stephen's calling to art comes, he feels, from within the depths of his soul. Though we can see this most clearly in the ecstatic passages at the end of chapter IV, it is implied by a paragraph earlier in the chapter, when the true course of Stephen's destiny begins to become clear to him:

> He was passing at that moment before the Jesuit house in Gardiner Street, and wondered vaguely which window would be his if he ever joined the order. Then he wondered at the vagueness of his wonder, at the remoteness of his soul from what he had hitherto imagined her sanctuary, at the frail hold which so many years of order and obedience had of him when once a definite and irrevocable act of his threatened to end for ever, in time and in eternity, his freedom. The voice of the director urging upon him the proud claims of the church and the mystery and power of the priestly office repeated itself idly in his memory. His soul was not there to hear and greet it and he knew now the exhortation he had listened to had already fallen into an idle formal tale. He would never swing the thurible before the tabernacle as priest. His destiny was to be elusive of social or religious orders. The wisdom of the priest's appeal did not touch him to the quick. He was destined to learn his own wisdom apart from others or to learn the wisdom of others himself wandering among the snares of the world. (pp. 161–62)

Several aspects of this passage deserve attention. We should mark especially the statement that "his destiny was to be elusive of *social* or *religious* orders," further supporting the claim that in Stephen's mind the religious perspective is paired with the social as representing external forces (my terms *social* and *religious* for chapters I and III derive from this sentence).

Also, the passage testifies in various ways to the "externality" of the priest's exhortation: Stephen's soul is not there to hear or greet it; the appeal does not "touch [Stephen] to the quick"; and he contrasts that ineffectual call with "his own wisdom."

The climax of the chapter—the scene on the beach when Stephen sees the wading girl and realizes that his true calling, his destiny, is to be an artist—is also the climax of the novel. That is, the calling to all that Stephen feels in this lyrical, ecstatic passage is his valid calling. While it does require the whole of this famous passage to convey Stephen's ecstasy, I quote only those aspects that show how fully the experience derives from within Stephen's psyche, Stephen's soul, with relatively little provocation from the "external world."

> A girl stood before him in midstream, alone and still, gazing out to sea. She seemed like one whom magic had changed into the likeness of a strange and beautiful seabird.
> ... when she felt his presence and the worship of his eyes her eyes turned to him in quiet sufferance of his gaze, without shame or wantonness. ...
> —Heavenly God! cried Stephen's soul, in an outburst of profane joy.
>
>   * * *
>
> Her image had passed into his soul for ever and no word had broken the holy silence of his ecstasy. Her eyes had called him and his soul had leaped at the call. ... A wild angel had appeared to him, the angel of mortal youth and beauty, an envoy from the fair courts of life, to throw open before him in an instant of ecstasy the gates of all the ways of error and glory. (pp. 171–72)

The passage expresses the depth and completeness of Stephen's feeling that he has now found his true life's calling, and clearly Stephen is expressing something that he senses as coming from within himself, not something foisted upon him from the public, external world. The cry that Stephen utters comes straight from his soul, and his communion with the wading girl has nothing of the social or the institutional about it. Undoubtedly Stephen's ignorance of who the girl is facilitates her serving as an objectification of what is welling forth from within him.

Stephen arrives at his artistic calling on an inward swing of his psychic pendulum. What this implies, and what is borne out by various aspects of chapter V, is that Stephen's conception of art and the artist arises from an inward, subjectivist orientation and thus implicitly expresses his commitment to a "symbolist" (rather than a "naturalist") understanding of art. This is not to say that his view of art is "caused by" his inner orientation; rather, it is characteristic of something deep in his psyche that he would come to a sense of this calling on an inner swing of the pendulum, rather than an outer (as Zola presumably would have). This subjective orientation reveals Stephen's symbolist/aestheticist conception of the artist which is very much a function of his milieu. Granted, not every artist who emerged around the turn of the century necessarily construed his calling in symbolist/aesthetic terms. But it is important that (as Marguerite Harkness has pointed out in the passage quoted above in chapter 3, footnote 22), most of them did construe the artist's calling in terms either of symbolism/aestheticism OR naturalism/realism, both of which Joyce regards as partial and incomplete. Precisely what predisposed Stephen toward the aestheticist approach to art rather than the naturalistic—i.e., why he implicitly feels art to be an expression of his soul rather than a documentation of the world around him we cannot fully explain. Doubtless the Dublin milieu depicted in *Dubliners*, which drives all sensitive persons into inward retreat (see "Araby" and "A Painful Case"), had something to do with it, as did the powerful examples of Pater, Wilde, and Yeats (though we should not forget that other young writers sought out the pattern of Zola and the brothers Goncourt). But Stephen's own distinctive temperament plays a large role in his construing the nature of the artist as he does. In any event, the fact that he discovers his artistic calling on an inward phase of his oscillating orientation enables us better to understand the biases and deficiencies of his view of the artist, and to appreciate what Stephen must begin to do in this novel and in *Ulysses* to redress that imbalance.[15] His problem in chapter V is to understand the meaning of this new-found calling.

Several elements in this scene on the beach suggest that this fourth realization is more substantial than those in the first three chapters. In the first three scenes Stephen makes his way to his climactic meeting by wandering through a maze or labyrinth—first in the school corridors, and then in chapters two and three, through the streets of Dublin. This motif invokes the treacherous maze that Daedalus made for King Minos of Crete, and suggests that in these scenes Stephen is wandering blindly. The climactic scene of the fourth chapter occurs on an open beach with a feeling of breadth and expansiveness, suggesting that this affirmation is qualitatively different from the others, and that the calling of artist is Stephen's true calling. Appropriately, the subject of chapter V, then, is not another violent rise and fall or orientation on Stephen's part, but the more mundane, less dramatic, question of Stephen's attempts to work out what his vocation as artist involves.

One interesting pattern among the four climactic scenes that undergirds the oscillation between external and internal influences is the sex of the other person involved in each of the scenes. In chapters I and III—those designated as the social and religious phases and manifesting an external claim—the climactic scene presents Stephen with a male figure of considerable authority (Father Conmee, and the priest), whereas in chapters II and IV, sensuous and aesthetic, involving an internal orientation, the other figure is a woman (the prostitute, and the wading girl). This is in keeping with Joyce's inclination throughout his canon to associate the male with some mode of external or social authority and the woman with the inner self or the soul. Though Jung had not yet articulated his ideas of the anima and the animus when *Portrait* was published, it seems clear that Joyce is here thinking in such terms. In chapters I and III, Stephen is responding to some "external," authoritative behest, represented in each case by a male figure (more specifically by a priest). In chapters II and IV, Stephen is responding to some deeply personal and internal call, in both cases epitomized in a female figure who objectifies this latent part of his psyche.[16]

In true *Bildungsroman* form, then, the very structure of the novel derives from and expresses the patterns and rhythms of Stephen's development—its rises and falls, its swings from outer to inner. Each chapter climaxes with a new and presumably fuller understanding on Stephen's part of how to live life, and each succeeding chapter shows this orientation dissolve under the influence of other more compelling demands.

I agree with the consensus that the end of chapter IV is the climax of the novel.[17] The validity of Stephen's aesthetic calling is borne out not only by the remainder of this novel, but by *Ulysses* as well. That Stephen has not yet become a successful or full-fledged artist even by the time we leave him in *Ulysses* does not disprove that art is his calling; rather, it simply reflects his not yet having found an orientation, a life-grounding, out of which to write. Such a *point d'appui* must, among other things, involve Stephen's getting beyond the dualism that now holds him in thrall—i.e., his coming to understand that matter is not the enemy of spirit, but is the indispensable means of its manifestation.

But Stephen's discovery of his artistic calling is not the only thing that happens at this crucial point in the novel, and from the perspective of the themes that we are tracing, perhaps not the most important. The fundamental theme that emerges here is that of Stephen's self-awareness and self-determination, rendering this scene the novel's climax because Stephen sees himself as no longer the passive product of the forces acting upon him, but the arbiter of his own destiny. This is reflected, of course, in his discovering his artistic calling, but it is reflected even more profoundly in Stephen's remaking, redefining for himself, the meaning of various aspects of his experience. In Stephen's own view this episode is a crucial step toward his self-understanding and self-determination, toward his becoming captain of his fate and master of his soul. Now that he has realized the implications of his name—realized who he is—he is no longer a mere pawn, no longer the creature of forces acting upon him, but is actively creating his own self: "his soul had arisen from the grave of boyhood, spurning her graveclothes. Yes! Yes! Yes! He would create proudly out of the freedom and power of his soul, as the great artificer whose name he bore, a living thing, new and soaring and beautiful, impalpable, imperishable" (p. 170). But we shall see that this idea of self-creation, grounded as it is in Stephen's superficial modernist sense of the self, is naive and unfeasible.

Stephen's presumption of taking responsibility for his own destiny generates a change in tone from chapter IV to chapter V that has been noted by many critics.[18] But while Joyce does to some extent recede from his character, he does not lose sympathy with him. In the period that intervenes between chapters IV and V, Stephen has assumed the mantle and the mannerisms of self-determination. He has become more circumspect, more defensive. Like Lucifer, he has made claims to self-sufficiency, and he must assume the burdens of that claim. Gone is the naive young boy who was so vulnerable to forces sweeping over him from within or without. And as a result of this defensiveness and presumptuousness, Stephen is less appealing than he was in the preceding chapters. But this too is a necessary phase of his overall development, a phase that has not yet been completed even in *Ulysses*, though there are promising signs in that novel.

We can trace in chapter V various effects of Stephen's aspirations to self-knowledge and self-determination, and of his construing his artistic calling subjectively. One of these is his implicit view of freedom as escape, which exemplifies my earlier claims about the way that theme often works in the *Bildungsroman*. As we have seen, the character and the author of the novel often conceive of freedom differently, which provides the thematic basis for irony. This may seem surprising, since we think of the *Bildungsroman* as an autobiographical form, and often identify the author and his character. For many readers, Stephen Dedalus is Joyce, Eugene Gant is Thomas Wolfe, Paul Morel is D. H. Lawrence. But scrutiny of most *Bildungsromane* will confirm the distance between author and protagonist a distance that usually manifests itself (among other ways) in two contrasting conceptions of freedom. The young hero, in his late 'teens or early twenties, sees freedom as escape, lack of restraint, as utter self-determination; the author, writing from the perspective of his late twenties or early thirties, sees this view as simplistic and escapistic, and is more likely to regard freedom as a realization of one's potentialities, necessarily involving a degree of social relatedness—or at least the acknowledgment of the social nature of one's own self—that the young protagonist finds intolerable. In this situation the writer must find a way to convey this ironic distance between his character's views and his own.

Stephen's elaboration of his aesthetic theory is another effect of his aspiration to self-knowledge and self-control. In this chapter it becomes clear that Stephen is more adept at aesthetic theorizing than he is at writing works of art. He develops a subtle and overwrought theory of art which he derives from Aristotle and Aquinas. But his only artistic creation is his effete, narcissistic villanelle.[19] Perhaps some modicum of theorizing about life and art is necessary to the growth of the artist, but Stephen is in danger of taking refuge in theorizing, rather than engaging life and art. Apparently Stephen feels that he cannot become an artist until he has fully formulated an aesthetic theory, which he sees as simply a part of his being totally self-aware. But I argued earlier that an important turning point came for Joyce when he understood that his being an artist did not require his developing a full–fledged theory of art (see above, pp. 50–52).

This aesthetic theory has been the subject of a great deal of critical commentary, dealing with the nature of the theory itself, and its relationship to Joyce's own ideas and to his works. For the purposes of my present argument the specific philosophic claims of the theory; or its autobiographical status, are not so important as are the manner and the motives of Stephen's presentation of it, and his devoting so much of his energy to theoretical issues. That is, we should recognize that the primary function of this theorizing in *Portrait* is not to present Joyce's ideas on art, but further to characterize Stephen.[20] Joyce's distancing from Stephen here manifests itself not in regard to the theory itself—which I find not only coherent but very close to what Joyce himself believed—but in the tenor. and the purposes of its presentation, and in Stephen's resort to it to maintain some control over his experience. This theorizing on Stephen's part, then, involves one of the most fundamental questions that Joyce is exploring here and in *Ulysses*—the question of how much abstract, theoretical knowledge one must have in order to be an artist.

Stephen's subjectivist orientation toward art and the artist also puts him in danger of what Joyce considers an even worse failing—the use of his art, or his role as an artist, as a refuge from unpleasant aspects of life. Joyce was keenly aware that for some artists art becomes not a means of engaging reality, but of escaping from it. While such an attitude may not be a logical corollary of a subjectivist conception of art, the inward turn of the aestheticist does easily involve his regarding the "exterior world" as something to be retreated from. Perhaps the classic text here is Wilde's statement (through the persona of Gilbert in "The Critic as Artist") that "it is through Art, and through Art only, that we can realize our perfection; through Art, and through Art only, that we can shield ourselves from the sordid perils of actual existence" (Oscar Wilde, p. 274).

But attractive as this view may be to Stephen, Joyce himself did not see things this way. Quite the contrary, Joyce felt that the artist had an obligation far beyond that of the "ordinary person" to face up to every aspect of life, including those that might seem coarse or sordid. The story is told that, soon after the publication of *Ulysses*, Joyce met his cousin Kathleen, daughter of his favorite aunt, Josephine Murray, in London, and he asked her how her mother had responded to *Ulysses*. Kathleen replied, with embarrassment, that her mother had said the book was not fit to read. "If *Ulysses* isn't fit to read," Joyce replied, "life isn't fit to live" (*JJ II*, p. 537). Joyce's reply conveys his belief that the artist must face up to life squarely, that he cannot use his art as a crutch or an escape.[21]

That Stephen has not yet learned this is shown by several passages reflecting his attempts to use his art as a means of distancing or protecting himself from life's less appealing aspects. Consider this passage describing his morning walk to the university through one of the lower sections of Dublin:

> His morning walk across the city had begun, and he foreknew
> that as he passed the sloblands of Fairview he would think of
> the cloistral silverveined prose of Newman, that as he walked
> along the North Strand Road, glancing idly at the windows of
> the provision shops, he would recall the dark humor of Guido
> Cavalcanti and smile, that as he went by Baird's stonecutting
> works in Talbot Place the spirit of Ibsen would blow through
> him like a keen wind, a spirit of wayward boyish beauty, and that
> passing a grimy marinedealer's shop beyond the Liffey he would
> repeat the song by Ben Jonson which begins:
>   *I was not wearier where I lay.* (p. 176)

Stephen's inclination to use the realm of art as a retreat from the sordid reality of the external world is clear here, and is one sign that he has not come to terms with the implications and responsibilities of his calling.[22]

While on one level Stephen is sincerely striving to see what it means to be an artist, on another he is merely playing out the current stereotype of the artist that derives from Walter Pater and Oscar Wilde and other fin de siècle aesthetes whose names are now obscurity.[23] It involves seeing the artist as sensitive, almost too sensitive for life, as inherently misunderstood by the Philistines around him, and as therefore necessarily alienated and outcast. Such an attitude shows through in several of Stephen's characteristic comments and stances toward his fellow students, and in certain of the diary entries that close the novel (e.g., 20 March; 21 March, night; 3 April). But if we look closely, we will see as well some of those deeper and better qualities in Stephen that remind us Joyce's ironic perspective on Stephen is essentially sympathetic and even admiring. (I referred briefly to some of Stephen's more appealing, self-effacing qualities in footnote 18 above.)

Consider the April 15 diary entry, on the next-to-last page of the novel:

> Met her today pointblank in Grafton Street. The crowd brought us together. We both stopped. She asked me why I never came, said she had heard all sorts of stories about me. This was only to gain time. Asked me, was I writing poems? About whom? I asked her. This confused her more and I felt sorry and mean. Turned off that valve at once and opened the spiritual-heroic refrigerating apparatus, invented and patented in all countries by Dante Alighieri. Talked rapidly of myself and my plans. In the midst of it unluckily I made a sudden gesture of a revolutionary nature. I must have looked like a fellow throwing a handful of peas into the air. People began to look at us. She shook hands a moment after and, in going away, said she hoped I would do what I said.
>
> Now I call that friendly, don't you?
>
> Yes, I liked her today. A little or much? Don't know. I liked her and it seems a new feeling to me. Then, in that case, all the rest, all that I thought I thought and all that I felt I felt, all the rest before now, in fact ... O, give it up, old chap! Sleep it off?
> (p. 252)

This interesting and complex passage focuses the problem of Stephen's inadequate personal relationships, especially with women. He is snide and sarcastic to Emma, then feels sorry and mean, then attempts to retreat into a Platonic relationship by turning off the valve of human sympathy and turning on the spiritual-heroic refrigerating apparatus that Western culture has learned from Dante. But most important is his statement in the last paragraph, which suggests that this liking—not passion, not adoration, but *liking*—might be the doorway to fuller and more meaningful personal relationships for Stephen. But if that is the case (he asks himself), what about all the supposed isolation of the artist, all that Stephen had thought he thought and felt he felt? But he opts to sleep it off. Apparently he is not yet ready to pursue the difficult, tangled path of relationships with others; he still prefers the heady heights of aesthetic isolation. But the seed of social relatedness is there, and will germinate.[24]

The last two diary entries also contain interesting implications in regard to Stephen's autonomy:

> *26 April*: Mother is putting my new secondhand clothes in order. She prays now, she says, that I may learn in my own life and away from home and friends what the heart is and what it feels. Amen. So be it. Welcome, O life! I go to encounter for the millionth time the reality of experience and to forge in the smithy of my soul the uncreated conscience of my race.
>
> *27 April*: Old father, old artificer, stand me now and ever in good stead. (pp. 252–53)

Stephen here seems to take a softer attitude toward his mother, acknowledging her love and sympathy for him, and sensing that her love may well be—as Cranly has told him (pp. 241–42)—the most real thing in life. Later Stephen himself wonders whether a mother's love may not be the "only true thing in life" (*U*, 2.143 and 9.843). But he cannot pause now to consider that—he is about to set out to create the conscience of his race.

The image he uses in the final diary entry recalls Stephen's earlier thought of the fabulous artificer, Daedalus, and the story of Daedalus and Icarus, who attempted to fly from their island of Crete to the mainland. But if we reflect on this, we realize that Stephen, wittingly or unwittingly, calls upon the father, Daedalus, thus casting himself as the naive and exuberant son. Does he realize this? Probably not, but Joyce does, and wants us to. (For fuller discussion of this passage, see pp. 144–45, below.) In this, too, the novel is typical of the *Bildungsroman*, in that Stephen is regarded by his creator with sympathetic irony. Stephen will eventually find the meaning of his calling as an artist, and will accept its challenges and responsibilities. For now, though, he remains naive and romantic. Joyce is willing to have us see this and understand that this promising young man yet has some way to go.

NOTES

1. From Gaggi's *Modern/Postmodern: A Study in Twentieth-Century Arts and Ideas* (Philadelphia: Univ. of Pennsylvania Press, 1990), pp. 157–58. Gaggi is drawing upon Jonathan Culler's discussion of "the anti-humanistic implications of semiotics and structuralism, which suggest that 'the self is dissolved as its various functions are ascribed to impersonal systems that operate through it.' The individual ceases to be centered in an *a priori* 'self' but becomes instead a locus where various signifying systems intersect" (Gaggi quotes from Jonathan Culler's *The Pursuit of Signs: Semiotics, Literature, Deconstruction* [Ithaca: Cornell Univ. Press, 1981], p. 33. Chapter 2 of Culler's book discusses how the self is dissolved into the cultural nexus]. R. B. Kershner's reading comes very close to eliding Joyce and Stephen into the various cultural influences and texts that act upon them. He

says for example that "much of *Portrait* reflects—or embodies—Stephen's possession by the languages that surround him, and his attempts to appropriate them in turn" (*Joyce, Bakhtin, and Popular Literature: Chronicles of Disorder* [Chapel Hill: Univ. of North Carolina Press, 1989], p. 154); "For long stretches, during this phase of his development, Stephen's thoughts simply are not his own" (Ibid., p. 157); and "Stephen is a product of his listening and reading, an irrational sum of the texts, written and spoken, to which he has been exposed. . . . the very structure of his consciousness is dependent upon these texts" (Ibid., p. 162); and Kershner refers to Stephen's being "'spoken through' even in his private thoughts, in a sort of mental ventriloquy" (Ibid., p. 164). John McGowan's discussion of the self, in "From Pater to Wilde to Joyce: Modernist Epiphany and the Soulful Self," *Texas Studies in Literature and Language* 32 (Fall 1990): 417–45, sees modern and postmodern conceptions of the self as involving either a heroic self created ex nihilo, or a denial of the constraints of selfhood; he posits no healthy alternative, and he presumes that Stephen's heroic view of the self is sanctioned by Joyce. (For other critics who would dissolve the self into its linguistic and cultural components, see the citations of Hugh Kenner's "*Ulysses,*" Colin MacCabe's *James Joyce and the Revolution of the Word*, and Cheryl Herr's *Joyce's Anatomy of Culture* in Chapter 3, footnote 38.)

2. Richard Ellmann also cites this observation of Stanislaus' and says "for *A Portrait of the Artist as a Young Man* is in fact the gestation of a soul, and in the metaphor Joyce found his new principle of order" (*JJ II*, pp. 296–97). He goes on to describe the unfolding of Stephen's character in keeping with this metaphor. Fritz Senn also stresses the developmental and process-oriented aspects of the novel in his "*A Portrait*: Temporal Foreplay," *Etudes Irlandaises* No. 12 (December 1987): 65–73.

3. "Strings in the Labyrinth: Sixty Years with Joyce's *Portrait,*" in *Approaches to Joyce's "Portrait": Ten Essays*, ed. Thomas F. Staley and Bernard Benstock, (Pittsburgh: Univ. of Pittsburgh Press, 1976), p. 20. Maurice Beebe, in *Ivory Towers and Sacred Founts*, speaks pointedly of "the structure of the novel, which is identical with the development of Stephen . . ." (p. 268).

4. Since virtually every discussion of Stephen's character, including those of various psychological motifs, involves the novel's structure, a review of the critical literature relevant to this issue would survey a large proportion of what has been written about it. (As early as 1964 Robert J. Andreach apologized for offering yet another discussion of the novel's structure, in his *Studies in Structure* (New York: Fordham Univ. Press, 19641.) The discussions that I have found most provocative or helpful are the following (chronologically listed): Hugh Kenner, "The *Portrait* in Perspective" (1948, 1955); Dorothy Van Ghent, *The English Novel: Form and Function* [New York: Rinehart and Company, 1953]; Grant H. Redford, "The Role of Structure in Joyce's *Portrait,*" *Modern Fiction Studies* 4 (Spring 1958): 21–30; Robert J. Andreach, *Studies in Structure* (1964); David Hayman, "*A Portrait of the Artist as a Young Man* and *L'Education Sentimentale*: The Structural Affinities," *Orbis Litterarum* 19 (1964): 161–75; J. E. Hardy, "Joyce's *Portrait*: The Flight of the Serpent," in *Man in the Modern Novel*, pp. 67–81 (Seattle: Univ. of Washington Press, 1964); Thomas Van Laan, "The Meditative Structure of Joyce's *Portrait,*" *JJQ* 1 (Spring 1964): 3–13; Evert Sprinchorn, "A Portrait of the Artist as Achilles," in *Approaches to the Twentieth-Century Novel*, ed. John Unterrecker (New York: Crowell, 1965), pp. 9–50; Sidney Feshbach, "A Slow and Dark Birth: A Study of the Organization of *A Portrait of the Artist as a Young Man,*" *JJQ* 4 (Summer 1967): 289–300; Lee T. Lemon, "*A Portrait of the Artist as a Young Man*": Motif as Motivation and Structure," *Modern Fiction Studies* 12 (Winter 1967–68): 441–52; K. E. Robinson, "Stream of Consciousness Technique" (1971); H. O. Brown, *James Joyce's Early Fiction* (1972); Diane Fortuna, "The Labyrinth as Controlling Image in Joyce's *A Portrait,*"

Bulletin of the New York Public Library 76 (1972): 120–80; William A. Gordon, "Submission and Autonomy: Identity Patterns in Joyce's *Portrait*," *Psychoanalytic Review* 61 (Winter 1974–75): 535–55; Bernard Benstock, "A Light from Some Other World: Symbolic Structures in *A Portrait of the Artist as a Young Man,*" in *Approaches to Joyce's "Portrait,"* ed. Thomas F. Staley and Bernard Benstock (Pittsburgh: Univ. of Pittsburgh Press, 1976), pp. 185–211; Hans Walter Gabler, "The Seven Lost Years of *A Portrait*" (1976); J. Delbaere-Garant, "From the Moocow to Navelless Eve: The Spiral Growth of Stephen Dedalus," *Revue des langues vivantes* [*Tijdschrift Voor Levende Talent* 43 (1977): 131–41; Jon Lanham, "The Genre of *A Portrait of the Artist as a Young Man* and 'the rhythm of its structure,'" *Genre* 10 (1977): 77–102; Sheldon Brivic, *Joyce Between Freud and Jung* (Port Washington, N.Y.: Kennikat Press, 1980); Thomas E. Connolly, "Kinesis and Stasis: Structural Rhythm in Joyce's *Portrait*," *Irish Renaissance Annual II* (1981): 166–84; Rita Di Guiseppe, "The Mythos of Irony and Satire in Joyce's *Portrait*," *Quaderni di Lingue e Letterature* 6 (1981): 33–48; Margaret Church, "How the Vicociclometer Works: The Fiction of James Joyce," in *Structure and Theme: "Don Quixote" to James Joyce* (Columbus: Ohio State Univ. Press, 1983), pp. 135–67; Richard Peterson, "Stephen and the Narrative of *A Portrait of the Artist as a Young Man*," in *Work in Progress: Joyce Centenary Essays*, ed. Richard F. Peterson, Alan M. Cohn, and Edmund L. Epstein (Carbondale: Southern Illinois Univ. Press, 1983), pp. 15–29; John Paul Riquelme, *Teller and Tale in Joyce's Fiction: Oscillating Perspectives* (Baltimore: Johns Hopkins Univ. Press, 1983); J. F. Carens, "Portrait" (1984); B. L. Reid, "Gnomon and Order in Joyce's *Portrait*," *Sewanee Review* 92 (1984): 397–420; Marguerite Harkness, *Aesthetics* (1984); Elliott B. Gose, Jr., "Destruction and Creation in *A Portrait of the Artist as a Young Man*," *JJQ* 22 (Spring 1985): 259–70; Joseph A. Buttigieg, *"A Portrait of the Artist" in Different Perspective* (1987); Gerald Doherty, "From Encounter to Creation: The Genesis of Metaphor in *A Portrait of the Artist as a Young Man*," *Style* 21 (Summer 1987): 219–36; and Phillip Herring, *Joyce's Uncertainty Principle* (1987). While I do not agree with all of these claims for structural patterns in the novel, neither do I feel that they necessarily contradict one another, for Joyce has woven innumerable overlapping and intersecting structural patterns into Stephen's development.

5. I might pose this first point as a question: Can we, in this quintessential *Bildungsroman*, discover any aspect of the novel's structure that is not simultaneously an aspect of Stephen's psyche? In the subsequent discussion of the novel's style, we shall see how difficult it is to discover any image, even any metaphor or simile, that we can regard simply as part of an artifactual design of the novel or an authorial perspective, and that does not in some way enter either into Stephen's "individual" psyche, or form some part of his cultural psyche. This issue involves interesting problems about the relationship between the unity of an aesthetic work and that of the individual psyche. For example, since the protagonist's self is still in process of formation even as the work ends, is there not an inherent discrepancy between the structures of the novel and those of Stephen's psyche? Must not the structures of the novel "round out" at the end in a way that those of the self cannot? Phillip F. Herring points to this problem when he says "the form [of *Portrait*] must therefore be incomplete or indeterminate because its autobiographical aspect can never catch up with its fictional denouement, or Joyce might have shown us Stephen beginning to write the work of which he is the subject" (*Joyce's Uncertainty Principle*, p. 172). R. B. Kershner also touches upon these issues: "in a book as dependent upon the protagonist's consciousness as is *Portrait* we find it difficult to ascribe the 'shape' of a chapter or an episode either to the impress of Stephen's consciousness in the organization that he imparts to his experience, on the one hand, or to the aesthetic intention of Joyce, on the other. . . . Nonetheless, there are areas, such as those involving the structure of the entire book, in which it is not practical to ascribe the primary

role to the protagonist, whose mind, language, and sense of structure are in continual change" (*Joyce, Bakhtin, and Popular Literature*, p. 153). Not surprisingly, some critics have claimed that *Portrait* is written by Stephen—however baffling that may be to common sense; see J. P. Riquelme, *Teller and Tale in Joyce's Fiction*, pp. 51 ff., and K. E. Robinson, who proposes that the first 164 pages of the novel are "recollection," the subsequent pages Joyce's authorial presentation ("Stream of Consciousness Technique," p. 63)—an idea endorsed by Jon Lanham, "The Genre of *A Portrait of the Artist*," pp. 100–01. In the next chapter we will discuss the tendency, noted by Dorrit Cohn, in her *Transparent Minds: Narrative Modes for Presenting Consciousness in Fiction* (Princeton: Princeton Univ. Press, 1978), to treat novels that skillfully employ narrated monologue as if they had no narrator. Herring's objection, though, overlooks both the unaccountable degree to which the self does have considerable "unity" at every stage of its progressive unfolding, and the capacity of a literary work to project its structures beyond its ending. One study that proposes a pattern in the novel that it seems could hardly apply to Stephen's psyche is that of Evert Sprinchorn ("A Portrait of the Artist as Achilles"), who argues that there is a regular pattern of inverse repetition throughout the novel, by virtue of which sections 1, 2, 3, 4, etc. throughout the first half of the novel are recapped in opposite order in the latter half, 4, 3, 2, 1. (The text of *Portrait* in which Sprinchorn discovers this pattern has seventeen "sections" rather than the nineteen of the 1964 text edited by Chester G. Anderson. For Sprinchorn's defense of his choice of text, see footnote #7 of his essay.) But there is some such structure in Stephen's psyche, though not so symmetrically, insofar as the "mature" Stephen goes back over his youthful experiences, trying to re-read or re-make them. Richard F. Peterson develops the salutary point that the narrative of *Portrait*, including such things as the cycles of the seasons, has an existence apart from Stephen's subjectivity, such that even when he thinks mistakenly about things, he nonetheless must perceive the ineluctable reality of this world around him. As Peterson puts it, "the reason for the undeniable movement of the seasons and the irresistible rhythm of tides within and without in *A Portrait* is to assure us that the body of reality has its own identity" ("Stephen and the Narrative of *A Portrait*," p. 27). I very much concur, but would stress that this body of reality is experienced by Stephen not as "inert matter," but as a public psychic entity—not "subjective" (in the sense of residing solely within Stephen), but psychic nonetheless.

6. Lee Lemon recognizes this implication and suggests that Joyce's use of motifs as motivating elements in Stephen's psyche necessarily involves very implicit stimuli. See Lemon, "Motif as Motivation and Structure," pp. 43, 44, 51.

7. Perhaps the most assiduous Freudian reading is Chester G. Anderson's "Baby Tuckoo: Joyce's 'Features of Infancy,'" in *Approaches to Joyce's "Portrait": Ten Essays*, ed. Thomas F. Staley and Bernard Benstock (Pittsburgh: Univ. of Pittsburgh Press, 1976), 135–69. While I do concur with psychoanalytical readings in seeing Stephen's psyche as involving subconscious elements, there are crucial differences between such approaches and my own: they ascribe undue importance to sexuality, they presume the forces or patterns they explore to be virtually deterministic, and they do not see the dynamics that they discuss as an integral part of a larger, positive process of "individuation." Other psychoanalytical readings of the novel include William A. Gordon's "Submission and Autonomy"—an intelligent, perspicacious essay), Calvin Thomas's "Stephen in Process/Stephen on Trial," and Sheldon Brivic's *The Veil of Signs*.

8. As we have already seen (Chapter 3, footnote #37), Maurice Beebe has defended Joyce's style as a brilliant effort to show how the typical young artist of his time viewed the world ("*Portrait* as Portrait," p. 29). I am claiming that this veridicality necessarily extends to the structure of the novel, since that structure is an expression of his underlying view of reality.

9. I had used this figure for the novel's structure in class discussions long before coming across B. L. Reid's similar description. Reid says "the action of chapter I [which he sees as a paradigm of the whole] can be crudely abstracted as an inclined plane slanting upward, beginning low and moving gradually then suddenly high. That is a coarse graph of the whole action of the novel, and it works for each of the five pans" ("Gnomon and Order," p. 406). Later Reid says ". . . one sees a succession of five inclined planes slanting from low to high. The eye . . . then tends to draw a mental dotted vertical line from each high end to the following low beginning" (p. 420). In my figure, the declining line slopes gradually and crosses the ascending one at about mid-chapter, to suggest that each successive approach erodes gradually as the next one arises.

10. Chiasmus as a structural element of the novel has been proposed by several critics, on various scales. Gabler ("The Seven Lost Years of A Portrait") and, more extensively, Sprinchorn ("A Portrait of the Artist as Achilles"), have described the larger structures of the book in these terms; Eliott B. Gose, Jr. has explored it on the level of phrase and sentence, and as it enters into Stephen's creative process itself. Gose sees chiasmic statements as attempts to balance inner and outer in Stephen's experience ("Destruction and Creation in *A Portrait*," p. 259). Hugh Kenner briefly discusses chiasmus on several levels in his Introduction to the Signet edition of *Portrait* (New York: Penguin Books USA Inc., 1991).

11. It may be questionable whether so ordinary, unimagistic a term as "the fellows" constitutes a psychological "motif" for Stephen, but these words are doubtless associated unpleasantly with the bewildering social forces the young boy is subjected to at this time. A glance at Leslie Hancock's Word Index to *James Joyce's "Portrait of the Artist"* (Carbondale and Edwardsville: Southern Illinois Univ. Press, 1967) shows the great preponderance of fellow, fellow's, and fellows in chapter I. And most occurrences of these words in subsequent chapters strongly carry the theme of social demands upon Stephen. For example, Mr, Dedalus says of the Jesuits, "those are the fellows that can get you a position" (p. 71). And in the single paragraph that involves most of the uses of these words after Chapter I, Mr. Dedalus, in Cork, advises his son, whatever he does to "mix with gentlemen," and says, "when I was a young fellow I tell you I enjoyed myself. I mixed with fine decent fellows" and the words occur five more times in this paragraph of quintessentially social, paternal advice (pp. 91–92). But by now it is obvious to Stephen how inappropriate and ineffectual such advice is. This flurry of fellow and fellows signals an important juncture in Stephen's turning his back on such social demands.

12. I have labeled this approach to life sensuous rather than sensual to suggest that the "inner" forces acting on Stephen at this time are not confined to sexuality. Here it is his belly that is counseling him. The word counseled invokes the motif of voices, which itself reflects Stephen's inner/outer predisposition, in that some of the voices that Stephen hears he regards as representing private needs, others public demands. Here he construes his belly as expressing a demand of his inner sensuosity. Interestingly, Stephen in *Portrait* never manifests the extreme modernist disjunction that would regard his body as outer, as alien to his self. The various somatic motifs of blood, heart, belly, are all read as aspects of Stephen's self. (In *Stephen Hero* we are at one point told "His body disturbed him and he adopted the expedient of appeasing it by gentle promenading" [*SH*, p. 69].) A more reflective Stephen in *Ulysses* does not feel so comfortable with his body and cannot so easily identify it with his self. He is aware of the decay of his teeth (*U*, 3.494), for which Mulligan mocks him (*U*, 1.708 and 1.412), and in Wandering Rocks, listening to the whirr of the dynamos in the powerhouse in Fleet Street, Stephen refuses to identify his self with either the outer or the inner: "Throb always without you and the throb always within. . . . I between them. Where?

Between two roaring worlds where they swirl, I" (*U*, 10.822–824). Regarding the body as outer or alien does occur in certain quintessentially modernist literary characters—Kafka's Gregor Samsa, who becomes a cockroach, or Sartre's Roquentin, whose hand becomes an alien object.

13. The sincerity—or at least the depth—of Stephen's social feeling is called into question by the image of the ants, and even more by an image two paragraphs earlier of "the sound of softly browsing cattle as the other boys munched their lunches tranquilly" (p. 125).

14. Stephen's unwitting reliance upon the Church in a variety of ways—most obviously his conception of the artist as a "priest of eternal imagination" (p. 221)—offers a tangible and persistent example of the novel's irony in regard to Stephen's presumed self-understanding. Stephen's debt to the church extends, however, not merely to abstract theological concepts, but to more implicit ways in which his very self (which he increasingly regards as a thing of his own making) is structured by the images, presuppositions, and attitudes of the church. James Carens says that even Stephen's gestures in chapters III and IV are institutional, devotional gestures ("The Motif of Hands in *A Portrait of the Artist as a Young Man*," *Irish Renaissance Annual II* (1981), 150; as an illustration, see *P*, p. 158.21–27). Stephen's simplistic subject/object dichotomy causes him to underestimate the continuing influence of the church on him once he has formally broken with it. Unable, that is, to understand the impossibility of separating inner from outer, he fails to see that while you can take the boy out of the church, you cannot so easily take the church out of the boy. Interestingly, in *Stephen Hero*, this realization is explicitly present in Stephen's own inner monologue, in the passage where Stephen hears the "embassy of nimble pleaders": "was it anything but vanity which urged him to seek out the thorny crown of the heretic while the entire theory, in accordance with which his entire artistic life was shaped, arose most conveniently for his purpose out of the mass of Catholic theology?" (*SH*, p. 205); and later in the same passage "can you be fatuous enough to think that simply by being wrong-headed you can recreate entirely your mind and temper or can clear your blood of what you may call the Catholic infection?" (*SH*, p. 206). The Stephen of *Portrait* is not so perspicacious on these points.

15. Others have acknowledged (though not *explained*) this predilection in Stephen. Marguerite Harkness says "Joyce is more precise and careful in his analysis of Aestheticism than of naturalism or realism because it is, for him, simultaneously the more attractive and the more dangerous tendency" (*Aesthetics*, p. 44). Charles Rossman says that Stephen in *Portrait* is "alienated from external reality" and "fluctuates between distorted perceptions of the outer world, scorn of it, and open flight from it," and that "eventually, a persistent gulf opens between the subjective world and the outer world, and Stephen soon prefers the 'adventure of the mind'" ("Stephen Dedalus and the Spiritual-Heroic Refrigerating Apparatus," pp. 114, 116).

16. B. L. Reid says of Stephen in chapter II, "he longs to meet his *anima*, his mystic salvatory female spirit . . ." ("Gnomon and Order," p. 407). Marguerite Harkness verges on a similar insight when she says "Each time that [Stephen] has accepted an order of his own making [i.e., what I am calling internal], he has 'seen' a woman" (*Aesthetics*, p. 27). Hugh Kenner also posits the similarity of odd and even numbered chapters, but does not pursue it along these lines; see *Dublin's Joyce*, pp. 123, 129). Another expression of this identification of the depths of Stephen's psyche with the female is that whenever Joyce refers to Stephen's soul he uses the feminine pronoun. For example, in the passage that we looked at above Stephen reflects on "the remoteness of his soul from what he had hitherto imagined her sanctuary" (p. 161). And just before the climactic beach passage, "His soul had arisen from the grave of boyhood, spurning her graveclothes" (p. 170), or a few pages later, "his soul was loosed of her miseries" (p. 176). For a good discussion of the uses to which Stephen puts

women, see Suzette Henke, "Stephen Dedalus and Women: A Portrait of the Artist as a Young Misogynist," in *Women in Joyce*, ed. Suzette Henke and Elaine Unkeless (Urbana: Univ. of Illinois Press, 1982), pp. 82–107.

17. Hugh Kenner long ago said matter-of-factly, "the climax of the book is of course Stephen's ecstatic discovery of his vocation at the end of chapter IV" (*Dublin's Joyce*, p. 131). David Hayman says of the "bird-girl passage" that "most critics consider [it] the novel's climax" ("Daedalean Imagery in *A Portrait*," in *Hereditas: Seven Essays on the Modern Experience of the Classical*, ed. Frederick Will (Austin: Univ. of Texas Press, 1964), p. 51), and Diarmuid Sheehan, in a recent Exemplar Notes publication on *Portrait* that is largely a mirror of critical opinion says of this scene "this is the climax of the novel" (*James Joyce's "A Portrait of the Artist as a Young Man"* [Ashbourne, Co. Meath: Exemplar Publications, Ltd., n.d.], p. 2).

18. Evert Sprinchorn, for example, begins his long essay on *Portrait* acknowledging that most readers feel "a sense of disappointment arising from the last chapter" ("A Portrait of the Artist as Achilles," p. 9), and trying to account for this feeling. John Edward Hardy finds in the chapter "an effect of falling-off that needs to be explained," and seriously asks "why did Joyce not end the novel with the triumphant vision of mortal beauty? Why doesn't Stephen simply take flight immediately in full glory?" And he finds "a distinct weakening of the heroic character in the final episodes" ("Joyce's *Portrait*," pp. 78–79). Hugh Kenner, who is very severe on Stephen, calls chapter V a "suspended chord" and says "there remains a moral ambiguity (how seriously are we to take Stephen?) which makes the last forty pages painful reading" (*Dublin's Joyce*, p. 121). Arno Heller more or less concurs, detecting in the last chapter a "complete change of tone and narrative texture [that) has led to a series of controversial interpretations which call for a reconsideration of the novel" ("Ambiguous Equilibrium: Joyce's *A Portrait* Reconsidered," *Literatur in Wissenschaft und Unterricht* 11 [1978], 34), and finding in Joyce's attitude toward Stephen in chapter V at best an "ambiguous equilibrium" (p. 39). A more imaginative and contrived explanation for the change that we feel at this point in the novel is offered by Jon Lanham—namely, that Stephen's own persona had narrated the novel until late in chapter IV, but then evaporates, and "the absence of this buffering personality wholly sympathetic to young Stephen is clearly felt in chapter V" ("The Genre of *A Portrait*," p. 101). (Marguerite Harkness rather surprisingly calls this chapter "the funniest in Joyce's novel" (*Portrait: Voices of the Text*, p. 771.) While I feel the negative qualities that these critics are troubled by, and I myself am arguing that some such difference is effected in Stephen by his aspiration to self-determination, I nonetheless find a great deal about the Stephen of chapter V to admire, to sympathize with, and even to like. He is several times shown to be vulnerable, wavering, self-critical. Consider for example his withdrawing the barb that his mind sends at MacAlister (pp. 193–94); his confusion about the tundish/funnel matter (pp. 188–89); his criticism of his own attempt to think of E___ C___ in sensual terms (p. 233); and his April 15 diary entry (which we shall look at later). His least appealing moments involve public scenes, when Stephen is concerned about the image he is projecting.

19. I will not review the extensive literature on the villanelle; briefly, I see it as an effete symbolist effusion on Stephen's part, not without some skill, but reflecting a pallid, callow sense of reality, very much in keeping with his subjectivist orientation. We know that Joyce wrote the villanelle much earlier, destroyed most of his juvenile verse, and disavowed even what he later published, and that in *Stephen Hero* the "Vilanelle of the Temptress" is referred to as "some ardent verses" inspired by a "trivial incident" (*SH*, p. 211).

20. I disagree, that is, with Maurice Beebe's view that this is a "theory of aesthetics propounded by Joyce through Stephen" ("The *Portrait* as Portrait," p. 14), and agree with

those earlier critics who have argued that the function of the theorizing is dramatic—i.e., that it characterizes Stephen. S. L. Goldberg says of the aesthetic theory that "its force in the novel is not so much philosophical as dramatic," and that it "serves to reveal not so much the nature of art as the nature of Stephen Dedalus; and to miss this, or to attempt to assess Joyce's work by the theory as he there presents it, is inevitably to distort his artistic achievement" (*Classical Temper*, p. 43). Charles Rossman says "Everyone agrees that Stephen's discourse on Shakespeare in *Ulysses* reveals more about Stephen than Hamlet; yet that the same is true of Stephen's aesthetics in the earlier novels has gone relatively unappreciated" ("Stephen Dedalus and the Spiritual-Heroic Refrigerating Apparatus," p. 102). Richard F. Peterson takes this same tack, saying "more than anything else Stephen's theories reflect his personal ordeals in the novels" ("Stephen's Aesthetics: Reflections of the Artist or the Ass?" *JJQ* 17 [Summer 1980] 427). Ben Forkner's unpublished Ph.D. dissertation, "Stephen Dedalus: Verbal Consciousness and the Birth of an Aesthetic" (University of North Carolina at Chapel Hill, 1975), makes an extensive case for regarding Stephen's theories dramatically.

21. That Joyce felt an obligation to include in his books aspects of life he may not personally have approved of is suggested by a story Italo Svevo tells: "Dedalus is loose-spoken, while Joyce one day called me to task because I allowed myself to make a rather free joke. 'I never say that kind of thing,' said he 'though I write it.' So it seems that his own books cannot be read in his presence" (E. H. Mikhail, *James Joyce: Interviews and Recollections*, p. 47).

22. James Naremore discusses Stephen's turning to art as an escape from sordid circumstances and says of this passage describing Stephen's morning walk that Stephen is "meditating on art in order to ward off reality" ("Consciousness and Society in *A Portrait of the Artist*," in *Approaches to Joyce's "Portrait": Ten Essays* [1976], ed. Thomas F. Staley and Bernard Benstock, p. 121). But what Naremore does with this insight is strange. Though he sees that Joyce is taking Stephen's measure in the novel, he ends by claiming ambiguously that while "Joyce could learn to criticize his life ... he could not change his entire consciousness and become another man" (p. 133). In effect he judges that Joyce was "untaught by the wisdom he has written or by the laws he has revealed," as Stephen says of Shakespeare in *Ulysses* (9.477).

23. The fullest discussion of Stephen's debts to Pater, Wilde, Yeats, and Aestheticism in general is Marguerite Harkness's *Aesthetics* (1984), which shows how debilitating the effects of Aestheticism are on Stephen. John McGowan's "From Pater to Wilde to Joyce" is not concerned with influences so much as with modernist and post-modernist conceptions of the self in these three writers. His discussion of Joyce is vitiated by his presuming that Stephen Dedalus' "willful heroic self that is created ex nihilo" (p. 418), expresses Joyce's own view.

24. S. L. Goldberg quotes this passage as reflecting "the first glimmering of Stephen's maturity ... and even a significant touch of *self*-irony" (*Classical Temper*, pp. 110–11). F. Parvin Sharpless sees this passage as an example of Stephen's having succeeded in moving from "kinetic involvement through detachment to pity" in his relationships with women ("Irony in Joyce's *Portrait*," pp. 104–5). James Carens, by contrast, says of Stephen's "Now I call that friendly, don't you?" "Stephen's only sign of maturity is the cynicism with which he mocks the gesture" [of her farewell handshake] ("Motif of Hands," p. 152).

DAVID LEON HIGDON

Gendered Discourse and the Structure of Joyce's "The Dead"

"At any rate, very careful composition," wrote Virginia Woolf in her "Dalloway Notebook" on 16 October 1922, "[t]he contrast must be arranged. . . . The design is extremely complicated. The balance must be very finely considered" (quoted in Novak 226–27). She was, of course, mapping the structure of *Mrs. Dalloway* being generated by the eventual intersection of the lives of Clarissa Dalloway and Septimus Smith. However, with equal appropriateness she could have been describing the structural features of James Joyce's "The Dead," for it, too, has an "extremely complicated" binary design whose "contrast . . . must be finely considered." In many ways, though, this design has been inadequately recognized and largely undescribed because the thematic and psychological macrostructures have eclipsed the microstructures of the story, particularly the patterns wherein music and noise images coordinate with female and male worlds, microstructures whose subtleties make the story a rehearsal for the "Sirens" episode in *Ulysses* and for the "melodiotiosities in purefusion by the score" of *Finnegans Wake* (222). Stanislaus Joyce indicated as much when he wrote that "[t]here is a mastery of story telling in the skill with which *a crescendo of noise and jollity is* gradually worked up and then *suddenly silenced* by the ghost of a memory" (527; emphasis added).

From *ReJoycing: New Readings of* Dubliners, edited by Rosa M. Bollettieri Bosinelli and Harold F. Mosher, Jr. © 1998 by the University Press of Kentucky.

Virtually every critical discussion of "The Dead" has taken place within the intellectual boundaries inscribed early by David Daiches and Brewster Ghiselin. In *The Novel and the Modern World* (1939), Daiches very deftly established three guiding principles regarding Joyce's story: its "expansive technique" (73), its self-conscious "working-out . . . of a preconceived theme" (74), and its "lopsided[ness]" (75) set it far apart from the other fourteen stories in the collection and make it a crucially transitional bridge into the ever increasingly complex novels, written "as it was at a time when Joyce was becoming increasingly preoccupied with the problems of aesthetics" (81). Daiches made clear that Gabriel Conroy's encounters with three women— Lily, Molly Ivors, and Gretta Conroy—which mark the several stages in his journey toward self-knowledge, constitute the heart and soul of the story's technique, theme, and pattern. In 1956, in "The Unity of Joyce's *Dubliners*," Ghiselin extended these areas into symbolic structure and "a pattern of correspondences" (75), such as found in *Ulysses*, and thus a critical template was firmly established in place.[1]

At present, most Joyce critics work almost exclusively in terms of these women and their roles in Gabriel's evening. Regardless of the theoretical map, the destination seems the same. The 1994 Lacanian approach of Garry M. Leonard, suggestive and persuasive as it is, sees "the story as three attempts by Gabriel Conroy, with three different women, to confirm the fictional unity of his masculine subjectivity" (289) and differs little from Gerald Doherty's 1989 Bakhtinian untangling of the metaphoric and metonymic dimensions of the text that leads to "Lily's bitter comment about men," "Miss Ivor's aggression," and Gabriel's "brief tiff with Gretta" (227) as features of the metonymic plot line. Richard Brown (1985) and Edward Brandabur (1971) had already reached similar conclusions, the former observing that "the story . . . seems tailor-made for feminist interpretation. Gabriel's evening consists of a succession of significant encounters with women" (92), the latter concluding that "throughout the story, personal encounters disturb [Gabriel's] poise until he finally gives in to the annihilation he has not only anticipated but invited" (116).

The recent Daniel R. Schwarz edition (1994) for St. Martin's very successful series "Case Studies in Contemporary Criticism" also takes us down this same familiar road whether the vehicle is psychoanalytic, reader-response, new historicist, or deconstructionist criticism. Schwarz sounds the familiar call in relating the autobiographies of Joyce and Conroy: "Gabriel expresses Joyce's fear of betrayal—*sexual, political, and personal*" (104, emphasis added)—abstractions of the views of, wounds inflicted by, and temptations posed by the three women. These designs adequately describe the "encounter scenes," but they rarely do justice to the sections separating them. By concentrating on the 618 lines in the encounters and essentially ignoring the structural significances of the remaining 1,042 lines, they fail to account fully for the "considerable formal differences" (O'Connor 305) between "The Dead" and the other stories and also overlook the subtle, complicated interplay of counterpointing rhythms, musical and sexual, among the scenes.

I propose that the Lily, Molly, and Gretta "encounter scenes," dramatizing the comfortable illusions Gabriel harbored about himself and about most other men, alternate with inverted scenes in which individual men threaten to disrupt, if indeed not to overthrow, the harmony and melody usually bodied forth in dance, song, and performance by the women. The main offenders—Freddy Malins, Mr. Browne, and Bartell D'Arcy—are eventually joined by Gabriel himself as the Lord of Misrule dethroning harmony this winter night.[2] Freddy's drunkenness and unzipped fly, Browne's coarseness and defiance, D'Arcy's rudeness and hoarseness, and Gabriel's smug sense of superiority and condescension threaten the spirited, celebratory world created by the three Misses Morkan, but only Gabriel emerges from the evening enlightened in any way.

In other words, the grand tonal shifts occurring between the endings and beginnings of chapters in *A Portrait of the Artist as a Young Man*, patterns so ably delineated by A. Walton Litz and Hugh Kenner, are fully anticipated and realized throughout "The Dead." Litz argues that "each chapter ends on a tone of intense lyricism, corresponding to Stephen's new-found hope; but then—as we move into the next chapter—there is an abrupt change in language which reflects the decline in Stephen's resolution" (69), movement from lyrical triumph to Icarian plummet. This is a more sophisticated, more aesthetic observation on structure than Kenner's remarks on the alternations between dream and reality, but both capture the binary clashes that generate structure. Thus, in "The Dead," there is a constant juxtaposition of male/ female, past/present, public/private, and other binaries that cluster together around thematic and structural poles as the three scenes in which the female "wounds" the male's self-image, leaving him pondering in silence how to respond and how to defend his ego—a pattern of exclusion, alienation, interior monologue, and silence alternating with a pattern of inclusion (whether in dance, song, or feasting), sharing, and sound. The female rhythm in this story directly points toward Molly Bloom and Anna Livia Plurabelle.

Following the tightly designed opening scene (*D* 175.1–176.33) and Lily "encounter" episode (*D* 176.34–179.20), Joyce's story appears to concentrate randomly for the next few pages on unrelated groups of characters at the party, giving first this man or that woman his or her moment of attention.[3] The story's structure thus alternates between the private moments of Gabriel and a woman (first Lily, then Molly, and finally Gretta) and the public world of the party in which men boorishly endanger the social balances, proprieties, and melodies—perhaps a hostess's most serious but unvoiced fear. Gabriel is, of course, actually alone with both Lily in the "little pantry" (*D* 175) downstairs where he insults her with the improperly given tip and Gretta in the hotel. In one way or another, Gabriel consciously insults each significant woman in the story, and he clearly intends his words to wound, as when he reminds Gretta of her violation of clear social distinctions in her relationship with Michael Furey and even ventures to question her fidelity to him (*D* 219).

It has been less clear, perhaps, how he insults Lily. Of course, the scene lacks the complexity and significance of the other two "encounter scenes," and Gabriel must be quick and more spontaneous in his response. The crux is the coin he gives Lily, which is less a muted sexual insult than it is a gross violation of the etiquette of his class and period. No houseguest would tip his or her hostess's servant unless remaining in the house overnight, and never on the guest's arrival. Redoubtable Elizabeth L. Post still firmly decrees, "No tip—ever—for servants in a private house at a dinner party" (403), and such measures would have been even more pronounced at the time of the Misses Morkans' party, especially given the social pretensions of the family. Gabriel attempts to mask his act as one of generosity authorized by the season, but Lily sees beneath the mask an unmistakable rudeness and insensitiveness.

Although his encounter with Molly takes place on the dance floor, fellow dancers become aware of their conversation only after their voices are raised, an obviously intended effect since Joyce originally had Gretta remarking on "the row" Gabriel had had with Molly (Scholes 29). The private, male, illusioned world endangered by the female though is abruptly swept away by the roisterous, good-natured, public, female rhythms, and the two rhythms ultimately fuse in the final scene of the story.

In the first of the female-ordered worlds (*D* 179.21–187.18), the females triumph, even though the "pretty waltz" (*D* 183) with its accompanying "stamping and shuffling of feet" (*D* 177), the quadrilles announced by "a red faced young woman" (*D* 183), and Mary Jane's showy concert piece, designed more to highlight her masterful technique than the work's substance, could at any moment be disrupted. Aunt Kate fears that Freddy Malins is "screwed" (*D* 182), but he seems "hardly noticeable" as he crosses the floor "on rather shaky legs" (*D* 185). Browne threatens more serious disruption as he leads not one but three young ladies "into the back room" (*D* 182), drinks "a goodly measure of whisky" (*D* 183), and attempts "a very low Dublin accent" (*D* 183) in his coarse joke. In the rush to pair men and women for the quadrilles, however, Mary Jane and Aunt Kate avert further disruptions and sweep the guests up in dance, but not before Aunt Kate has satisfied herself that Malins is under control and has chastised Browne "by frowning and shaking her forefinger in warning to and fro" (*D* 185), thus leaving them alone and silenced in their own disorder and evading, for the moment, the disruptions that a habitual drunk and a socially displaced boor could inflict on the party.

Following Gabriel's more serious encounter with Molly Ivors (*D* 187.19–192.27), the story moves to the second female-ordered scene (*D* 192.30–213.30), one much more highly fragmented and potentially disordered than the first; as might be expected, the men are again much more disruptive than the women. Browne escorts Aunt Julia to the piano so that she may treat her guests to a song. After she finishes the song, Freddy Malins continues applauding long after everyone has stopped and further embarrasses Julia with his overeffusive compliments. Unexpectedly, too, a near quarrel erupts among Malins, Browne, Kate, and Mary Jane. At fault is another man, Pope Pius X, who has declared that since "singers in churches have a real liturgical office . . . women . . . cannot be admitted to form part of the choir or of the musical chapel" (Gifford 119). Aunt Kate "had worked herself into a passion" (*D* 194), we are told, and the group has become "very quarrelsome" (*D* 195). At this point, Molly Ivors says her farewells, though not in the ill humor we might have expected after her exchange with Gabriel.

For a while, "a great deal of confusion and laughter and noise" (*D* 197) reigns as the dinner proceeds, and, as Warren Beck has pointed out, the guests' "nearest approach to a common interest is not Irish nationalism but *music, and more especially singers*" (305; emphasis added). Talk of the Negro tenor at the Gaiety, though, soon has Freddy questioning "sharply" (*D* 198) and Browne speaking "defiantly" (*D* 199) and "incredulously" (*D* 200), as the talk eventually grows "lugubrious" (*D* 201), turns to monks' coffins, and then lapses into silence. Gabriel's speech, with its embedded insult to the now-absent Molly, follows, loudly interrupted several times by Browne's effusive, noisy protestations (*D* 202, 203). Despite all of its compliments to his aunts and his cousin, it harshly judges the moderns for living in "a less spacious age" (*D* 203), and we sense its many hypocrisies because Gabriel had earlier dismissed the company for its low "grade of culture" (*D* 179) and his aunts as "only two ignorant old women" (*D* 192). The revenge Gabriel takes on Lily with his impolite tip and on Molly through insults shows how mean-spirited he can be and just how unfairly his patriarchal values enable him to treat servants, colleagues, and wives. Ruth Bauerle quite rightly perceives that "scarcely a woman has encountered Gabriel without being disdained, overruled, or interrupted" (117).

As the guests leave, again the men threaten disorder: Freddy with his "resounding knock" (*D* 208); Browne by holding the front door open far too long, letting in cold air, and creating confusion in the "cross-directions and contradictions and abundance of laughter" (*D* 209) as the cabdriver attempts to sort out his fares' wishes; Bartell D'Arcy with his shockingly rude, "rough" reply that takes the women "aback": "'Can't you see that I'm as hoarse as a crow?'" (*D* 211). He, of course, also supplies the ultimate thematic and psychological disruption by singing the song, "The Lass of Aughrim," which triggers Gretta's tearful memories of Michael Furey and strips Gabriel of his last marital illusions. In light of these examples, it is difficult not to see Gabriel's "wild impulse of . . . body" (*D* 215), his "desire to *seize*" Gretta (*D* 215; emphasis added), "the thoughts . . . *rioting* through his brain, proud, joyful, tender, valorous" (*D* 213; emphasis added), and his "keen pang of lust" (*D* 215) as being an attack on Gretta—"mate-rape," Bauerle has called it; Gabriel does, after all, long "to be master of her strange mood" (*D* 217) and wish "*to crush* her body against his, to overmaster her" (*D* 217; emphasis added), phrases with very strong connotations of noisy action.

Throughout these six scenes, three voices, fully available to reader and author but not uniformly available to characters and narrator, dominate the story—a point considered in great technical detail by John Paul Riquelme (121–30), who finds in this medley "clearly the stylistic proving ground that makes possible the configuration of technique in the later work" (123). First, there is the voice of the individual character in dialogue, asking, responding, cajoling, offering, in ways that reveal what the character wishes to show forth to the world as well as what the author wishes to unveil. Second, there is the interior monologue voice of the characters, that aspect of the story so inadequately communicated to the audience in John Huston's 1987 film adaptation, which are unavailable to the other characters. Indeed, lack of access to this voice creates some of the key misunderstandings within the story, as when Gabriel blunders so in his reading of Gretta's thoughts and provokes such an "outburst of tears" (*D* 218) that he is left nonplussed by his own reflection in the mirror. The third voice, primarily available to Joyce and his reader, usually appears in such rhetoric as the adverbial speech tags and descriptive passages. For example, Gabriel mentions that the cab window "rattl[ed] all the way" (*D* 180), and the narrator that Gabriel went down the stairs "noisily" (*D* 182) and that Bartell D'Arcy spoke "roughly" (*D* 211), but only Joyce and the reader are intended to discern in these words the gradual evolution of a pattern in which certain actions, certain speeches, certain attitudes are associated with noise. In discussing *Finnegans Wake*, Clive Hart presciently notes that "there are unmistakable signs at least as early as 'The Dead' of the deliberate use of verbal motifs for structural and tonal effects" (162), and we can see that this deliberate use belongs largely to the third voice, which is fully capable of defining and exploiting the unique qualities of "The Dead" and also of creating complex symbolic relationships amongst melody, noise, and silence, available in the traditions of European literature since Pythagoras, who supposed the whole heaven to be a "*harmonia* and a number," a medley fully exploited as early as Geoffrey Chaucer's "The General Prologue."

Numerous unifying patterns of images have been identified in the text of "The Dead," and warnings concerning "denial of proportion" in relating imagery to the totality of the story have been firmly posted. Epifanio San Juan Jr., for example, has raised particularly sound objections against "the mistakes the formalist habitually commits, stemming from the denial of proportion by exaggerating the role of a part and making part and whole somehow equivalent" (215). If one turns to images of sounds, however, of which there are at least 345 in the text, one sees patterns develop in terms of harmony and noise, standing in direct relationship to the female and male divisions of the story.[4] Determining just what constitutes a sound image is, of course, subjective to a degree and thus probably admits no exact count.

Quite obviously, words such as "scraping," "squeaking," "stamping," and "shuffling" (D 177) gleaned from early in the story constitute sound images, as do the adverbial constructions "said gaily" (D 178) and "laughed heartily" (D 180). It is equally obvious that the first three images constitute noise or discord, whereas the latter suggest harmony or melody. Thus such speech tags as "nervously" (D 180), "almost testily" (D 181), "noisily" (D 182), "bluntly" (D 187), "lamely" (D 188), "warmly" (D 190), "moodily" (D 191), "coldly" (D 191), "loudly" (D 197), "defiantly" (D 199), "archly" (D 206), "roughly" (D 211), and "ironically" (D 219) have been grouped together as noise images with such verbals as "clanged" (D 175), "exploded" (D 185), "stuttered" (D 190), "tapped" (D 192), "coughed" (D 201), "puffing" (D 208), "shouted" (D 209), "muttered" (D 216), and "mumbled" (D 216) and such substantives as "bitter and sudden retort" (D 179), "sidling mimicry" (D 183), "habitual catch" (D 185), "a kink of high-pitched bronchitic laughter" (D 185), "loud applause" (D 193), "clatter" (D 200), "broken only by the noise of the wine and by unsettlings of chairs" (D 201), "shrill prolonged whistling" (D 206), "confusion" (D 208), "thumping" (D 215), and "sobbing" (D 221). On the other hand, "peal of laughter" (D 180), "lovely voice" (D 184), "opening melody" (D 187), "soft friendly tone" (D 188), "distant music" (D 210), "old Irish tonality" (D 210), and "merry-making" (D 222) have been categorized with the verbals "murmured" (D 181), "laughed in musical echo" (D 183), "singing" (D 199), "strumming" (D 206), and "call . . . softly" (D 214) as harmonic or melodic images, appropriate to this Twelfth Night celebration.

Consideration of the roles of music in *Dubliners* in general and in "The Dead" in particular would take us in several directions, some already well covered. We could look at the role of music in Joyce's own life, especially as it relates to his great-aunts whose party was the source of the party in the story; we could look at the specific allusions to songs, operas, and composers in *Dubliners*, material already more than adequately catalogued by Matthew J.C. Hodgart, Mabel P. Worthington, Zack Bowen, Timothy Martin, and others; we could look at the uses of music in relation to the characters and themes. All three approaches carry their own satisfactions.

Joyce's contemporaries recall again and again that music reigned in his household. Jacques Mercanton remembered Joyce, sitting at a piano, "carried away by his own delight in [an Irish folksong]," singing and accompanying himself "in a voice melodious and vibrant, though a little ragged" (231). Robert Haas has shown how pervasive musical references are throughout *Dubliners* in the daily lives of the characters, references that finally "serve to enrich" (20) all the stories but especially "The Dead." Bruce Avery has even successfully fused the biographical data with the textual allusions to demonstrate that the numerous "musical references in the text signal that 'The Dead' is concerned with hearing and sound in much the same way that 'Araby' concerns itself with vision and sight" (475). Indeed, Avery anticipated my key point when he wrote that music "even affects the language of the narrator, whose figures compose aural images drawn from the terminology of music" (474). The critical ground has been well prepared for sowing the idea that sounds are key elements in the figurative structures of the story.

Approximately 119 sound images are associated with the men, 137 with the women. (The remainder belong to the company in general, as with "[a]n irregular musketry of applause" [*D* 192], or simply constitute a sound, neither melody nor noise.) Considered more closely, 69 noise images and 50 harmony images are associated with the men's actions, thoughts, and comments—the latter figure slightly unbalanced since so many of the harmony images emanate from Browne while he is discussing opera singers. Specifically, 32 noise images are associated with Gabriel, 15 with Freddy Malins, 8 with Browne, and 6 with Bartell D'Arcy. In sharp contrast, the 137 sound images associated with the women, who are dancing, singing, playing the piano, or chatting pleasantly throughout the story, divide into 104 harmonic images and only 20 clearly noise images, most of which fall within the "encounter scenes." In other words, it is even money that men will produce either harmony or noise; however, women are five times more likely to produce harmony than noise. We do hear Lily respond "with great bitterness" (*D* 178), Molly Ivors speak "bluntly" (*D* 187), "frankly" (*D* 188), and "warmly" (in the sense of annoyed or piqued [*D* 190]), and Gretta burst into tears (*D* 218) and choke with sobs (*D* 221), but these are exceptions to the generally harmonic images accompanying the speeches and actions of the women and do indeed appear in the malice-governed scenes. In her discussion of *Dubliners* criticism, Florence L. Walzl cogently observed that "over half" of the 200 music teachers listed in the *1904 Thom's Directory* were women and that "no field seemed more promising or safer for young women of talent" (*"Dubliners"* 198), a point most relevant to the lives of the Misses Morkans in Joyce's story.

Perhaps we could expect no more than noise from Freddy Malins, described as he is from the first as a potentially disruptive force: "His face was fleshy and pallid, touched with colour only at the thick hanging lobes of his ears and at the wide wings of his nose. He had coarse features, a blunt nose, a convex and receding brow, tumid and protruded lips" (D 184). Freddy may be "laughing heartily" (D 184) at times, but usually we hear his "habitual catch" (D 185) or "resounding knock" (D 208) or find him clapping loudly, speaking "sharply" (D 198), or beating time with a pudding fork, perhaps on the tabletop or even against his glass (D 205). Browne, equally unpromising with his "stiff grizzled moustache and swarthy skin" (D 182) and "sidling mimicry" (D 183), generates some "mirth" (D 185), does "laugh very heartily" (D 193), and shows his appreciation of operatic voices, but he also speaks "defiantly" (D 199), "warmly" (D 199), and "loudly" (D 203), asks questions "incredulously" (D 200), and creates "a good deal of confused talk" (D 208). Donald T. Torchiana has suggested the importance of Browne as a structural device when he observed that Joyce uses Browne "to punctuate almost every scene at the party with something like a full stop" (D 226). Bartell D'Arcy, more a presence than a character in the story most of the time, responds to Browne "warmly" (D 199) and to his hostesses "roughly" and "rudely" (D 211), always speaking "hoarsely."

Even such minor male figures as the four young men with their "vigorous clapping" (D 187), the cabman with his "rattling" vehicle (D 209), and the hotel porter who "mutters" and "mumbles" (D 216) Gretta and Gabriel to their room create noise. Although much is said about the vocal abilities of Michael Furey, the only sound he actually produces in Gretta's narrative comes from the gravel he flings against her bedroom window. The noisiest male, though, is Gabriel Conroy himself. He "scrapes" his shoes "vigorously" (D 177); descends the stairs "noisily" (D 182); speaks "slightly angered" (D 181), "lamely" (D 188), "shortly" (D 189), "moodily" (D 191), "coldly" (D 191), "loudly" (D 205), "abruptly" (D 216), and "ironically" (D 219); adopts "a false voice" (D 217) and a "tone of cold interrogation" (D 220); and once must "restrain himself from *breaking out* into *brutal* language" (D 217; emphasis added). Indeed, the story ends with him listening to the "few light taps" (D 223) the snowfall makes against the Gresham Hotel window.

In *Joyce, Bakhtin, and Popular Literature*, R.B. Kershner maintains "that within a society in which women are disempowered there should arise an opposing imaginative scenario in which women are omnipotent" (147). Indeed, "The Dead" contains just such a scenario within the three very private scenes when Lily, Molly, and Gretta evade the rhetoric Gabriel has scripted for them and "defeat him," Lily by rejecting his money, Molly by leaving before his insult, Gretta by simply going to sleep. Within the party scenes, the harmonies of the women also overrule the threatened disorder of the men. Margot Norris's feminist discussion makes much of the interplay between "two texts: a 'loud' or audible male narrative challenged and disrupted by a 'silent' or discounted female countertext. . . . 'The Dead' itself thematizes these complicated textual operations in the homely gesture of what I call 'the stifled back answer'" (192), but, as I have shown, the answers given by the women, available through the imagery in Joyce's story, are anything but silent or stifled. Paradoxically, Gabriel becomes threatened not only by his wife's revelations but also by Michael Furey's ghostly presence, thus fusing the male and female patterns and the two strands of intertwined images. The story, however, ends in an ambiguous impasse, as so many of the thematic discussions have concluded; neither noise nor music penetrates the silence of the closing sentences.

Paradoxically, closure in "The Dead" brings images of neither concord nor discord, but rather a profound and ambiguous silence that lends itself to contradictory readings of the story's final page. The reader does not know what will eventually result from Gabriel's silence because the pattern established in his encounters with Lily and Molly remains incomplete and there is no third "party" scene. Women in Gabriel's world both wound and heal, both pet and correct. Gabriel could not be wounded or corrected, however, were there not already some inner vulnerability in his self-image, some inner awareness that he has indeed lightly flirted with Lily, politically compromised himself for a few books, and ungenerously insulted his wife. Gabriel has been a highly disruptive individual in the tightly constituted world of his family and the restrictive world of his culture. His disruptions and noises, however, have been obliterated by the gender-inflected music of independent, capable, and talented women, rhetorical and thematic sisters to Molly Bloom and Anna Livia Plurabelle. The noise of the self is ultimately silenced by the music of the group. Only if we cease to let the diachronic action of Gabriel Conroy entice us away from the synchronic structures of the entire story does it become entirely clear to what extent gender has permeated every aspect of "The Dead," from the psychology of the encounter scenes, to the culturally charged public scenes, to the highly gendered discourse patterned by melody and noise attached to the female and male.

Notes

1. I found it very puzzling that in 1982, Florence L. Walzl's insightful "*Dubliners*: Women in Irish Society" would remark that "[i]t is significant that the plot progresses by a series of confrontations Gabriel has with women" (50), adding in a note that "[t]he fact that all the main confrontations of 'The Dead' are with women has not received as

much critical attention [as the self-perceived assaults on Gabriel's ego]" (56). Almost more puzzling is that R.B. Kershner could write in 1989 that "surprisingly, few critics have noted that Gabriel's significant encounters in the story are all with women, especially the three encounters with Lily, Molly Ivors, and Gretta" (140).

2. Thomas Dilworth briefly discusses the Mock King of Twelfth Night festivities and concludes that "the resemblance of the Morkans' party to the ancient celebration of the god of sowing and husbandry may have symbolic resonance with the party's occurring in a house shared by the office of a 'cornfactor'. . . a grain and seed merchant" (114).

3. Hereafter cited as *D* followed by page and line numbers, the divisions are as follows: prologue (*D* 175.01–176.33), Lily encounter scene (*D* 175.34–179.20), party scene (*D* 179.21–187.18), Molly Ivors encounter scene (*D* 187.19–192.27), second party scene (*D* 192.28–213.03), Gretta Conroy encounter scene (*D* 213.04–222.02), and Gabriel Conroy recognition scene (*D* 222.03–224.04). Discussions of "The Dead" mention from two to five "parts" or "divisions." Robert Scholes's edition, used for this essay, prints the story with only one break. The Yale manuscript clearly indicates breaks on page 17 ("Gabriel could not listen while Mary Jane was playing") and page 74 ("She was fast asleep"); the Cornell composite typescript-manuscript indicates the former (page 9) but not the latter and has an additional break on page 31 ("the piercing morning air came into the hall . . ."); see Michael Groden 489, 497, 513, and 535.

4. Late in my work on this essay, I read what I consider to be an exemplary essay relating motifs to gender issues: Earl G. Ingersoll's "The Gender of Travel in 'The Dead.'" Fusing structuralist, psychological, and feminist thought, Ingersoll remarks: "Of particular interest in 'The Dead' is evidence of the metaphor of travel, with its associations of freedom and the phallocentric, and metonymy, with its associations of servitude and the neglected 'feminine'" (42). His success in explicating the implications of the spatial language of the story enforced my belief that sounds in "The Dead" are inextricably intertwined with gender. I found the following critics quite useful for spurring thought about Joyce and women—Richard Brown, Bonnie Kime Scott, Karen Lawrence, Shari Benstock, and Hana Wirth-Nesher—although none of these individuals seemed to make a particularly strong statement about "The Dead" and Gabriel's relationship with women.

WORKS CITED

Avery, Bruce. "Distant Music: Sound and the Dialogics of Satire in 'The Dead.'" *James Joyce Quarterly* 28 (1991):473–83.

Bauerle, Ruth. "Date Rape, Mate Rape: A Liturgical Interpretation of 'The Dead.'" In *New Alliances in Joyce Studies*, ed. Bonnie Kime Scott, 113–25. Newark: Univ. of Delaware Press, 1988.

Beck, Warren. *Joyce's Dubliners: Substance, Vision, and Art.* Durham, N.C.: Duke Univ. Press, 1969.

Benstock, Shari. "City Spaces and Women's Places in Joyce's Dublin." In *James Joyce: The Augmented Ninth*, ed. Bernard Benstock, 293–307. Syracuse, N.Y.: Syracuse Univ. Press, 1988.

Bowen, Zack. *Musical Allusions in the Works of James Joyce: Early Poetry through Ulysses.* Albany: State University of New York Press, 1974.

Brandabur, Edward. *A Scrupulous Meanness: A Study of James Joyce's Early Work.* Chicago: Univ. of Illinois Press, 1971.

Brown, Richard. *James Joyce and Sexuality.* Cambridge: Cambridge Univ. Press, 1985.

Daiches, David. *The Novel and the Modern World*. Rev. ed. Chicago: Univ. of Chicago Press, 1960.

Dilworth, Thomas. "Sex and Politics in 'The Dead.'" *James Joyce Quarterly* 23 (1986): 157–71.

Doherty, Gerald. "Shades of Difference: Tropic Transformations in James Joyce's 'The Dead,'" *Style* 23 (1989): 225–36.

Ghiselin, Brewster. "The Unity of Joyce's *Dubliners*." *Accent* 16 (1956): 75–88.

Gifford, Don. *Joyce Annotated*. 2d ed. Berkeley: Univ. of California Press, 1982.

Groden, Michael, ed. *Dubliners: A Facsimile of Drafts and Manuscripts, The James Joyce Archives*. Vol. 4. New York: Garland, 1978.

Guthrie, W.K.C. "Pythagoras and Pythagoreanism." In *The Encyclopedia of Philosophy*, ed. Paul Edwards, 7:37–39. New York: Macmillan, 1967.

Haas, Robert. "Music in *Dubliners*." *Colby Quarterly* 28 (1992): 19–33.

Hart, Clive. *Structure and Motif in Finnegans Wake*. Evanston, Ill.: Northwestern Univ. Press, 1962.

Hodgart, Matthew J.C., and Mabel P. Worthington. *Song in the Works of James Joyce*. New York: Columbia Univ. Press, 1959.

Ingersoll, Earl G. "The Gender of Travel in 'The Dead.'" *James Joyce Quarterly* 30 (1992): 41–50.

Joyce, James. *Dubliners*. Ed. Robert Scholes. New York: Viking, 1968.

———. *Dubliners: Text, Criticism, and Notes*. Ed. Robert Scholes and A. Walton Litz. 1969. Reprint, New York: Penguin, 1976.

———. *Finnegans Wake*. New York: Viking, 1959.

Joyce, Stanislaus. "The Background to *Dubliners*." *Listener* 51 (1954): 526–27.

Kenner, Hugh. "The *Portrait* in Perspective." In *James Joyce: Two Decades of Criticism*, ed. Seon Givens, 81. New York: Vanguard 1948.

Kershner, R.B. *Joyce, Bakhtin, and Popular Literature*. Chapel Hill: Univ. of North Carolina Press, 1989.

Lawrence, Karen. "Gender and Narrative Voice in Jacob's Room and *A Portrait of the Artist as a Young Man*." In *James Joyce: The Centennial Symposium*, ed. Morris Beja, Phillip Herring, Maurice Harmon, and David Norris, 31–38. Urbana: Univ. of Illinois Press, 1986.

Leonard, Garry M. *Reading Dubliners Again: A Lacanian Perspective*. Syracuse, N.Y: Syracuse Univ. Press, 1994.

Litz, A. Walton. *James Joyce*. 2d ed. Boston: Twayne, 1972.

Martin, Timothy. *Joyce and Wagner: A Study of Influence*. Cambridge: Cambridge Univ. Press, 1991.

Mercanton, Jacques. "The Hours of James Joyce." In *Portraits of the Artist in Exile: Recollections of James Joyce by Europeans*, ed. Willard Potts, 206–52. New York: Harcourt, 1986.

Norris, Margot. "Not the Girl She Was at All: Women in 'The Dead.'" In *The Dead*, ed. Daniel R. Schwarz, 190–205. New York: St. Martin's, 1994.

Novak, Jane. *The Razor Edge of Balance: A Study of Virginia Woolf*. Coral Gables: Univ. of Miami Press, 1975.

O'Connor, Frank. "Work in Progress." In *Dubliners: Text, Criticism, and Notes*, ed. Robert Scholes and A. Walton Litz, 304–15. New York: Penguin, 1976.

Post, Elizabeth L. *Emily Post's Etiquette*. 14th ed. New York: Harper, 1984.

Riquelme, John Paul. *Teller and Tale in Joyce's Fiction: Oscillating Perspectives*. Baltimore: Johns Hopkins Univ. Press, 1983.

San Juan, Epifanio, Jr. *James Joyce and the Craft of Fiction*. Rutherford, N.J.: Fairleigh Dickenson Univ. Press, 1972.

Scholes, Robert. *In Search of James Joyce*. Urbana: Univ. of Illinois Press, 1992.

Scholes, Robert, and A. Walton Litz, eds. *Dubliners: Text, Criticism, and Notes*. New York: Penguin, 1976.

Schwarz, Daniel R., ed. *The Dead*. New York: St. Martin's, 1994.

Scott, Bonnie Kime. *James Joyce*. Atlantic Highlands, N.J.: Humanities, 1987.

———. *Joyce and Feminism*. Bloomington: Indiana Univ. Press, 1984.

Torchiana, Donald T. *Backgrounds for Joyce's Dubliners*. Boston: Allen, 1986.

Walzl, Florence L. "*Dubliners*." In *A Companion to Joyce Studies*, ed. Zack Bowen and James F. Carens, 157–228. Westport, Conn.: Greenwood, 1984.

———. "*Dubliners*: Women in Irish Society." In *Women in Joyce*, ed. Suzette Henke and Elaine Unkeless, 31–56. Urbana: Univ. of Illinois Press, 1982.

Wirth-Nesher, Hana. "Reading Joyce's City: Public Space, Self, and Gender in *Dubliners*." In *James Joyce: The Augmented Ninth*, ed. Bernard Benstock, 282–92. Syracuse, N.Y.: Syracuse Univ. Press, 1988.

KLAUS REICHERT

Shakespeare and Joyce:
Myriadminded Men

When Freud was asked, around the year 1900, which were for him the most urgent problems waiting to be solved by scholarship and science, his answer was: first, what is the state of the unconscious?; second, who was Shakespeare? This conjunction sounds rather strange, as if there had been no more imminent problems to be taken up by psychoanalytic theory. Of course Freud was much interested in the biographies of great men. Thus, in a bookseller's inquiry about ten great books to be recommended to a general reading public he includes Mereschkowski's *Leonardo da Vinci*,[1] of which he makes ample use in his own study of Leonardo, which sets out to elucidate the enigmatic smiles on the faces of his figures by paying close attention to biographical detail. But why Shakespeare? Was it because his very identity as a writer had been questioned and was about to disappear behind the masks of Bacon, Rutland, or Southampton? As late as 1936 and 1937, while writing his Moses—another demolition of a given or an alleged identity—Freud was fascinated by the problem and opted for the earl of Oxford, Edward de Vere.[2] Is it important, one may well ask? No, if one is interested only in the finished result of writing or if one assumes with young Stephen in Joyce's *A Portrait of the Artist* that "the artist, like the God of the creation, remains within or behind or beyond or above his handiwork, invisible, refined out of existence, indifferent, paring his fingernails."[3] Questions of the artist's

From *Shakespeare and the Twentieth Century: The Selected Proceedings of the International Shakespeare Association World Congress, Los Angeles, 1996*, edited by Jonathan Bate, Jill L. Levenson, and Dieter Mehl. © 1998 by Associated University Presses.

biography are important, however, if one is interested in the creative process: why did he do what he did, why was he obsessed by certain themes, why did he shape and reshape them under various guises, how did he transform the "sluggish matter" of his personal life into something impersonal, an "impalpable imperishable" work of art?[4]

Young Joyce was beset by these questions. It was only when he discarded the first draft version of *A Portrait*—a thinly disguised autobiographic account of his early years up to maturity—and rewrote what was to become his first novel, that he began to square the circle: to use personal material in such a way that a fictitious character emerged who had his reverberations in myth, history and literature, but was at the same time "real" in the sense that Joyce paid close attention to the actual facts of life in Dublin and Ireland around the turn of the century. Indeed, Joyce had his artist remain "within or behind or beyond or above" his work, but the artist is Joyce, not Stephen. The problem, however, of fact and fiction, personal matter and impersonal work, was neither settled nor discarded. Joyce returned to it and restated it at one remove, I believe, in the Shakespeare theory that the Stephen of *Ulysses* expounds to four or five incredulous listeners in the Irish National Library.

Of course Shakespeare has been around right from the start in *Ulysses*.[5] In the first chapter Stephen is presented in his Hamlet garb: dark hat and clothing, gloomy mood, he is a "bereaved son," and thoughts of his mother, who has recently died and who will appear to him as a ghost later in the book, constantly cross his troubled mind. The whole of the initial setup has indeed been likened to the first court scene in *Hamlet* with Buck Mulligan, who is called "usurper," as Claudius. But the setting on top of the tower, which is later expressly associated with Elsinore, also recalls the night watch in *Hamlet* with Mulligan as Horatio. And when Stephen later leaves the tower in the company of Mulligan and Haines, the Englishman, he has the feeling of walking between traitors who wish to pry into his thoughts, veritably the pair Rosencrantz and Guildenstern. Thus, even though Stephen may on one level certainly be seen as a new Hamlet, recently called back across the sea from his university because of the untimely death of a parent, such a fixation will not hold true for the other characters. They coalesce briefly with certain figures of the play but are detached from them again equally quickly, glimpses in Stephen's mind, sequels of an interior monologue as if he were playing, like Richard II, "in one person many people, / And none contented" (5.5.31ff.). Thus the works of Shakespeare, and in particular *Hamlet*, function as a projection plane for the character of Stephen to gain contour beyond that of an impoverished would-be Dublin writer. Furthermore, we may remember that the title of the chapter is "Telemachus," pointing to a son in search of a father. From another angle this ties in again with the Hamlet theme, and Stephen sets out on his journey to find a father who will not be his physical father but, as it were, a ghostly one or what he calls—"What's in a name?"—a "consubstantial father," young Hamlet and old Hamlet or Stephen and Bloom.

The library chapter, where Stephen expounds his Shakespeare theory, is the ninth, the ninth out of eighteen, which means that it attains a special place as a centerpiece: it is the theoretical core of the book. The title of the chapter is "Scylla and Charybdis," which is to say that Stephen steers his course through perilous waters; dangers are lurking everywhere, which he tries to avoid or takes up boldly; and which he does not overcome unhurt. The time is two o'clock in the afternoon, the pagan ghost hour or the holy hour in Dublin, when pubs are closed. Joyce provides his character with all the knowledge available about Shakespeare in 1904, in particular about the controversial debates as to his identity or that of some of his characters. Stephen knows the great biographies of Georg Brandes and Wilhelm Elze, recently translated into English; knows the work of Sidney Lee, Karl Bleibtreu, and the juicy life by Frank Harris; is familiar with Wilde's "Dark Lady of the Sonnets" and the witticisms of Shaw;[6] mentions the options as to who wrote the plays that do not seem to stimulate his mind greatly: "Rutlandbaconsouthamptonshakespeare or another poet of the same name in the comedy of errors wrote Hamlet" (866).[7] Since for Joyce identity is not a fixed entity, it is absurd trying to pin it down. It may come as a surprise, however, that Stephen undertakes to do just this, but this is precisely the point: to distill a personality out of many variables and unknown givens just as, reversely, apparently identifiable persons—all the people in the book who have "a local habitation and name"—are being dissolved into "airy nothings"; the unknown becomes known, the known unknown. In a way similar to Joyce's, who believed Dublin could be reconstructed from his book, Stephen sets out to reconstruct Shakespeare's life from his work—the artist within his handiwork.

Stephen's Shakespeare is Aubrey's butcher boy who was seduced by a woman eight or nine years his senior, Anne Hathaway. The gist of this affair went into his first epic poem, *Venus and Adonis*, aging damsel seducing inexperienced boy, and was the basis of his female characters in the comedies: "his boywomen are the women of a boy" (254). But by the time he wrote *Venus and Adonis* he had already left Anne with child and had escaped to London. Did the death wound inflicted upon the boy Adonis have something to do with it, the blow at his vital parts he could parry only by taking to his heels? The cliché of the cruelty of women, their sinfulness and frailty, is everywhere to be seen in the great tragic heroines, but Stephen derives it from personal experience: Anne was the adulteress who haunted Shakespeare's mind and forced him to return to the subject over and over again, either as imagined adultery (as in the cases of Desdemona or Hermione), or as "real" (as with

Gertrude or the Lear daughters). Worst of all, Stephen contends, his own brothers Richard and Edmund made him a cuckold; and this is the reason, Stephen holds, why the two most heinous villains of the plays, Richard III and Edmund in Lear, bear their names. On the other hand, time and again Shakespeare returned to Stratford and to Anne, begot more children, bought real estate, died there, and bequeathed his second-best bed to Anne, who survived him.

Joyce did not have Stephen recount the poet's life in order to show off his own erudition or that of his sharp-witted Stephen figure, though this may be partly the case with the latter. In choosing any material Joyce always puts it to use, functionalizes it for the overall structure of his book: everything ties in with everything else. Thus Joyce presents Molly in the first Bloom chapter as seductress, the nymph Calypso, whom the hero has to leave in order to set out on his odyssey; but in the last chapter she becomes Penelope, the in-no-way stainless wife waiting for her husband to return to her. And Bloom, the cuckold, is meandering through his day driven by jealousy. These major themes, which constantly pop up in the mind of Bloom and structure his actions and misactions, are projected by Joyce onto the plane of Stephen's consciousness and are extrapolated by him in his redaction of Shakespeare's life story as a concentration of the themes of the book as a whole. Moreover, Stephen has not yet met Bloom; he is neither jealous nor a cuckold. But by letting the subjects of Bloom's and Stephen's thoughts converge, Joyce gives a first instance of the interweaving of the two characters, unknown of course to both of them. There is only a slight hint at the connection when, right in the middle of the chapter, Bloom briefly appears, hardly seen, hardly identifiable—"A patient silhouette waited, listening" (597)—in order to check something in the library. He turns up like a specter out of nowhere, "a bowing dark figure," which may alert the reader that Bloom's story, too, is being told under the guise of Shakespeare's. And shortly after, Stephen launches into his theory of cuckoldry as a major Shakespearean theme, adding money and seduction into the bargain of themes. Also the question of identity arises: was Shakespeare a Catholic or perhaps a Jew? All of this was reeled off by the brief apparition of Bloom, the Jew, who was a Protestant twice over.

Central to Stephen's arguments is his Hamlet theory. Hamlet had been a great preoccupation with Joyce for a long time.[8] In winter 1912 he delivered twelve lectures on "Amleto di G. Shakespeare" at the Trieste University Popolare, none of which have survived. What did survive are some sixty pages of excerpts made for preparing the lectures.[9] What we find is much of the material from Brandes or Sidney Lee he later used in *Ulysses*, but besides this there are copious excerpts from contemporary writers such as Marlowe, Stubbes, Sidney, Spenser, Bacon, Overbury, and from Dover Wilson's recently published *Life in Shakespeare's England*, mostly attached to a specific scene from *Hamlet* in order to establish its context. Thus, for the brief comparison of Ophelia with Jephthah's daughter he copied out the whole narrative from the *Book of Judges*. By and large the excerpts testify to his wish to re-create Elizabethan atmosphere—everyday life, theater practice, patronage, character types, trade, exploration, licentious living, etc.—and in the library chapter Joyce follows a double strategy: giving Stephen his "dagger definitions" for arguing his theory, yet at the same time, in some of the argument, but mainly in Stephen's interior monologue, making the reader sense that other world in a detailed, though fragmented, pastiche of allusions and quotations that serve to identify Stephen as one of the period on a linguistic plane. (The ironic point is of course that the discussion takes place in a library; a borrowed identity has come out of books, like that of Don Quixote or Madame Bovary mentioned in the notes.)

Joyce himself, when preparing the lectures, was so much involved with the figure of Hamlet that he identified with it, as we can see in the Trieste prose piece he wrote at the same time, posthumously published under the title of *Giacomo Joyce*. It is the story of slighted love, of jealousy, of arrogance, of the ludicrous discrepancy between a father and a daughter, much of it interspersed with Elizabethan phrasing. There is even a direct reference to the Trieste lectures:

> I expound Shakespeare to docile Trieste: Hamlet, quoth I, who is most courteous to gentle and simple is rude only to Polonius. Perhaps, an embittered idealist, he can see in the parents of his beloved only grotesque attempts on the part of nature to produce her image.... Marked you that?[10]

The connection is obvious: in the same way that Ophelia is not created in the image of Polonius, the beloved of the prose piece does not resemble her overbearing father. But another thing is also obvious: that Joyce took no pains at camouflaging the connection but rather implied it, thus laying bare the deep structure of his intent, for example, the repetitions or reverberations of a given set of constellations throughout history under various disguises, as he was to find it formulated much later in Vico's theory of history, but as he would use it for the conception of *Ulysses*. The shift of the Jamesey of *Giacomo Joyce* to the Stephen of *Ulysses* is as significant as that of the Stephen of the early autobiography to the Stephen of *A Portrait*: a transformation of the personal into the impersonal form of art as allegedly Shakespeare had done. Thus, Stephen's Shakespeare theory is a description of Joyce's own creative process in disguise.

Among the excerpts there is one that ties in with Joyce's assumption of the protean quality of human character in general and that of Hamlet

in particular. It is taken from *Rosencrantz and Guildenstern* (1891), a farce
by William Schwenck Gilbert (the collaborator of Sullivan). Ophelia is
asked by Guildenstern "what's he like?" and she reels off a list of his various
identities:

> Alike for no two reasons at a time.
> Sometimes he's tall—sometimes he's very short—
> Now with black hair—now with a flaxen wig—
> Sometimes an English accent—then a French—
> Then English with a strong provincial "bun"—
> Once an American and once a Jew—
> But Danish never take him how you will![11]

And she goes on to list the contradictory answers devoted to the question
whether or not he is mad. Joyce made no apparent use of the passage, but the
reason why he copied it seems fairly obvious: apart from the multifariousness
of character, it was a deft instance of the metamorphoses mythic figures went
through in history, or upon the stage, and the farcical flavor of it anticipated
what Joyce himself was to do on a large scale.

Of all the plays *Hamlet* is most closely linked to Shakespeare's life,
according to Stephen—or Brandes for that matter. Hamnet, Shakespeare's
only son, had died in 1596 at age eleven. In the winter of that year, Shakespeare
wrote *King John*, and the most moving death scene of young Prince Arthur
in that play was written, Stephen suggests, to commemorate this tragic
event. But some six years later Shakespeare came back to it and devised a
more dignified memorial for his son in writing *Hamlet*, which is to say that
Hamlet is meant to be Hamnet, killed before he reached maturity, sexually
unresponsive, as an eleven-year-old boy would be. By the time Shakespeare
wrote that play, he would have made up his mind as to responsibilities, and
he set a whole Ibsen-like family drama in motion with Anne as the guilty
queen who had ousted William from her bed, for example, symbolically
killed him. Consequently Shakespeare himself must be old Hamlet's ghost, a
speculation which ties in with an assumed fact that he indeed acted the ghost
on the stage. As for Claudius, he must be one of the brothers, but Stephen
does not opt for either one.

How do these correspondences connect with *Ulysses*? Stephen's Hamlet
identification may briefly be summarized: he, too, is the "bereaved" and, as
he styles himself, the "dispossessed" son. The friends he thought he had have
betrayed him or are about to do so. Throughout the day he is haunted by the
ghost of his dead mother, and the repeated "List, list, o list" in the chapter
points to her presence in his thoughts. He is suspected of not meaning seriously
what he says—when asked whether he believes in his own theory he bluntly

says "No"—and hides behind the mask of paradoxical or provoking statements showing off his superiority. He is isolated, or isolates himself, by his talk, a solitary figure, crossed in his ambitions. Repeatedly there is mention of a literary gathering in the evening to which he, the aspiring writer, is not being asked, just as Shakespeare was held to be an "upstart crow" and was slighted by the intellectual coterie of his day. All he can do in the situation is "to take arms against a sea of troubles," but he cannot, by opposing, end them. The revenge he feels called upon to take boils down to inane threats in his mind that resemble the helpless soliloquies of his protagonist—"the improbable, insignificant and undramatic monologue" (77) he calls Hamlet's "to be or not to be" speech, unaware that he is characterizing his own mutterings. As for the ghost, he would in the context of the novel be Bloom, who in fact did lose a son in his boyhood whose death he still bemoans, and who has an unfaithful wife on whom he cannot take revenge because he is incapacitated, not physically as old Hamlet's ghost is, but mentally and emotionally. On another plane, within the framework of Stephen's esoteric musings, Bloom would be his "consubstantial father" in search of whom he sets out on his journey during the rest of the day, not knowing that he was so close to him in the library. In his own smart way, Bloom devises his kind of revenge by wishing to present Stephen to Molly as her new lover, a lover he can accept, since he would be, on another plane again, his consubstantial son. Thus, energy seems to be floating from Shakespeare's life into the constellation of his play, from there into the triangle of *Ulysses* with the division of the fathers, and from there into Joyce's own life situation with its heart-rending drama of jealousy[12] at about the time he devised the *Hamlet* lectures; and from there it is projected back again onto Shakespeare. Incidentally, for a man deeply convinced of magic numerology as Joyce was, the coincidence that Hamnet was christened on the day Joyce was born, on 2 February, must have functioned as a "proof" for Joyce that his identification was correct, or in Stephen's words about Shakespeare: "He found in the world without as actual what was in his world within as possible" (1041).

Clear-cut and definite as these ascriptions to *Hamlet* may seem, they are only a half-truth. As one of Stephen's interlocutors remarks: "The truth is midway, he affirmed. He is the ghost and the prince. He is all in all" (1018). Stephen agrees: "All in all. In *Cymbeline*, in *Othello* he is bawd and cuckold." Earlier Stephen had claimed that Shakespeare had disseminated his name in many places: "He has hidden his own name, a fair name, William, in the plays, a super here, a clown there, as a painter of Italy set his face in a dark corner of his canvas. He has revealed it in the sonnets where there is Will in overplus" (921). Now he assumes that Shakespeare is "all in all," that each character, "ostler and butcher," villain or saint, is created in the image of this "myriadminded man,"[13] claiming for him a godlike omniscience and omnipotence. And it does not come as a surprise when Eglinton, another one of the interlocutors, strengthens the link by quoting "Dumas *fils* (or is it Dumas *père?*). After God Shakespeare has created most" (1028). (It is, incidentally, this assertion which Joyceans have transferred to their hero when they say: "After Shakespeare Joyce has created most.") And again, "like the God of the creation," the artist "remains within or behind or beyond or above his handiwork." It is, nevertheless, Stephen's intention, like that of any youthful theologian, to track down this god. One way has been biographical identification—after all there was Renan's *Vie de Jésus*, which Joyce valued; another way is instanced by the thematic obsessions deduced from it. I have mentioned jealousy, a Bloom theme, and betrayal, a Stephen theme, the former being also a self-characterization of God, the latter tying in with Jesus. Another theme would be banishment, which indeed is central to Joyce's work without Stephen having to alert us to it. Stephen states it thus: "the note of banishment, banishment from the heart, banishment from home, sounds uninterruptedly from *The Two Gentlemen of Verona* onward till Prospero breaks his staff. . . . It doubles itself in the middle of his life, reflects itself in another, repeats itself" (999). This sounds like a self-characterization of Stephen from *A Portrait* right through to the end of *Ulysses* and up to the Shem figure of *Finnegans Wake*. This theme, or one should rather say experience, was paramount in Joyce's mind: as a young man he styled himself an exile, had gone into real exile; his one play, written between *A Portrait* and *Ulysses*, was called *Exiles*; and his epics were actually written in exile. On the basis of the many Jewish reverberations in the book, it would not be surprising if Joyce had also God in exile in mind, the Shekhina of the Kabbalists: God roaming about the earth bemoaning his fallen creatures until the coming of the Messiah. This leads to a final cluster of themes, set into motion by original sin. In Stephen's words: "it was the original sin that darkened his [Shakespeare's] understanding, weakened his will and left in him a strong inclination to evil. . . . An original sin and, like original sin, committed by another in whose sin he too has sinned. . . . Beauty and peace have not done it away. It is in infinite variety everywhere in the world he has created" (1006). Does this insinuate a God guilty of the fall because he created the world, as will be a major theme in *Finnegans Wake*? Clearly the theme is Stephen's, as we know from the guilt-ridden boy and adolescent of *A Portrait*, and guilt feelings towards his dead mother loom large in the pages of *Ulysses*. But it is Bloom, like King Lear a man "more sinned against than sinning," who ponders sin time and again, wondering, questioning, curious, as he has no real use for this Christian obsession but feels guilty all the same, slyly trying to eat from any forbidden tree about him.

According to Stephen Shakespeare has very few themes, just as Joyce has, but they are played through "in infinite variety," to take up Enobarbus's description of Cleopatra, taken up by Stephen. Like Shakespeare's they are doubled, trebled, reflected in others, repeated. Shakespeare's method, more so than anybody else's, even Homer's, was the method adopted by Joyce, his consubstantial son. In the "Oxen of the Sun" chapter, where the course of English literature is parodied from Anglo-Saxon times to the present day, there is no mention of Shakespeare—because he was sacrosanct or because he was, as Beckett said of Joyce, a continent of his own? Yet Shakespeare is on every page, not only in the innumerable open or hidden allusions, but also in the very technique. Shakespeare's mixed metaphors, the reeling off of a thought in various directions, the cramming-in of incongruous materials, always controlled by rhythm and sound, may have given Joyce the idea of his interior monologue. Then there is the mixture of styles, the high and the low next to each other, the multiple variety of idioms and in particular idiolects; there are the cascades of puns and quibbles that are unique with these two authors. The overruling principle perhaps lies in the demand they both make on the active participation of the readers or onlookers. "Work, work your thoughts," the Chorus in *Henry V* implores (3.25); "Piece out our imperfections with your thoughts; / Into a thousand parts divide one man" (1.23–24), or "'tis your thoughts that now must deck our kings, / Carry them here and there, jumping o'er times, / Turning th' accomplishment of many years / Into an hour-glass" (1.28–31). Shakespeare spread out his hundreds of characters in a multitude of imagined locations and times upon a single stage. Joyce, "jumping o'er times," condensed them into a single day and into one book but gave us the totality of their lives—if we but work our thoughts. And the story of their lives recalls in the memory theater of Stephen's and Joyce's minds all the lovely or terrible, quaint, grand, passionate or insignificant fragments that made up the characters of their precursor.

NOTES

1. "Antwort auf eine Rundfrage *Vom Lesen und von guten Büchern*" (1906), in *Gesammelte Werke*, Nachtragsband. Texte aus den Jahren 1885–1938 (Frankfurt: S. Fischer, 1987), 662–64.

2. Letters to Arnold Zweig (22.6.1936 and 2.4.1937), in Sigmund Freud, Arnold Zweig, *Briefwechsel* (Frankfurt: S. Fischer, 1968), 142, 149–50.

3. *A Portrait of the Artist as a Young Man*, ed. Chester G. Anderson (New York: Viking, 1968), 215.

4. Ibid., 169.

5. William M. Schutte, *Joyce and Shakespeare* (New Haven: Yale University Press, 1957), chap. 2, 17–29.

6. William H. Quillian, "Shakespeare in Trieste: Joyce's 1912 *Hamlet* Lectures," *James Joyce Quarterly* 12, (1974/1975): 7–63 (7–17).

7. Quotations from *Ulysses* are from the Gabler edition (New York: Garland, 1984). The figure in parentheses gives the line in episode 9.

8. As shown by Vincent Cheng, Joyce also used *Hamlet* as "an all-encompassing matrix for his purposes in *Finnegans Wake*." See his *Shakespeare and Joyce: A Study of "Finnegans Wake"* (Gerrards Cross: Colin Smythe, 1984), 72.

9. Quillian, "Shakespeare in Trieste," 18–63.

10. James Joyce, *Giacomo Joyce* (New York: Viking, 1968), 10.

11. Quillian, "Shakespeare in Trieste," 59.

12. Letters to Nora Barnacle (6 and 7 August 1909), in *Selected Letters*, ed. Richard Ellmann (London: Faber & Faber, 1975), 157–60.

13. This is Coleridge's word for Shakespeare, *Biographia Literaria*, chapter 15.

ROY K. GOTTFRIED

"The Comic Irishman in the Bench Behind": The Portrait with Two Heads

For Stephen, a model schoolboy, scenes in a pedagogical setting are capital moments in *Portrait*; for the reader they are equally essential moments of instruction and enlightenment. Classrooms are not only obviously an important part of a student's life, they are also places in which the novel's quality entity as a *Bildungsroman* obtains. Education is an essential element of *Bildung*; moreover, instruction compliments the intellectual component of the novel, adding to the sense of weighty issues being entertained. The classroom is a place of authority, which must be both obeyed and defied for the growth of the protagonist. In *Portrait* that authority limns at a distance the control of colonization and, because Stephen is taught by religious men who add dogma to the order of other powers of the classroom, they are certainly guardians of the power of the Word and, by extension, of the world. A classroom is—or should be—a place where those various authorities impose order and rile, directing while teaching about the world. Stephen must accept and adapt to this order, his response to the instruction he receives—and then transforms or rejects—operates as an analogy to the activity of the reader, who reads the text and must transform or reject what happens to Stephen, and it is here that irony plays its part in the reader's response to the novel's instruction. The classroom has a purpose to advance the student, much as the generic plot of the novel of development has a purpose to advance to its

From *Joyce's Comic Portrait*. © 2000 by University Press of Florida.

predisposed end. Stephen finds a sense of superiority and otherness in class, befitting his sense of special calling, and so he demonstrates these qualities. In the order of the class, however, there is disorder, and Stephen often misses what happens in the class around him. The reader, because he focuses on Stephen, similarly misses much of what goes on elsewhere in the classroom. And so often what happens in these instructional moments that Stephen fails to note is a sense of chaos and misrule. It is there that the comic spirit surfaces, in acts of humorous capering. Much as the novel's serious drive is interspersed with moments of tumbling, the classroom's pedagogical thrust is alternated with antic behavior. It was in such classrooms as the mathematics class at Belvedere that the notion of the alternate comic tumbling was found; in the physics class at UCD that the image of the capering clerics occurs. The reader, like Stephen a model schoolboy, takes seriously or takes offense at what happens in the instruction; the comic element occurs just beyond notice, as an alternative to the direction of the class.

In addition to the mathematics class and the physics lecture, four other classroom scenes bring into light the workings of *Portrait* as something comic, as alternately over the shoulder. Stephen ofttimes falls short in these classes, and sometimes he is merely present, standing by while something occurs. Much like his slaying to the side during the rough and tumble rugby in the first term at Clongowes, Stephen is a bystander here to moods, activities, concepts that go on just behind him, and *these* things, indeed, are active and amusing, much like sport or a game. He partakes as little of this fun as he did of sports. These scenes are discussed here not in their order in the plot, because the elements of the comic that peer through each scene follow their own alternate process of comic misrule. Jumping around the chronology of the plot defies the authority of the genre and allows the comedy to emerge from the rules. The chronology of these scenes makes them appear accretive, as Stephen grows into his sense of his own powers; to displace that order is to see the ways in which Stephen's tumbling and error are themselves independent, equal moments of humor, comedy allowing no hierarchy. The first scene discussed is one of the last, and it is only fantasy—the English class Stephen imagines on his way to Newman House, having already missed the class proper, the second is that actual physics class where something more appears beyond the scene of uncloistered revelry occasioned by the ribald comment. After these, a transgressive move jumps back to the very first class, the one at Clongowes in which he is pandied, and then to an English class at Belvedere in which Stephen is threatened with punishment when accused of heresy. These two classes in which Stephen is in error then yield to the meeting with the dean of studies, before the actual physics class, in which, although Stephen more than holds his own in intellectual discussion, a comic sense pervades the encounter. The last classroom considered is a return to that class of mathematics in the winter term at Belvedere, where the idea of comic tumbling is first recognized, to see that the class yet contains something else besides. While these scenes defy the logic of plot and chronology, they obey comedy's antic sway.

So the classroom is a particular, important area for both the serious development of the novel and the skewed presence of the comic. By his university years, Stephen has begun to slacken in his studiousness; his own home is misruled by a clock that is wildly inaccurate, and he even fails to know what weekday it is and so only realizes on his way that he will miss his English class. He imagines being there, envisioning the other students with heads "meekly bent," dutifully taking notes while his "own head was unbent" (178), as if resisting the ideas of the lecture. He sets himself apart yet again as different, another kind, as he has been in all his school days, even in a classroom he only imagines. The head is a major feature of this imagined scene, surely because the head is the main object of the classroom's instructional intent (and heads are so prominent in the tiered auditoria to both student and instructor alike). So the focus on heads seems appropriate (and necessary) to the novel's serious intellective purpose. That prominence is why the classroom provides such a capital setting in the book. The presences of heads, Stephen's up and others' meekly bent, also localizes the figure of the body to stress its most revealing feature, the one that is the absolute center of a portrait.

After imagining the English class he actually missed and then entering the physics theatre and meeting the dean, Stephen attends the physics lecture. Like mathematics, its subject is rule and authority; it is also a subject of the actual world. This last class presented in the novel is no culmination of Stephen's education. Rather than a matriculated finish to his learning, one that would drive the telos of his development, this class is riddled with confusion and unruliness. The tedious lecture is spiced with marginal commentary by Moynihan. In particular, the one vulgar aside he makes about ellipsoidal balls produces in Stephen the image that recognizes the comic tumbling around the somber ideas of his life. In the order of science lurks the ribald biology of youthful raillery, just as within the somberness of the priests and the earnest youthfulness of the narrative lurks a comic impulse. Moreover, even as Stephen's imagined scene of the cavorting priests gives antic misrule and tumbling to the somber, principled drive of the plot, so this scene in the physics class also gives comedy something else, its particular position and place. We will not be surprised to find that it lies just over the shoulder, like the humeral veil, displaced from the apparent center. Throughout the lecture Moynihan's voice from the back is in contrast to the subject matter presented at the front of the auditorium, as serious matters are always foregrounded in the novel: as the front of the room is for serious material, so the back of the classroom is the place for vulgar speech. At the outset of the class, when the roll is taken and there is no answer to the call of Cranly's name, "Try Leopardstown! said a voice from the bench *behind*"; and the instructional hour ends as "Moynihan's voice called from *behind* in echo to a distant bell:— dosing time, gents!" (191, 194, emphasis added). Behind the authority of instruction and questions is the jocular exclamatory countervoice, the back of the classroom being the place for the unruly students. Moynihan is the very figure of the antic that Stephen evokes when he hears his ribald comment about "ellipsoidal balls": his "snoutish face" (191) is the face not only of scabrousness but of satire, marking its etymological derivative from satyr.

There are other voices around Stephen and their presence makes up the real world that eludes him or that he avoids. In the middle of the lecture, during the teacher's demonstration of electrical current, one other student asks a question: "A sharp Ulster voice" asked whether students would be responsible for questions of applied science. This to Stephen is the voice of the other again, which always intrudes upon his thoughts. He sees it as another head, Protestant, northern, alien. The intrusion of other voices always forces a shift away from the intense foregrounding of Stephen's own serious thoughts; they present alternative tones to the monovocal quality of the narrative. He only recognizes in such other voices the authority of their dutiful obligatory imperative and seeks to free himself from the conformity they demand: "the constant voices . . . urging him to be a gentleman . . . to be a good catholic . . . to be strong and manly . . . to be true to his country" (83–84). Together, they all create "the din . . . hollowsounding." His escape from them is into "the pursuit of phantoms," certainly not a freedom achieved in the real world. Yet there are other voices that Stephen fails to hear, and these are ones from the real world around him that do not urge duty but misrule, not purpose but playfulness.

In many instances, such as this one from the different student, the "other voice" is heard within the tumult and disorder of the classroom that Stephen, self-absorbed and highly intellectual, ignores. We have remarked on Stephen's self-absorbed catechetical questions about the Real Presence of the Divine in the Eucharist that continue despite the comic intrusion of his classmate's noting the return of the rector with "Here he is!" Again at Belvedere, and similarly, when Stephen is greatly moved by the rhetoric of the presentation of hell at the retreat, he imagines "his brain was simmering and bubbling within" the skull, flames bursting from that skull "shrieking like voices:—Hell! Hell! Hell!" (125). What is actually going on around him is that his fellow students, completely unmoved, are remarking and joking about the sermon to others not at the retreat: "Voices spoke near him:—On hell.—I suppose he rubbed it into you well.—That's what you fellows want: and plenty of it to make you work." With a sense of the comic that appears obliquely, a reader should sense that the raucous voices of Stephen's fellows make such likely sophomoric jokes as "it was a hell of a scrim" of "it was hell to sit through it" that causes the repetition of the word "hell, hell." Such voices around Stephen, unnoticed by him, mark the chaotic nature of the classroom and the comic life of the real world. Those voices always contrast humorously with Stephen and his (here) genuine, conscience-stricken self-absorption. Importantly, those voices do not ironize his response, but offer an alternative in another tone, a comic presentation that takes place just over his shoulder.

Back in the physics theatre, the sharp Ulster voice of this practical Scot asking questions about the material annoys Moynihan, who "murmurs from behind" Stephen, "—Isn't MacAlister a devil for his pound of flesh?" (193), as he conflates Scottish parsimoniousness with Shakespeare's Jewish usuriousness. Stephen, sitting on his bench, is stuck between MacAlister before and Moynihan behind, posed between earnestness and comedy, positioned in the same space as his own autobiographical novel, doubled in between earnest development and comic otherness. A bench is also equally two things, partaking of the doubleness of diction that often produces comic paronymy: a bench is the *banc* of law, or authority and rule, yet it is also at the same time the *banc* climbed upon by the huckster, the joker, the mountebank of misrule and tumbling. Two voices, two benches suggest another focus and location to the portrait, riffled otherwise with a tension between the serious and the ironic.

This sort of doubleness is clearly continued by Stephen's heavily configured thought about MacAlister's head: "Stephen looked down coldly on the oblong skull beneath him" (193). Stephen is so firmly tied to his self, so narcissistically connected to his own portrait, that he often gazes at his own reflection. He "gazed at his face for a long time in the mirror of [his mother's] dressingtable" (71) trying to write a poem for E. C.; or he wonders what his face looks like to others, whether "there was something in his face which made him look like a schemer and he wished he had a little mirror to see" (53). It is by solipsistic extension that he so often notices the heads of his classmates, primarily as an egoistic reflection of his own search for a portrayed identity (and partially because his eyesight would limit him to noticing only what was directly before his face). Each head, of course, is a portrait that connects to the central representation of the novel, but each one is of someone other, and thus is a counterimage to the one of Stephen that occupies so much space in the novel. Many of these heads offer lesser alternatives to Stephen's exalted image within the text, and we will not be surprised to see that these offer comic alternatives to the serious sitting of *Portrait*. Stephen, bidding his mind think a "willful unkindness" about that head of MacAlister, considers that "the student's father would have done better had he sent his son to Belfast to study and have saved something on the train fare by so doing" (193), displaying solicitude for money and fatherhood Stephen has never before shown. Yet it is a thought with less malice in it than Stephen has elsewhere shown himself capable. What follows is an odd exchange in Stephen's mind: "The oblong skull beneath did not turn to meet this shaft of thought and yet the shaft came back to its bowstring: for he saw in a moment the student's wheypale face" (193). The passage has a certain quality as a set piece, a polished period of prose: "shaft," "bowstring," "wheypale." (This last is a description Joyce cherished enough to use with variation in "Proteus" when Stephen looks at the face of Sargent.[1] "Wheypale" must in Stephen's mind be associated with mother's milk and the firstborn, as he thinks in regard to Sargent; if MacAlister is a firstborn, Stephen has found in him another semblance.) It is Stephen's intent to think here, to speak weightily to himself, and the willful verbalizing is always in danger of being over-embroidered because it is conscious and deliberate.

Yet the words "shaft of thought" and "bowstring" are odd figures for Stephen, resembling the adventure stories read by the boys in "An Encounter"; their strangeness suggests the strained effort by Stephen to be literary. Too often, when he consciously reaches as he does here for artistic efforts, the results exceed his grasp and become empurpled with excessive rhetorical blooms that make an inviting target for the action of comic tumbling, tripping them down from an undeserved lofty perch. Some of these figures owe their debt to Stephen's allusive mind, one that already has had suggestions of Shakespeare in Moynihan's clichéd "pound of flesh." Surely Stephen's disavowal of intent immediately following his insult to MacAlister resembles Hamlet's odd apology to Laertes about his lack of aforethought, "that I have shot mine arrow o'er the house / And hurt my brother" (V, ii, 253–254). In that speech Hamlet claims to be another Hamlet ("If Hamlet from himself be ta'en away"), and Stephen with MacAlister's skull is portraying himself as another. Stephen has found two heads for himself, as if there are two Stephens figured in any image he makes or in any other person he sees; in this alternative and doubling lies the possibility of comic effect.

This sense of otherness, of something just behind, is continued with the head of MacAlister phrenologically observed as "oblong," a shape that is like an ellipsoid. When Stephen sees that MacAlister does not respond to his sharp thoughts (the shaft of his thought came back to the bowstring), he wishes to disavow his unsuccessful witticism: "That thought is not mine, he said to himself quickly. It came from the comic Irishman in the bench behind" (193). It is not clear whether Stephen's denial of "that thought" refers to his practical one (about the train fare) or to his metaphoric one (of the bowstring); if the former, he seeks to undo his unkindness; if the latter, his awkward metaphorizing. This is the Stephen unsure of his identity and unwilling to assert it as is Hamlet; it will be the same when he goes to Paris (as he remembers in "Proteus") and keeps police tickets to prove an alibi: "*Lui, c'est moi*" (*U* 3.183). His comment here is another alibi, literally, to be somewhere else, neither in the one thought nor in the other. Disavowal is a doubling, a making of another, an alternative. In the need to deny either an unkind thought or an inelegant word choice, Stephen seeks the erasure of himself by positing a double, a similar but alternate entity. It is an entity neither practical nor poetic, one more humorous than earnest It is more likely that he refers not to any thought of his, practical or metaphoric, but rather he disavows the comic thought of Moynihan. Stephen puts the blame for levity somewhere else, on someone else; that is why he is so rarely funny.

Stephen may mean to say something quite literal and correct when he says that "thought was not mine . . . it came from the comic Irishman in the row behind": that the thought he disavows was the comment "Isn't MacAlister a devil . . ." and that it was Moynihan who made it, the Moynihan of the ellipsoidal balls who sets the tumbling sabbath of misrule in Stephen's mind. He is indeed seated in the bench behind, from whence comes the thought, and he is comic.

Yet the very notion of the comic Irishman behind in Stephen's disavowal would well describe the comic counter-narrative of the novel. There is comedy always just behind the text that focuses with directed intensity on Stephen; the text quite clearly localizes it: humor is always just over the shoulder of Stephen, that shoulder of the humeral veil. The very same comedy is always indirect, not only just "behind" (where Moynihan is always located in all these exchanges), but also just to the side, laughing "in the sleeve" as Lynch had noted of Stephen's comic use of Aquinas. That comedy is always the other side to the novel of development, in "another head" portrayed in the text a head other than his filled with serious thoughts; *Portrait* may produce a doubled but alternate view, an opposition to serious direction.

The comic Irishman is neither the artist nor the serious boy (nor is he Joyce, exactly); he is someone other just in the margins of the text.[2] It is he who tumbles over and over in undirected antics, rather than rising to higher levels; he is misrule rather than rule, carnival rather than career. He is always displaced just behind. Ellmann, speaking of the more open humor of Stephen in the last passages of the novel, notes that comedy had before been "almost undisclosed" in the earlier chapters; he fortuitously notes that obscured and cloistered nature of the comic *Portrait*.[3] This disposition of comedy, a closeting away from the seriousness of the plot, is necessary on several grounds, although being necessary does not mean that the novel cannot be comic.

The reasons for this displacement, for the comedy appearing in the bench behind, are many—historical, psychological, artistic, and critical. There is first the subordinate condition of the colonial, for whom, as critics note, comedy is the response to imperial power. The comic Irishman is always the alternative figure standing in humorous comic dissipation and powerlessness against the authority of the imperium, much as the hapless students must use chaotic ribaldry to resist the power of parochial educational authority.

Portrait, in fact, has several hegemonic forces against which evasion and subterfuge are necessary. The political system of imperialism is not the only force that demands of its colonial subjects a surface conformity and appropriate behavior that result in a subversive humorous counterrebellion; religion is one of perhaps greater effect in Ireland and certainly within Portrait. The Church is the force of censure and censoring, a particular threat to the artist.[4] While politics seeks to suppress native feeling, the Church seeks to censor pagan impulses. For the late nineteenth century, of course, these were one and the same: native feeling was uncivilized, primitive, and pagan. So Portrait, because it centers on a protagonist caught in the system of a Church and living in a country controlled by the system of an imperium, is a novel in which the repressive forces are foremost in the events and must be challenged by the individual for a necessary outcome. (One might argue that Bildungsroman is the prime locus for the expression of a self liberated from all hegemonies.) Yet the very heavy presence of those two repressive systems of church and state (to which might be added others, such as culture) suggests that Portrait is in greatest need for humor that finds its way out from underneath oppression's weight and out from behind the powerful enfranchised systems. The pagan forces against which the Church marshals its power are those very ones associated with the body—sexuality and license—the body that is the source of comedy.

Yet there is another powerful order and authority that surrounds the text rather than appearing in it; it is an order that is artistic. The novel's very genre must also be resisted in the same ways as political order, authority, dogma, and tradition are generic as well as hegemonic and must be resisted by carnivalesque tumbling; that may be Joyce's first overthrow in revolution. To resist reading the directed plot and seriousness of Portrait as a novel of development is to resist the order and direction that are the main implements of power, both literary and imperialist. To read the novel as comic is to resist all orders.[5]

Freud has argued that the techniques of comedy—caricature, parody, and travesty—"are directed against . . . objects which lay claim to authority and respect, which are in some sense 'sublime.'"[6] While it is evidently true that much of Joyce's humor is directed against church and state, and even against aspects of culture and family, it should be also argued that his humor is directed against the authority of the artistic forms he chooses to employ, the esthetic sublime. Certainly the deconstructive parodic aspects of Ulysses work against the demands of the epic and novel form, those established norms which are for the artist an authorizing enfranchisement. *Portrait*'s very genre represents the challenge of the protagonist to all forms of authority, yet within the plot of *Bildungsroman* such a challenge is rarely humor-laden. The humor of *Portrait*, however indirectly, works against the very precise claims to authority of its particular genre because the form is itself the authority that gives direction and structure. The comedy of *Portrait* is at war with the very authority it generates itself; it is little wonder that the humor must be so covert.[7]

Stephen's sloughing off of Moynihan as the comic Irishman is a critical judgment as well. He disdains the typical literary caricature of the stage Irishman as an unstable influence, belligerent, chaotic, and unserious.[8] Stephen wishes to make his own elevated art of the esthetic, as witnessed by the ephemeral villanelle. He only has to hear of an old peasant from the west, who reacts to Mulrennan's question about the universe and the stars with the comment, "there must be terrible queer creatures at the latter end of the world" (251) for him to "fear him. I fear his redrimmed horny eyes." Stephen feels he must struggle with him, resisting the Antaeus-like pull of the Irish soil that Yeats embraces because Joyce sees it as sluggish matter that will keep him from soaring with elevated art. Yet the comic Irishman behind Stephen, just over his shoulder, is his future as it was Joyce's (a point that will be discussed at some length in chapter 3); and that figure will overtake Stephen when he comes to live with Mulligan in the Martello tower at the start of the next work. The writer Stephen might become (and Joyce does) is a comic writer, one who takes his stand against all authority, Church, imperium, and literary tradition—all, through the use of comedy that he adapts to his own purposes and not to those of an exclusive national identity. The comic figure resides within the frame of *Portrait*, limited by the narrative, always there just behind, just beyond; he makes another head that is imperfectly seen in the alternative portraiture.

Scenes of instruction in the classroom, with heads attentive or not, are thus fundamental to *Portrait*, itself a depiction of a head, and to its genre as novel of intellectual development, of education. Classrooms are instructive for the attentive reader, too, if the reader can just look beyond the foregrounded absorption of Stephen and hear beyond Stephen's dominant voice, and past the directed drive of the novel that centers both; the comic alternative appears in capering confusion in that space behind, as the classroom situates the comic impulse. Such notions as comic tumbling, presented in the mathematics class at Belvedere (a class that will be revisited again in this chapter), and the image of the sabbath of misrule in the physics theatre at UCD, revisited above, are places where the reader can learn. In these classes the reader has been instructed already in two essential features of the comic: its tumbling sense of capering aimlessness and its temporary respite from the serious, and now a third, the displacement of the comic as different and behind.

There are further classroom scenes showing Stephen in less than successful achievement, indeed they show his shortcomings, his confusions, the otherness of his ideas. While Stephen is central to and his thoughts predominate the narrative, both causing and caused by the interiorization of the novel, and the classroom experiences encapsulate the internal workings of his mind, the fact that he is brought up short and seen as inadequate in these moments of instruction suggests that the scenes offer something more, and something other, than the directed drive of the seriousness of development. Stephen is often implicitly contrasted in these scenes by other, duller students and with obtuse masters: this contrast, while it works to elevate Stephen, also adds a sense of otherness and difference; it suggests the world outside of Stephen. Other voices here emerge, such as the ones noted at the retreat or at the university, and these voices give articulation to things that are different from the novel; and because the novel is so serious, that difference is often humor. This otherness is not the irony that arises within the indirect style in the disparity between Stephen and the narrative.[9] Otherness is the distance between Stephen and text, making the space behind that opens up the alternative to seriousness: in comic otherness, in the bench behind, there is a glimpse of the carnival of misrule rather than the sobriety of ironized instruction.

It is transgression and misrule we find that prompt the first two classroom scenes in the plot of novel. The initial one, in Stephen's first school, is in many ways the most complex and determined in the novel, the scene of pandying, when Stephen falls afoul of authority without any action on his part; it is an exceptional event in Stephen's otherwise and subsequent obedient school career. Yet, in addition to the issues of authority and justice that are important to the text, the scene also establishes the primacy of the classroom setting in the novel, and establishes the places within it of the serious and the funny. Fleming is a recognized idler and dullard, with a blotted copy book and a grasp of grammar so weak as to suggest that the noun sea has no plural; he probably deserves flogging as an idler; even before Dolan appears looking for one, Father Arnall claims that Fleming is "one of the idlest boys" (47) he ever met. Yet Fleming's intellectual failings are placed in equal standing with Stephen's physical one of not being able to see, and Stephen feels an injustice in being considered a similar idler. He feels this equality especially as the two students are placed together when they are usually set so differently in the classroom. Stephen has a highly developed sense of place; he is insistent even in the physics theatre, in a class he no longer cares about, when he notes that Moynihan is in the bench behind. He is just as scrupulous at the outset of his academic career at Clongowes. Fleming is made by Father Arnall to kneel in the middle of the class, to come out of his place in the last row of seats, a place assigned due to his poor academic performance. The text locates him: "Fleming moved heavily out of his place and knelt between the two last benches" (47). Like the joker Moynihan at university, Fleming is in the bench behind. Stephen, or course, sits in the front row, as befitting his status as head scholar and leader of Yorkists; his is first of place, that of seriousness and achievement. He is summoned by Dolan to the middle of the class, where his punishment reduces and positions him *inter pares* with his classmates. What justified resentment Stephen feels in this scene about being beaten unfairly must be colored by his disdain at getting equal placement with a fellow student far his inferior, one in fact from the last benches, that place in the classroom of foolishness and misbehavior. In his very first class, Stephen seeks to disassociate himself from the unruly elements in the back of the class, even as he continues to do so up to the last class, where he disavows the comic comments from the row behind. (As a sign of his seriousness at the retreats in chapter 3, Stephen is twice located "in the front bench of the chapel" [108] and "again in the front bench" [126].) Order is restored after the beating when Father Arnall tells the different malefactors, "You may return to your places, you two" (51). Places are hierarchical, awarded on merit in the classroom; there Stephen receives his just deserts. The benches behind, from whence issue the ribald, the comic and the chaos, are ones with which Stephen has no wish to associate. They represent the misrule that here is punished but elsewhere lives in the world around Stephen, whether he will acknowledge it or not.

The second classroom scene in the novel occurs at the end of the first term at his next institution, Belvedere, and also involves a failing of Stephen's, this one of the intellect and not of the body. He remembers, invoked by Heron's beating him to confess Byron a heretic, an incident in which he is accused by the English master of having heresy in his essay. "Mr Tate withdrew his delving hand and spread out the essay.—Here. It's about the Creator and the soul. . . . Ah! *without a possibility of ever approaching nearer*. That's heresy. Stephen murmured:—I meant *without a possibility of ever reaching*. . . . It was a submission and Mr. Tate, appeased, folded up the essay and passed it across to him, saying:—O . . . Ah! *ever reaching*. That's another story" (79).

The gap in this brief moment of heresy, spiritual misrule, and submission is one that further opens up the possibility of the comic. "Approaching nearer" and "ever reaching" might well be a slip of the pen (especially by someone with weak eyesight, the cause of the other classroom confrontation); the eye might slip by omitting "approaching" and misreading "reaching" for "nearer." (The diphthong *ea* in both is always elided when the name Dedalus appears, making another sort of gap.) The distinction between "nearer" and "reaching" (like that of Tennyson's "reach" and "grasp") is something that falls just short of absolute control or completion; it is, in fact, much like the comedy of the novel that never actually reaches the forefront of the text but always approaches nearer, over the shoulder, in the last row or the bench behind. And the echo of Tennyson must surely stand comically behind the confrontation of Heron with Stephen, who must defend Byron against Heron's choice of the Laureate. The interconnections of this classroom scene with the confrontation with Heron can be given a comic gloss. Further elements of a comic language are to be found in the memory of the beating by Heron that evokes the classroom scene with Mr. Tate: as the teacher has asked Stephen to "submit" a paper, so Heron commands Stephen to "admit"; words can seem much the same and yet humorously different. The instructor is pleased with Stephen's retraction and restatement of his essay, its being a "submission" to indicate that Stephen is subservient to authority. Yet a submission, so rare a thing from the proud Stephen, is also an activity done every time a student hands in an essay, an activity Stephen is eager to do; this alternate meaning of language makes for comic possibility. When at Belvedere, the young Joyce sought to submit comical sketches to *Tit Bits*, showing not only his eagerness for submission for public fame but also a tendency to humor in contrast to the somber self-portrait at this same chronological point in the novel.[10] Admission, as confession, and submission, as placing beneath, are the movement of Stephen's life; but their interplay in the text is a comic shadow of Stephen's development and rebellion.

The delving hand of Mr. Tate as he sifts the submitted essays resembles that of Father Dolan at the pandying; the strong arm of authority ends with forceful hands. Yet that delving hand, going beneath the papers, can also be viewed as the hand behind which the priests whisper their laughter when Stephen imagines them in misrule. The subject matter of Stephen's essay is serious: the soul and its relation to God, a relationship that has its analogue in *Portrait* obviously in Stephen's relation between his soul and the world; the relation also pertains to the space between the character and the author, that source of irony. The gap between God and the soul replicates that seemingly unbridged gap in the novel between Stephen and the world outside, so that he only glimpses and faintly hears its misrule and comedy far behind him. The idea of nearing but never reaching also obtains between the reader and the text. The idea of otherness, of distance between God and the soul, or of Stephen's soul and the world, and the reader and the text, is continued by the fact that his error in the essay is itself something else; it is not intentional but a *lapsus scripsi*, that is, a tumble that opens up comically misunderstood possibilities within orderly dogma. A gap, within a word or in a text, is a likely place for comedy, where something falls short of an ideal, where something is less than intended, or other than expected. When Stephen submissively notes his error, the teacher offers in reconciliation that his essay is something else, another type of literature, "that is another story." As another story it is like the alternate *Portrait*, not serious but funny, whose missteps are places of comic discovery.

The originary failing of Stephen in the classroom at Clongowes, that of his pandying, makes up "another story" told twice in *Portrait*; in fact, this story is told once as the noble history of justice served after the beating and the second time as farce. It is what Simon Dedalus calls "that story about you" (72) he heard from Father Conmee, who gave "a great account of the whole affair." It, too, is another story: *Manly little chap! . . . You better mind yourself, Father Dolan, . . . or young Dedalus will send you up for twice nine*" (72). This repetition is a doubling over, and it is an emblem of the way in which the comic appears in the novel: first a serious account, told from Stephen's interior point of view, and then a more antic rendition told—or frequently glimpsed alternately from outside. As the text presents the father's recounting of Cone and his "great account," the novel has something told, retold (recounted), and valued ("account")—all the function of literature but also the substance of fanciful stories, *contes*. In the discussion of Stephen's admission to Belvedere (the place in which so many instructional moments occur in which the serious is mingled with the comic) there is something humorous. Simon begins by telling Stephen that his "long holiday" from school is over, which is to say that the sabbath of idle pleasure is now to come to an end with new application to order and discipline; comic freedom is to give way to serious purpose. When it is clear that there has been an "arrangement" about Belvedere, Simon then remembers that Stephen's brother Maurice is also to be included in it. Marginalized in the text (this his only mention) and here brought in only as Simon's afterthought, "Holy Paul, I forgot about Maurice," this brother is a completely comic figure: "they'll teach you to spell c.a.t cat. And I'll buy you a . . . handkerchief to keep your nose dry" (72). Maurice "grinned at his father and brother," apparently accustomed to being the butt of such low bodily humor; just behind Stephen in years, he is another figure of the comedy that surrounds the major character. Yet that first son and prime focus of the novel is himself in this account an unaccustomed source of humor to others: Conmee says, "Father Dolan and I had a great laugh over it . . . We had a famous laugh together over it. Ha! Ha! Ha!" (72). By way of comic exaggeration and repetition, this punch line is repeated for a third time, the text setting it in italics so as to suggest that it has become a source of legend for a circle wider than the original two: "*Father Dolan and I and all of us we had a hearty laugh together over it.*" This account, with its vocalized laughter ("Ha! Ha! Ha!"), contrasts with the solemnity with which Stephen undergoes this experience of visiting the rector (and there is an echoic similarity and difference, as the laughter "Ha! Ha! Ha!" contrasts with the historic landscape feature of the school, the ha-ha). Stephen is first presented as purposeful and solemn, and yet this scene described by Simon offers a counterexample of accounting and recounting that is quite raucously funny. Conmee's account is one of comedy. It has a reversal, a misrule, in that Stephen will now mete out punishment to his superior. As well, the retelling has inversion: Stephen, then elevated on the shoulders of his schoolmates, is now the figure of contradiction, as both "manly" and "little." The retelling also has exaggeration, where Stephen's two hits are enlarged gargantuanly out of justice to the threat of twice nine.

As he quietly goes up the storied and historical long dark corridor to the office at Clongowes, Stephen imagines what he does is sanctioned by history "by some great person whose head was in the books" (53); again he situates the serious at the site of the intellect, the head. Yet portraiture has many sittings and other poses; the other story about Stephen is quite loud. The "hearty" laugh of Conmee is situated in an organ in contrast to the head and its intellection, an organ of the body that is the source of humor (hence the belly laugh); the contrast between the head and the *hearty* and *great* and *famous* laugh is the alternate portraiture of the novel.

These classroom scenes of pandying and heresy are Stephen's lapses, if both inadvertent and excused; they are two lapses of a sort not normally granted model schoolboys, if in the real world such missteps are common. St. Stephen, for the similar lapses perceived by his elders in authority, was dilapidated. Unlike the saint his namesake, however, Dedalus achieves a victory of sorts in discussion with the elder dean of studies. This is another pedagogical scene, which takes place in the empty physics theatre just before Stephen's next class, in which he will envision the misrule and locate the comic Irishman. The meeting with the dean is more a tutorial than a class, where Stephen interacts with a lesser member of the hierarchy, the exchange with the dean being one in which Stephen smugly maintains his superiority. Here Stephen feels he is the instructor. His points about "the esthetic question" seem to convince the Father temporarily. The culmination of the conversation is in the discussion of the word *tundish*, where Stephen seems to defeat the dean by asserting that the word is common and English. English things are to be disdained, but so too are things too Irish; all are too common for a young man who wants to be distant from the real world of the vulgar. Indeed, much of the discussion about language is about otherness and displacement. The dean is an Englishman, an outsider to the Irish Stephen, and more, he is an outsider brought into the Church by conversion, a figure of change or turning about. As such, he is another figure behind or just to the side who, fittingly with the sense of otherness and displacement in language, is a source of comic possibility.

The language in which we are speaking is his before it is mine. How different are the word *home, Christ, ale, master*, on his lips and on mine! ... His language, so familiar and so foreign, will always be for me an acquired speech.... My soul frets in the shadow of his language. (189)

Stephen feels further displacement because he considers that the language spoken is the dean's before it is his; for Stephen, it is an acquired speech (although an alert reader might ask for whom is language not acquired speech? And as to Stephen's claim that the language was the dean's before it was his, surely the difference in their ages makes that an idle and self-concerned piece of pathos). The secondariness of the language, however, seems to be a pertinent condition for a comedy situated behind; and the words that Stephen chooses to suggest that he and the priest have a different purchase on language all contain enough dissimilarity to suggest comic alternatives: *home, Christ, ale, master*. The first and third are English words, as simple as "tundish"; the second is Greek, the last Latin, as is "funnel." While the list begins with the familiar and common, it moves next to the special and unique; back then to common ("ale") and then returns to the superiority that Stephen always seeks. The list has its own comic possibilities, unknown to Stephen; it might resemble a list Stephen makes for Bloom in "Circe" which he knows to be funny, but pitches the humor beyond Bloom to maintain the sort of superiority he tries to gain with the dean of studies: "Cicero, Podmore. Napoleon, Mr Goodbody. Jesus, Mr Doyle."[11] Doyle is the anointed *one*, the Christ and the master, Cicero is connected to Latin; so the comic connection of these two lists spans several years and texts in Joyce's mind (and Stephen's). Such connections, we have observed, confirm the presence of the comic in both *Ulysses* and *Portrait*. In Stephen's first list, "home" and "ale" are common, "Christ" and "master" are superior, the list has its chiastic conflation. "Home" is familiar, "Christ" is unique (and there is also the connection of the Gospel, "in my father's house there are many mansions"). The anointed one must be anointed, and ale could function in that way, especially as it is a fermented spirit (and again, the miracle at Cana occasions Mulligan's jokes about free drinks [*U* 1.590]). Language at odds here creates the sort of gap or distance out of which the comic can peer. Stephen seems unaware of the connotations of the words he uses; in that space between connotation and denotation is *another* spot for humor. The sense of distance and displacement is continued with Stephen's bathetic claim that "his soul frets in the shadow of his language," which he takes to suggest his art languishing in the tenebrous power of the other culture. But the space between the soul and language is a place just behind and over the shoulder, and a distance maintained from language can be a virtue, because in that space verbal comedy can be forged.

Stephen is not merely unaware that what he thinks could be humorous; he is too serious about his own displacement to see that language, when displaced, can be comic. Extending the idea of distance between Stephen and language, what is additionally comic is the way that the language of the passage refers to a world outside Stephen which he refuses to recognize and that gives a comic and deflationary tumble to the weight of his ideas and the metaphoric language in which he expresses them.[12] The actual figure of the dean is a good place to start; he is described in the homely task of removing candlebutts from his soutane. The man who will be the butt of Stephen's smug superiority and university-wit nimbleness (and Stephen remarks to himself on the way to UCD that it was the home of Buck Whalley of the Hellfire Club) was called in *Stephen Hero* Father Butt, so that the object he takes out and his function are more comically evident in that earlier text; in the *Portrait* the name has been displaced and redirected into oblique anonymity, relegated to the behind bench of an earlier version to hide the obvious comedy. (More of this issue of how the overtly comic earlier text of *Hero* frets in the shadow of the *Portrait* will be discussed in chapter 4.)

To his action of removing the remnant of candles, Stephen thinks of the dean as humbly serving "without growing towards light" and that his body and soul both had "waxed old" (185). Although the dean in fact lights the fire, Stephen can find in him "no spark" of Ignatius's enthusiasm (186). The dean's simple task is to light an actual fire in the empty physics theatre, and he manages to bring actual light and heat when Stephen, not yet achieving his esthetic, speaks of those qualities only as metaphoric substitutions for knowledge and fervor. All of Stephen's diction, even before the choice of "tundish," is attenuated and unreal thinking about esthetic "by the light of" Aristotle and Aquinas, of using and guiding himself "by their light" and of trimming the lamp if it smells (that is, if the thoughts are unhelpful) is clearly his tongue-in-cheek way of ridiculing the figure before him. When, to Stephen's use of lamp as a metaphor for reading and lucubration, the dean asks about Epictetus and his actual lamp, Stephen linguistically extinguishes the conversation by noting "coarsely" that Epictetus was "an old gentleman . . . who said that the soul was very like a bucket of water" (187), the water extinguishing the metaphors of the light Stephen tries to shed. Characteristically, Stephen turns to make metaphor, in large part to maintain his superiority to those around him, as he had always held his higher position among his classmates. Yet the clash of reality with his metaphors makes a comic turn; the intellectual light Stephen sheds, metaphorizing and theorizing, creates humorous shades in the scene portrayed. The discussion with the dean is crucial to Stephen's burgeoning sense of an artist thinking on his own, yet it has comic elements. The scene can stand in for *Portrait* itself, as one of the meanings of the root *protrahere* is "to bring to light" and thus not only to elucidate but to alternate light and shadow, seriousness and comedy.

The use of the lamp metaphorically or actually, Stephen claims, is a contrast between literary tradition and the marketplace; yet giving the difference to these term overweighs the argument with a value judgment. The question is directed not only to the use of words as poetic or vulgar, highly valued or cheaply employed (the subsequent subject of chapter 4), but also to the use of words as literary or as actual, as belonging to the realm of the isolated artist and not to the world of common experience. By stressing the realm of the isolated and rarified artist, the context of literary words, Stephen can too readily catch the dean with Newman's use of the word "detain," which the father hears as simply a social phrase; it is a poor joke too easily bought. Common experience Stephen always neglects and diminishes; and it is that experience that forms the antic comedy of the novel. Stephen catches the dean with a piece of arcane diction; yet he himself is always tripped into comedy by the common language of others around him.

When the conversation takes its turn from the metaphoric lamp to the actual one of Epictetus (before Stephen's bringing the whole conversation to an end by extinguishing it with the "bucket of water"), the realm of the actual intrudes. As Stephen's mind is checked "in a false focus" (187), "a smell of molten tallow came up" as the actual candle brought by the unnamed (and erased) Father Butt, who has waxed old in service, has had an actual effect in the useful arts. Reality intrudes everywhere to create a similar comic effect; humor lies in the ordinariness of the world (especially when it comes up against Stephen's isolated otherworldliness). The dean's genuine surprise at the word "tundish" causes him to mutter, "I must look that word up. Upon my word I must" (188); he naturally and realistically repeats himself to a comic effect (and also mixes literal with metaphoric "word"): this, Joyce knew, is the way events happen to fall out and tumble up humorously in actual life. Alongside this humor is the more prominent foregrounded seriousness of Stephen's esthetic considerations, to which this undercurrent of humorous touches makes a pleasing contrast of shadow. Until Stephen sees that such tumbling and commonness can be art, he will not be an artist, despite his working in the light of ideas.

So the otherness that Stephen strives to maintain in the exchange in the empty classroom between himself and the lesser-ranked and -gifted dean, between himself and the use of English, and between himself and the world of actual words and things, turns out to be the otherness that always separates him from the world of confusion and material life that breeds the comic. In the same way, the reader frequently is separated from the real world around Stephen and consequently from its humor. Stephen's serious feelings about esthetics are genuine, and the scene does not ironize

Stephen's feelings; however, his seriousness of purpose, his impetus to special separateness, keep him (as they do the reader) from glimpsing the possibilities of comedy in the actual actions and conversation. In a similar way, we have seen how Stephen's further theorizing about art with Lynch had comic elements that did not reflect ironically on Stephen. The fact that Stephen ridicules the dean shows that he is aware of what can be humorous, but the fact that he uses his wit only for ridicule says much about his selfishness and immaturity. His exchange takes place in an empty classroom, and, like much of Stephen's efforts in the novel, it is a vain and empty activity, producing neither heat nor light.

It is to the physics theatre, where he will find the image of carnival and the figure of the comic Irishman, Stephen has come, arriving late and missing his English hour, where he imagined the heads of students. In that reverie which takes place before he talks to the dean and hears Moynihan and MacAlister in the physics lecture, he also fancies yet "another head than his," that of his friend Cranly; still walking to Newman House, his thoughts become increasingly complicated by the sort of otherness and difference that filled the exchange with the dean or the recognition of the other, comic Irishman in the bench behind. "Another head," Cranly's, is like "another story" that Conmee laughingly tells of Stephen's triumph; it is the depiction of yet another head of a fellow student of Stephen's. This other head is a contrast and a compliment to Stephen's own, a further alternative as tumbling is to falling and as a pun is an alternative to denotative single meaning.

One reason for Stephen's question, "Why was it that when he thought of Cranly he could never raise before his mind the entire image of his body but only the image of his head and face?" (178), is due to the nature of portraiture always at the center of the novel's focus: the image portrayed on canvas, as it is also conveyed to Stephen's mind, is focused on the head. The prominence of heads in the novel so titled makes Stephen's question almost rhetorical; and he notices many other heads. As Stephen mediates Cranly by not remembering his actual face but only an image in mind, so too does the portrait present not the actual features but an image mediated by art. The artful and yet attenuated nature of Stephen's thinking about Cranly's image is further suggested by the distant allusion to a text Stephen has certainly read, "Macbeth," with its suggestion that "there is no art to find the mind's construction in the face" (I, iv, 12). Yet in that small art lies the possibility for Stephen to imagine Cranly's portrayed head as an image increasingly out of the ordinary and grotesque, finally being so extended as to collapse into the comic: "he saw it before him like the phantom of a dream, the face of a severed head or deathmask, crowned on the brows by its stiff black upright hair as by an iron crown" (178). The fantastic and the revenant are the ultimate others, outside and beyond the rational; they hover in shadow just over the shoulder of reality as does the comic. The severed head also leans to the legends of hagiography, the Baptist precursor to Stephen's own Jesus with His crown of thorns, and the iron crown in particular points not only to royalty but nationality: the Iron Crown of Hungary, that country whose political situation was a model for Irish nationalism, was kept even as late as Stephen's university years in Vienna's St. Stephen's Cathedral. Thus in many ways, inevitably, on that face of "another head than his" Stephen sees and reads his own face, doubled into possibilities, alternatives, extremes that lead to grotesquery. He, who has rejected the pastoral calling, calls Cranly's head "priestlike" (178), seeing in Cranly's demeanor his own until recently, and because Stephen acknowledges that he has confessed to Cranly, a compliment to him. Yet the similaic "priestlike" face and pallor indicates another difference, another space between one head and another, as Cranly tumbles from the power of the priesthood into the impotence of being unable to grant absolution to Stephen for his confessed sins: "a guilty priest who . . . had not power to absolve . . ." (178). Stephen's sins are falls into what he terms "tumults and unrest and longings of his soul" and all the words apply to what he calls the "life" of his father's house, the unrest of the actual, vegetable world, in which are the tumult of tumbling and the comedy of misrule.

Cranly's head has further sources of difference and comic confusion, related to the sorts of "longing" to which Stephen confesses. Longing is an appetite, a source of desire and therefore potentially of the comic; Cranly's face is doubled in gender to serve other desires. The "priestlike" face is intended by celibacy to be neuter, but in that it is guilty of hearing Stephen's confession of sexual "longing" without being able to absolve, it is impotent, and thus its "guilt" is marked in his face by the difference of "dark womanish eyes" (178). For Stephen, viewing the unsure sexuality of the celibate and the too close proximity of a male friend, begins to turn that other head even further into something completely other, the opposite sex: one head may confusedly contain two genders. (And here again the image of the head on a platter connects not only to the Baptist, but also to the Wilde play of *Salomé*.) To imagine Cranly's head as womanish is to make him completely other, yet, insofar as Stephen reads his own face in Cranly's, his own portraiture contains a potential doubling comedy of sexual confusion.

The literal confusion of this sort of two-headedness, Stephen/ Cranly or man/woman, leads to further confusions: these are to be found in language. In its possibilities of comic alteration, there is an inevitable interplay of puns here in Stephen's thinking that show potential comic misunderstanding. The elevated introspection of Stephen about Cranly, which occurs in an imagined scene, is tripped up to tumble into humor. To Cranly's "gaze of . . . dark womanish eyes," Stephen extends his reverie; he regards the feminine listlessness of Cranly as an opiate, a "deadly exhalation" of "nightshade." The exotic image appeals to Stephen's reading, the decadent aura of narcotic hebetude and sexual attraction, and thus fits well with a portrait of Cranly as esthetic priest or object of desire. (Particularly suggestive in this is the "dark cavern of speculation," seemingly Platonic, but also homoerotic.)[13] Yet into this dreamily allusive speculation intrudes the antic comedy of paronymy: "Dark womanish eyes"—or woman's eyes made dark—are those of actual temptresses (such as prostitutes in "Circe," with Zoe's eyes *ringed with kohol* [15.1319], or the women Little Chandler evokes) or imagined sirens such as Pateresque Mona Lisas; all cosmetically enhanced their eyes and made them more lustrous and provocatively languid by the application of "nightshade." Thus the elaborate portrayal of Cranly's head as "other," like Stephen's priestlike but also like a woman's, is doubled further into anticness by language that makes a comic turn in diction, so that the purple exoticism of the languid plant and the temptress hidden in Cranly's head is humored by language into a comic capering. Another synonym for "nightshade," because of this very cosmetic use, was "belladonna," also a beautiful woman. Thus there is a turning over and constantly tumbling from Cranly as priest to Cranly as woman, from dark womanish eyes to nightshade and finally to belladonna; that tripping and tumbling prizes the confusions of gender and language and lets misrule have its sway in the earnestness of Stephen's thoughts. The actual word "belladonna" is hidden, just beyond the margin of the text, in that place behind where the comic Irishman resides, speaking the language of ribald misrule. It is unlikely that Stephen sees the humor of his thoughts, in no small measure because he is afraid of what he feels about Cranly; yet the text can interpose from behind him a note of levity. Cranly's head, imagined by Stephen, has two identities conflated together to make a comic effect, a prophet with priestlike seriousness and a female with exotic allure. Stephen's thinking about that head opens up language so that it plays, turning (unbeknownst to him) paronymically into a comic pairing of "nightshade" and the figure of a belladonna. It is a comic turn mischievously just behind the serious language of Stephen's inner thoughts.

Heads, doubled as alternates to the seriousness of Stephen's education and the development of his life in the novel, thus appear in classrooms where those heads are to be instructed with information conveyed in language. Language is also potentially to be doubled, two-faced or twin-voiced, and behind this doubling effect lies comedy. Puns give language two heads simultaneously: one meaning is serious and direct, the other humorous and oblique; one is in the foreground, the other behind. This combination comes to a point in the very mathematics class in which dusk came "tumbling clownishly" for Stephen, the place where the first suggestion of the countermovement of the plot of the novel arose. We should return to that class, as a student must go repeatedly and regularly to a class meeting, to find there another idea that opens up the places within language, behind and oblique, where the comedy of *Portrait* is to be found.

Unlike his earlier years, Stephen commits no error in this class, yet he is not interested, either. He is sitting to the side of the teacher's instruction and comment, but his thoughts are filled with his lapse into sin, which is the ultimate misrule but with tragic, not comic, consequences. He works on an equation in his scribbler, which begins "to unfold itself slowly and to spread abroad its widening tail. It was his own soul going forth to experience, unfolding itself sin by sin . . . " (103). The equation, like error, has its own graph and balance sheet. Yet the phrasing of "going forth" and "spreading" echo the etymology of a "portrait" as "dragging forward, drawing to a conclusion." Mathematics is knowledge, irrefutable and authoritative, much like physics. Yet it is in this class that the dusk came "tumbling clownishly," a motion that Stephen later (and the reader then) should recognize as the antithesis of order, the notion of misrule. Even in the class of mathematics there is an alternative to fact and certainty.

When the instructor intrudes on Stephen's musing to correct a dull student, what he says presents the very same contrasting alternative. The instructor berates a student, much like the idler Fleming, one in contrast with the model Stephen; yet Stephen here is conveniently inattentive to the lesson, deeply introspective, and seems no less censurable than is this Ennis. The instructor asks: "—Well now, Ennis, I declare you have a head and so has my stick! Do you mean to say that you are not able to tell me what a surd is?" (104). Ennis gives no answer.

The teacher's comment is banal, suggesting colloquially that Ennis's intellect is wooden. It may as well evoke a very particular feature of Irish education in the common hedgerow schools, where students had a stick suspended around their necks with notches, each for a lapse into Gaelic.[14] This fall from the superior language, a *lapsus linguae*, replicates what has happened to Stephen in his sin (where the prostitute's tongue is clearly mentioned); the stick is a sign of both language and lapse. Yet the prominence of the head suggests that there is something more in the example. The teacher's attempt at humor must surely evoke in Stephen his own early sense of language as doubled, possessing, Janus-like, two faces; he, after all, came early to the recognition that a belt round his pocket was also used to give a fellow a belt. Suck, too, had two meanings, one clear, one metaphoric; one right in some contexts, wrong in others; one direct, one humorous. He will note in his discussion with the dean of studies that a lamp may be figurative as well as literal. Heads can have contradictory countenances, and these often stand in comic alteration and cancelling.

There is even more in the instructor's comment; unlike the certitude and authority of mathematics, language is deceptive and ambiguous, so that what he says resonates through the novel (beyond merely having chided Ennis). The teacher's joke is an admission of a futility: as the head—the seat of the intellect—is the intended target for all the pedagogical activity of a class, the authority of the classroom and the nature of *Bildung* in the novel are compromised when both sticks and men have heads. Esthetics is also seriously tumbled: the answer to Stephen's question of esthetics as to whether the bust of Sir Phillip Crampton is epical, lyrical, and dramatic, has as its answer the same comic point: the bust, too, has a head.

The surd in mathematics is an irrational number, yet a surd also defines an entity in language, an unvoiced sound. So not only are there two heads, on people and on sticks, there are two terms for surd, irrational and unvoiced. In concert with the spirit of a *Portrait* with two heads, something alternate as a comic counterpart in the bench behind, there is something just beyond the surd, something other: the absurd. And the absurd is the realm of comedy; it marks the boundary between rule and misrule, the place where language is both one thing and another. Wordplay, so dear to Joyce, always embraces the absurd: to pun is to make two heads, a doubling alternative to meaning that often undermines the foregrounded serious purport of language. And as the surd is silent, it is like the comedy of "laughing in your sleeve" (as Lynch says, 209) or of whispering silently "behind their hands" (192) by the imagined cavorting priests; and as the absurd stands beyond, so too does the comedy stand just beyond the seriousness of mathematics of Stephen's own charted growth in the novel. The humor of heads is that they are absurdly doubled, they make comedy by interjecting over the shoulder from the bench behind.

Hitherto we have seen the comic otherness of *Portrait* in scenes and situations, those elements of the plot, but there is a more oblique and indirect presence of humor in the language, a humor essential and integral to the text. It is with verbal comedy that Joyce makes his largest and most displaced effect, with multiple possibilities making for comic confusion, and the language of *Portrait* is subject to a comic doubleness of diction that undercuts and makes tumble its highest solemn moments. Language is the essential means of comedy in *Portrait* as events are always secondary to the means to think about and describe them; more attention will be paid in subsequent chapters to the issue of language in terms of the notions raised, in the class above, of surd and absurd, silent and silly. We will see the effect of popular comic journals on the style of *Portrait* as another version of the comic Irishman behind (in chapter 3). *Portrait* obscures but saves vulgar speech like Moynihan's in contrast to Stephen's prim rhetorical strivings, as it places its earlier comic version of *Stephen Hero* behind (the subject of chapter 4). Immediately, the next chapter will focus on the further meaning of the teacher's question, which is to extend the portraiture into comedy by a language which itself has two heads.

Notes

1. *Ulysses* 2.166, whose mother had fed him with her "wheysour milk."

2. Kershner, in his essay "The Artist as Text: Dialogism and Incremental Repetition in *Portrait*," suggests that when Stephen disavows the comment on MacAlister, the reader recognizes that it comes "from Simon Dedalus, whose language Stephen so reluctantly shares" (in *Critical Essays on James Joyce's A Portrait*, edited by P. Brady and J. Carens [New York: G. K. Hall, 1998], 241). Simon as a comic figure is similarly eclipsed and replaced in *Portrait*.

3. *James Joyce*, 355.

4. Krause: "In an insular and parochial country such as Ireland ... comic renewal has often been greeted with suspicion, violence, or censorship" (20). He also speaks of the antagonism of the jester with the priest (54).

5. In discussing the political effect of subversive humor, Dettmar claims that, in order to "destroy Stephen's aesthetic [of Romanticism), Joyce needed to adopt a guerilla position. This he doesn't do in *A Portrait*.... Thus *A Portrait* has a difficult time laughing at Stephen" (136). I would argue that the humor, literally subversive and to the side, is in fact the guerrilla activity, the laughter of the suborned of the text, and does laugh at Stephen to the political end of undermining all the novel's authoritative orders. Dettmar finds the humor of "Telemachus" as "the carnivalization of *A Portrait*" (136). He notes, with respect to "Aeolus," that the changing polyphony of *Ulysses* is "a guerrilla action, from the outside" (187). As demonstrated, this study finds such polyphony in *Portrait*, so that there is this sort of political action within but just behind that text.

6. *Jokes and Their Relation to the Unconscious* (Norton, 1963), 200.

7. In his discussion of whether *Portrait* is ironic, Scholes considers the tension between serious and satirical in terms of Frye's patterns of comedy, where the tendentious part of the text functions as the *alazon*, the humorous as the *eiron*. Scholes's main point is that the balance of these features is to be found in Stephen, "himself as both *eiron* and *alazon*" in *In Search of James Joyce*, 10. The places where I claim comedy is to be sought and found extend beyond Stephen even to the countermovement of the genre itself, such as here.

8. That figure, as Maureen Waters discusses, is a convention of the late nineteenth century; see especially her chapter 3.

9. From Booth onward, the distance between Stephen and the narrative (or the world around him) is seen as an esthetic one exclusively in the service of irony. Staley gives an overview of the criticism in his "Sixty Years with Joyce's *Portrait*," as does James Sosnowski's review of esthetic distance in "Reading Acts and Reading Warrants." Buttigieg (40–41) sees irony as a means to assert the novel's autonomy as a work of art and the necessary demand for stasis that made it so appealing to New Critical approaches (such as Sharples, "The Stasis of Pity," reprinted in Schutte, 96–106). Gillespie finds that there is a polyphony in the "sophisticated reading of *Portrait*," and that the "emphasis given to irony will vary from reader to reader [as] ... the tones of Stephen and the narrator become implicit commentaries on one another" (153). Yet that distance need not be bridged by knowing, purposeful irony but rather capering humor.

10. Kershner, 6; Ellmann, 50.

11. *Ulysses* 16.362.

12. Thornton, 126, gives a very original analysis of the way in which Stephen's mind is affected by what is going on around him, although Stephen resolutely fails to acknowledge that anything is: "Consider how subtly Stephen's 'inner' psychic processes reflect his sensations and his perceptions of the outer world . . . images and metaphors . . . are engendered in Stephen's mind by the public objects and events in the scene before him"; for example, how the candles the dean lights makes Stephen think, "His very body had waxed old in lowly service."

13. For the relationship of Stephen and Cranly, see Joseph Valente, "Thrilled to His Touch: Homosexual Panic and the Will to Artistry in *A Portrait*," *The James Joyce Quarterly* vol. 31, no. 3, spring 1994, particularly 184–186.

14. See Waters, 4: "The children in some districts wore sticks, suspended from their necks, on which notches were carved to indicate any lapse into Irish, for which punishment was duly meted out." Humor in Joyce can always gesture to political oppression.

MARGARET McBRIDE

The Ineluctable Modality: Stephen's Quest for Immortality

*U*lysses opens as the story of an artist; more specifically, it opens as the story of an artist haunted by death. As a consequence, the young Stephen vows to compose an ageless masterpiece. And Stephen's masterpiece will perhaps turn out to be *Ulysses*, a work that carries intimations of Homeric and Ovidian immortality. Consequently, the timeline of the novel, which initially appears to be confined to June 16, 1904, may extend far beyond a day. Indeed, both *récit* and *discours* may include the key inscription "Trieste–Zurich–Paris / 1914–1921" since the critical event of the novel could be the novel's composition. As one comes to appreciate these broader architectonics, the elegantly Aristotelian groundings of the tale emerge. In a sense, for all its embrangled stylistics and verbal acrobatics, this work is, on one level, a *Künstlerroman*, a story about *becoming*. The main focus is the writer-protagonist's movement from the dark and limited point of view of youth to the brilliant vision embodied in the final text.

Hence, any study of Joyce's aptitude for self-reflexive fiction might do well to begin with the basics of Stephen's story, that is, the plot and characterization introduced in the Telemachiad. In these essentials—in Stephen's temporal fixation, in his fascination with the circular, in his explicit meditations on Homer—lie the seeds of *Ulysses*. But though this novel, at the start, appears to resemble a traditional *Künstlerroman*, the tale

From Ulysses *and the Metamorphosis of Stephen Dedalus.* © 2001 by Associated University Presses.

will move beyond this frame. It will also move beyond the usual clichés about art and immortality. The text manipulates its novelistic form in striking ways in order to challenge the intrinsically timebound conventions of narrative. As I hope to show, one of the work's most compelling turns involves Stephen's conceptualization of time as a medium linked closely to "the audible," that is, to *the word*. This all-important premise allows the reader to grasp the full import of the ingenious—and atemporal—diegesis buried in Bloom's story, a story told, in the main, through a series of eloquent silences. The "inaudible" dimension that pervades Bloom's odyssey strongly points to Stephen as its likely artificer. And, significantly, when Bloom is so unmasked—as no more and no less than a clever, fictional construct of Stephen's—Stephen, the implied narrator, is likewise revealed to be a fiction, the supreme fiction, for he too is no more and no less than a series of words found within the pages of *Ulysses*. Thus Joyce's account of a young writer's development ultimately succeeds in both constructing and deconstructing its narrative source. And through this Penelopean weaving and unweaving, Joyce's *Künstlerroman* manages to revolutionize the genre: Stephen's story appears to culminate with, ironically, the disintegration of its own artist figure.

THE INELUCTABLE MODALITY

Critics as diverse as Wyndham Lewis, Margaret Church, and Udaya Kumar agree that *Ulysses* has, as a central feature, a focus on time. Lewis attributes this controlling component to the "time-mind" of James Joyce. But the "time-mind" behind the text may belong to Stephen Dedalus. Stephen is obsessed with time. Stephen sees it as an "ineluctable modality," and its relentless linear progression is evident everywhere throughout his portions of the novel. As the narrative traces his morning, the episodes are presented in neat hourly units, possessing almost horologic precision. The events within each chapter unfold at a pace that effects a fusion of the time of the fiction and the time of the narration, an isochronism that serves to foreground time's ceaseless movement. The temporal format of the text's opening could be described with Stephen's own words in "Wandering Rocks." As he stands before a clockmaker's,[1] Stephen observes of the universe, "Very large and wonderful and keeps famous time" (10.828). It is against such a clockwork frame that the novel's protagonist initially appears to reveal his own temporal fixation. All Stephen's thoughts and actions are focused on time, a force that seems to be leading him only, and inevitably, toward death.

Stephen's dread of time is clear in the novel's initial scenes, where Stephen is tortured by memories of his mother's death. It is almost a year after the event, yet Stephen still harbors a grudge against Buck Mulligan for a remark that the medical student made on the day Stephen had visited him after the loss of his mother.

Stephen cannot shake Buck's reference to his mother as "*beastly dead*" (1.198–99). Stephen is not angry merely at the insult to his mother's memory. He says that he is thinking also "Of the offence to me" (1.220). The death of May Dedalus has impressed upon Stephen the reality of his own mortality. Buck's epithet is a vivid reminder to the young man of his own fate. Stephen hears Buck's words in highly personal terms.

The youthful Stephen perceives his whole world from a similarly self-centered point of view. Though Stephen may appear to be dispassionately contemplating various "medieval abstrusiosities" (3.320), beneath his intricate and allusive mental machinations there runs a single *idée fixe.* his fear of death at the hands of time. It is as if all scenes are a replay of his gazing in the mirror in "Telemachus" and wondering "Who chose this face for me? This dogsbody to rid of vermin" (1.136–37). "Vermin" is simply Latin for "worms."

For Stephen all time moves to one end: his own. In "Nestor," as he ponders the meaning of history, he focuses on the end of Pyrrhus and the assassination of a Caesar (2.48–49). The meaning of time is also apparent in literature, as Milton's *Lycidas* (2.64–66) elegizes a dead man. It is no wonder then that in this same chapter Stephen provocatively imagines an end to time itself. "I hear the ruin of all space, shattered glass and toppling masonry, and time one livid final flame" (2.09–10).

Similarly, as "Proteus" opens, Stephen contemplates space, the "ineluctable modality of the visible" (3.01). Stephen seems to be objectively evaluating Aristotle's definition of colors. But one of Aristotle's points is that colors do not exist without a body: "But he [Aristotle] adds: in bodies. Then he was aware of them bodies before of them coloured. . . . Limit of the diaphane in. Why in?" (3.04–5; 7). Stephen questions not only why colors must exist in bodies but why life must exist in them. To Stephen the body symbolizes man's mortal nature. As he continues his consideration of space, the domain of the body, he pictures himself falling through it to death, falling "over a cliff that beetles o'er his base . . . through the *Nebeneinander* ineluctably" (3.14–15). It is clear that Stephen rejects his physical body (as these opening chapters are, appropriately, assigned no organs in the *schema*). Stephen wants to live outside the body in order to escape its decay. He wishes to confine his reality to the rarefied intellect. For the Stephen of the Telemachiad, corporality and corpseness are all too closely linked.

In his subsequent ruminations on the most obscure theological questions, Stephen's last thoughts are also about, finally, death—the death of the heretic Arius:

> In a Greek watercloset he breathed his last: *euthanasia*. With
> beaded mitre and with crozier, stalled upon his throne, widower
> of a widowed see, with upstiffed *omophorion*, with clotted
> hinderparts. (3.52–54)

The word *euthanasia* appears a cruel and ironic form of oxymoron. Stephen
must wonder how a syllable meaning "death" and a syllable meaning "good"
could ever be yoked.

As "Proteus" proceeds, Stephen comes to inhabit, more and more,
his own world, a world overshadowed by his fear of the temporal and the
mortal. He watches with macabre fascination as a mongrel roaming the
beach happens upon the remains of another dog (3.347–52). Stephen is once
more confronting his own mortality as he clearly identifies with the living
dog which faces the image of its eventual fate. One day Stephen too will
resemble the carcass buried in sand, the "poor dogsbody" (3.351) which lies
so "beastly dead."

Stephen remembers that a dead man is supposed to surface sometime
later in the day. He conjures up a fantasy of the decomposing body:

> Bag of corpsegas sopping in foul brine. A quiver of minnows,
> fat of a spongy titbit, flash through the slits of his buttoned
> trouserfly. God becomes man becomes fish becomes barnacle
> goose becomes featherbed mountain. Dead breaths I living
> breathe, tread dead dust, devour a urinous offal from all dead.
> Hauled stark over the gunwale he breathes upward the stench of
> his green grave, his leprous nosehole snoring to the sun.
> A seachange this. . . . (3.476–82)

Proteus is the God of change and, in this chapter, it seems that the only
change is death and disintegration. It is "Houses of decay, mine, his and all"
(3.105).

Stephen's inability to deal with death, the ultimate change that time
brings, is apparent in his inability even to utter the syllable. As he recalls a
graveyard scene from Boccaccio's *Decameron*, Stephen stops short: "But the
courtiers who mocked Guido in Or san Michele were in their own house.
House of . . ." (3.318–19, author's ellipsis[2]). The missing word is "death."
But death is not confined only to the graveyard. It enters and pollutes the
great river of life. Water, a symbol of renewal and regeneration, signifies to
the hydrophobic Stephen yet another medium for dying. This is evident in
the grotesque picture of the drowning man that constantly plagues him. It is
a man whom Stephen both wishes and fears to save:

Do you see the tide flowing quickly in on all sides, sheeting the lows of sands quickly, shellcocoacoloured? If I had land under my feet. I want his life still to be his, mine to be mine. (3.326–28)

So too in these early episodes, Stephen's God is not God the Creator, image and archetype of the artist, but rather God the Destroyer. He is the "*dio boia*, hangman god" (9.1049), a "Ghoul! Chewer of corpses" (1.278). In "Oxen of the Sun," Stephen also calls him

> an omnivorous being which can masticate, deglute, digest and apparently pass through the ordinary channel with pluterperfect imperturbability such multifarious aliments as cancrenous females emaciated by parturition, corpulent professional gentlemen, not to speak of jaundiced politicians and chlorotic nuns. (14.1286–91)

It is for this reason that Stephen has refused to pray at his dying mother's bedside. He believes that as one of those "cancrenous females, emaciated by parturition," she has been willfully destroyed. "Someone killed her" (1.90), Stephen says. He does not go down on his knees to this God of Death.

The perversity of Stephen's vision is especially pronounced in the images of cadaverous females that float before his mind's eye. In "Telemachus" Stephen confronts a withered old milkwoman. He observes her "Old shrunken paps" and imagines her "Crouching by a patient cow at daybreak in the lush field, a witch on her toadstool, her wrinkled fingers quick at the squirting dugs" (1.400–402). She is a personification of Old Ireland herself. During one of the hallucinations in "Circe," she reappears as "*Old Gummy Granny . . . the deathflower of the potato blight on her breast*" (15.4578–80). She calls Stephen to arms, to defend her, though it may mean his death (15.4736–39). Stephen cries out against her: "Aha! I know you, grammer! Hamlet, revenge! The old sow that eats her farrow" (15.4582–83).

A second set of female figures is the pair of women Stephen glimpses walking along the beach at the start of "Proteus." Stephen imagines that they are midwives but in his fantasy they do not carry with them a new-born infant. Their bag contains a "misbirth" (3.36). These same women will inspire Stephen's later story, *The Parable of The Plums*, in which, while eating the juicy fruit and staring up at Nelson's Pillar, they are depicted as "spitting the plumstones out between the railings," onto the street. In his tale of infertility, their sterile and empty nature is further emphasized by the fact of their fifty- and fifty-three-year-old virginity. These women are no givers of life.

As "Proteus" closes, Stephen watches the gypsy woman on the shore, a strolling "mort" as he calls her, his diction indicating her deathly nature. She comes to represent all women, indeed, all life, and Stephen sees her moving ever westward, toward death:

> Across the sands of all the world, followed by the sun's flaming sword, to the west, trekking to evening lands. (3.391–92)

Like the old woman, she too is a daughter of Eve, "the serpent's prey" (1.421–22), a woman who brings death. And it is to this same end that all flesh must come: "*Omnis caro ad te veniet*" (3.396–97).

The most deadly avatar of all is Stephen's mother. Since, for Stephen, life means death, woman's reproductive power becomes a death-dealing force. Stephen thinks of her "allwombing tomb" (3.402). His mother, who has given him life, has, simultaneously, contaminated him with mortality. Her life-giving faculty has also hastened her own demise: the hangman God feeds more easily on cancer-ridden women who have been "emaciated by parturition" (14.1289). And, as Stephen visualizes the moment of his own conception, he sees "a ghostwoman with ashes on her breath" (3.46–47). Women, because of their menstrual cycles, seem to carry the river of time within them: "Tides, myriadislanded, within her" (3.393–94). Yet to Stephen the river of time leads only to death. His mother's death by cancer becomes, in his mind, a succumbing to that river, a drowning. In his closing thoughts about the drowned man, the gender of the pronoun shifts:

> A drowning man. His human eyes scream to me out of horror of his death. I . . . With him together down . . . I could not save her. Waters: bitter death: lost. (3.328–30, author's ellipses)

The image of his mother's drowning clearly shapes Stephen's perception of his sister. In "Wandering Rocks," he sees Dilly as doomed to an identical fate:

> She [Dilly] is drowning. Agenbite. Save her. Agenbite. All against us. She will drown me with her, eyes and hair. Lank coils of seaweed hair around me, my heart, my soul. Salt green death. (10.875–77)

The sister resembles the mother as she too is drawn into the pattern of women who are associated with death.

Memories of his mother, which continually intrude upon Stephen's thoughts, depict her not merely as dying but as summoning Stephen to death as well:

Silently, in a dream she had come to him after her death, her wasted body within its loose brown graveclothes giving off an odour of wax and rosewood, her breath, that had bent upon him, mute, reproachful, a faint odour of wetted ashes. . . . The ring of bay and skyline held a dull green mass of liquid. A bowl of white china had stood beside her deathbed holding the green sluggish bile which she had torn up from her rotting liver by fits of loud groaning vomiting. (1.102–5; 107–10)

And,

In a dream, silently, she had come to him, her wasted body within its loose graveclothes giving off an odour of wax and rosewood, her breath, bent over him with mute secret words, a faint odour of wetted ashes.

Her glazing eyes, staring out of death, to shake and bend my soul. On me alone. The ghostcandle to light her agony. Ghostly light on the tortured face. Her hoarse loud breath rattling in horror, while all prayed on their knees. Her eyes on me to strike me down. *Liliata rutilantium te confessorum turma circumdet: iubilantium te virginum chorus excipiat.*

Ghoul! Chewer of corpses!

No, mother! Let me be and let me live. (1.270–79)

As "Telemachus" closes with Stephen walking away from the beach to begin his day, he hears in the distance the bells of a church. In their three chimes there is a deathknell, the *Liliata rutilantium* of his mother's final ordeal:

He walked along the upwardcurving path.
Liliata rutilantium.
Turma circumdet.
Iubilantium te virginum.[3] (1.735–38)

At the day's end, as he and Mr. Bloom listen to the bells of St. George's, Stephen hears it again (17.1230–31).[4]

All time signifies death. This is the meaning of the eleven o'clock riddle, an enigmatic rhyme that, on one level, is a displaced reference to the death of May Dedalus. The riddle is told twice during the day and always with the suggestion that it is the hour of death:

The cock crew,
The sky was blue:

The bells in heaven
Were striking eleven.
'Tis time for this poor soul
To go to heaven. (2.102–7)

When repeated in "Circe," the riddle conjures May Dedalus from beyond the grave. The mention that it is "long after eleven" (15.3560) provokes Stephen to recite it again. In this version, however, when the bells strike eleven, "'Tis time for *her* poor soul / To *get out of* heaven" (15.3580–81, emphasis added). And this "her soul" seems to do, as May Dedalus now appears to her son in the brothel, her body in an advanced state of decay. The message that she carries back from the grave is that Stephen too shall die. This is his fate, and time will bring him to it:

THE MOTHER

(*with the subtle smile of death's madness*) I was once the beautiful May Goulding. I am dead. . . . All must go through it, Stephen. More women than men in the world. You too. Time will come. (15.4172–74; 4182–84)

She reaches out to Stephen:

THE MOTHER

(*her face drawing near and nearer, sending out an ashen breath*) Beware! (*she raises her blackened withered right arm slowly towards Stephen's breast with outstretched finger*) Beware God's hand!

(*A green crab with malignant red eyes sticks deep its grinning claws in Stephen's heart.*)

STEPHEN

(*strangled with rage, his features drawn grey and old*) Shite! (15.4216–23)

Stephen then enacts a fantasy first contemplated in "Nestor." In the schoolroom, as noted, he had envisioned the end of time as a blazing destruction of light: "and time one livid final flame" (2.10). In "Circe," a drunken Stephen lashes out at the chandelier, crying "*Nothung!*" He "*lifts his ashplant high with both hands and smashes the chandelier. Time's livid final flame leaps and, in the following darkness, ruin of all space, shattered glass and toppling masonry*" (15.4242–45). In his hallucination (though only in his hallucination) Stephen succeeds in destroying the ineluctable modality.

But the rebellious gesture only underscores the futility of his struggle against time. The would-be poet engages in the darkest inversion of the archetypal act of creation, "*Fiat lumen.*" Moreover, he fails to destroy time. In fact, he does not even destroy the chandelier. He manages merely to damage its chimney (15.4285). The light, time's symbol, persists. It is impossible to escape the ineluctable.

Stephen's storyline, as it unfolds on June 16, 1904, is a narrative that implies that there is no escaping time. Even the temporal ordering of the plot, as it proceeds from morning to midnight, is a linear progression that, near its close, serves up this graphic *memento mori* scene from "Circe," a scene that offers a most potent reminder of Stephen's inevitable end. Thus Stephen's basic plotline follows and foreshadows the larger timeline that is his life; it is a timeline that moves Stephen ever nearer death.

ART AND IMMORTALITY

If Stephen's tale is limited to June 16, 1904, the chronicle can possess no successful denouement; there is, that day, no method of escape from time. But Stephen's storyline, as stressed, may span more than a single day. His plot perhaps extends to the narration of *Ulysses* itself. And in this self-begetting arc, the significance of the tale's heroic embellishments at last emerges. When Stephen is seen as the text's putative Author, the epic devices serve to parallel him—deliberately and directly—to artists like Homer and Ovid, who have achieved immortality through the telling and retelling of Greek myth.

Interestingly, even as a child, Stephen dreamt of a kind of literary athanasia:

> Books you were going to write.... Remember your epiphanies written on green oval leaves ... copies to be sent if you died to all the great libraries of the world, including Alexandria? Someone was to read them there after a few thousand years, a mahamanvantara.... When one reads these strange pages of one long gone one feels that one is at one with one who once.... (3.139; 141–46)[5]

Through the word the writer lives on. Stephen can sit in a library in the year 1904 and read the philosophy of Joachim Abbas (3.107–8), or Aristotle (2.68–70), centuries, even millennia, after their deaths. As Stephen ponders

the life and works of Shakespeare, another artist who has attained the kind
of fame that Stephen seeks, the scene is the National Library. Surrounded
by volumes that have survived the ages, Stephen realizes that lore as old as
ancient Egypt is kept alive in "spice of words":

> Coffined thoughts around me, in mummycases, embalmed in
> spice of words. Thoth, god of libraries, a birdgod, moonycrowned.
> And I heard the voice of that Egyptian highpriest. *In painted
> chambers loaded with tilebooks.* (9.352–55)

Stephen sees the hieroglyphic archives as a kind of library ("*painted chambers
loaded with tilebooks*"). The Egyptians so valued these records that they gave
them the god Thoth as a protector. Stephen repeats to himself the rhetoric
of "Aeolus": "*It seemed to me . . . that I stood in ancient Egypt and that I was
listening to the speech of some some highpriest of that land*" (7.830–33). The
thoughts of the hieratic scribes can, in a sense, be heard still; they are as
perfectly preserved as any mummified pharaoh "in spice of words."

The point is made again during the discussion of Shakespeare. As
Russell aptly and succinctly puts it, "We have *King Lear:* and it is immortal"
(9.188). Stephen agrees, asserting that Hamnet Shakespeare has "died in
Stratford that his namesake may live for ever" (9.172–73).

Stephen has seen this phenomenon illustrated in "Nestor" as well, in
an episode that also centers around books. In the schoolroom, as the pupils
review their lesson, it becomes apparent that, though Pyrrhus and Caesar
have died, their stories continue in the pages of history. In fact, Pyrrhus
seems to be remembered almost solely because of his (and Plutarch's) words.
The students in "Nestor" recall neither the site of the battle ("I forget the
place, sir" [2.11]) nor the manner of Pyrrhus's death (2.19). But they do
remember his words: "And he said: *Another victory like that and we are done
for*" (2.14). Stephen pauses to consider the force of such rhetoric:

> That phrase the world had remembered. A dull ease of the mind.
> From a hill above a corpsestrewn plain a general speaking to his
> officers, leaned upon his spear. Any general to any officers. They
> lend ear. (2.15–17)

The theme is reiterated moments later in *Lycidas*. While its contents
provide another image of a drowned man, the poem itself holds intimations
of immortality. Sunk though he be beneath the watery floor, Lycidas—and
Edward King—live on. They live on, not so much through "*the dear might of
Him that walked the waves*" (2.78) but through the power of the poet. It is the
printed elegy that gives them their immortality.

And it is not Lycidas alone who is immortalized. Milton too achieves a form of immortality. So do all the authors whose words appear in *Ulysses*. Throughout the novel, Dante and Aquinas, Aristotle and Sabellius, Shakespeare and Blake, all live on into the twentieth century. They live most obviously in the mind and meditations of the erudite Stephen Dedalus, but the richly allusive texture and intertextuality of *Ulysses* suggests that reverberations of their works sound all over Dublin this day, from Buck's passing allusion to Ovid ("Your absurd name, an ancient Greek" [1.34]) to O'Madden Burke's lighthearted "Lay on, Macduff" (7.898). References to earlier writers are found on calendars that feature "Quotations every day in the year" (11.905); they are on the lips of the schoolboys and the old Professor. They filter through the thoughts of Leopold Bloom and even his semiliterate wife, Molly.

Nowhere is the diuturnity of great literature more evident than in the numerous recapitulations of Homer that Stephen hears. In "Telemachus" Buck cites, possibly verbatim, a poet who has been dead two thousand years: "*Epi oinopa ponton*" (1.78). The phrase haunts Stephen as he later translates, "*oinopa ponton*, a winedark sea" (3.394). Homer's story is also the source for Deasy's diatribe against women: "For a woman who was no better than she should be, Helen, the runaway wife of Menelaus, ten years the Greeks made war on Troy" (2.390–92). In "Aeolus," MacHugh filters Homer through Virgil: "*Fuit Ilium!* The sack of windy Troy" (7.910). The Professor then observes that Antisthenes "took away the palm of beauty from Argive Helen and handed it to poor Penelope" (7.1038–39). And when Stephen later encounters Bloom, the two talk of "sirens, enemies of man's reason" (16.1889–90). The citations seem to reach a pinnacle in "Scylla and Charybdis": "the life of Homer's Phaeacians" (9.110), "like another Ulysses" (9.403), "a Penelope stay-at-home" (9.620), "poor Penelope in Stratford" (9.649), "Antiquity mentions famous beds" (9.718). It is in this same episode that Mulligan expressly invokes Homer as the ultimate paradigm for an author; in a somewhat hyperbolic literary review, Buck imagines a modern epic: "The most beautiful book that has come out of our country in my time. One thinks of Homer" (9.1164–65).

Stephen hopes one day to write such a book himself. He calls it his "postcreation." Through the postcreation, the poet, or "maker," can transform the temporal into the eternal:

> Mark me now. In woman's womb word is made flesh but in the spirit of the maker [the poet] all flesh that passes becomes the word that shall not pass away. This is the postcreation. *Omnis caro ad to veniet.* (14.292–94)

The last line, from the Psalms, has been seen before. Stephen used it in "Proteus," referring to death (3.396–97). In "Oxen," he now uses it to refer instead to the artist's ability to transcend time.

In "Oxen" Stephen also rejects mere procreation, an act that is too much a part of the temporal process, an act that creates only more death. Stephen vows not only not to die himself but not to create anyone or anything that will die (14.438–43). When Stephen creates, what he creates will be immortal. It will be art.

Stephen makes this rather inflated claim in the midst of a chapter that, through its form, asseverates the olamic power of the word. Much of the stylization in this fourteenth episode is a monument to authors long dead as the parodic mode draws on memorable prose writers of English, from the earliest of Anglo-Saxon chroniclers to novelists like Sterne and Dickens. It is with these enduring masters that Stephen wishes to be aligned. Thus, at the height of his drunken braggadocio, Stephen attempts to encircle his own head "with a coronal of vineleaves" (14.1116–17), the symbol of poetic achievement. One of Stephen's boon companions then reminds him that

> those leaves ... will adorn you more fitly when something more, and greatly more, than a capful of light odes can call your genius father. All who wish you well hope this for you. All desire to see you bring forth the work you meditate, to acclaim you Stephaneforos. I heartily wish you may not fail them. (14.1118–22)

Lenehan thoughtlessly interjects, "O no ... Have no fear. He could not leave his mother an orphan" (14.1122–23). At the witticism, Stephen becomes dejected:

> The young man's face grew dark. All could see how hard it was for him to be reminded of his promise and of his recent loss. (14.1123–25)

Stephen falls despondent, not simply because of the reference to his dead mother, but because of the reminder that all his boasting is simply that—boasting. He has yet to produce his masterpiece.

The incident, with its explicit reference both to Stephen's "promise" and to "the work" that Stephen meditates, makes overt the crucial forward thrust of the plot. Stephen's story cannot be complete or completed on June 16, 1904. It reaches far beyond a solitary day. His tale stretches far into the future, to a time when Stephen, as realized artist, composes his postcreation.

There is irony, then, in Stephen's attempt to shatter the chandelier, his private symbol of the temporal. The one thing that Stephen Dedalus needs in order to transcend time is, paradoxically, time itself. And Stephen knows this. Stephen even seems to know how much time he needs: a decade. At least this is what he has told Buck Mulligan. In "Wandering Rocks," as Buck sits in the D.B.C. eating scones, he repeats to Haines Stephen's prophetic words:

—Ten years, he [Buck] said, chewing and laughing. He [Stephen] is going to write something in ten years.
—Seems a long way off, Haines said, thoughtfully lifting his spoon. Still, I shouldn't wonder if he did after all. (10.1089–92)

It is a long way off and not simply in terms of years. The lonely figure introduced at the novel's opening has a lengthy personal odyssey ahead of him before he can shape the events of this day into a work of art that will rival the poetry of Ovid and Homer. Stephen must move from the isolated, solipsistic world of the Telemachiad into the unbounded realm of the imagination. And it is Stephen's development into that epic artist that this proleptic text simultaneously forecasts and emblematizes.

TRIESTE–ZURICH–PARIS, 1914–1921

That this novel can be seen as a self-begetting artifact, one illustrating its poet-protagonist's maturation, may be the meaning of the closing legend. The date "1914" is especially noteworthy since it reveals that Stephen has met his self-imposed deadline of "ten years" (10.1090). As noted, what Riquelme writes regarding *A Portrait* is thus applicable to *Ulysses*: "The last—that is, the most recent—stage of Stephen's development as an artist is presented through the narration, not in the narrative."[6]

Similarly, the place names "Trieste–Zurich–Paris," words usually affiliated with Joyce, are about Stephen; the triadic entry indicates that he does indeed abandon Dublin for "a continental . . . manner of life" (17.21). The inscription, then, is furnishing concrete geographical data about an event that, while unchronicled within *Ulysses*, is anticipated throughout: Stephen's Ovidlike exile. Stephen's story, as it unfolds during an eighteen-hour frame in June, insinuates that such a move is inevitable if he ever desires to fulfill himself as an artist. Stephen knows that he can never achieve greatness in Ireland: in Ireland his place as poet has been usurped. Hence, the issue of Stephen's imminent departure deserves further exploration, for this eventual self-banishment is closely bound to the all-important motif of usurpation, a theme that dominates not only Stephen's day but ultimately all his art.

A Portrait ends with Stephen's flight from his homeland. When *Ulysses* opens, the reader learns that the young man has returned unexpectedly because of his mother's death. After a year in Ireland, however, Stephen seems to be contemplating exile once more. Visions of the wild geese filter through his meditations (3.164; 216; 249; 264). In "Scylla and Charybdis," as he stands on the library steps, he remembers searching for a sign or omen from the birds: "Here I watched the birds for augury. Aengus of the birds. They go, they come" (9:1206–7). When he glimpsed these avine portents in *A Portrait*, he wondered if they were not a "Symbol of departure."[7] And as *Ulysses* draws to a close, the last glimpse the reader has of Stephen is his exiting Bloom's house; this scene is fraught with images of exile. The leavetaking is called an "exodus" (17.1021) and is accompanied by the words of the 113th Psalm, "*modus peregrinus*" (17.1030), or "the mode of going abroad."[8]

What impels Stephen to expatriation is his commitment to the postcreation. Stephen knows that it will never be written in Ireland. There is no place in Ireland for the serious artist. As Stephen's story makes clear, in Ireland the artist's place has been usurped.

The idea of usurpation pervades Stephen's thoughts. The topic is introduced early in "Telemachus" in the scene with the old milkwoman, who represents Ireland. Stephen watches scornfully as she pays homage to Buck and even the Englishman Haines but ignores Stephen (1.418–23). It is the "bonesetter" (1.419), the priests, and even the British conqueror that Ireland bows before, not her poets. The last word in "Telemachus" is, literally, "Usurper." Stephen glances back at Buck:

> A voice, sweettoned and sustained, called to him from the sea. Turning the curve he waved his hand. It called again. A sleek brown head, a seal's, far out on the water, round.
> Usurper. (1.741–44)

The idea recurs in Stephen's Shakespeare story, where he projects onto his protagonist his own feelings of betrayal: "the theme of the false or the usurping ... brother ... is ... always with him" (9.997–99). And it is always with Stephen. When, well after midnight, Stephen meets Bloom, their conversation turns inevitably to "usurpers, historical cases of the kind" (16.1891). The theme starts and ends Stephen's day.

Stephen's belief that his rightful place has been preempted appears well-grounded. In the National Library, Stephen sits silently as other writers are elevated and celebrated while his abilities are overlooked. He has made this visit to the library in the first place only because Haines said he wished to hear him on *Hamlet*, but Haines has stood him up, preferring to go in search of a book of poems by Hyde: "I couldn't bring him in to hear the discussion. He's gone to Gill's to buy it" (9.94–95). In the middle of Stephen's presentation, Buck is invited to share the limelight and himself expound on Shakespeare. Lyster observes, "Mr Mulligan, I'll be bound, has his theory too" (9.503–4). Wilde's performance on Shakespeare is praised as "The most brilliant of all" (9.522).

To the meeting of Dublin literati, Buck and Haines the foreigner have already been invited. Eglinton says to Buck, "We shall see you tonight. . . . Moore says Malachi Mulligan must be there" (9.1098–99). Stephen's invitation comes belatedly, and he is requested to "Bring Starkey" (9.324). When it is revealed that Russell is "gathering together a sheaf of our younger poets' verses" (9.290–91), one assumes that Stephen's poetry is not numbered among them.

Stephen says to himself, "See this. Remember" (9.294). And, "Listen" (9.300). And, as he listens, he hears all around him enthusiasm for second-rate talents and nothing for himself.

> Young Colum and Starkey. George Roberts is doing the commercial part. Longworth will give it a good puff in the *Express*. O, will he? I liked Colum's *Drover*. Yes, I think he has that queer thing genius. Do you think he has genius really? Yeats admired his line: *As in wild earth a Grecian vase.* Did he? I hope you'll be able to come tonight. Malachi Mulligan is coming too. Moore asked him to bring Haines. . . . James Stephens is doing some clever sketches. We are becoming important, it seems. (9.301–6; 9.312–13)

Notably, it is Moore, not Stephen, who is seen as the one who will write "Our national epic" (9.309). Stephen feels, understandably, the sorrow of "*Cordoglio*" (9.314). He is also like the dispossessed Cordelia, whose true worth has been scorned while those inferior to her are praised in her stead.

Stephen must leave Ireland. That he is contemplating such a move is tacit in his attempt to break with Buck. In *A Portrait* it is Stephen's similar disaffection with Cranly that sets him free to leave:

> Away then: it is time to go. A voice spoke softly to Stephen's lonely heart, bidding him go and telling him that his friendship was coming to an end. Yes: he would go.[9]

By the day's end, Buck and Stephen have separated. Stephen will not return to the Martello Tower (3.276). Nor will he return to the job at Deasy's school (16.157–58). Stephen, like Ovid, will write in exile. And, within ten years, just as he has predicted, he begins *Ulysses*. It is Stephen, not Moore, who pens Ireland's "national epic."

STEPHEN'S ARISTOTELIAN DECADE: THE CREATION OF BLOOM

Stephen says of *Hamlet*, "The boy of act one is the mature man of act five" (9.1020). A similar statement can be made about *Ulysses*. the young artist of "Telemachus" is the mature artist of "Penelope." Stephen may at first seem an unlikely source for the masterpiece in which he appears, but this is because the youth of the Martello Tower is merely a *potential* artist. Before he can create his great work, Stephen must become an actual artist. While this maturation process is not dramatized within the text, it is evinced by the text. The book itself, through its mere existence, can be taken as evidence, metafictionally speaking, of Stephen's development into a fully realized writer. The contrast between the struggling poet of the work's overture and the consummate artist behind the completed text is the very point of the story.

Critics who dismiss Stephen as the work's author because of limitations in his character may be failing to grasp the importance of the decennium that intervenes between his callow twenty-second year and "Trieste–Zurich–Paris, 1914 . . . "[10] Time is moving Stephen toward, not merely death, but his destiny as an artist. Hence the view of time that informs the larger narrative is not the narrow fixation of the inexperienced Stephen but instead a wiser and more humanistic vision: time can lead to growth and fulfillment.

This emphasis is Aristotelian. Aristotle and his singular notion of "becoming" provide the very foundation for the novel's dual role as *Künstlerroman* and self-begetting text as the significance of the inferred time span encompassed by the tale depends on the idea that Stephen will, and must, change over time. A brief review of Aristotle on this issue of fulfillment shows just how explicitly *Ulysses* draws on his theories.

Aristotle perceives all of nature in a constant process of change: "Nature has been defined as a 'principle of motion and change',"[11] and the most fundamental kind of motion, or change, is from potential to actual. At one point, Aristotle defines motion exclusively as the movement from potential to actual: "the fulfillment of what exists potentially, in so far as it exists potentially, is motion."[12] (Stephen echoes in "Nestor": "It must be a movement then, an actuality of the possible as possible. Aristotle's phrase . . ." [2.67–68].)

So much of the *Physics*, *Metaphysics*, and *De Anima* are devoted to this idea that the movement from potential to actual is almost a hallmark of

Aristotle's vision of the universe. For Aristotle, the cosmos is in a continuous state of becoming as all things *fulfill* themselves in time.

> So, we have Aristotle's general definition of physical motion: such motion is strictly not spatial, but dynamic change, a passage from potentiality to actuality.[13]

Time is the essential ingredient for such change, or "movement," because time and motion are inseparable:

> Not only do we measure the movement by the time, but also the time by the movement, because they define each other.[14]

Allusions to Aristotle, particularly to his focus on the movement from potential to actual, substantially shape Stephen's storyline, reinforcing its implicit forward trajectory. As already noted, Stephen cites the Physics during "Nestor." In the National Library and in "Circe," he also considers the concept of "entelechy" (9.208; 15.107), a term that, as used by Aristotle, can signify the condition of a being whose essence has been fully realized and also the vital force that impels a being toward fulfillment.[15] In a somewhat jumbled and unfinished thought, Stephen refers to himself as

> I, entelechy, form of forms, am I by memory because under everchanging forms. (9.208–9)

Stephen sees himself as in transition, in an Aristotelian state of becoming. He acknowledges that "Life is many days" (9.1097), and he has, as he says, "much, much to learn" (7.915). He contemplates a future time when he will look back on this day from a different perspective, with greater distance and maturity:

> —As we, or mother Dana, weave and unweave our bodies, Stephen said, from day to day, their molecules shuttled to and fro, so does the artist weave and unweave his image. And as the mole on my right breast is where it was when I was born, though all my body has been woven of new stuff time after time, so through the ghost of the unquiet father the image of the unliving son looks forth. In the intense instant of imagination, when the mind, Shelley says, is a fading coal, that which I was is that which I am and that which in possibility I may come to be. So in the future, the sister of the past, I may see myself as I sit here now but by reflection from that which then I shall be. (9.376–85)

In that future, when Stephen can look back from a different vantage point, what he will have "come to be," of course, is the Author of *Ulysses*. In order to reach that goal, however, Stephen must first actualize his potential. Thus he tells himself, "Act. Be acted on" (9.979). These words too are from Aristotle; they filter throughout his disquisitions and are suggestive of the ways in which potential is fulfilled or realized. In the *Physics* Aristotle speaks of "the fulfilment of what can act and what can be acted on."[16] In the *Metaphysics*, he remarks on "potencies either of merely acting or being acted on."[17] When Stephen tells himself to act and be acted on, he is encouraging his own development and self-realization along deliberately Aristotelian lines.

Stephen's richest and most direct allusion to Aristotle is drawn from *De Anima*, where Aristotle calls the soul the "form of forms." The soul is, for Aristotle,

> all existing things; for existing things are either sensible or thinkable, and knowledge is in a way what is knowable, and sensation is in a way what is sensible: in *what* way we must inquire.
>
> Knowledge and sensation are divided to correspond with the realities, potential knowledge and sensation answering to potentialities, actual knowledge and sensation to actualities. Within the soul the faculties of knowledge and sensation are *potentially* these objects, the one what is knowable, the other what is sensible. They must be either the things themselves or their forms. The former alternative is of course impossible: it is not the stone which is present in the soul but its form.
>
> It follows that the soul is analogous to the hand; for as the hand is a tool of tools, so the mind is the form of forms and the sense the form of sensible things.[18]

Stephen twice quotes this passage from *De Anima* in "Nestor," as he recalls an experience in Paris and, in retrospect, perceives what had been "the darkness of his soul's potentiality":[19]

> in my mind's darkness a sloth of the underworld, reluctant, shy of brightness, shifting her dragon scaly folds. Thought is the thought of thought. Tranquil brightness. The soul is in a manner all that is: the soul is the form of forms. Tranquility sudden, vast, candescent: form of forms. (2.72–76)

The movement from darkness to brightness is a movement from potential to actual.

Goldberg persuasively argues the intensely Aristotelian vision of *Ulysses* when it is treated as Stephen's story.[20] The novel may be read almost entirely in terms of the ever-expanding growth of Stephen's soul, as he acts and is acted on, as he realizes all the potential within himself, as human being and as artist.[21]

For Goldberg, the meeting with Bloom, a man whom Stephen must somehow embrace or emulate, symbolizes Stephen's ultimate maturity:

> "That lies in space which I in time must come to, ineluctably."
> . . . And as he [Stephen] decides this, Bloom passes by. Bloom, we must remember, is also compared with Christ, and it is he who, at a crucial moment, speaks out for Love. In short, Stephen must learn to accept the world outside him, and in accepting, to love. . . . Stephen, the bitterly critical Antisthenes, must grow to the maturity figured in Bloom.[22]

Goldberg's claim is an important one. If *Ulysses* is Stephen's story, then the novel's meaning turns on the Aristotelian—and *Künstlerroman*—theme of Stephen's ever-widening vision and understanding. But as one considers the novel more closely, particularly the Aristotelian element in Stephen's own Shakespeare theory, it appears that Goldberg's reading may not be telling the whole story. There is more to the novel's plot than Stephen's comprehending or appreciating Bloom. For the novel to make its greatest statement, Stephen, as artist, must *create* Bloom. Indeed, Stephen must create all of *Ulysses*.

This crucial, self-reflexive purport first surfaces in "Scylla and Charybdis," where Stephen reinterprets Aristotle, particularly Aristotle's concept of the soul as "the form of forms." Stephen explores at length the ramifications of this definition when it is applied *to the artist*. Stephen contends that in the writer's finished work is seen the writer's soul; this claim provides the critical link between Stephen's own *Bildungsroman* and the complex epic confronting the reader.

Stephen's focus on the soul as the "form of forms" has note because Stephen is a poet, or *maker*, and the poet's goal is not merely to know or understand the factual, external universe: it is to *create* a fictive universe. And he must do so from within. Whatever characters and themes a poet realizes through his work are manifestations of realized potentials within the artist. The richness of the artist's finished product is the result of the artist's development, of the inner potential that has been actualized. There is an important corollary to this proposition. Any gifted artist who aspires to greatness must, in order to fashion a masterpiece, develop the resources within himself. He must expand his soul, or imagination, so that his "form of forms" can furnish him with the infinite forms necessary for his art. The lesson for Stephen is obvious.

Stephen's acknowledgment of the interplay between personal growth and poetic achievement is stressed frequently in the Shakespeare theory, which, on one level, is simply Aristotle's metaphysics brought to bear on the poet, as the presentation's diction makes evident. Stephen says of Shakespeare, "He acts and is acted on" (9.1021–22). Shakespeare

> found in the world without as actual what was in his world within as possible. (9.1041–42)

Shakespeare's life is a constant process of self-actualization, continuous motion. And with his death, observes Stephen (echoing Shakespeare's words in *Romeo and Juliet*), "The motion is ended" (9.1033–34).

As evidence of the potential realized within Shakespeare, Stephen turns, not to biographical data, but to, significantly, the plays and poems. The final and most compelling portrait of the artist, according to Stephen, is the work. In this respect, when Shakespeare peruses *Hamlet*, he is, literally, "*lisant au livre de lui-même . . . reading the book of himself*" (9.114–15). Each play is "*Pièce de Shakespeare*" (9.121), a piece of its author, and, as such, attests to the artist's success in realizing the potential within. As Stephen repeatedly makes such an argument for Shakespeare, he implicitly makes it for himself as well. The Stephen of June 16, 1904, is inviting his audience to see that the proper end to his own chronicle, a chronicle so centered around the question of his future fulfillment as an artist, will be found, not in some later story about Stephen, some sequel to *Ulysses*, but rather in a later story by Stephen—*Ulysses* itself.

The inevitable role that a complex, all-encompassing text like *Ulysses* must play in any account of Stephen's development is thus portended in his praise here of the variegated *dramatis personae* of Shakespeare. Stephen believes that Shakespeare has mined deep within himself to evoke this diverse assortment of beings, who are all aspects of their creator. All so different and all so lifelike, they seem to constitute an entire race that Shakespeare has fathered forth, as postcreation and procreation become one:

> When Rutlandbaconsouthamptonshakespeare or another poet of the same name in the comedy of errors wrote *Hamlet* he was not the father of his own son merely but, being no more a son, he was and felt himself the father of all his race, the father of his own grandfather. (9.865–69)

It is the "infinite variety everywhere in the world he has created" (9.1012–13) that adduces the manifold potential within himself that Shakespeare has fulfilled. Stephen says that Shakespeare has drawn "Shylock out of his own long pocket" (9.741–42)—and Hamlet *père* and Hamlet *fils*. And Othello. And Iago. When Eglinton observes that the Bard is both "the ghost and the Prince. He is all in all" (9.1018–19), Stephen concurs:

> —He is, Stephen said.... All in all. In *Cymbeline*, in *Othello* he is bawd and cuckold.... His unremitting intellect is the hornmad Iago ceaselessly willing that the moor in him shall suffer. (9.1020–24)

So prodigious is Shakespeare's achievement that he not only deserves to be compared to God ("After God, Shakespeare has created most" [9.1028–29]), but now serves as the model for the Creator. At the close of the discussion, Stephen goes so far as to compare the God of Genesis to the playwright (9.1046–50). The artist, like God, is "all in all in all" (9.1049–50) of his creations.

This emphasis on the depth and range of the characterization found in Shakespeare establishes a metafictional context that gives meaning to the numerous and complex portraits found in *Ulysses*; above all, it gives meaning to the appearance of the Mr. Leopold Bloom who surfaces in episode four of the surfiction. Mr. Bloom is a creation of Stephen's; Bloom's tale, a story within a story. His twentieth-century odyssey has been spun into being by Stephen, in his guise as a modern Ovid or a modern Homer. Thus the many and marked contrasts, which at first seem to separate Stephen and Bloom, actually evidence the degree to which Stephen has developed and evolved over time. Like Shakespeare, Stephen has plumbed the depths of his own soul in order to fabricate the contrapuntal Mr. Bloom, who clearly represents all that the Stephen of 1904 is not.

Bloom is a middle-aged, family man, a pragmatist. He possesses a Jewish heritage. Unlike Stephen, the hydrophobe, Bloom is "the water-lover" (17.183). The intensely physical Bloom eats "with relish the inner organs of beasts and fowls" (4.01–2), savoring "grilled mutton kidneys which gave to his palate a fine tang of faintly scented urine" (4.04–5). Stephen, as already noted, denies the body, denies the physical. He seems to go the entire day eating almost nothing. The youthful writer is an intellectual, a scholar steeped in Dante and Blake. The middle-brow Poldy, if steeped in anything, is steeped in *Matcham's Masterstroke* (4.502). Stephen spends his day absorbed in the literary theories of Aristotle; the closest Bloom can come to a poetics is his observation that "That is how poets write, the similar sounds. But then Shakespeare has no rhymes" (8.64–65). As Stephen moves about the city, he contemplates the postcreation; Bloom wanders the same streets composing doggerel about "The hungry famished gull" (8.62) that "Flaps o'er the waters dull" (8.63).

One can hardly imagine two males more different or disparate; in fact, reams of Joyce criticism are devoted to comparisons between the pair. But the larger thrust of the antithesis emerges only after one realizes that Stephen is Bloom's creator. Indeed, the myriad voices and visions within *Ulysses* must be seen as springing from the pen and mythopoeic powers of Stephen Dedalus. Stephen fathers forth *all* the characters: Bella Cohen and Gerty MacDowell, Buck and Haines, Ben Dollard and Si Dedalus. Stephen is the source of the multiple narrators in "Cyclops"; of the numerous parodies of "Oxen"; of the hallucinations in "Circe." Most amazing, Stephen is the creative force behind Molly Bloom.

Molly is the novel's true climax as the erudite Stephen allows a sensuous, adulterous, Dublin matron to take center stage in his masterpiece. This mythic anima figure is an alter ego of Stephen's. (The "artist weave[s] and unweave[s] his image" [9.377–78], says Stephen.) Molly caps perfectly the theme of his ever-evolving maturity as all the negativity of the initial chapters will give way to her final "Yes" (18.1609). The callow poet of "Telemachus," whose dread of the mortal led him to reject entirely the corporeal, has become, by "Penelope" (and through "Penelope"), the artist who can imagine, in his mind's eye, a woman so carnal that she is virtually defined by her body. Stephen, haunted earlier by the terrifying vision of a drowning man, now conjures into being a micturating, menstruating female who symbolizes and celebrates the great river of life. In her wake are washed away the deadly matrices of the novel's opening: the strolling mort, the midwives with their strangled misbirth, the ghastly May Dedalus. "Penelope" closes Stephen's story on a note of endless affirmation[23] as the episode signifies the implicit inner odyssey that Stephen has made: it is a journey that has taken him from the dark Martello Tower to his marvelous, almost dazzling, vision of Molly Bloom.[24]

Stephen is the narrator who is "all in all in all" of *Ulysses*. By creating the book, he completes his story, fulfilling himself as poet and also displaying his growth as human being. He has gone far beyond the egocentric concerns of the Telemachiad. He has accomplished a boundless and all-encompassing artistry, one identical to that of his Shakespearean ideal. Stephen's achievement is manifest in the infinite variety everywhere in the world *he* has created—*Ulysses*.

In such an analysis, *Ulysses* can, quite readily, be interpreted as a grander rendering of the *Bildungsroman* found in *A Portrait*, with the later, far more complex, novel assuming the same basic contours of the earlier *Künstlerroman*. In this reading, *Ulysses* serves primarily as Stephen's postcreation, a reworking of an ageless Greek myth. But *Ulysses* has more intricate currents running through it. While the narrative begins with an almost Romantic presentation (or re-presentation) of an artist-protagonist seeking immortality, the work soon reveals a highly sophisticated, and distinctly Modern, concern with the temporal nature of narrative. The novel's circularity will not depend on some vague leap of faith that Stephen leaves Eccles Street and somehow goes out to compose *Ulysses*. Several identifiable, and self-conscious, seeds of the finished text are scattered, repeatedly and very specifically, throughout the events of June 16, 1904. The appearance of these clear foreshadowings indicates that Stephen has set his sights beyond simply an Ovidlike retelling of a timeless myth: his poetic theories, as delineated on this day in June, set in motion a series of neverending cyclings and recyclings that exploit the eternal looping possible only in self-depicting texts.

NOTES

1. Gifford and Seidman, *"Ulysses" Annotated*, 276.

2. I use the deliberately ambiguous phrase, "author's ellipsis" because of the nature of my argument, that is, that Stephen is the work's understood author.

3. See the ingenious discussion of this passage by Clive Hart in his and Leo Knuth's *A Topographical Guide to James Joyce's "Ulysses"* (Colchester, England: A Wake Newslitter Press, 1975), 23–24. Hart explains that the dispersing of the Latin phrase into three tiers indicates that it is 8:45 in the morning.

4. Joseph Prescott, in his *Exploring James Joyce* (Carbondale: Southern Illinois University Press, 1964), discusses the "sound of the peal of the hour of the night by the chime of the bells in the church of Saint George" (17.1226–28) in "Ithaca," stressing the onomatopoeic quality (29).

5. This last ellipsis is the author's.

6. Riquelme, *Teller and Tale*, 62.

7. Joyce, *A Portrait*, 226.

8. Gifford and Seidman, *"Ulysses" Annotated*, 581.

9. Joyce, *A Portrait*, 245.

10. They also align with the faithless Buck, who similarly sees no future for Stephen. The mere fact that the unlikable Buck confidently predicts Stephen's failure may be one more reason to believe in Stephen's success. While the original Malachi was a prophet, his namesake is consistently depicted as an ineffectual and "flippant prognosticator" (14.1217). He labels Stephen an "*impossible*" person (1.222, emphasis added). All Buck's overt references to Stephen as artist are never serious; it is "you dreadful bard" (1.134) and "The bard's noserag" (1.73). Buck states explicitly that Stephen "can never be a poet" (10.1074). (Buck here echoes Dryden's remark to Swift [Gifford and Seidman, *"Ulysses" Annotated* (51, 281)].)

The joke will be on Buck, however, as Stephen enjoys the last laugh. In the finished novel, Buck frequently does presage, though always unwittingly, the grand metafiction in which he appears (a work, note well, that this Malachi has predicted will never be written).

11. Aristotle, *Physics*, from *The Works of Aristotle*, ed. W. D. Ross (Oxford: Clarendon Press, 1908–52), 200^b: 10–15. Unless otherwise noted, all Aristotle quotes throughout the text of this work are from Ross.

12. Ibid., 201^a: 10–11.

13. Frederick J. E. Woodbridge, *Aristotle's Vision of Nature*, ed. John Herman Randall Jr. (New York: Columbia University Press, 1965), 67–68.

14. Aristotle, *Physics*, 220^b: 15–17.

15. Roy K. Gottfried, in *The Art of Joyce's Syntax in "Ulysses"* (Athens: University of Georgia Press, ca. 1980), sees this principle operating not only in plot and characterization but in the very style of the narrative. This idea runs throughout Gottfried's discussion, but see, for a specific example, page 87 of his study.

16. Aristotle, *Physics*, 202^b:26–27.

17. Aristotle, *Metaphysics*, 1046^a:16–17.

18. Aristotle, *De Anima*, 432^a: 1–3.

19. Goldberg, *The Classical Temper*, 74.

20. Goldberg, in *The Classical Temper*, devotes much of his chapter, "Art and Freedom" (66–99), to an exploration and explanation of the novel's Aristotelian emphasis on Stephen's maturation process. Goldberg's reading is a thorough one, and I refer the reader to his analysis.

21. Goldberg, *The Classical Temper*, 97.

22. Ibid., 97–98.

23. In a well-known letter, Joyce underscores Molly's affirming nature. See *Letters of James Joyce*, ed. Stuart Gilbert and Richard Ellmann (New York: Viking, 1957–66) 1:170.

24. In 1925, Joyce wrote Harriet Weaver about his long-standing interest in Giordano Bruno, an author Joyce cited as early as "The Day of the Rabblement"; Joyce stresses Bruno's emphasis on the way in which one must develop an opposite as part of the process of self-realization. See *Letters of James Joyce*, 1:226.

KERI ELIZABETH AMES

The Rebirth of Heroism from
Homer's Odyssey *to Joyce's* Ulysses

Safe!

(U 8.1193)

There she found Odysseus among the bodies of the murdered, splattered with blood and gore like a lion who comes from devouring an ox from a farm; and his whole chest and his cheeks on both sides are covered with blood, and he is dreadful to look upon, just so had Odysseus been splattered, his feet and his hands above.

(Od. 22.401–6)

So Leopold Bloom in Joyce's *Ulysses* is delighted to escape confronting his wife's lover, Blazes Boylan, by turning into the National Library, whereas in Homer's *Odyssey* the nurse Eurykleia discovers Odysseus after he slaughters Penelope's suitors standing fearsome and awesome (deinos), drenched in blood like a lion who has just finished eating.[1] Odysseus has already killed so many suitors that "the whole floor flowed with blood" (*Od.* 22.309), and his house must be washed and purged with sulfur before he can reunite with Penelope (*Od.* 22.437–94). In contrast, Bloom chooses to return silently to a marriage bed befouled by his wife Molly's sexual encounter with Blazes Boylan:

What did his limbs, when gradually extended, encounter?

From *Twenty-First Joyce*, edited by Ellen Carol Jones and Morris Beja. © 2004 by Ellen Carol Jones and Morris Beja.

> New clean bedlinen, additional odours, the presence of a human
> form, female, hers, the imprint of a human form, male, not his,
> some crumbs, some flakes of potted meat, recooked, which he
> removed. (*U* 17.2122–25)

Such a pitiful cuckold seems like the antithesis of Homeric heroism and
Joyce's proof of its demise. So, at first glance, Joyce's depiction of heroism
appears to supersede Homer's entirely: the extraordinary victor has become
an ordinary victim.

Yet perhaps this position only allows us to dismiss the significance of
Joyce's title too precipitously, for in his notes to his only play, *Exiles*, Joyce
observes, "Since the publication of the lost pages of *Madame Bovary* the
centre of sympathy appears to have been esthetically shifted from the lover
or fancyman to the husband or cuckold" (*E* 150). With the choice of his title
Ulysses, Joyce focuses upon precisely this problem. Just as Molly has become
the adulteress Penelope is not, so Bloom has become the cuckold Odysseus
could never be. Yet if we consider the possibility that such contradictions
between the Blooms and their Homeric counterparts do not simply serve to
present a parody of the Homeric intertext invoked by Joyce's title, a remarkable
convergence between Joyce's and Homer's conceptions of love and heroism
emerges.[2] The obvious contradiction between Penelope's chastity and Molly's
adultery can be reconciled to a certain degree with the acknowledgment that
both marriages are fraught with ambivalence and infidelity.[3] In the same
vein, how might the heroism of the cuckold in *Ulysses* and the heroism of
the avenging husband in the *Odyssey* depend upon the same heroic virtues?
One answer may be found in the way in which Homer's and Joyce's uses of
the word "hero" (eros) function to create and confirm a remarkably similar
meaning of heroism, thus endowing Joyce's title with great resonance.[4] Let
us then explore the idea that certain instances in which Homer and Joyce
use the word "hero" (eros) serve to define one particular kind of heroism that
Odysseus and both attain.[5]

We first encounter the word "hero" (eros) in the *Odyssey* in the context
of divine aid and wrath, a context that reveals what constitutes this sort of
heroism. Athena has just sprung into action on behalf of Odysseus, after
receiving Zeus' permission to help him return home: "So she spoke, and
beneath her feet she bound beautiful sandals, immortal, golden, which bore
her over both the deep waters and the boundless land with the breath of the
wind. And she seized her strong spear, tipped with sharp bronze, heavy,
huge, and stout, with which *she overpowers the ranks of hero-men* (andron
eroon) whoever are the kind that tend to anger her, that daughter of an
oh-so-powerful father" (*Od.* 1.96–101; emphasis added).[6] Being a hero, the
audience learns here, is the task of a man. Previously, the word "hero" is quite

noticeably absent from the proem (*Od.* 1.1–10), where Homer initially refers to Odysseus only as a man without even mentioning his name, accentuating his humanity and his masculinity rather than his heroic status: "Tell for me the man, muse" (*Od.* 1.1). We next find the words "man" (aner) and "hero" together in the genitive case, with the grammatical effect of denoting "a connection or dependence between two words. . . . The substantives may be so closely connected as to be equivalent to a single compound idea" (Smyth 314). I justify my hyphenation of "hero-men" based upon the interdependence Homer's grammar accentuates, emulating how Smyth hyphenates his examples. By inextricably binding up his first use of "hero" with "man" in the grammatical sense, Homer announces that his heroes are definitively not gods, but ordinary mortal men who quiver and suffer beneath the gods' wrath.

Hero-men must cope with force, symbolized by Athena's spear. For Athena does not only come to the aid of hero-men like Odysseus; she frequently subdues them (damnemi) with her spear when they anger her. Homer's use of an aorist subjunctive (kotessetai [*Od.* 1.101]) implies that her anger is customary (Stanford, *Homer 218*). By introducing his hero-men as those who suffer from habitual divine wrath, Homer implies that they cannot avoid being mastered by the gods. The hero-men beneath the spear exemplify the complexity of the heroic task: Homer's heroes face the double task of knowing when to suffer patiently the forces beyond their control and when to use the force at their disposal for their own benefit. Heroic endurance depends upon negotiating a very delicate balance between accepting what cannot be changed and fighting to alter what can be changed. Joyce gestures toward this idea in the "Scylla and Charybdis" section with an incredible economy of words: "Act. Be acted on" (*U* 9.979). This duality encapsulates the heroic task in the *Odyssey* and *Ulysses*. Just as Athena controls hero-men with the force of her spear, so hero-men must control their own forces, the desires of the heart (thumos), in order to endure.[7] Hero-men must resist being entirely overcome by external forces while overcoming the forces that emanate from within. As hero-men, their challenge, and the test of their endurance, is taming themselves.

By presenting this image of Athena in conjunction with his first use of the word "hero," Homer portrays a kind of heroism to which every human being can aspire, and in which every human being alive can and must participate. Everyone faces the task of controlling desire (thumos) while suffering forces beyond one's control. Because suffering itself, regardless of its source, provides the opportunity for human distinction, even the most ordinary person has the same chance of becoming heroic as an epic warrior does. R. Havard comments upon the chances of attaining such heroism: "Pain provides an opportunity for heroism; the opportunity is seized with surprising frequency" (Lewis 157). Extraordinary endurance within ordinary human life lends this heroism its special quality. Since rising to the challenges of suffering is its only imperative, one can qualify for this sort of heroism just as easily in Dublin in 1904 as in ancient Ithaca, or in the United States in the twenty-first century. Still, such heroism is ordinary only because it is possible for ordinary people in any time and place. It requires a strength that is quite extraordinary.

The first person upon whom Homer bestows the title "hero" epitomizes the demands and requirements of such an ordinary brand of heroism. Athena names him while speaking to Telemachus, after arriving at the home of Odysseus, disguised as Mentor: "Our fathers were guest-friends from long ago, which you would learn if you just go and question *old-man-hero-Laertes*, who, so they say, no longer comes to the city, but far away in the fields suffers pains, together with an old woman servant, who puts out food and drink for him, once exhaustion has seized his limbs as he struggles to move up the hill of his vineyard" (*Od.* 1.188–93; emphasis added). Surprisingly, Laertes is much like Bloom, suffering pitifully without any obvious resistance to his plight. Later, Penelope begs for the suitors' patience until she can finish "a funeral shroud for Laertes-hero" (*Od.* 2.99), while the goat-herd Melanthius holds an old, stout shield, speckled with rust, the one belonging to Laertes-hero, which he would always carry during his youth" (*Od.* 22.184–85). Young Laertes used to fight in battle. Now, like his rusty shield, he is old and worn, leading Thomas Falkner to suggest, "Like the dusty shield . . . Laertes' heroic abilities are hidden from sight. . . . in spite of his age, Laertes retains his heroic ability" (45, 46). By endowing Laertes with the title "hero" on these occasions, Homer emphasizes that heroes can be old, decrepit, and unquestionably vulnerable to suffering and death, but no less heroic for that condition. He portrays how hero-men bravely extend their mortal existence with every effort.

Other old fellows are worthy of the appellation "hero" as well. Aegyptius is also infirm: "Among them then Aegyptius-hero was the first to speak, who was bent with old age and whose wisdom was past measure" (*Od.* 2.15–16). Like Laertes, he is bent (*kuphos*) by old age, but not broken. Homer manages to include the reason why Halitherses is a hero at the same time as he overtly names him as such: "Then among them spoke old-man-hero-Halitherses, son of Mastor, for he alone excelled all of his contemporaries in knowledge of bird omens and in speaking according to fate" (*Od.* 2.157–59). Far beyond anyone else, Halitherses knows the pain the future holds. As the last hero explicitly titled in the poem, Halitherses cautions the families of the suitors about the consequences of the suitors' recklessness, imploring them to shun violence (*Od.* 24.454–62). Halitherses is named a hero while counseling restraint, not vengeance, stressing how crucial self-control is for this kind of heroism. Such temperance, along with great perseverance, earns hero-men a considerable degree of respect.

Hence Homer's actual use of the word "hero" refutes the idea that heroism is connected to the transient vitality of youth usually presumed to be one of its immutable requirements.[8] Homer's extension of the idea of heroism to include elders raises endurance to the same status and prestige as more traditionally heroic actions like battle. The youthful, martial heroism of the *Iliad* has thus been transcended and replaced with a new brand of heroism in the *Odyssey*, as Falkner observes: "Where the *Odyssey* differs from the *Iliad*, with regard to old age as with so much else, is in reformulating and even redefining the nature of heroism and heroic values" (35).[9] In the *Odyssey*, Homer's use of the word "hero" betrays how endurance itself has become a worthy form of heroism.

Homer's language further expresses how Laertes' extraordinary endurance distinguishes him as a hero. When Odysseus goes to the orchard to greet his father upon his return home, he finds Laertes gardening, digging dirt around a plant while "penthos aexon" ("fostering his pain") (*Od.* 24.231). This verb "aexo" literally means to increase, but it can also mean to foster, nourish, exalt, glorify, grow, or help to flourish or blossom (Liddell and Scott; Cunliffe). The verb describes crops thriving with rain (*Od.* 9.111, 9.358), waves rising (*Od.* 10.93), Telemachus growing (*Od.* 13.360, 22.426), and the day waxing toward noon (*Od.* 9.56). Eumaeus uses it to characterize how the gods reward labor and make his efforts prosperous (*Od.* 14.65, 66; 15.372). It seems like a very odd verb to apply to one's pain until we recognize what it connotes: the heroic embrace of the pain that fate and the gods inflict upon us. Laertes makes his pain bloom, just as a gardener tries to make a plant bloom. For Laertes relishes his suffering just as he relishes life. He cherishes his pain not because he is a masochist and enjoys suffering, but because he has no other options if he wants to survive. Since he has not yet found any remedy for the triple wound of losing his only son and his wife and being besieged by the suitors, he must persevere. For Homer, Laertes is heroic because he keeps struggling to live just as he struggles to inch through his orchard. He values life no matter how agonizing living has become. By naming him as the first hero in the poem, such endurance is presented as a kind of heroism.

Remarkably, Homer and Joyce each name Odysseus and Bloom directly as their heroes in the context that best illustrates what this heroism of endurance comprises: the context of earning homecoming. Bloom receives the title "our hero" in the "Eumaeus" section, when he finally decides to return home with Stephen: "I propose, *our hero* eventually suggested after mature reflection while prudently pocketing her photo, as it's rather stuffy here you just come home with me and talk things over. My diggings are quite close in the vicinity" (*U* 16.1643–45; emphasis added). Bloom is proposing that he and Stephen seek homecoming (nostos), while our narrator is proposing that Bloom deserves to be accepted as our hero. We may be inclined to interpret this naming ironically or sarcastically, but Bloom is truly "our hero" when he is rescuing Stephen at the same time as he is rescuing himself. "After mature reflection," he tries to withstand the pain of Molly's adultery, pocketing her old picture and his memories along with any rancor. Bloom, like Laertes and Odysseus, refuses to give up on life and on love, resolved in his belief that "talking things over" at home is the best possible course of action.

With striking similarities, only once in the *Odyssey* is Odysseus named a hero directly. While he is telling the story of his endurance to the Phaeacians, Odysseus describes how Kirke told him to travel to the rock in Hades where the two rivers meet, the very edge of death itself. Then he quotes her next instructions: "There and then, *hero*, draw near, just as I order you and dig a pit of a cubit on each side, and around it pour a libation to all of the dead . . . and then right away the prophet [Teiresias], leader of the people, will approach you, and he will tell you your way and the extent of your journey and your return [nostos]" (*Od*. 10.516–18, 538–40; emphasis added). Kirke addresses Odysseus as a hero when he is attempting to return home by gaining and following this advice from Teiresias: "Still, despite everything, you may yet return, even though suffering many evils, if you resolve to restrain your desires and those of your companions [ai k etheles son thumon erukakeein kai etairon], as soon as you shall bring your well-benched ship to the isle of Thrinacia, fleeing the violet sea, and grazing there find the cattle and good flocks of Helios" (*Od*. 11.104–9). Teiresias warns Odysseus that only through self-restraint will he accomplish his homecoming to Ithaca. As Kalypso confined Odysseus in her caves (eruko) (*Od*. 1.14), so Odysseus must curb his own desire (thumos) so as not to devour the oxen of the sun. Again the utter duality of Odysseus' task cannot be ignored: as he was being restrained, he must also restrain himself. He must resist enough to restore his agency but must still resist any reckless impulses. Thus Kirke names Odysseus a hero while sending him to Hades to learn the importance of the self-restraint, patience, and determination that Bloom displays when he pockets Molly's photo and invites Stephen home.

Odysseus previously erred in this effort, for he is not the perfect hero in perfect control of himself. He sometimes fails to master his own desires and passions (thumos), and the context in which Kirke names him a hero also calls attention to his inconsistency in this regard. Barely a hundred lines earlier, Eurylochus has accused him of having lost his men to the Cyclops through his own recklessness (*Od*. 10.431–37), recalling how Odysseus' comrades were reputed to have destroyed themselves in the same way by eating the oxen of the sun and how Halitherses condemns the suitors' folly (atasthalie) (*Od.* 1.7, 10.437, 24.458). Odysseus stifles the urge to kill him (*Od.* 10.438–45), and Kirke invites the men to stay, claiming that they need to seize desire (thumos) in their chests again, because so much suffering has made them withered (askeles) and without desire (thumos) (*Od.* 10.456–65). Desire has dried up and shriveled, like a plant without water, and now requires cultivation. So they remain with Kirke, feasting and drinking wine, until Odysseus' men caution him to remember his home (*Od.* 10.466–74). Up to this point, Odysseus forgets his own return for an entire year, so busy and content is he cultivating and satisfying his heart (thumos)! Even though he then takes full credit for his decision to leave, never alluding to his comrades' intervention when he announces to Kirke: "My heart (thumos) is now eager to go, as are those of my comrades" (*Od.* 10.484–85), we the audience witness how his ability to control himself wavers.

Only in this context, the context of the crisis of controlling desire (thumos), does Kirke call Odysseus a hero. The location of his heroic naming stresses the quality that fuels Odysseus' endurance and characterizes his heroism: the willingness and the self-control to endure pain. Joyce names Bloom "our hero" at the same kind of critical juncture. For Bloom too has hesitated about returning home, thinking, "Go home. Too late for *Leah. Lily of Killarney.* No. Might be still up" (*U* 13.1212–13). Bloom delays his own return on purpose until Molly will be asleep, while Odysseus forgets his return while luxuriating with Kirke. Both then proceed to accomplish homecoming by following the advice that Odysseus gives to Aias in Hades, precisely the sort of advice that Odysseus himself previously received from Teiresias: "Subdue your passion [menos] and your daring spirit [thumos] damason de menos kai agenora thumon]" (*Od.* 11.562). Notably, Odysseus uses the verb "damazo," meaning to tame, master, control, which correlates very closely with the verb "damnemi," which conveys how Athena overpowers hero-men with her spear (*Od.* 1.100; see Liddell and Scott; Cunliffe). Heroes must treat desire (thumos) in the way Athena treats men with her spear, once again highlighting the duality of the heroic task in trying to subdue one's internal forces while being threatened by external ones. Only the proper balance between initiative and submission makes homecoming possible.

Odysseus further clarifies the nature of this task to Telemachus when they are plotting revenge against the suitors, counseling him to resist his urge to intercede too soon: "Even if they insult me within the house, still let the dear heart [ker] endure in your breast while I am suffering evilly" (*Od.* 16.274–75). Father and son agree upon the nature of their task of endurance, so Telemachus responds, "Father, most certainly, I think in time to come you will know my heart [thumos], for no weakness at all has a hold on me" (*Od.* 16.309–10). Earlier, Telemachus described how passionate wrath rose within him while desiring revenge against the suitors ("aexetai endothi thumos) (*Od.* 2.315). But as the suitors insult his disguised father, he increases his own pain rather than yielding to his desire, enabling him to abstain from immediate action and plot revenge in silence as his father requested ("mega tenthos aexe") (*Od.* 17.489ff.). During the bow contest, Homer is careful to inform us that Telemachus frustrates his desires by restraining himself: "Three times he made it [Odysseus' bow] quiver with his strength [bie], hoping in his heart [thumos] to string the bow and shoot an arrow through the iron. And now, finally, trying to pull it on the fourth try, he would have strung it with his strength [bie], but Odysseus shook his head and held him back, even as eager as he was" (*Od.* 21.126–29). At his father's silent command, he sacrifices his own success, relying upon his strength to conceal itself rather than exhibiting it. Valuing patience over bold and brazen initiative, he masters himself accordingly through the fierce control he exercises over his force (bie) and his passions (thumos). Telemachus shares with his grandfather and father the ability to foster his pain and control his desires, rather than engaging in self-destructive behavior.

Joyce is admittedly somewhat ironic in his depiction of this kind of Homeric heroism, but not in such a way that relegates heroism to meaninglessness. His narration of how Bloom acts "heroically" mocks Homer's conception of ordinary heroism in the *Odyssey* at the same time as he justifies its worth. His parody of heroism functions to confirm its persistence in a new form, not to render it null and void. Consider this example from the "Eumaeus" section, after Bloom fails to hail a ride, the only time in *Ulysses* in which the word "heroically" appears:

> This was a quandary but, bringing common sense to bear on it, evidently there was nothing for it but put a good face on the matter and foot it which they accordingly did. So, bevelling around by Mullett's and the Signal House which they shortly reached, they proceeded perforce in the direction of Amiens street railway terminus, Mr Bloom being handicapped by the circumstance that one of the back buttons of his trousers had, to vary the timehonoured adage, gone the way of all buttons though, entering thoroughly into the spirit of the thing, he *heroically* made light of the mischance. (*U* 16.31–39; emphasis added)

Here is nurturing pain ("penthos aexon") in more absurdity than we could have imagined. Bloom remains undaunted by a lost button, while Odysseus and Laertes remain undaunted by nineteen years of misery! Yet despite Joyce's switch from the epic to the comic, Bloom does bear up bravely and patiently, exactly like his Homeric predecessors, despite the contrast in their circumstances. The heroic thing for Bloom to do is to endure—not to whine or complain, nor to try to find a safety pin with which to effect a repair. Bloom is heroic because he refuses to be discouraged. By subscribing wholeheartedly "into the spirit of the thing," he resigns himself to his bad luck that his button has "gone the way of all buttons." Like Laertes, he accepts the necessity of his own suffering. Like Odysseus, he returns home handicapped by mischance, but with great determination, refusing to be deterred by anything.

Of course, the most significant pain that Bloom suffers on Bloomsday is Molly's sexual betrayal. That the button has gone the way of all buttons means only a little embarrassment. But Bloom does not want his wife to go the way of all wives, so to speak, and leave him. The pain that he cherishes is the pain of cuckoldry. Bloom accepts the pain that loving Molly inflicts upon him rather than trying to escape from it by getting divorced. Joyce captures the various ramifications of this decision when Bloom kisses his wife's rump in bed, thinking, "Divorce, not now" (*U* 17.2202). Bloom is impressively forgiving and desperately pathetic as he tries to save his home and his marriage. Yet the patience that sustains Bloom and fuels his efforts to save his home mirrors the same patience with which Odysseus salvages his home. Despite the violence with which Odysseus finally punishes the suitors, that triumph operates through the self-restraint that preceded it. Only by waiting patiently and preparing shrewdly for the right moment will he be victorious, as Athena impressed upon him beneath the olive tree: "So endure even by necessity, and tell no one of them all, neither man nor woman, that you have come back after your wanderings, but in silence suffer many pains, submitting to the force [bie] of men" (*Od.* 13.307–10). Bloom has exercised exactly that sort of restraint by deciding to return home with Stephen in tow. "Prudently" pocketing his wife's photo (*U* 16.1644), he reins in his emotions, what Homer would name desire (thumos), for the sake of his homecoming. Still preserving his self-control, he later brushes out of his bed without a word the potted meat that Molly and Boylan shared (*U* 17.2125) in an impressive display of "equanimity" (*U* 17.2155, 2177, 2195). Joyce names Bloom "our hero" (*U* 16.1643) when he is exhibiting the virtues of restraint and patience that Odysseus learned in Hades and from Athena beneath the olive tree. Bloom is described as acting "heroically" (*U* 16.38) when he is relying upon the silence and forbearance Odysseus also exercises in order to restore his home, ignoring the wounds to his dignity.

Given this congruence, Homer's *Odyssey* and Joyce's *Ulysses* both depict a very ordinary kind of heroism at the same time as they portray an extraordinary way to triumph. In avowing that "Joyce wrote *Ulysses* about a new kind of hero, an ordinary hero. In a way, so did Homer. . . . Like Odysseus, if Bloom is to be a hero, he must find a new kind of heroism" (Nelson 63, 79), Stephanie Nelson is observing how the *Odyssey* reformulates the heroism of the *Iliad*. Consequently, the ordinary kind of heroism that Joyce's *Ulysses* represents is not an invention by Joyce at all, but an embrace of the kind of heroism depicted in the *Odyssey* and an implicit rejection of the heroism depicted in the *Iliad*. Odysseus and Bloom are the same kind of ordinary human hero who triumphs through extraordinary endurance. Odysseus, an extraordinary hero in an extraordinary situation, endures by very ordinary means, controlling his impulses. Bloom is in an ordinary situation, yet he endures in an extraordinary way by the same ordinary means. Despite Joyce's objection that "A writer . . . should never write about the extraordinary. That is for the journalist" (*JJ* 1470), his focus upon the ordinary unveils how the extraordinary is not only hidden within the ordinary but emerges from it.[10] Any ordinary mortal can aspire to the heroism of endurance, but only extraordinary ones can achieve it. The endurance of heroism between the *Odyssey* and *Ulysses* is demonstrated by the heroism of endurance, exemplified by Laertes, Odysseus, Telemachus, and Bloom.

So, in a complex intertextual echo, Joyce portrays how Bloom remains an unconquered hero like Odysseus despite his humiliations. To this end, Lenehan makes this pronouncement about Blazes Boylan: "See the conquering hero comes" (*U* 11.340). Blazes is the conqueror who ravishes Molly and makes the Blooms' connubial bed jingle on Bloomsday. But that is only part of the story, for, "Between the car and window, warily walking, went Bloom, unconquered hero. See me he might" (*U* 11.341–42). Again Bloom prefers to avoid any encounter with Boylan, as he has already done earlier at the National Library. Bloom's tactics of evasion while "warily walking" may seem disgraceful when compared to ancient standards, yet in the modern context, they reflect the degree to which his patience, perseverance, and self-restraint enable him to preserve his home. Joyce exploits his contrasting uses of the word "hero" to prove how extraordinary and impressive Bloom actually is even when coping with such a degrading situation.[11]

Bloom's choice to avoid confrontation with his wife or with her suitor on Bloomsday and thus to acquiesce impassively to being cuckolded may seem antiheroic, but the choice to avoid struggle is often Odysseus' best strategy as well.[12] As Pietro Pucci remarks, the "choice—to do nothing—seems implicitly the best thing to do . . . the posture of endurance emerges repeatedly as the solution Odysseus embraces, it being the more advantageous for his survival and protection" (74–75). In both cases, our hero-men seem less than admirable, mostly because, as Pucci concedes, "'enduring' necessarily implies survival, and so a questionable form of heroism" (49).[13] This skepticism about the merit of such heroism may be countered by the acknowledgment that the qualities promoting such endurance are commendable. For the manner of Bloom's reentry into bed names those qualities and establishes why he is much more like Odysseus than we first imagined possible.

How?

> With circumspection, as invariably when entering an abode (his own or not his own): with solicitude, the snakespiral springs of the mattress being old, the brass quoits and pendent viper radii loose and tremulous under stress and strain: prudently, as entering a lair or ambush of lust or adders: lightly, the less to disturb: reverently, the bed of conception and of birth, of consummation of marriage and of breach of marriage, of sleep and of death. (*U* 17.2114–21)

Bloom returns to his bed with the same degree of self-discipline and caution with which Odysseus returns home: "with circumspection . . . solicitude . . . prudently . . . lightly . . . reverently," Odysseus' return in disguise, his testing of Penelope, and his decision to unveil himself to his son and recruit his help in killing the suitors all occur in a similar manner and by a similar method as Bloom's return to bed. But Odysseus' rage at the suitors has become so suppressed in Bloom that he manifests it only with the flick of the wrist with which he cleans off his sheets and with his private condemnation, "Is there anything more in him that they she sees? Fascination. Worst man in Dublin" (*U* 6.201–2). As Bloom counsels himself over his tormenting thoughts about Molly's affair—

> Touch. Fingers. Asking. Answer. Yes.
> Stop. Stop. If it was it was. Must. (*U* 8.591–92)

—he resigns himself to the pain of her infidelity as necessity because he "must," much as Odysseus accepts his hunger on Thrinacia and his humiliation by the suitors while in disguise.

Bloom, however, refrains from inflicting pain on others as punishment or revenge, as Odysseus and Telemachus relish during the slaughter (*Od.* 22.171–93, 462–77). Violence for Bloom is not an option: "Duel by combat, no" (*U* 17.2201–02). Herein lies one instance of a "revelation of the irreducible differences" that Wolfgang Iser finds an inevitable result of Joyce's Homeric intertext (Iser 200). Still, both Odysseus and Bloom prevail due to their extraordinary patience and capacities for self-restraint. Joyce employs the word "hero" in *Ulysses* to endorse this sort of heroism portrayed in the *Odyssey*, even as he purposely transforms how such heroism is expressed in a new place and time. *What* Bloom endures in *Ulysses* is very different from *what* Odysseus endures in the *Odyssey*, but *how* they endure is the same. As with Odysseus, Bloom's patience and self-control generate his endurance, an endurance that constitutes a particular kind of heroic excellence and that makes homecoming possible. So, while the expressions of enduring heroism have changed between the *Odyssey* and *Ulysses* due to the modern context, the meaning of this kind of heroism has not. For this reason, Joyce's conception of heroism simultaneously revolutionizes Homer's conception and reinforces it.

This insistence upon enduring and remaining unconquered despite enormous sufferings unites the Homeric and Joycean conceptions of heroism. Homer's inclusion of the title "hero" at the point when Odysseus is about to visit Hades while still alive draws attention to his choice to remain mortal and heroic, joining his father in embracing suffering. Kalypso offered Odysseus immunity from suffering, aging, and death: "I told him I would make him without death and old age for all his days" (*Od.* 5.135–36), she confides to Hermes. But in spite of Kalypso's admonition that if he knew the extent of his future suffering, he would stay with her (*Od.* 5.206–10), Odysseus aspires to become an old-man-hero who dies at home, gently, out of the sea, as Teiresias predicts (*Od.* 11.134–37), accepting suffering, old age, and death as the necessary prerequisite of his heroic glory. Odysseus' absolute refusal to yield in this regard causes him to endure like a hero instead of living like a god, because accepting the invulnerability of immortality would mean the death of his humanity and of his heroism. Life, suffering, and death are the horizons of heroism for Homer; to try to escape them is to lose any eligibility for heroism. For this reason, Jean-Pierre Vernant insists that accepting Kalypso's offer is the equivalent of rejecting heroism: "Sharing divine immortality in the nymph's arms would constitute for Odysseus a renunciation of his career as an epic hero" (188). Homer's gods enjoy a transcendence of time that heroes cannot share. As Jasper Griffin confirms, "If the hero were really godlike, if he were exempt, as the gods are, from age and death, then he would not be a hero at all" (92–93). Kalypso's offer therefore presents Odysseus with a choice of deaths: the death-in-life of immortality, or a heroic death in Hades. His choice lends veracity to Dean Miller's conclusion that "Death therefore is the limit—the only limit—the hero accepts without demur" (383–84).

Heroic endurance thus requires an extraordinary will to live and the tenacity to welcome suffering until a fully inevitable death arrives. Joyce's fascination with the hero's need to endure life's pain until a fully fated and inevitable death arrives is borne out by his notes. Two passages of the *Odyssey* cited in Joyce's notes, "*Od.* XI.118.130–XXIII.250.275" (Herring 28), betray Joyce's attention to Odysseus' decision to endure pain until his fated death. Joyce notes Teiresias' prediction to Odysseus: "You will make them [the suitors] pay the penalty for their violence [bie] when you come home" (*Od.* 11.118); and Odysseus' pronouncement to Penelope: "Hereafter there are still countless toils, many and difficult, which I must complete in full"

(*Od.* 23.249–50). The rest of both citations detail Odysseus' next journey, wandering until he finds the man who calls his oar a winnowing fan, at which point he must plant it in the ground and make offerings to Poseidon. Only then can he return home for good. Joyce's notations comprise his recognition that Odysseus must punish the suitors and then leave home again to finish the full measure of his suffering. Joyce's notice of the lines in the *Odyssey* establishing why Odysseus' homecoming is only temporary alerts us to a curious and crucial connection between Bloom and Odysseus. They share the same need to endure suffering as they try to return home, knowing they must only leave again. After all, every new day in Dublin is a new journey, regardless of who prepares breakfast. Despite the banality of that daily departure, love always seems to require another return in both texts. Homecoming is not a single, discrete task, but a constant and continual effort.

In that endeavor, why do Odysseus and Bloom sustain the will to live? They may very well have learned from the examples of their parents' failure to do so. That Bloom's father Virag is a suicide is no surprise, but Odysseus' mother, Antikleia, is not typically categorized as one. She is normally described as dying of a broken heart. Why is she too a suicide, and in whose opinion? In Hades, Odysseus asks her what fate of sad death overwhelmed her (damazo) (*Od.* 11.171ff.). She attributes her death to her longing for the extraordinary kindness of heart of her son, his unmatched aganophrosune (*Od.* 11.203, a full *hapax legomenon*): "Nor did the sharp-sighted archer attack me in my halls with gentle arrows and kill me, nor did any sickness come to me, such as the wretched wasting away that removes the spirit [thumos] from the limbs. No, it was longing for you and for your advice, shining Odysseus, and for your kindheartedness [aganophrosune] that stole my honey-sweet will to live [thumos]" (*Od.* 11.198–203). Death conquers Antikleia because she cannot master her own desires. She later enumerates how death ensues once desire (thumos) has left the bones: "For the sinews no longer keep the bones and flesh together, and the strong force of the blazing fire destroys them, as soon as the spirit [thumos] leaves the white bones behind, and the soul [psuche] like a dream, floats away, to hover and drift" (*Od.* 11.219–22). In death, Antikleia details the cause of her own death. She explains that the pain of her yearning for her son was so strong that it erased her will to live, forcing Odysseus to confront the fact that death is often the consequence of failing to control desire (thumos).

Moreover, Antikleia recognizes that Laertes is managing to endure what she could not, telling Odysseus, "[your father, Laertes] lies grieving in the orchard and nurtures great pain [penthos aexei] in his heart, longing for your return" (*Od.* 11.195–96). Unlike her husband, who is able to endure his agonies, her longing for her son kills her, leading to Joyce's judgment in his notes that her death is tantamount to suicide: "Antikleia dies of grief (suicide) / Laertes goes to country" (Herring *15*). Joyce also wrote "Suicide 15.356" and beneath it, "Sisyphos—Antikleia" (Herring 30). Antikleia failed to endure her pain, whereas Laertes and Sisyphos submitted to its necessity. In the passage Joyce cites, Eumaeus tells the disguised Odysseus, "Laertes still lives, but he is always praying to Zeus that his spirit [thumos] may pass away from his limbs in his halls. For relentlessly he grieves for his absent son, and for his lawful and respected wife, whose death agonized him most of all and brought him to old age before his time" (*Od.* 15.353–57). Joyce specifically marks *Od.* 15.356, the line in which Laertes grieves most of all for Antikleia, the only place in the *Odyssey* where the depth of his grief for his double loss of wife and son is emphasized. He is so devastated by losing his beloved wife that he wishes for death, but he nonetheless renounces suicide and tolerates his agony. Joyce's consideration of Eumaeus' description of the extent of Laertes' grief justifies the suspicion that Joyce intended to emulate Homer's focus upon the need to endure grief from the loss of loved ones. *Ulysses* demonstrates how Joyce learned the same lessons that Odysseus did from Teiresias and Antikleia in Hades, and that he appreciated their implications for the meaning of heroism.

Odysseus, like his father, succeeds where his mother failed. Bloom too succeeds, but where his father failed.[14] Virag and Antikleia died for the same reason: grieving for a lost beloved. Bloom remembers finding his father after his suicide and ponders what death incites: "No more pain. Wake no more" (*U* 6.365). Virag's suicide note states that life has ceased to hold any attraction for him in his grief: "it is no use Leopold to be . . . with your dear mother . . . that is not more to stand . . . to her . . . all for me is out" (*U* 17.1883–85). Choosing to commit suicide is the ultimate failure of this kind of ordinary heroism that extends and values human life above all else. Virag seems to have made that choice by poisoning himself: "Verdict: overdose. Death by misadventure" (*U* 6.363–64, see also 6.529). His note indicates that he sought his own death for the sake of joining his wife, while Antikleia just pined away until she died.

Love, then, has the power to kill in *Ulysses* and in the *Odyssey*. As Bloom muses, "Poor papa too. The love that kills" (*U* 6.997). The pain that belongs to love killed Virag and Antikleia. Neither one can recover from grief, and so the loss of love kills them. Stephen has not yet experienced the pain of love: "Pain, that was not yet the pain of love, fretted his heart" (*U* 1.102). But the pain that has not yet become the pain of love for Stephen is fully in bloom for Bloom, Virag, Odysseus, Antikleia, and Laertes. Recalling Stephen's declaration that "*Amor matris*, subjective and objective genitive, may be the only true thing in life" (*U* 9.842–9:3), we wonder how to interpret the pain of love. No one has any love for pain in the objective genitive sense. But Bloom and Odysseus do feel the pain that belongs to love, in the subjective genitive sense. They know that to survive love's pain, they must follow Laertes' example. Only by cultivating pain ("penthos aexon") can they resist succumbing to death. Treasuring pain has become another part of treasuring life. The insistence of Laertes, Odysseus, and Bloom upon the value of living and loving is the hallmark of their heroism.

By the standards of the heroism of endurance, Virag is no hero. Heroes are supposed to save lives, not end their own. Ironically, given the title of Joyce's *Stephen Hero*, Joyce relies upon Stephen to protest that he is not a hero at all for this very reason, telling Buck Mulligan, "Out here in the dark with a man I don't know raving and moaning to himself about shooting a black panther. You saved men from drowning. *I'm not a hero, however*. If he stays on here I am off" (*U* 1.60–63; emphasis added). Because the only life Stephen is trying to save is his own, he maintains that he is no hero. But by this measure, Odysseus is not a hero either, because as the only hero to come home, in the end he saves only himself. After all, Odysseus is the hero who does not even try to save drowning men! Instead, when Zeus strikes their ship with a thunderbolt after his men have eaten the oxen of the sun, he paces their sinking ship and watches his men drown: "Like sea crows they were tossed upon the waves around the dark ship, and the god stole from them their homecoming" (*Od.* 12.418–19). No examples of altruistic, heroic rescue like those to which Stephen avers are enacted by Odysseus in the *Odyssey*. In the *Odyssey* and *Ulysses*, heroism first requires saving one's own life, not sacrificing it for the sake of others.

Exposing such complexities in the notion of heroism, while insinuating that heroism may actually be much more ordinary, and even more pitiful or contemptible than one normally presumes it to be, was likely one of Joyce's aims in selecting his novel's title. Joyce's words to his brother Stanislaus reveal that heroism was not a universal ideal he sought to embrace and glorify, but an illusion he sought to dispel: "Do you not think the search for heroics damn vulgar—and yet how are we to describe Ibsen? . . . I am sure however that the whole structure of heroism is, and always was, a damned lie and that there cannot be any substitute for the individual passion as the motive power of everything—art and philosophy included" (*Letters* 1180–81). Setting aside the problem of Ibsen here, Joyce's notion of heroism as a lie veiling the potency of a single individual's capacities is borne out by Homer's *Odyssey*. The prominence Homer gives to the power of desire (thumos), and the hero's need to master it and yield to it at the right moments, constitute exactly the individual motive power to which Joyce alludes. For in some sense, Odysseus, the victor of the Trojan War who devised the stratagem of the Trojan horse, gives up on the "damn vulgar" search for heroics in the *Odyssey* for the sake of simply surviving and returning home. Odysseus is both victor and victim as he seeks homecoming. Thus, by creating a conception of heroism fraught with ironies, tensions, and contradictions, the *Odyssey* demands the reconsideration and revision of its own premises.[15] Both Homeric poems critique the very notions that they depict, simultaneously accomplishing the presentation and the revision of those notions. Joyce's *Ulysses* engages in the same struggle with traditional heroic values, assuming the same posture of self-reflexivity, self-critique, and self-contradiction, exposing why "the whole structure of heroism is, and always was, a damned lie." Heroism deconstructs itself in the *Odyssey* and in *Ulysses* by discrediting the lie that only the extraordinary is heroic. In both texts, heroism is ordinary and extraordinary at the same time, without becoming entirely ineffable or incommensurable.

The preceding inquiry thus confirms Hugh Kenner's suspicion that Odyssean and Ulyssean heroism might somehow intersect in the realm of meaning in spite of the undeniable contrasts in its forms: "Was Odysseus perhaps a Bloom perceived through Ionic hexameters? . . . is this 1904 Ulysses perhaps the same man, reclad in circumstance as also in headgear and idiom? In Homer he seems different, very; may we say, though, thanks only to parallax?" (Kenner, *Ulysses* 106). Of course, Bloom shares Kenner's preoccupation with parallax, wondering, "what's parallax?" (*U* 8.578). Joyce provokes his readers to ask the same question about heroism, having imposed parallax on heroism itself by transplanting the story of homecoming into a new cultural and historical context. In so doing, Joyce has not subverted Homer's heroism but given it a new birth in a new guise. His readers must resort to the patience and perspicacity of Bloom and Odysseus if they are to appreciate the rebirth of heroism in Dublin. Yet from the stance of patience and endurance, there is no heroic parallax whatsoever between the *Odyssey* and *Ulysses*. Bloom is Ulysses is Odysseus, who "would somehow reappear reborn above delta . . . and after incalculable eons of peregrination return" (*U* 17.2019–20).

NOTES

1. I thank Morris Beja, Wendy Doniger, Paul Friedrich, John Gordon, David Grene, Ellen Carol Jones, Patrick McCarthy, Stephanie Nelson, Fritz Senn, and Anthony C. Yu for their comments on earlier versions of this essay. All quotations are from the Greek text of Homer's *Odyssey*, edited by T. W. Allen. All translations are mine. Citations refer to book and line number.

2. Ezra Pound first called Joyce's Homeric correspondences simply "a scaffold, a means of construction" (406). Most recently, Morton Levitt argues that *Ulysses* "makes use of Homer only as an aspect of its parody and social satire, in order to demonstrate the inversion of mythic values in modern times" (32, 53), joining the general consensus proclaimed by Richard Madtes that "little is to be gained from a study of Homeric references" (30; see Ames, "Convergence" 1–11, for a review of the literature). Like Constance Tagopoulos, who disputes how "Joyce scholarship has termed the Homeric parallels in *Ulysses* incomplete, idiosyncratic, and noninstrumental to the work" (184) in her study of return, disguise, and

recognition in the two texts, I seek to affirm the value of intertextual reading of the *Odyssey* and *Ulysses* by establishing how their glaring divergences conceal the same brand of heroism, thus beginning to nullify Kenner's old but still valid complaint: "That the fundamental correspondence is not between incident and incident but between situation and situation, has never gotten into the critical tradition" (*Dublin's Joyce* 181).

3. Therefore, despite the gender switch of the adulterous partner, *Ulysses* can be understood to affirm Homer's depiction of "real love . . . between married folk" (*U* 16.1385–86) in a new time and place. For my full argument concerning why Molly and Penelope should both be viewed as faithful wives in loving marriages, see Ames, "Oxymoron."

4. While Homer's use of epithets and formulae may have depended more upon metrical expedience than any intentional pattern, it is intriguing to contemplate how certain words complement the contexts in the poem in which they occur. Alice Radin makes a compelling case for why Homer's repetition of a single, apparently inconsequential word can connote enormous meaning through its context: "Homer limits the temporal conjunction *emos* . . . to link a proverbial, time-reckoning event to an event that is actually happening within the narrative . . . the clause derives its meaningfulness from a view of time as cyclical. In Homer, emos always connects a recurring point in cyclical time to a specific moment in the linear narrative" (293). I submit that Homer uses the word "hero" (eros) to great effect as well, inserting it at moments that express the special kind of heroism he is depicting in the *Odyssey*.

5. Homer uses "hero" (eros) forty times in the *Odyssey*, while Joyce uses "hero," "heroine," and its adverbial and adjectival forms twenty-seven times in *Ulysses*. An exhaustive analysis of all such uses lies beyond the scope of the present inquiry but can be found in "Convergence."

6. Only here in the *Odyssey* does Athena ever wield her own spear. A. P. David noted to me that shortly thereafter Telemachus puts her spear in a rack, where it rests with Odysseus' abandoned spears for the entire poem, never to be mentioned again (*Od.* 1.120–29; personal conversation, the Committee on Social Thought at the University of Chicago, June 5, 1998). Athena's spear watches over the action of the household, just as it hovers over the actions of men, unacknowledged but ever-present.

7. Caroline P. Caswell superbly explores how the semantic range of thumos creates "approximations in meaning which range from 'soul' to 'anger,' but it is clear that these words do not adequately express what was intended by the Greek" (1). I offer various translations in this essay for the sake of conveying its depth of meaning, in concurrence with Caswell's claim that "the uses of thumos are so varied, covering almost every important aspect of human experience, that it seems possible only to translate each occurrence as is fitting to that passage without attempting consistency" (1).

8. Falkner discusses how the *Odyssey* depicts another kind of heroism that does not depend upon victory in battle nor upon youth: "While the word eros in Homer may not be age-specific, heroism clearly means youthful heroism . . . there is within the heroic line of Laertes a rich agricultural tradition, one characterized specifically as an alternative to heroic warfare" (30, 43). Homer's valuation of heroes beyond the bloom of youth perhaps contributed to the evolution in the meaning of heroism in ancient Greece discussed by Douglas Adams: "The Greek words [hero (eros) and Hera (Nra)] can now be seen as the regular outgrowth of an important Indo-European cultural emphasis on youthful vitality. This cultural perspective had lost some of its power in the classical Greek polis but had still been very much alive in the heroic age" (177). Further, see Adams and Mallory 362ff., and Frisk 644ff.

9. For more on classical attitudes toward old age, see Falkner and deLuce, eds.

10. David Hayman comments that Joyce "has managed to show the extraordinary as a quality of the ordinary" (17), while Richard Ellmann speaks of Joyce's "need to seek the remarkable in the commonplace" (*JJII* 156). For Ellmann, "Joyce's discovery, so humanistic that he would have been embarrassed to disclose it out of context, was that the ordinary is the extraordinary" (*JJII* 5).

11. Heroism thus depends upon one's reaction to circumstances, regardless of the nature of those circumstances, as Francis Mackey implies of Bloom: "Heroic, undaunted, he has refused to bow to the sad fate that seems to await him, that coincidence and chance seem to assure" (62). John Henry Raleigh agrees that Bloom is "indomitable and thus heroic. . . . The really splendid originality of Joyce's conception was to place his hero in the most unheroic of circumstances" (595).

12. Odysseus' lineage raises doubts regarding his heroic status. Of his grandfather Autolycus, S. G. Farron states, "It would be difficult to imagine a more unheroic or unaristocratic ancestor" (64). W. B. Stanford contends that Joyce echoes this ambiguity: "Though Odysseus in Homer is (by mere convention) an aristocrat, much of his conduct and many of his associates are far from aristocratic, especially in the *Odyssey*. . . . Homer was no snob. When Joyce is criticized for unheroic elements in Bloom, he is all the more clearly in the traditional succession" ("Ulyssean Qualities" 126).

13. This equivocal sort of excellence accounts for why Morris Beja praises Bloom for his lack of histrionics, albeit cautiously: "Bloom's attitude toward Molly's infidelity may in part—not entirely, to be sure: I am trying not to exaggerate but to set up what I perceive as a proper perspective—be correct, arguably heroic, even wise" (119–20). Lauding Bloom's forbearance seems especially justified in light of how Odysseus too prevails by preferring equanimity to violence at certain points in time.

14. Both men resist any temptation to suicide. Odysseus considers whether to drown himself or continue to endure in silence after his comrades release the winds of Aeolus (*Od*. 10.49–54). He also loses his will to live momentarily when Kirke commands him to visit Hades (*Od*. 10.496–502). Bloom views neither murder nor suicide as a satisfactory remedy, fearing the abandonment of reason:

> What did he fear?

> The committal of homicide or suicide during sleep by an aberration of the light of reason. (*U* 17.1765–67)

He does consider hurting himself to be one kind of "retribution" (*U* 17.2200) he might seek: "Suit for damages by legal influence or simulation of assault with evidence of injuries sustained (selfinflicted), not impossibly" (*U* 17.2203–5).

15. Seth Schein makes a similar claim about the *Iliad*: "Its style, mythological content, and heroic themes and values are traditional, but it generates its distinctive meanings as an ironic meditation on these traditional themes and values. Through parallels, contrasts, and juxtapositions of characters and actions, a dramatic structure is created that forces us to consider critically the traditional heroic world and the contradictions inherent in this kind of heroism" (1).

Works Cited

Adams, Douglas. "Nros and Nra: Of Men and Heroes in Greek and Indo-European." *Glotta* 65 (1987):171–78.

————, and J. P. Mallory, eds. *Encyclopedia of Indo-European Culture.* London: Fitzroy Dearborn, 1997.

Ames, Keri Elizabeth. "The Convergence of Homer's *Odyssey* and Joyce's *Ulysses.*" PhD diss. University of Chicago, Committee on Social Thought, June 2003.

————. "The Oxymoron of Fidelity in Homer's *Odyssey* and Joyce's *Ulysses.*" *Joyce Studies Annual* 14 (Summer 2003): 132–74.

Beja, Morris. "The Joyce of Sex: Sexual Relationships in *Ulysses.*" In *Light Rays: James Joyce and Modernism*, edited by Heyward Ehrlich, 112–25. New York: New Horizon, 1984.

Caswell, Caroline P. *A Study of Thumos in Early Greek Epic.* Leiden: Brill, 1990.

Cunliffe, Richard John. *A Lexicon of the Homeric Dialect.* Norman: University of Oklahoma Press, 1963.

Falkner, Thomas M. *The Poetics of Old Age in Greek Epic, Lyric, and Tragedy.* Norman: University of Oklahoma Press, 1995.

Falkner, Thomas M., and Judith deLuce, eds. *Old Age in Greek and Latin Literature.* Albany: State University of New York Press, 1989.

Farron, S. G. "The *Odyssey* as an Anti-Aristocratic Statement." *Studies in Antiquity* 1 (1979–80):59–101.

Frisk, Hjalmar. *Griechisches Etymologisches Wörterbuch.* Heidelberg: Carl Winter, 1960.

Griffin, Jasper. *Homer on Life and Death.* Oxford: Oxford University Press, 1983.

Hayman, David. "*Ulysses*": *The Mechanics of Meaning.* Englewood Cliffs, N.J.: Prentice-Hall, 1970.

Herring, Philip. *Joyce's Notes and Early Drafts for "Ulysses": Selections from the Buffalo Collection.* Charlottesville: University Press of Virginia, 1977.

Homer's *Iliad.* Edited by David B. Monro and T W. Allen. In *Homeri Opera.* New York: Oxford University Press, 1902–20.

Homer's *Odyssey.* Edited by T. W. Allen. In *Homeri Opera.* Oxford: Oxford University Press, 1917–19.

Iser, Wolfgang. *The Implied Reader: Patterns of Communication in Prose Fiction from Banyan to Beckett.* Baltimore: Johns Hopkins University Press, 1974.

Kenner, Hugh. *Dublin's Joyce.* New York: Columbia University Press, 1987.

————. *Ulysses.* Rev ed. Baltimore: Johns Hopkins University Press, 1987.

Levitt, Morton R. *James Joyce and Modernism: Beyond Dublin.* Lewiston, N.Y.: Edwin Mellen, 1999.

Lewis, C. S. *The Problem of Pain.* New York: Collier, 1962.

Liddell, Henry George, and Robert Scott. *Greek–English Lexicon.* Oxford: Clarendon, 1968.

Mackey, Peter Francis. "Chaos Theory and the Heroism of Leopold Bloom." In *Joyce through the Ages: A Nonlinear View*, edited by Michael Patrick Gillespie, 46–65. Gainesville: University Press of Florida, 1999.

Madtes, Richard. *The "Ithaca" Chapter of Joyce's "Ulysses."* Ann Arbor: UMI Research Press, 1983.

Miller, Dean A. *The Epic Hero.* Baltimore: Johns Hopkins University Press, 2000.

Nelson, Stephanie. "Calypso's Choice: Immortality and Heroic Striving in the *Odyssey* and *Ulysses.*" In *Literary Imagination, Ancient and Modern: Essays in Honor of David Grene*, edited by Todd Breyfogle, 63–89. Chicago: University of Chicago Press, 1999.

Pound, Ezra. *Literary Essays of Ezra Pound.* Edited by T. S. Eliot. London: Faber and Faber, 1954.

Pucci, Pietro. *Odysseus Polutropos: Intertextual Readings in the "Odyssey" and the "Iliad."* Ithaca: Cornell University Press, 1987.

Radin, Alice P. "Sunrise, Sunset: emos in Homeric Epic." *American Journey of Philology* 109 (1988): 293–307.

Raleigh, John Henry. "Bloom as a Modern Epic Hero." *Critical Inquiry* (1977): 583–98.

Schein, Seth L. *The Mortal Hero: An Introduction to Homer's "Iliad."* Berkeley and Los Angeles: University of California Press, 1984.

Smyth, Herbert Weir. *Greek Grammar.* Cambridge: Harvard University Press, 1984.

Stanford, W. B. *Homer, "Odyssey" XIII–XXIV.* London: Bristol Classical Press, 1996.

———. "Ulyssean Qualities in Leopold Bloom." *Comparative Literature* 5 (1953): 125–36.

Tagopoulos, Constance. "Joyce and Homer: Return, Disguise, and Recognition in 'Ithaca.'" In *Joyce in Context,* edited by Vincent Cheng and Timothy Martin, 184–200. Cambridge: Cambridge University Press, 1992.

Vernant, Jean-Pierre. "The Refusal of Odysseus." In *Reading the "Odyssey,"* edited by Seth Schein, 185–89. Princeton: Princeton University Press, 1996.

JENNIFER MARGARET FRASER

Intertextual Sirens

Another way of analyzing the circular theme of loss and recovery, or initiatory death and rebirth, in Joyce's texts reveals itself if readers open themselves up to the singing of the Siren. The Siren leads us, as readers, astray; the seductive song lures us out of education's bounds, and we may discover our own voice in the process. And yet hearing the Siren's song may just as easily drown the writer-in-progress. A balance must be struck between wandering and return, centrifugal and centripetal movement (*U* 579.1214).

Stephen finally separates from the oppressive maternal ghost—with her breath of ashes—near the end of the "Circe" episode. Notably, when Bloom hovers over Stephen, he opens up Stephen's coat to finally allow the poet-in-progress to breathe: "Poetry. Well educated. Pity. (*he bends again and undoes the buttons of Stephen's waistcoat*) To breathe" (*U* 497.4936–37). In this scene, Bloom opens the literary novice to something beyond his confining education, which is linked to the death-dealing breath of his mother. What leads Bloom to open Stephen's coat is "Poetry," specifically Yeats's poetry. Significantly, the quote Stephen mutters from Yeats, as he lies near-unconscious, refers to piercing: "Who . . . drive . . . Fergus now / And pierce . . . wood's woven shade . . .?" (*U* 496.4932–33). Being pierced by an earwig; being deflowered by a god; being penetrated by Siren song: these are some of the ways in which Joyce conceives of the initiatory process of art.

From *Rite of Passage in the Narratives of Dante and Joyce.* © 2002 by Jennifer Margaret Fraser.

At the end of *Portrait*, Stephen Dedalus seems to be under the spell of Siren song as he composes his journal before setting off on his sea journey:

> The spell of arms and voices: the white arms of roads, their promise of close embraces and the black arms of tall ships that stand against the moon, their tale of distant nations. They are held out to say: We are alone. Come. And the voices say with them: We are your kinsmen. And the air is thick with their company as they call to me, their kinsman, making ready to go, shaking the wings of their exultant and terrible youth. (*P* 252)

Stephen's journal entry for April 16 echoes the opening to Virgil's *Aeneid*: "Arma virumque cano" [Arms I sing and the man; my literal translation]. In this dense diary entry there are two dominant themes: the relinquishing of the authorial voice and the seduction of intertextual influences. The most apparent difference in the journal's echo of the opening line of the *Aeneid* is the shift from "sing" to "spell"; moreover, in Stephen's rendering, the authorial voice foregoes primacy to become "voices." If we press further the change from "sing" to "spell," one fluid authorial voice gives way to an author who puts words together, who spells. And the words that the author puts together or transfers into voices are taken from other texts. Instead of the author singing of arms and the man, here the author is lured—caught in the spell of—other ways, other voices.[1]

While Virgil sings of arms and the man, Stephen's diary accords with the first part, the "arms," but "man" is replaced by "voices." The hero becomes the voices of other texts. And while "arms" for Virgil represent the combat necessary to found a new race and carve out a homeland, "arms" for Stephen represent artistic battles fought in the name of freedom to express one's soul.[2] In a letter to Nora Barnacle written while they were courting, Joyce describes the "secret war" he waged against the Catholic Church as a student; he forcefully adds: "Now I make open war upon it by what I write and say and do" (*Letters* 2.48). In the "Telemachus" episode of *Ulysses*, Stephen battles with the "lancet of [his] art." He wounds with his "cold steel pen" (*U* 6.152–53). With these battles Stephen hopes to shape the soul of his race and put his homeland on the map. Shortly before the diary entries of *Portrait*'s conclusion, Stephen declares to Cranly in oft-quoted lines that, in order to escape colonized, Catholic Ireland, he will use artistic means: "using for my defence the only arms I allow myself to use—silence, exile, and cunning" (*P* 247). Thus his diary conveys an aesthetic method: Stephen's literary tools, his "arms," will be coupled with the introduction of other texts, other "voices."

Joyce's unusual image of the "white arms of roads" is elucidated when set against the Dantean intertext: as I have noted, Ulysses leads his companions out on the ocean "road," and, as revealed in the pilgrim's dream, the Siren song of his own rhetoric is responsible for the drowning. White arms may well open in an embrace, and the notion of being under a spell suggests a Siren's embrace. In *Stephen Hero*, his mind wandering—appropriately enough during an Italian lesson—Stephen believes that his life, under the spell of Catholic Ireland, has inherited "a soul the steadfastness of whose hate became as weak as water in siren arms" (*SH* 194). In the context of Stephen's rebellious feelings toward his educational experience, the expression "siren arms" brings together Dante's Siren with the literary arms of Stephen's diary entry. Siren arms threaten the creative writer with a smothering textual embrace, as the shaping force of education, or as the dogma of the church, or as a powerful literary influence. Stephen's "white arms of roads" become the "black arms of tall ships," and this black-and-white color scheme generates the image of a page rather than that of a seascape. Dante likens his narrative to a seagoing voyage, with his poem figured as a ship; even more telling, one of his nautical metaphors likens the poem to a Siren:

O voi che siete in piccioletta barca,
    Desiderosi d'ascoltar, seguiti
    Dietro al mio legno the cantando varca,
Tornate a riveder li vostri liti,
    Non vi mettete in pelago; chè forse,
    Perdendo me, rimarreste smarriti.

[O you who in a little bark, eager to listen, have followed behind my ship that singing makes her way, turn back to see your shores again; do not put forth on the deep, for, perhaps, losing me, you would be left bewildered.] (*Par.* 2.1–6)

The ship of Dante's poem sings like a Siren leading the reader out to sea. Since in the final cantos of Purgatorio, Virgil has had to return to Limbo, the *Commedia* would now appear to have taken on the role of initiatory guide or Siren, an intertext that Dante knows from experience the reader fears losing.

Stephen's arms of roads and arms of ships tell a "tale of distant nations," and the voices "[shake] the wings of their exultant and terrible youth." Arms and voices seem to be conflated, since voices are more likely to tell tales, and arms more characteristically resemble wings. More important, *Ulysses'* signature line—making "of the oars wings for the mad flight"—with its self-reflective relationship to Dante's poetry, conflates sailing and flying. In a write of passage, silence appears to correspond with reading. Stephen must fly into the unknown, plunge into the sea of other texts, before he is born into the literary world, transforming like Dante from a literary pilgrim, a reader, into a poet. Lorraine Weir has argued the same point: "the novice must finally retreat into isolation in order to wait for the coming of his own song, his voice—precisely a semiophany rather than a theophany, a response which is language itself."[3]

Stephen Dedalus wields the literary arm of silence; he reads. He exiles himself literally, by leaving Dublin, and figuratively, by plunging into the sea of other texts. However, this is only a phase. Cast upon the shore of *Ulysses*, and recurring as Shem the Penman in the *Wake*, Stephen Dedalus, as the writer-in-progress, remains on the cusp of rebirth. Joyce perpetually defers the transformation from pilgrim to poet, for as soon as Stephen/Shem becomes the poet, then Joyce's texts assume the authority, the educational force, the capacity to silence, that he deplores. Joyce's fiction strives to incite creativity and transform its readers into writers. Nonetheless, Stephen's plunge into an intertextual sea, where he spends time as a reader, is a significant phase to explore.

Siren figures such as Buck Mulligan threaten to lead Stephen into a baptismal experience that would drown him. In contrast, it would appear that Bloom has the force to lead Stephen into transformative waters so that he may be provisionally reborn.

Bloom wanders into a Catholic church, and his description of the baptismal font recalls the "bowl" in Mary Dedalus's sick room, which in turn recalls Buck's hailing of the sea as the "great sweet mother": "He stood a moment unseeing by the cold black marble *bowl* while before him and behind two worshippers dipped furtive hands in the low *tide* of holy water" (*U* 68.458–60; my emphasis). The suggestion that the baptismal font contains the sea appears next in Stephen's thoughts, which are in a medieval context. Thinking of Dante's friend Cavalcanti, and rejecting "medieval abstrusiosities," Stephen considers once again the difference between Buck's saving of the drowning man and his own fear. First, he recalls "the basin at Clongowes," and then he imagines: "Do you see the *tide* flowing quickly in on all sides [. . .]. If I had land under my feet. I want his life still to be his, mine to be mine. A drowning man. His eyes scream to me out of horror of his death. I . . . With him together drown. . . . I could not save her. Waters: bitter death: lost" (*U* 38.326–30; my emphasis). Stephen cannot save those he loves with the "artificial respiration" that animates figures like Buck Mulligan (*U* 507.293). Notably, in this context Buck bears an uncanny likeness to Dante's Ulysses.

Ulysses suffers in Hell for being the male version of a Siren, a false counselor. He becomes a medieval character in the *Commedia* without forfeiting his status as a classical Greek; likewise, Buck resembles a "patron of the arts in the middle ages" (*U* 3.32–33), while his name has a "Hellenic ring" (*U* 4.42). More telling, however, is Buck's similarity to creatures that fly as well as to those that swim. He not only recalls the defining verse of Dante's Ulysses whose oars become wings, but he also appears with the birdlike attributes of Ovid's Sirens (5.156). Buck "[hops] down from his perch"; the night before Buck was with a fellow in the "Ship"; we see him "running forward to a brow of the cliff, flutter[ing] his hands at his sides like fins or wings of one about to rise in the air [. . .] fluttering his winglike hands" with his "birdsweet cries" (*U* 16.593–602). He wants to see Stephen at "The Ship." And finally, Buck "plunge[s]," and Stephen hears a "voice, sweettoned and sustained, [calling] to him from the sea" (*U* 19.741). Buck draws on all of the seductive attributes of Dante's Ulysses in order to lure Stephen into the maternal sea where he will drown.

Hardly surprising, since he often acts as an antidote to Buck's poisonous charms, Leopold Bloom appears safe from the Siren song of Dante's Ulysses. Jean-Michel Rabaté discovers that Bloom's ability to withstand the Sirens results from his ties to writing and also, I would argue, from his astute mode of reading.[4] In the "Calypso" episode, Bloom is reading a pamphlet that tries to lure him on a voyage comparable to the adventure that Dante has Ulysses sing to his crew. He recognizes: "Makes you feel young. Somewhere in the east: early morning: set off at dawn" (*U* 47.83–84). Ulysses and his elderly crew also set off "poop turned to the morning" (*Inf.* 26.124). Bloom recognizes the false counsel of the pamphlet: "Probably not a bit like it really. Kind of stuff you read: in the track of the sun" (*U* 47.99–100). What Bloom describes is the route taken by Dante's Ulysses, who voyages with his crew "in the sun's track" (*Inf.* 26.117). Bloom does not fall for the "fiction" of the pamphlet; instead, he codes the false counsel in terms of the destructive mother. The sea into which the reader is lured appears to Bloom all dried up: "Now it could bear no more. Dead: an old woman's: the grey sunken cunt of the world" (*U* 50.226–28). In contrast to Dante's Ulysses who willfully leaves home (*Inf.* 26.94–99), Bloom's horror at the "dead sea" causes him to hurry "homeward" (*U* 50.231).

In Nighttown, Stephen unwittingly exchanges companions: Buck disappears, and Bloom makes his entrance. Surviving the dark night of the soul and body, the symbolic father and son stroll toward Bloom's home; the two are chatting "about sirens, enemies of man's reason, mingled with a number of topics of the same category, usurpers, historical cases of the kind" (*U* 543.1889–91).[5] The key word for Buck Mulligan, "usurper"— which brings the "Telemachus" episode to a resounding halt (*U* 19.744)—is linked in the conversation of Bloom and Stephen with the deadly song of the "siren."

One of the ways that Buck may drown Stephen is by means of alcohol: "The Ship," where Buck spends his time and Stephen's money, is a pub. In another Dublin watering hole, the setting of the "Sirens" episode, bronze and gold Sirens are dispensers of alcohol. Joyce's epic parallels drowning one's liver in too much booze and drowning in the sea: Stephen notes, "Seadeath, mildest of all deaths known to man" (*U* 42.482–83); and in reference to Paddy Dignam's death by alcohol, Bloom remarks: "The best death [. . .]. A moment and all is over. Like dying in sleep" (*U* 79.312–14). Shortly after this comment, Bloom, musing in the carriage on the way to Paddy's funeral, imagines: "Dunphy's corner. Mourning coaches drawn up, drowning their grief. A pause by the wayside. Tiptop position for a pub" (*U* 81.428–29). Joyce scripts alcohol in general and Buck in particular as Sirens that lure their consumers to a death by drowning. However, Joyce also configures inebriation as a liminal sleep state that is a vital passage through which one must travel. In *Finnegans Wake*, the images of drinking, Sirens, and literary production are once again linked. Thus, "he drink up words" (*FW* 611.11), and yet the text advises the reader to protect him/herself against seeming Siren song: "Stick wicks in your earshells when you hear the prompter's voice" (*FW* 435.19–20). Joyce imagines the narrative as being under the influence of Aquinas, or as Joyce has it, "Thomistically drunk."[6]

In the "Kersse the Tailor" episode of the *Wake*, HCE dispenses both liquor and stories at his pub, so that his customers are "liquorally" (*FW* 321.1) and figuratively under the influence. The drunken stutterers in the *Wake* try as best they can to speak "alcoh alcoho alcoherently" (*FW* 40.5), which serves to remind us of the way in which being under the influence affects our speech. In calling HCE's bar a "bierhiven" (*FW* 315.22), Joyce implies that being dead drunk in a beer heaven and being dead to the world stretched out upon one's bier may well have a certain correspondence. Alcohol puts the self into a deathlike sleep, but it also wakes one up: "slake your thirdst thoughts awake with it" (*FW* 311.16–17). In the ballad "Finnegan's Wake" that lends to Joyce's text its main theme and title, it is whiskey, spilled in a drunken brawl at his wake, that brings the hod carrier Tim Finnegan back to life. The song blends sleep with death in the final verse, in which Tim rises from his "bed": "The liquor scattered over Tim; / Bedad he revives, see how he rises, / And Timothy rising from the bed, / Says, 'Whirl your liquor round like blazes, / Thanam o'n dhoul, do ye think I'm dead?'"[7]

Joyce heard the story of Kersse the Tailor and the hunchbacked Norwegian captain from his father, who had learned it from a relative, Philip McCann. McCann was a ship's chandler, and as Ellmann notes, he was the sponsor for Joyce at his baptism on February 5, 1882.[8] As did many minor details, the attendance at the baptism became a crucial theme for Joyce.

The "retelling" of the story of the Irish tailor appears in the *Wake* as a "retailing" bar scene. The economics of the pun are important for Joyce, for he wants to buy back Irish culture, which, according to Stephen Dedalus, has been pawned (*U* 21.47). In Joyce's retelling of McCann's story, where he bossily suggests that readers "mind the narrator" (*FW* 314.18), the tailor claims that he cannot make a proper suit for the captain because of the man's hump. The tailor's outrage is as much about sewing as it is about storytelling: "a hole in his tale and that hell of a hull of a hill of a camelump back" (*FW* 323.22–23). A parallel is drawn between the hole in the story and the hump on the client's back. The story has a "hole" because it must go around the hump, which thereby creates a gap in the narrative. But the hump is also likened to a "hull," and thus tailoring clothes, and telling stories, are connected to "sailsmanship" (*FW* 325.17), or "salesmanship," and the buying back of culture. HCE in his guise as publican retails McCann's story as he gathers money at the till, so that it resembles the "tiller" with which he steers the narrative ship. And as Shari Benstock reveals, the "blank space in the text, a gap in the storytelling," is fundamentally connected to the "O" of ALP, which becomes "the geometric figure for the vaginal delta through which her children enter the world."[9] The gap allows for an initiatory return to the womb, configured in the *Wake* as the death and rebirth of baptism.

The plunge into the baptismal font in the episode of "Kersse the Tailor" produces a "merman" (*FW* 324.9) as well as "O maremen!" (*FW* 312.10). The "merman" may suggest the mythological figure Glaucus, to whom Dante compares himself as he plunges into Heaven. The phrase "O mare-men!" if read as a French pun on the sea ("la mer") and the mother ("la mère") may in fact be a "mere-man," one who returns to the mother's womb. And how exactly is one supposed to return to the womb? In *Finnegans Wake* it would appear that storytelling "presently returned him" (*FW* 323.29) along the nine spheres of the starry heaven, or Glaucus's nine circles, or the nine concentric spheres of Joyce's embryological chart for "Oxen of the Sun," for they all function as narratively superimposed "circumcentric megacycles" by which sailors and tailors navigate (*FW* 310.7).

The "O maremen," still punning in French, may also be a crew of "Homère-men," perhaps even the Homeric crew who set out to cross through the Pillars of Hercules and who thus drown like Dante's Ulysses. The associations with baptism—being cleansed of original sin in a "brina-bath" (*FW* 313.9–10)—through the figure of the storyteller McCann, allow Joyce to play with all of the various levels of listening to Siren song, drinking in a bar, and plunging into water, as contributions to an intertextual initiation in which one is under the influence.

I need to examine once again the early scene in which Buck aggressively proclaims the affinity between the figure of the mother and the sea. He is so seductive because he appears to offer initiation; he draws upon Swinburne's "Triumph of Time," in which the poet addresses the sea in initiatory terms: "From the first thou wert; in the end thou art."[10] Ostensibly about the view from the tower, Buck Mulligan's declarations about the sea being a "great sweet mother" demonstrate the difference between his thoughts and those of Stephen on art.[11] Buck borrows Stephen's handkerchief and teases him with the declaration that it represents a "new colour for our Irish poets: snotgreen" (*U* 4.73). He continues his joke by linking the sea as a "great sweet mother" to the new color for Irish poets, "The snotgreen sea" (*U* 4.78).

At the outset of the "Proteus" episode, watching midwives no less, Stephen recalls Buck's allusion to Swinburne's poem and inserts himself into the position of novice contending with the great maternal sea: "Like me, like Algy, coming down to our mighty mother" (*U* 31.31–32). Buck's reference to Irish art being the color of snot anticipates a passage in "Proteus" in which Stephen appears to be drawing himself out of the "green grave" of the maternal sea; he imagines lunging forth with his nose, one would assume, filled with the "snotgreen" of traditional mothers and art, turned upward, seeking clear air to breathe: "Dead breaths I living breathe [. . .]. Hauled stark over the gunwale he breathes upward the stench of his green grave, his leprous nosehole snoring to the sun" (*U* 42.479–81). Stephen imagines surviving a near-drowning in this maternal sea that breathes forth death, like the ghost of his mother who breathes forth ashes. After his seeming escape from the embrace of the maternal sea, Stephen has a "rere regardant" glimpse of a ship that seems to move through the air, once again recalling Ulysses' vessel powered by wings rather than oars: "He turned his face over a shoulder, rere regardant. Moving through the air high spars of a threemaster, her sails brailed up on the crosstrees, homing, upstream, silently moving, a silent ship" (*U* 42.503–5). At the outset of *Ulysses*, Stephen finds himself in a comparable position to that of the pilgrim, who at the beginning of his epic journey anxiously looks over his shoulder at the symbolic body of water out of which he has barely emerged intact (*Inf.* 1.22–27). Notably, Stephen's glancing vision of the ship is connected by Joyce to the ostensibly naturalistic detail about Stephen not wanting anyone to see him pick his nose (*U* 42.500–2); however, the detail has more ramifications when we realize that Stephen's nose is full from a plunge into the snotgreen grave of the maternal sea, which Buck compares to Irish art. The combination nearly drowns the writer-in-progress. Buck Mulligan states that Stephen will never become anything but a sophisticated reader of poets such as Swinburne and Dante, that Stephen will never be such a poet himself, for he lacks the necessary force to propel himself through initiatory dynamics: "He will never capture the Attic note. The note of Swinburne, of all poets, the white death and the ruddy birth. That is his tragedy. He can never be a poet. The joy of creation" (*U* 204.1072–75).

In the "Oxen of the Sun" episode, Buck's assessment of Stephen's failure as an initiatory artist returns slightly altered and blended with the telegram

Stephen sends earlier in the day: "Password. [. . .] Ours the white death and ruddy birth. Hi! Spit in your own eye, boss. Mummer's wire. Cribbed out of Meredith" (*U* 347.1484–86). In "Oxen of the Sun" the cribbing of literary heritage—which occurs throughout the entire episode in the form of Joyce's parodies—is juxtaposed with the possibility of initiatory production.[12]

The clash between Buck and Stephen results from their different opinions as to how Stephen should have behaved in the final days before his mother's death. For Buck, the mother—linked to the sea, honored by tradition—acts as the source of art. For Stephen, the mother fills basins, which resemble baptismal fonts, with bile that drowns art. Buck Mulligan acts as though he will save from drowning those who are lured by his Siren song, which chants the Greek version of Ulysses' return and drowns out Dante's medieval tale that plunges him into the sea.[13] Buck tells only of Daedalus's flight; he elides the drowning of Icarus. And thus the breath he offers to save one from drowning is artificial. As Richard Ellmann points out, Stephen's refusal to his mother is linked to his denial of Buck: "Not to pray, and not to swim: Stephen will not accept their spiritual or physical purification. Mulligan's attempt to be clean is like his mother's ghostly demand for his soul's cleanliness."[14] As I have noted, the clean statue of Narcissus acts as another figure for stasis that contrasts with the forbidden vulgar and dirty words that the writer-in-progress must access.

Stephen will not participate in the Catholic ceremony that he realizes will fail to bring about his rebirth and that may even drown his art. Mary Reynolds notes that "Stephen's dread of water" is attached to "his sensitivity to the power of water as a metaphor."[15] And thus, when Harry Blamires asserts that Stephen's "dislike of contact with water is related [. . .] implicitly (by the words partial, total, immersion) to his rejection of his own baptism," the baptism signifies much more than a rebellious rejection of the Catholic faith.[16] The rejection also implies an inability to activate initiatory dynamics, crucial to the joyful creation of poets.

Stephen's fear of plunging into the metaphoric realm of water is juxtaposed with Bloom's pleasure in the watery realm. The initiation of *Ulysses* involves the plunge of Stephen, "hydrophobe," into the realm of Bloom, the "waterlover, drawer of water, watercarrier" (*U* 549.183–84). When a novice has successfully completed an initiation, he receives a new name. Notably, Bloom is the only one to voice Stephen's name, which he does in the scene I discussed at the opening of this chapter, the scene in which Bloom tries to rally Stephen after the blow from Private Carr. Richard Ellmann compares the scene to the one in the *Commedia* in which Beatrice names the pilgrim "Dante."[17] The two naming scenes differ in that the pilgrim is named Dante, who signs the *Commedia* as its poet, whereas Bloom names the fallen man "Stephen," and it is James Joyce who signs his name to *Ulysses*. While Dante hones in on the moment of transformation from pilgrim to poet, Joyce seems more interested in the process, and thus his texts pivot continuously around the writer-in-progress.

A new womanly man draws Stephen into a sea that is both maternal and paternal. "Lady Bloom" (*U* 399.1677) compares in this context to Dante's Virgil, whose "stream of speech" (*Inf.* 1.80) functions as both a "mamma" and the "sweetest father" (*Purg.* 30.44, 50).[18] As I discussed, Statius honors Virgil as a mother/poet and as the spark (or "spunk," to use Molly's term) that ignites the imaginations of would-be poets. Joyce parodies the paternal and maternal Virgil when he describes Bloom's member as "floating hair of the stream around the limp father of thousands" (*U* 71.571) and then parallels this male generative site with its female equivalent: the bath water in which Bloom anticipates soaking is described as "a womb of warmth" (*U* 71.567–68). In a seeming play on his own name, Bloom dreams of himself bathing in floral terms: he imagines his navel as a "bud of flesh" and his penis as a "languid flower floating" (*U* 71.570–72). In the "Proteus" episode, struggling to enact the transformation from pilgrim to poet, Stephen has been dreaming of these intertextual waters over which Bloom presides: "Vehement breath of waters [. . .]. In cups of rocks it slops: flop, slop, slap: bounded in barrels. And, spent, its speech ceases. It flows purling, widely flowing, floating foampool, flower unfurling" (*U* 41.457–60). The sea Stephen seeks is one that evokes Virgil's stream of "speech," as well as one that signals the watery realm of parodic Virgilian guide, Leopold Bloom, with its unmistakable image of the "flower unfurling." The naming of Stephen occurs when he joins Bloom, immersing himself in Bloom's sea.

One way of charting a transformation in *Ulysses* from pilgrim to poet—a transformation that is ambiguous at best—must involve Bloom, whose creative leap in the text is to treat Stephen as though he were a symbolic son. In this context, one might understand Bloom's compassion as literary, in that he births Stephen from the womb of his imagination rather than producing him by means of a physical encounter with a woman. When Stephen switches his companions from Buck to Bloom, I believe he exchanges the maternal sea—into which Buck plunges as though it were a bed (*U* 19.713)—for the bed of Bloom, which generates an imaginary son. Bloom addresses this symbolic son as "Stephen," and then he tries to nurse and nourish him. Bloom begins the process of becoming symbolic father when he mingles with Stephen's biological father, so that we have "Siopold!" as the culmination of a telling flight (*U* 227.752). Sebastian Knowles notes that the union of fathers occurs in the song "M'Appari," which he argues is the "central song of 'Sirens'; it is the musical heart of Joyce's book," and thus, "Stephen has one father, and the book, which is about the search of father for son and vice versa, is given its impetus for the rest of the day."[19]

In the words that Bloom utters after waking Stephen from the slumber inflicted by Private Carr's blow, he appears aware that he has saved his textual son from drowning in a sea of tradition: "in the rough sands of the sea . . . a cabletow's length from the shore . . . where the tide ebbs . . . and flows . . ." (*U* 497.4953–54). Bloom's words magically conjure up a fantastic image of his lost son, Rudy, who notably reads from "right to left," which recalls Bloom's father reading "backwards" (*U* 101.206–7). What makes Bloom think of his father reading Hebrew from right to left is watching the typesetter in the newsroom of "Aeolus" set the keys for Patrick Dignam's obituary: "mangiD kcirtaP" (*U* 101.206). The appearance of one's name in a newspaper is sure death, whereas the surfacing of Rudy at the end of "Circe" is a startling dramatization of how initiatory literature may activate a rebirth. The appearance of Rudy could only occur in literature—his attributes are all intertextual or imaginative; Bloom's projection seems to arise from his nurturing of Stephen as a symbolic son.

We have touched on Joyce's use of profane trinities in *Ulysses*, and the trinity he has spinning at the end of "Circe" appears to be Bloom, Stephen, and Rudy, which can be read alternatively as Father, Son, and Ghost. One can gain further insight into Joyce's use of the father/son/ghost trinity by examining one of his letters, in which he brings Shakespeare and Dante together in order to position himself as an artist: "I am 35. It is the age at which Shakespeare conceived his dolorous passion for the 'dark lady.' It is the age at which Dante entered the night of his being" (*Letters* 2.433).[20] In "Scylla and Charybdis," Joyce's personal sentiments—which clearly link his own artistic development to Shakespeare's and Dante's—recur in Stephen's theory about life's impact upon literature: "If you hold that he, a greying man with two marriageable daughters, with thirtyfive years of life, *nel mezzo del cammin di nostra vita*, with fifty of experience, is the beardless undergraduate from Wittenberg then you must hold that his seventyyear old mother is the lustful queen" (*U* 170.828–33). Joyce teases us with the possibility that the initiatory dynamics of his literary projects self-reflectively address his own process as a writer.

In his aesthetic theory, another of Stephen's statements superimposes Shakespearean pseudobiography on the Christian Trinity, which again evokes Dante's *Commedia*: "He is a ghost, a shadow now, the wind by Elsinore's rocks or what you will, the sea's voice, a voice heard only in the heart of him who is the substance of his shadow, the son consubstantial with the father" (*U* 162.478–81). The question of the substance and the shadow is posed by the pilgrim and acts as the catalyst for Statius's discourse on the generation of the embryo. The shadow that accompanies the pilgrim-son through the afterworld is Virgil, "sweetest father." The idea of sons generated by literary fathers—in the way that Dante configures Virgil as his "author"—gives a certain weighty insight to Stephen's otherwise bizarre and facetious theory of art. At another juncture, Joyce has Stephen conflate Shakespeare and Dante. Virgil has traveled from *limbo patrum* in order to act as the pilgrim's guide through the afterworld. Dante implies that the pagan author has been forgotten, and thus his voice is "per lungo silenzio parea fioco" [weak from long silence] (*Inf.* 1.63). In "Scylla and Charybdis," Stephen suggestively asks: "Who is the ghost from *limbo patrum*, returning to the world that has forgotten him? Who is King Hamlet?" (*U* 154.150–51). Moreover, Joyce has Stephen introduce the ghost of King Hamlet according to Virgil's striking introduction of himself. The pilgrim asks him if he is a shade or a man, a shadow or a substance, and Virgil replies: "Non uomo, uomo gia fui" ["Not man; once I was a man"] (*Inf.* 1.67). Stephen introduces King Hamlet in comparable terms to the gathering in the library: "It is the ghost, the king, a king and no king" (*U* 155.165–66). Joyce subtly connects these ghostly fathers from the literary past with his character Leopold Bloom, for when Bloom enters the newsroom in "Aeolus," MacHugh intones: "The ghost walks" (*U* 102.237). The idea of the father/ghost who directs son/Hamlet neatly overlaps with the father/ghost Virgil who guides son/Dante and serves to generate the complex father figure Leopold Bloom, who strives to lead Stephen Dedalus but is not quite sure of the right direction.

In the passage quoted above—in which once again the poet-in-progress considers the voice of the sea as he struggles against more traditional ideas about art—Stephen argues for hearing with the "heart."[21] And if we place his oblique ideas here into the initiatory context, it would appear that one's plunge into the intertextual sea means, on one level, becoming the substance of a shade. The trinity of literature may be imagined as the substantial reader conjuring up the shadowy ghosts of the literary past, who act as fathers textually producing sons.

The breakdown of the heart occurs in "Hades," the episode of death and burial. When Stephen argues in "Scylla and Charybdis" that sundering and reconciliation go hand in hand (*U* 160.397–98), one anticipates the mending of the heart or the initiatory pattern of rebirth from death. The sundering of the heart appears to climax in "Circe," which contains the tormenting ghost of Stephen's mother but also the healing ghost of Rudy Bloom. Perhaps reconciliation occurs through writing, which allows one to rediscover the lost son in the symbolic son; this literary act encourages the heart to heal. The conjuring of the son's ghost signals a vital change in *Ulysses*: from this moment on in the story, Stephen is offered an opportunity to escape the sea of tradition.

One of the ways in which Joyce represents tradition and authority—whose rules must be broken—is through his representations of education. Essentially Joyce's method is a reverse of traditional methods of education:

instead of telling the reader something, he uses open-ended texts to reveal a whole series of possibilities. In perfect paradoxical fashion, it may well be Joyce's Jesuit training that taught him his independence; as Stanislaus observes: "The Jesuit influence, not their system, is educational, because it trains those under it to educate themselves."[22] Put into Joyce's own terms: "I think I have unlearned a great deal" (*Letters* 2.182). Joyce makes his reader active in the unlearning and learning process: in the act of analyzing the options, making a choice, and articulating a response, the reader is creating and defining his/her individuality rather than having selfhood spelled out by an authoritative system.

In *Ulysses*, Joyce uses education as the backdrop to a striking scene of metamorphosis. The narrator of "Ithaca" asks: "Did they find their educational careers similar?" And the text responds: "Substituting Stephen for Bloom Stoom would have passed successively through a dame's school and the high school. Substituting Bloom for Stephen Blephen would have passed successively through the preparatory, junior, middle and senior grades of the intermediate and through the matriculation, first arts, second arts and arts degree courses at the royal university" (*U* 558.548–54). The two figures meet at a threshold, an initiatory liminal zone in which they blend and then separate, and one may assume they are both changed by the experience. Readers are reminded that learning does not necessarily occur in school, in reciting the alphabet, or in absorbing authorities. In *Ulysses*, Joyce makes readers ponder both what is taught in school and the way it is taught.

Joyce intimates in "Calypso" that school may simply teach its students to lack an identity; in fact, education may well have the power to erase an individual's "I." When Bloom walks by Saint Joseph's National School, he hears the children learning the alphabet: "Brats' clamour. Windows open. Fresh air helps memory. Or a lilt. Ahbeesee defeegee kelomen opeecue rustyouvee doubleyou" (*U* 48.136–38). Bloom does not hear the children learning the letter "I." Each vowel is sounded except the one that acts as the sign of identity. The letters "h-i-j" are all missing. Joyce has his reader focus on the construction of language and literature by returning to the process of learning the alphabet. Heightening the reader's sensitivity to the way in which letters provide the tools to articulate or bypass an identity, Joyce seems to call out to his reader three times: "r*you*st*you*vee double*you*." One may conclude that although certain schools will strive to erase your "I," the epic undertaking of a book like *Ulysses* is that it tries to reach "U" you, double you, all of you.

The relationship Joyce explores between how we are educated and how we create an identity also surfaces in the "Proteus" episode, and it would appear that Stephen's literary identity hangs in the balance: "Books you were going to write with letters for titles. Have you read his F? O yes, but I prefer Q. Yes, but W is wonderful. O yes, W" (*U* 34.139–40). In this self-mocking scene, the letter titles Stephen chooses also lack an "I," and yet the imagined books address the reader in a comparable fashion to the scene in which the children recite the alphabet: "W [doubleyou] is wonderful. O yes, W [doubleyou]." By means of Joyce's punning, we again hear the calling out to the reader, coupled with an anticipatory echo of Molly's ecstatic "O [. . .] yes," which will triumphantly punctuate the final episode of the epic (*U* 643.1598–99).

Joyce encourages us to contrast the failure of education with his own methods of teaching that provoke us to consider self and other. Authorities operate dressed in "riddletight raiding hats" (*FW* 622.34). While reading/raiding the texts of others, they encase their knowledge-filled heads inside hats that cannot be penetrated by riddles. As Patrick McCarthy explains, in *Ulysses* Joyce privileges the potency of riddles to teach the opposite of what the authorities impart, namely independent thought.[23] Stephen recalls a "riddling sentence to be woven and woven on the church's looms. Ay." He recalls a traditional riddle: "*Riddle me, riddle me, randy ro. / My father gave me seeds to sow*" (*U* 22.86–89). The answer to the riddle is "writing a letter."[24] Joyce's riddling methods rouse the reader to write a letter, to address someone in writing. Rather than merely follow the rituals woven by authority, Joyce suggests that readers pose riddles to the church in order to generate our "Ay," a striking, brief sentence that contains both the book's irrepressible affirmation and the book's homonym for identity. Molly suggests that when confronted with the question of God, being steeped in the authorities is not the answer; rather, one discovers by creating: "I wouldnt give a snap of my two fingers for all their learning why don't they go and create something" (*U* 643.1564–65).

Nonetheless, as Bloom recognizes, a university degree is an excellent way to market the self. In the "Eumaeus" episode, what leads Bloom to muse on the idea of the B.A. as a potent self-advertisement is a piece Stephen sings about Sirens: "an old German song of Johannes Jeep about the clear sea and the voices of sirens, sweet murderers of men" (*U* 541.812–13). Practical Bloom wants to encourage Stephen to use his education and his beautiful voice in order to pursue a career in singing; he just needs to be "properly handled by some recognised authority" (*U* 541.1822). As we have seen, Joyce constructs Siren song as a double force that may drown the writer-in-progress or facilitate his rebirth through a transformative plunge. Siren song acts as one of the lures that draw the literary novice into the maternal sea, which becomes connected to education. Once again authority appears to be a two-sided coin, for education—essentially reading—is integral to becoming a writer, and yet one thereby risks drowning in the intertextual sea, overcome by authoritative voices.

In *Dubliners*, Joyce constructs a character who anticipates Stephen by means of his ample education, which this character imagines to be his defining feature. Lacking the ironic self-mocking stance of *Ulysses'* Stephen, Gabriel Conroy advertises himself, even to himself, according to his B.A. (*D* 179).[25] Even more interesting, Joyce has Gabriel attribute his acquisition of a university education to his mother's support and influence; she is also instrumental in his brother's attaining a church position: "Thanks to her, Constantine was now senior curate in Balbriggan and, thanks to her, Gabriel himself had taken his degree in the Royal University" (*D* 187). However, as the story unfolds, it becomes apparent that Gabriel's education has functioned merely as a suit of armor that cannot be pierced by music, or by the arrows of love, or by intense feelings of any kind. In Gabriel's case, the mother stresses education, being a good reader, rather than opening oneself up and thereby becoming a creator.

The mother disapproves of Gabriel's wife, whose lack of schooling is insinuated in her maternal slight when she calls Gretta "country cute" (*D* 187).[26] However, it is Gretta who acts as the catalyst for Gabriel's initiatory journey. Garry Leonard describes this path in Lacanian terms: "Gabriel believes the time has come for him to set out on his journey westward away from the Dublin fictional self that he thought he knew, toward the Galway want-in-being that he has refused to acknowledge."[27] I read Leonard's "fictional self" as the one generated by parents, by education, by one's time and place (politics/religion/nationality); in contrast, by means of an identity crisis and an initiatory response, the writer seeks another kind of identity, one that Leonard identifies as "want-in-being." While his university-acquired culture seals Gabriel up into a tight waterproof package (once again as an anticipation of Stephen Dedalus), uneducated Gretta threatens to unwrap him with her story of passion.[28] Gabriel has been taught how to think and feel, and he has learned the lesson well. However, he must plunge into the watery realm enjoyed by his wife. Gretta laughs at Gabriel's fear of getting wet: "Goloshes! said Mrs Conroy. That's the latest. Whenever it's wet underfoot I must put on my goloshes. Tonight even he wanted me to put them on, but I wouldn't. The next thing he'll buy me will be a diving suit" (*D* 180). Gretta's wet realm is represented by her tears, which Gabriel recognizes as emblematic of her love, a feeling he does not know (*D* 224). In "The Dead," we have the earliest version of a theme that will be constant in Joyce's fiction: the necessity of taking an initiatory plunge that allows the reading self (formed by authorities) to die and the writing self (transformed by art) to be born.

Joyce's method of immersion occurs through literature; yet much of his idea of plunging into watery realms seems inspired by his lover, and ultimately his wife, Nora Barnacle, who is infamously nonliterary. In love letters to Nora, Joyce refers to her as his "dark-blue rain-drenched flower" (*Letters* 2.269) and to her eyes as "strange beautiful blue wildflowers growing in some tangled, rain-drenched hedge" (*Letters* 2.267). Moreover, the ballad that Michael Fury sings in "The Dead," which causes the piercing tears of Gretta and Gabriel, is about a woman and baby abandoned by the closed-off father to whom they make an appeal from out in the rain: "The rain falls on my yellow locks / And the dew it wets my skin; / My babe lies cold within my arms; / Lord Gregory, let me in."[29] The ballad that haunts Gretta, and through her, Gabriel, is about opening up the sealed-off self who prefers the dry security of the manor house to the wild rain-drenched night beyond. The woman, who beckons to the man within, is a figure for the feminine that recurs in Joyce's work as the force that demands the plunge into a piercing, opening, healing realm that is most powerfully expressed by tears. Notably, the qualities in Joyce's fiction that compelled his patron, Harriet Shaw Weaver, to not only publish his fiction but also financially support his writing, are his "searching piercing spirit" and the "startling penetration of [his] 'intense instants of imagination'" (*Letters* 3.445).

Gabriel's impenetrable self recurs in a different form in the *Wake*. In the "Game of Colours," Shem must guess the color of Issy's underwear, which as we have seen elsewhere is an indicator for the unconscious or secret self; however, he fails. Margaret Solomon notes that Shem "seems to be notoriously 'showerproof'" (*FW* 182.16), because "he is doomed to ineffectual action after his triple chance at the heliotrope riddle in the game of Colours."[30] In an echo of Gabriel, Shem is impervious because he wears "goodda purssia" (*FW* 224.2); or as Gretta has it, "Guttapercha" things like rubber boots (*D* 181). Gabriel shows himself to be equally "showerproof" when the first memory that he has of his romance with Gretta revolves around a letter enclosed in a heliotrope envelope: "Moments of their secret life together burst like stars upon his memory. A heliotrope envelope was lying beside his breakfast-cup and he was caressing it with his hand" (*D* 214).[31] Issy's heliotrope underwear envelops the sexual, creative part of her body just as the heliotrope envelope in the scene from "The Dead" contains the sexual, creative promise of the life that Gretta and Gabriel will intimately share. The envelope of the letter in *Finnegans Wake* undergoes comic scrutiny in the comparison of the envelope for the epistle to enveloping "feminine clothiering" that covers "the rere" (*FW* 109.31–33).[32] The reader learns in this analysis of the letter that one must go beyond the "literal sense" to the "sound sense" (*FW* 109.12–15). The allusion to "sound" leads one back to the significance of listening to "distant music" in "The Dead." Gabriel uses this phrase to describe the letter he wrote to Gretta: "Like distant music these words that he had written years before were borne towards him from the past" (*D* 215). What has the force to open Gabriel up to the possibility of initiation into new life is Gretta's letter, which becomes even more potent when we recognize its connection to the letter of *Finnegans Wake*.

The distinction between letters in the alphabet and letters that are exchanged is that the former do not create relationships, whereas the latter do, bringing together self and other. Patrick McCarthy maintains that *Ulysses* is all about self-encounters, and thus the letters of the epic bring together not only self and other, but also, perhaps more important, self and self, I and I, double you.[33]

In Joyce's fiction, it would appear that learning occurs in opening oneself up to another figure, an author, a character, an individual, and allowing the other to pierce one's emotional, spiritual, and intellectual defenses. Reading Joyce requires a plunge; hence all-encompassing *Finnegans Wake* ends with immersion: "carrying that privileged altar *unacumque* bath [. . .] a lector of water levels, most venerable Kevin, then effused thereby letting there be water where was theretofore dry land" (*FW* 605.31–35). In the final moment of the text, which is also its inception, ALP riverruns into the ocean. It would appear that the packaged-up characters—sealed off from life—need to enter into an initiatory process in order to become receptive, permeable, pregnable. Learning from Joyce's books opens up the reader to experience life rather than to live with a "riddletight raiding hat" perched upon one's head.

The turning point in "The Dead" occurs when Gabriel hears, wafting down the stairs at the end of the party, a song that brings him to a standstill and causes him to listen. With Gabriel's speech, Joyce leads Gabriel to the zenith of his pompous, condescending life; Joyce then composes a line that marks the beginning of Gabriel's descent: "The piercing morning air came into the hall" (*D* 207). In this passage, "air" functions as a telling pun, for it has a trinity of meanings: air that we breathe, air that rushes in from the outdoors, and air as a song. Important for Joyce, the air—whether the kind we breathe or the kind we hear—is drawn in and thereby expands and melds with our inner selves. To draw on the terms of the *Wake*, Gabriel is "balladproof" (*FW* 616.32) until the rain-drenched song of the mother and child impacts him: the ballad enters him like piercing morning/mourning air. Significantly, Gabriel has trouble hearing this song: "He stood still in the gloom of the hall trying to catch the air that the voice was singing" (*D* 211). Initially, all Gabriel can hear is "a few chords struck on the piano and a few notes of a man's voice singing" (*D* 211).

The *Wake* has no time for those who are impervious to "sound sense" and therefore cannot learn from ballads like the ones that sing of Tim Finnegan or Persse O'Reilly. Thus the book brashly commands the reader to: "stick this in your ear" (*FW* 622.32). In Joyce's fiction, it is the ear that acts as the window to the soul. The *Wake* characterizes being closed off in the following terms: "Once you are balladproof you are unperceable to haily, icy and missle throes" (*FW* 616.31–33). If one becomes sealed off from the "cold morning air" in "The Dead"—recalled in the *Wake* with the chilly terms "hail[y]" and "icy"—then one cannot hear the song "The Holly and the Ivy." One cannot be kissed under the mistletoe if one is wearing a "balladproof" vest, for it protects from kisses and "missle throes." One must run the risk of death, for as McHugh points out, the Norse god Balder was killed by thrown mistletoe. And yet in Joyce's fictional world, if there is not a sundering, there cannot be a reconciliation. If one does not die, one cannot be reborn. The Fall in the Garden of Eden—which means men cannot speak directly and thus must tell lies—is recovered by the Annunciation and brings the birth of the Word at Christmastime. As ALP tells us: "I wrote me hopes and buried the page when I heard Thy voice" and "left it to lie till a kissmiss coming" (*FW* 624.4–6). What awakens the sleeping beauty that resides within the sealed-off self—which is comparable to a maiden who has been lying (asleep) as well as lying (making up fictions)—is the one who kiss[es] [the] miss.

Bringing the story of Persephone full circle in the *Wake* involves recognizing that the Fall, which is about loss and thus grief, teaches a vital lesson. Persephone's eating of pomegranate, like Eve's eating of the apple, lands humanity in winter. As Joyce explores in "The Dead," *Portrait*, *Ulysses*, and *Finnegans Wake*, the season of death with its hail and ice and piercing air is painful but also, paradoxically, vital. When the "original hen" of the *Wake* begins digging up the letter out of the dump of culture, Joyce sets the scene in winter: it appears to be a day in "bleak Janiveer" (*FW* 112.26); thus it is "Midwinter [. . .] an iceclad shiverer" (*FW* 110.22–24). Humanity is in the throes of the season of death when suddenly the hen discovers "literature" (*FW* 112.27).

Persephone/Eve opens humanity to the piercing of death, and Demeter/Mary heals the wound, returning the rebirth of spring to humanity. The Annunciation motif surfaces at the end of *Finnegans Wake*, superimposed on Zeus's ravishing Leda in the form of a swan:[34] "If I seen him bearing down on me now under whitespread wings like he'd come from Arkangels" (*FW* 628.9–10). Of course, Gabriel is the archangel who brings to Mary the Word, and yet here Mary is conflated with the pagan Leda. According to Joycean poetics, Leda opens herself to deflowering in order to bloom in the eternal garden, the world without end, created by art: "Leda, Lada, aflutter afraida, so does your girdle grow! Willed without writing, whorled without aimed" (*FW* 272.2–5). Joyce superimposes Leda on Mary, as suggested by the echo of the rhyme "Mary, Mary, quite contrary, how does your garden grow?" Earlier, in the "Anna Livia Plurabelle" chapter, Joyce links the ravishing of Leda with the act of writing: "And ere that again, leada, laida, all unraidy, too faint to buoy the fairiest rider, too frail to flirt with a cygnet's plume" (*FW* 204.9–11).

As recorded in McHugh's *Annotations to "Finnegans Wake,"* "cygnet" is a river's name; however, it is also a combination of the French "cygne" [swan] with the tag "et[te]," which is associated with Issy as Persephone. Joyce reinforces the link between the two maidens with the combination of pure language falling from the self as pure urine: "while poing her pee, pure and simple" (*FW* 204.12–13). The swan, of course, reminds one of Zeus's form as he ravishes Leda; however, with the addition of the term "plume," one is encouraged to think of the swan in terms of a writing instrument, like Shem's "quillbone" (*FW* 229.30). Moreover, in French there is a neat homonym between "cygne" [swan] and "signe" [sign]; and thus we may imagine that Leda's opening up to divine ravishment—paralleled with Adam and Eve's transgression of the sign—allows her to compose a swan's song [Le chant du cygne], or as Joyce has it, a "birdsong" (*FW* 204.13). Through death, the reading self ("cygne") writes his or her final masterpiece, thereby birthing the writing self ("signe"). Moreover, the swan of the passage evokes Marcel Proust's "Swann," who falls but is unable to resurrect himself by means of art. Joyce further alludes to Proust—an invalid almost all of his life—with "too faint" and "too frail." Moreover, Joyce specifies Proust's literary production with the phrase "a whole drove of maiden hawthorns blushing" (*FW* 204.19–20); hawthorns figure prominently in Proust's fascination with Gilberte in *Combray*.[35] Hence, ALP at this moment in her streaming life blends with "marcellewaved" (*FW* 204.23), the other modernist writer who composed a swan song for the reading self, who dies as Marcel, penning his last words in order to be reborn as the author of *A la recherche du temps perdu*, the "fairiest rider," both the gayest and fairest writer.

In the *Wake*'s final scene of divine ravishment—whether one reads it as Leda opening up to Zeus or as Mary opening the tympanum of her ear to God's announcement—the context points unmistakably to "The Dead" and to the discussion of art in "Scylla and Charybdis." Once again one is encouraged to connect ravishing and writing.

As McHugh records, the following passage alludes to the historical moment when the river Liffey froze in 1338. Winter is the zone of the death that we encounter every year as the ravished Persephone leaves her mother and descends into the world of the dead. ALP remembers: "And I'd lie as quiet as a moss. And one time you'd rush upon me, darkly roaring, like a great black shadow with a sheeny stare to perce me rawly. And I'd frozen up and pray for thawe" (*FW* 626.23–26). When the self becomes frozen, one cannot be ravished; life becomes rigid and static until it transforms into its own inverse and the living conduct their days like mere shadows: "One by one they were all becoming shades" (*D* 224). In this scene, comparable to the recurring Wakean figure of Leda, ALP recalls a ravishing pagan god like Zeus, although here he comes as a black swan upon the female figure. The fear that this figure will pierce her overlaps with her freezing up like a frigid lover, and yet she "pray[s] for thawe," which earlier in the *Wake* Joyce has linked to storytelling: "Thaw! The last word in stolentelling!" (*FW* 424.35).

I would like to read this passage one more time in the context of Stephen's aesthetic theory: "And one time you'd rush upon me, darkly roaring, like a great black shadow with a sheeny stare to perce me rawly." While the Dublin literati discuss Shakespeare in the library, Bloom arrives seeking information for the Alexander Keyes ad. Buck Mulligan rudely identifies Bloom as "The Sheeny!" (*U* 165.605); Mulligan then tells of how he saw Bloom checking out the rear anatomy of the pagan statues at the museum and concludes his tale by implying that Bloom may well ravish Stephen Dedalus: "—He knows you. He knows your old fellow. O, I fear me, he is Greeker than the Greeks. His pale Galilean eyes were upon her mesial groove. Venus Kallipyge. O, the thunder of those loins! *The god pursuing the maiden hid*" (*U* 165.614–17). Buck's joke implies a homosexual ravishing, but Joyce's larger frame of reference suggests that the ravishing refers in a significant way to his ideas about art, for Buck calls Bloom "pale Galilean," and this phrase is taken from Swinburne's "Hymn to Proserpine."[36] One anticipates some kind of a fall.

One tends to think that Private Carr delivers the blow that topples Stephen; however, perhaps it is more significantly Bloom who brings about Stephen's fall, for it is his "sheeny stare" that pierces Stephen rawly. As he often seems to with Buck Mulligan, Joyce transforms Buck's joking and mocking slights into key elements of his literary production so that the author has the last laugh. Leopold Bloom ravishes Stephen Dedalus, but not in a sexual way; he ravishes him with kindness and thereby opens up the artist-in-progress to unexpected feelings. As Stephen himself has argued, the one who falls is the one who may well produce like Shakespeare, or as the "Ballad of Persse O'Reilly" has it, one may produce like: "Suffoclose! Shikespower! Seudodanto! Anonymoses!" (*FW* 47.19). Bloom sunders the defenses that have kept Stephen sealed up. And as Stephen himself argues, such ravishing is vital to the artistic process. In the "Cyclops" episode, Bloom's "sheeny stare" is described with different terms as a "cod's eye" (*U* 249.410). In the *Wake*, Hosty Frosty (a signifier for winter) sings the ballad of Persse O'Reilly (*FW* 45.25); at one point he compares him to a cod: "(Chorus) A Norwegian camel old cod. / He is, begod" (*FW* 46.22–23). The fishy qualities of Bloom and Persse O'Reilly, their capacity for piercing—whether with their stares or with their entries into the ear—parallel them and demonstrate Joyce's ongoing concern with the theme of ravishing the frozen self so that it may thaw.

With the needle of his "sewingmachine" (*FW* 626.15), Joyce stitches together a "langscape" (*FW* 595.4), but his work as a tailor/teller uses the needle to prick (needless to say, the pun is intended) his readers, putting them to sleep like the fairy-tale princess Sleeping Beauty: "That was the prick of the spindle to me that gave me the keys to dreamland" (*FW* 615. 27–28). What awakens Sleeping Beauty in the fairy tale is a kiss, and in the "Nightlesson," Issy claims to have this power: "there's a key in my kiss" (*FW* 279.F1). Joyce asserts at the end of the *Wake* that he has given us, his readers, the keys: "The keys to. Given!" (*FW* 628, 15). Thus we too are pierced, kissed, and awakened by the cyclical yarn he spins. One of the best-known features of both Stephen Dedalus and Leopold Bloom is that they are without keys. *Finnegans Wake* implies that they regain the keys in sleep. In the *Wake*, Joyce suggests that it is the vulnerability of sleep and dream—during which the self is truly exposed to penetration, out of one's control—that is the quality that allows one to gain the keys.[37] And one may well assume that these keys open up the self to ballads, bullets, animal horns, to dreamland and to piercing mourning air. Joyce puns in the *Wake* on latch keys and musical keys: "Dublin's all adin. We'll sing a song of Singlemonth and you'll too and you'll. Here are notes. There's the key" (*FW* 236.10–11). Thus there are at least two levels on which the "keys" Joyce has given us in *Finnegans Wake* open up the "balladproof" self.

Nothing opens a person up as blatantly as sex. The pagan ravishment of Persephone and the biblical seduction of Eve incorporate the erotic in telling ways.[38] Joyce's sexual reading of these myths is distinct and provocative, because he fundamentally connects the Fall into carnal knowledge with the attainment of independent learning.[39] In *Finnegans Wake*, Joyce presents an alternative education, one that extols the benefits of spending time with fallen women and listening to Siren song. Thus, Joyce elaborates Dante's nautical metaphor and entwines it with education, tale telling, and the spell of the Siren: "Dogging you round cove and haven and teaching me the perts of speech. If you spun your yarns to him on the swishbarque waves I was spelling my yearns to her over cottage cake" (*FW* 620.33–36). Joyce here alludes to a Dantean "langscape," one that is both sea and "h[e]aven." Moreover, Dante imagines his readers following the great seagoing ship of his poem in a "piccioletta barca" [little bark] (*Par.* 2.1–3), echoed here by Joyce's "swishbarque." As I have noted, Dante's poetic ship "singing makes her way," much like an intertextual Siren. And in the above-quoted passage, Joyce has ALP casting a spell of desires, what one yearns for, while the one being addressed sounds like a teacher of language and a spinner of tales, echoing a sailor who returns from adventures at sea. Earlier in the *Wake*, Joyce develops his ideas on Siren song in order to further his exploration of the opening up of the self, specifically in this instance through sexuality.

In a passage that evokes being deflowered by love or death, the intertextual Siren, Virgil, surfaces singing: "And the greater the patrarc the / griefer the pinch. And that's what your doctor / knows. O love it is the commonknounest thing / how it pashes the plutous and the paupe" (*FW* 269.24–27). In this passage of the "Nightlesson," Joyce signals "Pluto"—the Roman version of Dis—with "plutous" in a sentence that brings together the pagan story of the fall with the Christian version. However, Joyce focuses not on Eve but on the earthly representative of God and tantalizes his readers with the notion of the pope's or "paupe's" dallying with "love." Referring his readers to a well-known canto of the *Commedia*, Joyce charges this passage with the sexual/textual story of Paolo and Francesca, who tell the pilgrim they were seduced by a book.

As the canto is well known, I will supply only a brief summary of the relevant features.[40] The couple, Francesca, a married woman, and her brother-in-law, Paolo, are reading the story of Lancelot and Guinevere. The fateful moment in which the adulterous knight kisses the queen is simply too much for the amorous pair, who begin their own adulterous relationship; they are seduced by the book, which Francesca labels a "pander." Francesca is shot by her husband, and the two lovers are buffeted about in Dante's Hell with other lustful shades (*Inf.* 5). In the passage from the "Nightlesson" quoted above—which reminds readers that Virgil is Dante's teacher of rhetoric—Joyce transcribes the Italian "dottore" [teacher] as "doctor" in a telling reference to the literary lovers of Dante's *Inferno*. Joyce connects the story of Paolo and Francesca with the ravishing of Persephone and with the seductive, influential Siren song of teacher Virgil.

Joyce has connected Francesca previously with the image of a Siren in *Portrait*. Stephen likens the birdgirl, who fuels his initiatory launch into art, to a crane and a dove: "Her long slender bare legs were delicate as a crane's and pure save where an emerald trail of seaweed had fashioned itself as a sign upon the flesh." Further developing the simile, he writes: "Her bosom was as a bird's soft and slight, slight and soft as the breast of some darkplumaged dove" (*P* 171). In the Paolo and Francesca canto, Dante also refers to both cranes and doves (*Inf.* 5.46, 82). In *Ulysses*, the lure of the Siren—who, according to Ovid's account, is part bird, part girl—reappears, blended with the seduction of the sea: "Under the upswelling tide he saw the writhing weeds lift languidly and sway reluctant arms, hising up their petticoats, in whispering water swaying and upturning coy silver fronds. Day by day: night by night: lifted, flooded and let fall" (*U* 41.461–64). Stephen's musing brings together Siren imagery with a vision of Icarus, who "lifted" on mechanical wings, was "flooded" by his father's invention, and was "let fall."

In the *Wake*, Joyce again turns to the seductive book of Paolo and Francesca; he entwines their story with the erotic education offered by Abelard to Heloise: "Still he'd be good tutor two in his big armschair lerningstoel and she be waxen in his hands. Turning up and fingering over the most dantellising peaches in the lingerous longerous book of the dark.

Look at this passage about Galilleotto! I know it is difficult but when your goche I go dead" (*FW* 251.21–26). Joyce links this medieval account of a tutor seducing his pupil to the seduction in the Garden of Eden, where the teacher is in fact a "toucher": "since Headmaster Adam became Eva Harte's toucher" (*FW* 251.28–29). The tale of Lancelot and Guinevere, which Francesca calls a "Galeotto," recurs here and reminds us that literature may well function as a pander.

Joyce's "peaches" carry an echo of the French pun "peches" [sins]/ "peches" [peaches], which is reinforced by the echo of "tantalizing" in "dantellising," and thus he brings together the idea of sinning—of stumbling off the straight road into the dark wood—with the erotic and hence the pagan and Christian myths of the Fall.[41] Granted, this kind of sundering is a little more serious than bad manners; nonetheless, Joyce comically implies that both sins may result in a near-death of the soul: "when your goche I go dead." When Joyce refers to the intertextual Siren Dante, who educated him in various ways or led him astray along various routes, he succinctly conveys the initiatory pattern of intertextual reversal, for just as Virgil becomes a character on the stage of Dante's poem, Joyce here writes Dante: "dante [. . .] i sing."

The play on Dante's name—"dantellising"—suggests "dentelle," the French term for lace, and thus signals the association drawn in the *Wake* between weaving and song.[42] The Ovidian myth of Philomela has particular bearing on this link, because once again this is a tale of metamorphosis that begins in a rape and ends in the girl transforming into a nightingale, an appropriate bird for the *Wake* considering its connection to the night (6.175–83). Philomela is raped and her tongue is cut out so that she cannot tell her sister of the violation done to her by her brother-in-law. She communicates the trauma by weaving the story in a tapestry. Joyce puts the transformation from grief and trauma into woven form: "as wapt from wept" (*FW* 34.24). As one of Joyce's letters recounts, Nora suffered a traumatic sexual experience as an adolescent at the hands of a so-called teacher: "One night at tea [the curate] took her on his lap and said he liked her, she was a nice little girl. Then he put his hand up under her dress which was shortish. She however, I understand, broke away. Afterwards he told her to say in confession it was a man not a priest did 'that' to her" (*Letters* 2.72). The whole point of course is that he is *not* only a man who tries to seduce an unwilling girl; his position is that of a teacher, a shepherd of the flock, a model, a guide. Joyce translates the event into Wakese: "Sweetstaker, Abel lord or all our haloease, we (to be slightly more femmiliar perhips than is slickly more then nacessory), toutes philomelas as well as magdelenes, were drawpairs with two pinmarks" (*FW* 237.34–238.1). Joyce alludes once again to Abelard and Heloise and thus to their erotic educational encounter. Joyce refers to Philomela as another version of the fall of Persephone and Eve and brings this pagan tale of metamorphosis together with the Christian one of Mary Magdalen, the ultimate fallen woman. Likewise, appropriately in the "Nightlesson," Joyce has "Ovid. / Adam, Eve" brought together in one of the marginal notes (*FW* 306.L). In Leonard Barkan's book on Ovid, he discusses the myth of Philomela in terms applicable to Joyce's *Wake*, for he argues that the metamorphosis results from the hero's and heroine's "rebellion" against "rigid categories of family and society." Barkan explains that "once categories are attacked, similar things are diversified into opposites and opposites are made identical."[43] Nora's actual experience is offensive; however, Joyce transforms its meaning so that the breaking of rules, rebelling against categories, can itself become the potent teacher. The theme of piercing—the body erotically, the fabric socially, the self mythologically—occurs by means of these female figures who are "drawpairs with two pinmarks."

The kind of death one undergoes in being seduced by the Dantean intertext is to plunge into the sea as though following Siren song: "her pupils swimmed to heavenlies, let his be exaspirated, letters be blowed!" (*FW* 251.30–31). The "pupils" are schoolchildren, as well as eyes, which compare to those of Beatrice as she trains them on Heaven. The pilgrim gazes into her eyes at the outset of *Paradiso*, likens himself to Glaucus, and famously transcends humanity (*Par.* 1.64–72). The plunge into a deathlike baptism at sea is exactly what births sign making; or, as Dante describes it, God breathes in "spira" (the self-reflective soul)—echoed in Joyce's "exaspirated"—thus transforming the embryo into a speaker: "Letters be blowed!" In his passage about the seductive Siren song of the *Commedia*, Joyce singles out *Purgatorio* 25 and its discourse on the embryo. He suggests that Dante's exasperating, influential sea of Heaven causes the poet-in-progress to swim in Heaven- lies. After the Fall, after the loss of direct communication with the divine, the way one swims to heaven is by telling lies, writing fiction.

It would appear that one must return, go back, travel into the past in order to bring one's two selves together. The return takes one all the way back to the womb: "Pale bellies our mild cure, back and streaky ninepace" (*FW* 618.7). In his talking cure—"teaching me the perts of speech" (*FW* 620.33)—Joyce puts us through the nine paces of embryological development whose phases function as an analogue for the developing articulate self. As one acquires language, one's vital early memories are lost; those memories resemble an inarticulate self who accompanies one like a ghost or a recurring dream through one's waking life. The self that cannot speak—whether it is the self overcome with emotion, or the infant self, or the unconscious self, or the self full of memories that have slipped beyond the boundary of recollection—becomes a speaker in *Finnegans Wake*. Joyce's portmanteau term "daydreamsed" (*FW* 615.24) captures this overlapping zone of the unspeakable and the articulate. The daydream becomes the speaker: "daydream said." The way Joyce has constructed the term also alludes to a former time, for tacking on "ed" at the end of "daydreamsed" operates as a signifier for the past, and as we realize on every Joycean page, "the past pulls" (*FW* 594.26).

Joyce constructs the bringing together of the mute self and the speaking self as a return to "paladays last" (*FW* 615.25). The *Wake* takes one back to the "days" when the inarticulate and the articulate were "pals," when both of them were part of the "I": "Thi is Mi" (*FW* 607.19). In this paradoxical return to paradise through art, "The silence speaks the scene" (*FW* 13.2–3). The communion in the self is achieved through creative recollection, and thus one discovers in reading the *Wake* that "we've [always] lived in two worlds" (*FW* 619.11). However, it takes art, a *Commedia* or a *Finnegans Wake*, to bring these two usually separate realms into dialogue so that "life wends and the dombs spake" (*FW* 595.1–2). And it is the creative writer, Shem the Penman, who gives life to the silent selves within: "He lifts the lifewand and the dumb speak" (*FW* 195.5).

In the "Nightlesson," directly after the reference to Proserpina and her myth of the Fall and its impact on language, light floods the scene, and the silent self finds a voice, or as the *Wake* has it: "Where flash becomes word and silents selfloud" (*FW* 267.17). The conclusion to the *Commedia* describes a comparable transformation of the self into a creative writer. In a flash of light the talking pilgrim becomes dead silent, and the voice of the poem is born: Dante is silent and "selfloud" at the same time (*Par.* 33.139–41).

Finnegans Wake teaches that one needs to learn the language of the Sibyl if one is to read the oracular leaves she has scattered through the universe: "So mag this sybilette be our shibboleth that we may syllable her well!" (*FW* 267.20–21). In order for the writer-in-progress to become a speaker of the language of the combined Proserpina/Sibyl—which is brought together with the characteristic "ette" ending used previously in the same passage, "Proserpronette" (*FW* 267. 11)—it would appear that the writer-in-progress must put the syllables together him/herself. At the end of his poem, Dante claims that his vision of love is what binds the scattered Sibyl's messages into one volume:

Qual è colui che somniando vede,
   E dopo il sogno la passione impressa
   Rimane, e l'altro alla mente non riede;
Cotal son io, chè quasi tutta cessa
   Mia visione, ed ancor mi distilla
   Nel cor lo dolce che nacque da essa.
Così la neve al sol si disigilla,

Così al vento nelle foglie lievi
Si perdea la sentenza di Sibilla.

[From that moment my vision was greater than our speech, which fails at such a sight, and memory too fails at such excess. Like him that sees in a dream and after the dream the passion wrought by it remains and the rest returns not to his mind, such am I; for my vision almost wholly fades, and still there drops within my heart the sweetness that was born of it. Thus the snow loses its imprint in the sun; thus in the wind on the light leaves the Sibyl's oracle was lost.] (*Par.* 33.58–66)[44]

At the end of the "Nightlesson," Joyce has Issy—the maiden comparable to Persephone and Eve—offer in a concise footnote the pilgrim's final dreamlike experience in which he encounters God at the end of the poem: "Something happened that time I was asleep, torn letters or was there snow?" (*FW* 307.F5). Issy links the vision of the divine Creator to her own role as the alluring maiden in the meadow who must be the one to fall: "at that time of the dream and it was a very wrong thing to do, even under the dark flush of night, dare all grandpassia!" (*FW* 527.6–8).

The ravishing and ravished maiden is the one who holds the key to the realm of sleep, dream, death, and rebirth. In initiatory texts, memory and speech fail the dreamer, whose recollection compares to melting snow and oracular letters torn and tossed by the wind. And therefore the artist must tell a heavenly lie about an experience that is beyond recollection, for it took place in the womb and can only be dreamed about and reconciled with the waking self by means of creative writing.

ABBREVIATIONS

Conv. Dante, *Convivio.* Italian quotations from this work are from the Cudini edition (Milan: Garzanti, 1980). English translations are from *The Banquet,* translated by Christopher Ryan (Saratoga, Calif.: Anma Libri, 1989). Citations refer to book, chapter, and line numbers.

FW James Joyce, *Finnegans Wake* (New York: Penguin, 1976). Citations refer to page and line numbers.

Inf./Purg./Par. Dante, *La Divina Commedia.* In the Dante Panel of this book, all of the Italian quotations from the *Commedia* and their English translations are from *The Divine Comedy,* translated by John D. Sinclair. In the Joyce Panel of this book, all of the Italian quotations from the *Commedia* are from the Camerini edition that Joyce used (Milan: E. Sonzogno, 1904); the English translations of those quotations are from the Sinclair edition. Translations of Camerini's notes are my own. Citations refer to the canticle (*Inferno/Purgatorio/Paradiso*), followed by the canto and line numbers.

Letters James Joyce, *Letters of James Joyce*, vol. 1, ed. Stuart Gilbert (New York: Viking, 1966); vols. 2 and 3, ed. Richard Ellmann (New York: Viking, 1964). Citations refer to volume and page numbers.

P James Joyce, *A Portrait of the Artist as a Young Man*, ed. Chester Anderson and Richard Ellmann (New York: Viking, 1964).

SH James Joyce, *Stephen Hero*, ed. John J. Slocum and Herbert Cahoon (New York: New Directions, 1963).

U James Joyce, *Ulysses*, ed. Hans Walter Gabler (London: Penguin, 1986). Citations refer to page and line numbers.

VN Dante, *La Vita Nuova*. Italian quotations from this work, unless otherwise noted, are taken from the Berardinelli edition (Milan: Garzanti, 1989). English translations, unless otherwise noted, are from *La Vita Nuova (Poems of Youth)*, translated by Barbara Reynolds (London: Penguin, 1969). Citations refer to chapter and page numbers.

Notes

1. Weir expresses the sea change that occurs as "Stephen Dedalus becomes SD, the paradigm of the codes of his articulation" (27).

2. In *Finnegans Wake*, Joyce has literary arms that are charged with Virgilian power: "O, felicious coolpose! If all the MacCrawls would only handle virgils like Armsworks, Limited!" (*FW* 618.1–2).

3. Weir 16.

4. Rabaté 97.

5. For a different reading, see Reynolds (*Joyce and Dante* 99).

6. Noon 65.

7. R. Ellmann, *James Joyce* 544.

8. R. Ellmann, *James Joyce* 23.

9. Benstock 596–97.

10. Swinburne 1514.

11. Friedman writes that "[f]or Stephen, the sea images the dual aspect of his mother and his feelings for her. She is both 'a great sweet mother' and the green bile she vomits" (170). I think it is important to distinguish between Buck's reading of the sea as the "great sweet mother" and Stephen's reading of this same sea as a brutal image of his dying mother's vomit.

12. For an insightful and detailed analysis of "cribbing" in *Ulysses*, see Osteen (237–49).

13. In a letter to Stanislaus, Joyce reveals the ambiguity and hypocrisy of Gogarty (the model for Buck Mulligan) taking on the heroic role of saving drowning men: "Gogarty would jump into the Liffey to save a man's life but he seems to have little hesitation in condemning generations to servitude" (*Letters* 2.148).

14. R. Ellmann, *Liffey* 11.

15. Reynolds, *Joyce and Dante* 145.

16. Blamires 208.

17. R. Ellmann, *Liffey* 147.

18. Bowen supports this view (*"Ulysses" as a Comic Novel* 122); however, he cautions: "If Bloom is initially Stephen's Virgil in the beginning, the novel becomes Bloom's comic spiritual biography somewhere in the final episodes" (121). For a brilliant discussion of androgyny as it relates to Dante and Joyce, see Boldrini (*Literary Relations* 181–86).

19. Knowles, "That Form Endearing" 218–19.

20. The translation of Joyce's letter, which was written in French, is by Christopher Middleton.

21. In *Ulysses*, words may well wound or inspire the heart: "Stephen, shielding the gaping wounds which the words had left in his heart" (*U* 8.216–17); Joyce writes to Nora: "*I know* and *feel* that if I am to write anything fine or noble in the future I shall do so only by listening at the doors of your heart" (*Letters* 2.254).

22. S. Joyce 112.

23. McCarthy, *Riddles* 46.

24. Gifford n. 2. 88–89. p. 32.

25. Wheatley-Lovoy argues that what opens up the closed-off Gabriel are "songs and music" (189).

26. My reading of "The Lass of Aughrim" depends a great deal on Cheng's interpretation (*Joyce, Race, and Empire* 143).

27. Leonard, *Reading "Dubliners" Again* 308.

28. Leonard, *Reading "Dubliners" Again* 295. Cheng concentrates on Gabriel's education and also its implications (*Joyce, Race, and Empire* 139).

29. See R. Ellmann's note 4 in Joyce's *Letters* (2.240).

30. Solomon 16.

31. In *Finnegans Wake*, Joyce rewrites this scene, which reinforces the connection between this letter in "The Dead" and the letter of the *Wake*. Benstock reveals that again the theme of getting wet versus being showerproof is in play (597). Once again at breakfast, the letter is pierced by a professor's fork (*FW* 124.9–10). Benstock writes that "[s]he is portrayed as a letter whose covering must be slit open and whose message is ravaged in order to be read. The destructive instrument is a fork [here Benstock has the sigla of Earwicker pointing down like the prongs of a fork] whose 'therrble prongs' (628.5) ALP fears" (604). I read these prongs as forceps, and thus the ravaging, ravishing, piercing of the letter all contribute to the rebirth of initiatory dynamics.

32. Senn argues the significance of the "rear" in Joyce's construction of the *Wake*; he maintains that the text moves "in reverse order, backward, arriving at the 'rear' end" ("Reading Exercise" 50). See Benstock for a different discussion of sexuality and textuality in *Finnegans Wake* that hones in on terms consistent with my reading: "penetrating"; reading as "a kind of rape"; "textual/sexual vulnerability" (607).

33. McCarthy, *"Ulysses": Portals* xiii.

34. Drawing on the work of Foucault and late-nineteenth-century pornography, Leonard analyzes the Zeus/Leda motif in terms of an attempted erotic initiation in "The Dead" ("Power, Pornography" 615–65).

35. Proust 152–53.

36. Gifford n. 9. 615. p. 228.

37. McHugh describes reading the *Wake* this way: "It can sometimes appear to be unreasonable nonsense whilst remaining utterly coherent for the reader who holds the key" (*"Finnegans Wake" Experience* 76).

38. Jager 115. Jager identifies other key figures, ranging from Clement of Alexandria to Freud, who have written on the correspondence between Eve and Proserpina's fall (278). Although my focus is on his use of the Dantean intertext, Joyce may well have further developed his theme from other sources.

39. Van Boheemen analyzes Stephen's "penetration" in the scene with the prostitute and discusses in compelling terms Joyce's "rewriting of the scene of sexual initiation" (28).

40. Atherton notes Joyce's allusion to the canto and the way in which he manipulates it (80–81). Reynolds discusses in greater depth *Inferno* 5 and concludes that Joyce treats the Paolo and Francesca story in terms of a teacher seducing a student (*Joyce and Dante* 216).

41. Polhemus has produced a fascinating account of the "Peaches and Daddy Browning" scandal from the 1920s, which he argues greatly impacted Joyce and his writing of the *Wake*. For my purposes, what makes the article compelling is Polhemus's analysis of Joyce and his daughter: "Unconsciously or consciously, he used Peaches to offset and give perspective to the plight of the schizophrenic, multi-voiced Lucia and to his own murky guilt about her and what he came to feel was her sacrificial, Iphigenia-like relationship to the *Wake* and its 'crazy' language" (78). Lucia parallels the figures (Persephone, Leda, Eve) that are ravished by the Creator, and I cannot help but wonder if her name—meaning "light"—influences the initiatory passages in which a loss occurs on the biological level, and yet a literary illumination of value takes place.

42. Joyce uses the term "rapsods" (*FW* 43.34) to bring weaving, song, and intertextuality together, for the Latin term "rhapsodia" originates from the Greek "rhaptein," meaning to string or stitch together. Joyce adds to this linguistic layer the connotations of the *Wake*'s dream: "watching her sewing a dream together" (*FW* 28.6–7).

43. Barkan 58–59. McCarthy makes a similar point regarding the *Wake*'s riddles: "Like the solved puzzle, incest brings together elements doomed to remain separate: the son marries the mother, the brother marries the sister, *in the same way in which the answer succeeds, against all expectations, in getting back to its question*" (*Riddles* 28). Focused on Ovid in the *Wake*, Senn concludes that "most transformations are the consequence of transgressions" ("Ovid's Not-yet-icity" 402).

44. Joyce himself produced his fiction in ways that recall the oracles of the Sibyl; as he explains in a letter: "I make notes on stray bits of paper which I then forget in the most unlikely places, in books, under ornaments and in my pockets and on the back of advertisements" (*Letters* 3.415).

NEIL MURPHY

James Joyce's Dubliners *and Modernist Doubt: The Making of a Tradition*

As early as 1901, in a letter to Henrik Ibsen, the young Joyce indicated that the specific focus of his admiration was Ibsen's 'lofty impersonal power',[1] suggesting recognition of a quality that later came to be synonymous with Joyce's own mature fiction and became a subject of much interest to the major modernist poets. That Joyce was already formulating an aesthetic sense that was to be central to high modernism, prior even to his writing of the stories of *Dubliners*, is revealing. This essay seeks to illustrate that the epistemological crisis that dominates modernism is already implicit in Joyce's *Dubliners*, as well the ways in which this crisis has proven influential to several major contemporary Irish writers.

Theorists of modernism have tended to place *A Portrait of the Artist as a Young Man* at the beginning of their exploration of Joyce's modernity, largely ignoring *Dubliners*. Randall Stevenson, for example, in *Modernist Fiction*, claims that the stories are 'fairly conventional in their realistic, sometimes satiric, portrayal of drab lives in a city Joyce shows suffering from paralysis of will, energy and imagination', although he concedes that the narratives are 'focused around the minds and inward experiences', without offering further clarification.[2] There are, however, a few notable exceptions. David Daiches suggests that the stories of *Dubliners* are 'realistic in a certain sense' but insists that only 'The Dead' 'stands apart from the others', because only this

From *A New & Complex Sensation: Essays on Joyce's* Dubliners, edited by Oona Frawley. © 2004 by the Lilliput Press and individual contributors.

story 'implies comment' on the part of the author.[3] Peter Childs goes further in his listing of what he views to be *Dubliners'* modernist characteristics: 'uncertainty, particularly in the stories' endings, symbolism, linguistic intensity, an aesthetic rather than a moral focus, linguistic experimentation, a drive to throw off the old in favour of the new, and an interest in the internal workings of the individual mind as much as a shared external reality'.[4] Childs too, however, insists that only 'The Dead' 'approaches a Modernist form', an aberration explained by the story not having been a part of the original collection. Here Childs oversimplifies Joyce's sense of form and doesn't consider the revisions that Joyce made to the stories while he was working simultaneously on *Portrait* and 'The Dead'; Childs also fails to note that 'Two Gallants' and 'A Little Cloud' were themselves late inclusions to *Dubliners*.

Joyce, Ellmann has claimed (with regard to the effaced narration used in 'The Sisters'), 'cradles here the technique which has now become a commonplace of modern fiction';[5] but Joyce's realism, which *Dubliners* certainly reflects, is not merely infused with the early rumblings of modernism. Indeed, as I will argue, Joyce's *Dubliners* manages to retain and reconstitute its realist impulses while engaging with modernist themes that become prominent enough that the collection can be seen as a modernist text in its own right, embracing and inventing a host of narrative techniques central to modernist fiction thereafter. As a consequence, one is forced to reconsider the relationship between modernism and Irish literature. Rather than view the work of Joyce as having been 'accommodated within the tradition of English or British literature, international Modernism, the plight of humankind in the twentieth century', as Seamus Deane has bitterly complained,[6] one can argue that Joyce's work represents a significant early contribution to modernist fiction.

BEYOND REALISM: TOWARDS AN AESTHETICS OF MODERNISM

Both Kearney and McHale have written extensively about what they respectively see as the 'critical narratives of self-questioning' that underpin the Irish critical tradition[7] and the 'epistemological dominant' of modernist literature.[8] Kearney defines a crisis brought about by modernist dissatisfaction with the traditional novel form and then indicates some of the ways in which the second generation writers of his critical tradition (Higgins, Banville, McGahern, Jordan) have responded to Joyce, Beckett and Flann O'Brien: 'their writing becomes self-reflexive as it explores fundamental tensions between imagination and memory, narration and history, self and language. In short . . . these authors share, with Joyce and Beckett, the basic modernist project of transforming the traditional narrative of quest into a critical narrative of self-questioning'.[9] The radical self-questioning that produces such writing 'is at all times fundamentally problematic',[10] in that the work, written in the spirit of modernist epistemological doubt, generates a poetics dominated by the problems of knowing and communicating.[11]

The isolation of epistemological doubt or 'self-questioning' as the central characteristic of modernist literature has significant consequences for *Dubliners*, because, initially at least, the realist impetus of the stories does not seem to accommodate epistemological doubt. Even the essentially self-reflexive *Portrait*, long considered an example of an early modernist text, retains a traditional quest motif, in the sense that the novel charts the aesthetic and intellectual journey of the protagonist, culminating in an unambiguous resolution. In this *Portrait*'s ending significantly differs from the higher levels of ambiguity that one discovers in *Ulysses*. *Dubliners* too nominally retains a quest motif, but significantly alters its structure to contain many modernist elements. These elements are evident in the text's repeated use of ambiguity and ambiguous closure; in the treatment of time and spatial form; in the narrative technique's reflection of social paralysis; in the precise nature of the epiphanic 'knowledge' that is typically gained; in the frequent use of ellipses; and in what Rabaté terms the 'problematics of silence' apparent in many of the stories.[12]

The opening first person narratives of 'The Sisters', 'An Encounter' and 'Araby' all conclude in resounding ambiguity. A quality of mystery, insecure meaning and uncertainty characterizes each story; and the repeated use of ellipses at crucial moments in 'The Sisters' generates a sense of incompletion. Old Cotter, for example, assures us from the outset that he will tell us his 'opinion' (*D* 10) about Father Flynn, but never does so, instead faltering into digression, ellipses and silence. Nevertheless, in the three opening stories, the first person narrators are all forced into an extremely vivid sense of awareness that reconstitutes the nature of their relationship with their world. However, while the epiphanies are certainly foregrounded in each story, as in the conclusion to 'Araby' when the narrator gazes 'up into the darkness' and sees himself 'driven and derided by vanity' (*D* 35), the precise logic that accompanies these discoveries is never made explicit and we can infer meaning from the stories' conclusion with only limited certainty.

Joyce's use of the effaced narrator from the third story onwards further emphasizes the absence of declared meaning. Stephen Dedalus was to declare his aesthetic belief in the refinement 'out of existence' of the personality of the artist (*P* 233),[13] and the stories of *Dubliners* are testament to the fact that the young Joyce was already constructing his narratives according to Stephen's principles. One of the consequences of the effaced narrator is the overwhelming sense of freedom of interpretation offered to the reader; in this Joyce's stories appear to embrace the multiplicity of potential meaning that consistently characterizes modern fiction. From 'Eveline' onwards, up to and including 'Grace', the stories refuse to concede finality of meaning and frequently project multiple meanings. One such instance is the sharing of the point of view between Mrs Mooney, Polly and Mr Doran in 'The Boarding House'. The rapidity of the juxtaposition ensures that the reader's sympathies are not allowed to rest on any one character, or to prioritize one 'version' above another. The conclusion to the story further emphasizes uncertainty by allowing us access to Polly's private reverie, remarkable in that she temporarily escapes from her dubious anxiety, forgetting the empirical world and erasing the actual landscape from her consciousness. Polly retreats, in effect, from the proper material of the realist text: 'she no longer saw the white pillows on which her gaze was fixed or remembered that she was waiting for anything' (D 68).

This essentially non-realist tactic is mirrored in the repeated authorial refusal to resolve the plots. We are never allowed access, for example, to what really happened to Father Flynn in 'The Sisters', just as Eveline's reasons for not leaving Dublin are never fully disclosed. This is evidence of epistemological uncertainty on the parts of individual characters as they struggle to make sense of themselves or their decision-making processes. Equally significant, however, is the aesthetic declaration that is implicit in the act of withholding information about the plotted events. Irresolution of plots and the attendant ambiguity draws the reader into the construction of meaning in a way that is rarely the case in realist fiction. If the fictional ontologies prove to be a locus of unmeaning, then the possibility of fixed interpretation dissolves.

'Eveline' exemplifies the use of free indirect style: the primary role of the narrator is to facilitate almost continuous access to Eveline's consciousness, without taking the leap into interior monologue. While free indirect style is not a specifically modernist technique, having been used extensively by Jane Austen and others, Joyce's particular application differs because he has us follow his unlikely heroine across multiple temporal zones, despite her spatial immobility. This results in a dislocation of temporal sequence and an extension of the traditional use of free indirect style. The temporal sequence is disrupted in a number of key ways, resulting in what Joseph Frank has called 'spatial form' in modern literature. This is effected by constructing what Frank names, based on his readings of Madame Bovary and Ulysses, a 'simultaneity of perception'.[14] Joyce's 'Eveline' reflects such a disruption of temporal sequence by juxtaposing the protagonist's memories and private reflections with external description of the room and the avenue. By repeatedly escaping from the present into other temporal zones, the narrative diminishes realism and effects a slowing of time, particularly in the first two-thirds of the story.

In addition, the story builds up a series of references and cross-references that, in Frank's words, 'relate to one another independently of the time-sequence of the narrative'.[15] Vidan argues that this type of temporal play produces spatiality, which is essentially at odds with sequentiality: 'The idea of spatial form is usually associated with . . . the recurrence and juxtaposition of verbal motifs, operative words, and key themes'.[16] These are precisely the effects achieved by the patterns of reference in 'Eveline', in, say, the alternative communicative force generated by the repeated references to 'dusty cretonne' (*D* 36, 39) or 'dust' (*D* 37). This type of resonance is established, too, between the promise Eveline has made to her mother and the 'promises made to Blessed Margaret Mary Alacoque' (who was associated with domestic security), as well as in the repeated seafaring or emigrant images that are finally underpinned by the avalanche of imagery associated with the sea and drowning in the final paragraphs. The physical locus of the story is also used to generate spatiality; throughout, the specific descriptive references to the avenue outside are imbued with a significance that mirrors the journey into mind that Eveline is undertaking. Initially, the evening 'invade[s]' (*D* 36) the avenue, and by the near-conclusion of the tale, the evening 'deepened in the avenue' (*D* 39). Of course, the avenue is also a focal point for her fond memories of childhood. The juxtaposition of references destabilizes temporal sequence, appropriate to a story in which the thematic centre revolves around time 'running out' (*D* 39). In fact, a central pattern of ideas relates to departures, or to those who have gone away, or to Eveline's own emigration, 'like the others' (*D* 37). This particular linkage of phrases and ideas is essentially in opposition to the temporal freezing that is generated by the spatial narrative and partially accounts for the temporal disorientation experienced by the reader.

'The Boarding House' similarly plays an extended temporal game with the reader. The first third of the story follows conventional temporal sequence, but the procession of time is severely compromised upon the mention of the 'little gilt clock' (*D* 64), which coincides with Mrs Mooney's decision to confront her lodger, Mr Doran. From this point until the end of the story, there are a series of references to time, and, in particular, to the specific moment—'seventeen minutes past eleven' (*D* 64)—at which Mrs Mooney's interior reflections begin, and to the near-exact time—'nearly the half-hour' (*D* 65)—at which she is ready to confront Doran. During the narratively compressed thirteen minutes, the reader is privy to a series of plans, reflections and general observations, all of which have a non-temporal life, separated as they are from the immediacy of the clock that we nevertheless know continues to unwind in the room. The point of view then switches to Doran, who polishes his glasses 'every two or three minutes' (*D* 65) and stews in the shortening time before he meets Polly's mother, while simultaneously worrying about the potential loss of his job (which, in a clever echo of the compressed thirteen minutes of deliberation we have just witnessed via the mind of Mrs Mooney, he has held for thirteen years) if the situation with Polly is publicized. The implicit contrast between these two temporal spaces has a disquieting effect on the reader; by the time access is allowed to Polly's point of view, one's ironic sense of the differing temporal possibilities is acute. Joyce's text then compounds the juxtaposed temporal variations by depicting Polly's private reverie in an arguably self-reflexive manner. Initially, Polly sits 'for a little time on the side of the bed' and then, swiftly, as her reverie deepens, she regards the pillows 'for a long time', and then, eventually, 'no longer' sees them (D 68). This rapid expansion and erosion of temporal experience can be interpreted as a Joycean commentary on what we have encountered in the story as a whole: a continual play on the varied, internalized temporal modes that can be experienced by the apprehending mind. The effect is significant, particularly in a text that depends so much on what Mrs Mooney and her daughter 'had been waiting for' (D 69). The story thus clearly echoes the modernist concern with the narrative mechanics of representing time, and the ways in which the mind alters and affects what one even means by time.

SILENCE AND THE EPISTEMOLOGICAL VOID

While such subversions—of various characters' grasp on meaning, of the ambiguous endings, as well as of the deliberate withholding of information in the stories—all significantly decentre meaning, there is also a recurring pattern of communicative breakdown and speechlessness in the stories. As Rabaté has convincingly illustrated, this finds expression in many distinct ways in *Dubliners*. The faltering into silence that we frequently encounter is but one of various kinds of silence in the stories. There are also many significant omissions or what Rabaté terms 'blank spaces' in the various plots, just as there are numerous examples of economy of information.[17]

The 'persistent silence' (D 63) that takes up residence in 'The Boarding House' has been present in the collection from the first story, 'The Sisters', in which the narrator is continually in a state of uncertainty as he attempts to assemble half-scraps of information. The story is punctuated by numerous references to muffed body language (pointing, nodding, walking on tiptoe), and muttering or murmuring in lieu of lucid speech. In addition, there are numerous references to non-speech: Eliza gazed into the grate 'without speaking' (D 17); 'A silence took possession of the little room' (D 17); the boy and his aunt 'waited respectfully for her to break the silence' (D 17); and, as the fiction moves towards finality, 'there was no sound in the house' (D 18). Knowledge and meaning, of whatever kind, exist in curious complicity with silence.

Silence also pervades in 'Eveline', in which the protagonist's 'silent fervent prayer' (*D* 41) predicts her final aphasia at the close. But Eveline is just one of many characters who register the incapacity of human expression in the collection and she, like the child narrator of 'The Sisters', may be viewed as a fledgling expression of the more sustained and dominant treatment of silence in 'The Dead'. Gabriel Conroy meets Lily's curt retort about men with averted eyes and without offering a response; Miss Ivors' political barracking is greeted with shocked silence, while the empty rhetoric of Gabriel's dinner speech is akin to epistemological silence. Gabriel also fails to hear the music that so spellbinds Gretta. These examples predict his general communicative incapacity in a story that closes with the sound of snow only 'faintly' heard.

Joyce's collection acts both as an acknowledgment of the frailty of human expression and as a demonstration of the power of silences as *acts of communication* in their own right. Or, as Rabaté puts it, 'Silence is not a mere symptom then, it defines the vanishing point of all assertion, exhibits the empty space which the writing of the text constantly re-covers and recovers, in its multiplication.'[18] The writing out of the epistemological and communicative lapses in human experience is itself an act of recovery, echoed perhaps in 'The Boarding House', in which Mrs Mooney and Polly inadvertently communicate in 'persistent silence'.

By the close of 'The Dead', the deep uncertainty that pervades Gabriel's consciousness has become overwhelming in its subversion of his grasp on the familiar aspects of his own life and self:

> His soul had approached that region where dwell the vast hosts of the dead. He was conscious of, but could not apprehend, their wayward and flickering existence. His own identity was fading out into a grey impalpable world: the solid world itself which these dead had one time reared and lived in was dissolving and dwindling. (*D* 223)

This epiphany is prompted by a series of destabilizing incidents throughout the evening and reaches a climax with the understanding that he has utterly misconstrued his relationship with his wife and, hence, his life. In this the author has universalized human epistemological failure and the closure of the final story not only registers Joyce's expression of fundamental doubt of the kind that characterizes modernism but also acts as a retrospective commentary on the assumptions with which many of the characters in the previous stories live.

The stories of *Dubliners* reflect an intellectual paralysis that Joyce's Dublin and its fictional inhabitants predict in modern, urbanized Europe. In its repeated depiction of communicative lapses and faltering silences,

Dubliners self-reflexively implies the limits of knowing and, ironically, the limits of many of the assumptions of realist fiction. Seamus Deane claims that *Dubliners*, through its 'registration of the detail of Dublin life, takes "realism" to the point of parody, because life becomes a kind of curious "inventory"'.[19] The realism that has for so long been viewed as the commanding generic force in Joyce's early fiction is thus a kind of wooden horse containing the seeds of modern parody, irony, ambiguity and a deep crisis of knowing. Joyce's 'realism' proves a useful way to speak of epistemological problems. That *Dubliners* doesn't look like modernist fiction in terms of its apparent lack of narrative experiment is itself a fictionalized illusion. Embedded in the carefully particularized settings and characters is, as we have seen, a range of quietly subversive elements that finally prevent resolution for readers as much as for the frail characters. In this, Joyce the modernist is everywhere evident in the stories.

DUBLINERS AND THE WRITERS OF THE COUNTER-TRADITION

The profound influence of Joyce's *Dubliners* on contemporary Irish writers is still evident, particularly in the work of those that Kearney includes in his 'second generation' of writers in the critical tradition: Aidan Higgins, John Banville and Neil Jordan. Each began his writing career with a collection of stories, and beyond this superficiality lies a shared responsiveness to the epistemological concerns that beset modernist writing in general. In attempting to discern patterns of connection among these contemporary fiction-makers and *Dubliners*, it is useful to consider the central focus on epistemological concerns, the representation of temporal and spatial zones and a registering of the distinctive quality of ambiguity.

According to Rüdiger Imhof, John Banville's first, and only, collection of stories, *Long Lankin*, is greatly indebted to *Dubliners*: 'the stories form groups which strikingly correspond to those in Joyce's collection: childhood, adolescence or early manhood, and maturity. The twin themes: the destruction of human happiness and the dissolution of a close relationship between two persons hold them together'.[20] While some of these may be tenuous assertions, Imhof is more accurate with his suggestion that Banville's 'The Possessed', the long final story in Banville's collection, was written in imitation of 'The Dead'.[21] Like Gabriel, Ben White attempts to discover the meaning of his own existence while attending a party of friends which, like the dinner party in 'The Dead', is followed by an epiphanic moment in the life of the previously deluded hero that heralds a climactic decision to go on a journey. In addition there is much talk of the significance of the past, and Ben is told by Livia that 'the dead can only touch us if we let them'.[22]

Molly Ivors' narrow, discordant nationalism in 'The Dead' is echoed by Colm in 'The Possessed', whose 'social conscience'[23] is presented as a disruptive force; Colm's association of frivolity with Englishness further intensifies the connection.

More significant, however, are the ways in which Banville repeatedly charts his characters' movement towards moments of epiphanic discovery, as in 'A Death', in which Stephen acquires 'strange clarity of vision and thought',[24] or in 'Sanctuary', in which Julie, 'in this new silence . . . seemed to hear vaguely someone screaming, a ghost voice familiar yet distant'.[25] Frequently, the epiphanic moment is closely associated with 'silence', and there is a continual play on music, and the inability to hear, similar to that which one finds in 'The Dead'. Banville's collection exhibits none of the technical versatility that is omnipresent in *Dubliners*, but it is nonetheless clear that Banville is attempting to work his way through a series of epistemological issues.

More closely reminiscent of Joyce's variation of temporal sequence, spatial form and general complexity of construction is Aidan Higgins' first collection of stories, *Felo De Se*. 'Killachter Meadow',[26] arguably the most accomplished story in the collection, recounts a series of vignettes plucked from the dull lives of the sisters Langrishe. Varied temporal zones commingle as pasts, present and drab imagined futures congeal to form the basis of the narrative space. The specificity of an exact temporal *now* is submerged beneath a multidimensional, indolent and directionless state that embraces the lives of the four sisters. This narrative spatiality is effected most convincingly in the closing stages of the story, when we are privy to Emily-May's Ophelia-like suicidal drift to death, a death about which we have been aware from the beginning:

> She passed through. Beyond March's bare trees she saw the sun hammering on the river: the water flowed by like a muscle, the summer returned, something turned over in Emily-May and she became young and voluptuous once more (she had never been either).[27]

Emily's mind wanders freely, seeing her sister Helen at once as a child and an adult, replete with unnerving adult disguises, so much so that when the final moment arrives, at the close of the story, one is left with the sense that her death actually occurred many years previously. This does not simply amount to analepsis and/or prolepsis: time zones are superimposed on one another to the point where the mind emerges as a receptacle of multiplicity and the very concept of a fixed present is undone.

Implicit in the narrative construction is the suggestion that the mind is anything but linear; in this Higgins' work echoes the Joycean layering of temporal zones in stories like 'The Boarding House', and may even clarify and/or extend the evocation of paralysis that one finds in *Dubliners*. Throughout *Felo De Se*, Higgins creates well-defined characters that suffer from credible human shortcomings, but the plots rarely remain within the confines of sequential narrative. Instead, the author creates spatial narratives within which the temporal sequence is subverted in order to painstakingly focus on vibrant moments. The consequence is that, as Patrick O'Neill claims, Higgins' characters typically 'emerge abruptly out of nowhere, are subjected to a portrait painter's penetrating scrutiny, and disappear again into the darkness from which they came'.[28] Hence their essentially plausible natures are subverted by the non-linear quality of their existence.

Higgins advances Joyce's 'paralysis' with a claustrophobic quality in the stories, achieved primarily by the author's use of intensely descriptive language. This has the effect of imbuing the characters' lives with a sense of immobility and narrow compression. The hazard of such stylistic construction is evident in the response of Roger Garfitt, who argues that 'the external world of experience is accurately perceived, but it is rendered into a dense, highly subjective linguistic structure, which becomes finally a bulwark against the experience itself. Reality is internalised.'[29] Garfitt's difficulty with Higgins' short fiction is similar to that experienced by readers of Joyce's *Dubliners*, in which the world is frequently filtered through a web of private thoughts and ambiguous meaning. In short, the fictional worlds that we encounter in both writers are shaped by the modernist emphasis on the shape of linguistic expression more than by the illusion of realist construction.

More recently, Neil Jordan has written of his early desire to write without being swamped in the language and mythology of Joyce: 'the only identity, at a cultural level, that I could forge was one that came from the worlds of television, popular music, cinema which I was experiencing daily'.[30] While on this level Jordan clearly found a personal utterance, the influence of his predecessor remains clear in his first collection of stories, *Night in Tunisia*. Like Joyce's, many of Jordan's stories deal with the difficulties and the oddness of everyday life. The need, for example, to feel authentic in a world that refuses to remain static fuels both 'Skin' and 'Outpatient': 'And she discovered to her surprise that she thirsted for pain and reality.'[31] The characters, like Joyce's, are not generally presented as social outsiders, and this is precisely where their strength lies. Because of the ordinariness of their lives they suggest a kind of universal social malaise.

Jordan's work too echoes the interrogative focus of modernist fiction when his narrators repeatedly question human modes of knowledge. The present is depicted as a complexity that challenges their capacity to comprehend, while the past represents an even more unyielding problem: 'She had been shrewish, he told himself as her memory grew dimmer, her hair had often remained unwashed for days . . . Thus he killed the memory of another her neatly.'[32] Jordan alters the past at will and his characters accept the foibles of memory as normal: 'As I remember you I define you, I choose bits of you and like a child with a colouring book, I fill you out.'[33] So too with Jordan's characters' communicative problems: 'She wondered about phrases, how they either retain the ghost of a meaning they once had, or grope towards a meaning they might have.'[34] The vague suggestiveness of these lines reveals little except the author's willingness to consider the possibility of another less exact significance to language.

In the title story, 'Night in Tunisia', Jordan constructs a narrative alternative to realism by generating a staccato of vignettes that resonate, with almost musical precision, in order to suggest the narrator's consciousness. Music acts as the central metaphor and becomes suggestive of human expression: 'He fashioned his mouth round the reed till the sounds he made became like a power of speech, a speech that his mouth was the vehicle for but that sprang from the knot of his stomach, the crook of his legs.'[35] Verbal communication is bypassed, and another kind of language emerges. Liberated from the demands of linguistic communication momentarily, the narrator comprehends his own self for the first time:

> He played later on the piano ... all the songs, the trivial mythologies whose significance he had never questioned ... as he played he began to forget the melodies of all those goodbyes and heartaches, letting his fingers take him where they wanted to, trying to imitate that sound like a river he had just heard.[36]

The natural man, long since named and invented by language, is restored and his frustration, so evident in the story, is somehow momentarily healed.

Equally revealing is Jordan's attempt to evade the linearity of sequential narrative. With 'Last Rites', the narrative continually shifts temporal focus: at an early stage the suicide victim's/narrator's body is discovered, after which we revert to the hours immediately preceding his suicide and accompany the narrator through his final hours. The effect is harrowing in its stark emphasis of the finality of the death of his consciousness. It also adds a powerful sense of pathos to the present, knowing, as we do, the finale. In addition, the story doesn't limit itself to the interior monologue of the narrator, offering us glimpses of the minds of the. other characters who too are showering, emphasizing not just the narrator's alienation but that of all the others.

Much more inventive is the technique used in 'Night in Tunisia', which conspires to communicate the protagonist's consciousness. The narrative voice is the only gelling agent for the diffusion of images and impressions as they imply the sheer complexity of experience. Images from the past, present and future mingle in the narrator's 'imagined place', particularly near the close. Only taken collectively is their suggestiveness revealed. There are no certainties here, no formalized fictional solutions for the chaos of experience. Jordan, like Joyce, tries to reinvent the rules to accommodate the relationship between his vision of life and the craft he uses, and central to this process is an inquiry into the ways in which we perceive and order experience, both on temporal and spatial levels. In this Jordan, like Banville and Higgins, makes a significant contribution to the tradition of epistemological questioning in contemporary Irish writing.

Beckett's diagnosis of 1931 that there was 'no communication because there are no vehicles of communication'[37] has clear implications for *Dubliners*, just as it does for the writers of Kearney's counter-tradition. Kearney's counter-tradition is significant in tracing an essentially non-realist tradition in Irish writing that questions the modes of human knowledge. That Joyce's *Dubliners* is a key early expression of this tradition is clear from the repeated evocations of ambiguity, the economy of information, the embracing of the potent metaphor of silence, the continuous investigation into the meaning of human communication, as well as from the sophisticated narrative arrangements of time and space. The early works of Banville, Higgins and Jordan all make significant contributions to Kearney's Irish counter-tradition, but it is a tradition that Joyce's *Dubliners* helped to initiate, particularly with regards to epistemological doubt. That Joyce was, as early as *Dubliners*, already in imaginative engagement and dialogue with both the early practitioners of, and precursors to, international modernist literature renders such national distinctions rather tenuous. Also ineffectual, however, is the notion that literary traditions born out of distinct, shared national cultures are without enormous significance. It is perhaps most fruitful to allow ourselves to view Joyce's resounding influence in terms of a tradition of epistemological doubt, both nationally and internationally: in addressing a work that is already so embracing of ambiguity, it is perhaps appropriate that we allow a commingling of the national and international to shape our focus, and embrace ambiguity ourselves.

NOTES

1. R. Ellmann, *James Joyce* (Oxford 1982), p. 86.
2. R. Stevenson, *Modernist Fiction: An Introduction* (Essex 1998), pp. 48–9. Other modernist critics who have marginalized *Dubliners* are Leon Surette, who doesn't mention *Dubliners* at all in his *The Birth of Modernism* (Quebec 1993), and M. Bradbury and J. McFarlane, whose authoritative *Modernism: A Guide to European Literature 1890–1930*

(London 1991) makes reference to Joyce's 'three major works', excluding *Dubliners* from consideration (p. 405). Even Ezra Pound, in '*Dubliners* & James Joyce' in *The Literary Essays of Ezra Pound* (Norfolk 1954) congratulated Joyce, the 'realist', for writing stories that give 'the thing as it is' (p. 399).

3. D. Daiches, *The Novel and the Modern World* (Chicago 1965), p. 66.

4. P. Childs, *Modernism* (London 2000), p. 200.

5. Ellmann, p. 84.

6. S. Deane, 'Introduction', *Nationalism, Colonialism and Literature: Essays by Terry Eagleton, Frederic Jameson, Edward Said* (Minnesota 1990), p. 11.

7. R. Kearney, *Transitions: Narratives in Irish Culture* (Dublin 1988), p. 83.

8. B. McHale, *Postmodernist Fiction* (London 1996), p. 6.

9. Kearney, p. 83.

10. R. Kearney, 'A crisis of imagination' in *The Crane Bag Book of Irish Studies* (Dublin 1982), p. 400.

11. McHale also characterizes modernist fiction as being 'dominated by epistemological issues' (p. xii).

12. J.M. Rabaté, 'Silence in *Dubliners*' in C. McCabe (ed.), *James Joyce: New Perspectives* (Sussex 1982), p. 46.

13. This aesthetic sentiment is echoed in Eliot's 'Tradition and the individual talent' in F. Kermode and J. Hollander (eds), *The Oxford Anthology of English Literature Vol. II* (Oxford 1973). Both Stephen and Eliot's association of the artist with the erasure of personality has clear implications for the stories of *Dubliners*, particularly to those stories that use an effaced narrator.

14. J. Frank, 'Spatial form in modern literature' in M.J. Hoffman and R.D. Murphy (eds), *Essentials of the Theory of Fiction* (Duke 1988), p. 87.

15. *Ibid.* p. 88.

16, I. Vidan, 'Time sequence in spatial fiction' in M.J. Hoffman and P.D. Murphy (eds), *Essentials of the Theory of Fiction* (Duke 1988), p. 437.

17. Rabaté, p. 45.

18. *Ibid.* p. 68.

19. S. Deane, 'Heroic styles: The tradition of an idea' in C. Connolly (ed.), *Theorizing Ireland* (New York 2003), p. 20.

20. R. Imhof, *John Banville: A Critical Introduction* (Dublin 1997), p. 24.

21. *Ibid.* p. 39.

22. J. Banville, *Long Lankin* (London 1970), p. 106.

23. *Ibid.* p. 111.

24. *Ibid.* p. 35.

25. *Ibid.* p. 57.

26. 'Killachter Meadow', originally published in *Felo De Se*, was most recently reprinted as 'North Sea Holdings' in *Flotsam & Jetsam* (Chicago 2002). I make references to both versions.

27. A. Higgins, *Felo De Se* (London 1960), p. 99.

28. P. O'Neill, 'Aidan Higgins' in Rüdiger Imhof (ed.), *Contemporary Irish Novelists* (Tübingen 1990), p. 95.

29. R. Garfitt, 'Constants in contemporary Irish fiction' in *Two Decades of Irish Writing—A Critical Study* (Cheshire 1975), p. 225.

30. Neil Jordan in M. Pernot-Deschamps, 'Neil Jordan's short stories—A question of Irishness', *Asylum Arts Review*, 4 (Winter 1997), 19.

31. N. Jordan, *Night in Tunisia* (London 1988), p. 91.

32. *Ibid.* p. 41.
33. *Ibid.* p. 112.
34. *Ibid.* p. 99.
35. *Ibid.* p. 69.
36. *Ibid.* p. 62.
37. S. Beckett, *Proust* (New York 1931), p. 47.

VICKI MAHAFFEY

Love, Race, and Exiles:
The Bleak Side of Ulysses

The first thing I want to explain is my use of the adjective "bleak" to describe an aspect of *Ulysses*. I have chosen the metaphor of bleakness advisedly, because although it means "exposed and barren and often windswept . . . lacking in warmth or kindliness," it derives from the Middle English word *bleke*, meaning "paleness."[1] By referring to the colder, more hopeless side of *Ulysses* as bleak or pale rather than dark, I hope to draw attention to the way that *Ulysses*, unlike *Star Wars*, emphatically refuses to equate darkness with evil. Or, to put it another way, Joyce sees a moral equivalency between light and darkness that is reinforced by the verbal similarity of "black," "blanc," and "blank."[2] Everyone knows that the male heroes of *Ulysses* are two dark horses in the human race who win that race against long odds. The fact that these men are dark (dressed in black) and associated with waste (through the winning horse's name, "Throwaway") shows that Joyce takes a bold minority view of the contest among races, upholding the value of currently disadvantaged or "dark" races, preferring unknowns to favorites.[3] Not only Bloom and Stephen but also Molly is associated with darkness; like the two rivals in Shakespeare's sonnets, Stephen and Bloom are drawn together through their almost gravitational attraction to this "dark lady."

Ulysses, then, is a book in which the protagonists, although they are racially "white," are all metaphorically dark. Joyce depicts them as dark partly

From *Joyce Studies Annual* 2007 (Winter 2007): 92–108. © 2007 by Fordham University Press.

to underscore the downtrodden status of the Irish and the Jews, which enables him to predict their unexpected resurgence. It is essential, however, to realize that the victory of these "dark" horses is *not* depicted, as it usually is, as a triumph of resistant nationalism, but as a triumph of ethics and, specifically, a triumph of heterodoxy. Bloom, Stephen, and Molly do not represent one side of an oppositional conflict; they represent *both* sides, and the possibility of dialogue between them. This is to say that they are not only dark but also white; the heterodoxy that Joyce would have us embrace might best be represented as chiaroscuro, in which an artful management of light and shade displaces the dominance of conventional or thoughtless morality. Ultimately, I will return to the question of why the protagonists of *Ulysses* not only do but also must signify the symbiosis of opposite extremes. It is worth pointing out that, although I am currently picturing those extremes as darkness and light, they could just as easily be defined as male and female or gentile and Jew. But in order to appreciate the ethics of the chiaroscuro perspective that Joyce so carefully offers to the reader, we must first consider his depiction of darkness and brightness, because Joyce's construction of the meaning of both differs so sharply from the way they are usually interpreted. Darkness, typically understood as "evil" in the popular imagination, is for Joyce not only a social and political index of the untapped power of ghettoized peoples, but also represents a more general attitude of mind, an attentiveness to the unknown. Psychologically and spiritually, what makes Stephen, Bloom, and Molly extraordinary is that like Averröes and Moses Maimonides, whom Stephen calls "dark men," they have the power to apprehend "the obscure soul of the world, a darkness shining in brightness which brightness could not comprehend."[4]

What does Stephen mean by "the obscure soul of the world?" Later in the "Nestor" episode, Joyce helps to clarify the difference between popular views of darkness and Stephen's revisionary ones through Stephen's verbal joust with Mr. Deasy. Deasy sees Jews as both dark and evil because, as he alleges, they "sinned against the light. . . . And you can see the darkness in their eyes. And that is why they are wanderers on the earth to this day" (2.361–63). Stephen counters by asking, "Who has not?" (2.373). In Stephen's mind, everyone has sinned against the light; everyone has darkness in his or her eyes, and everyone is a wanderer, an exile, in search of a home that is as elusive to us as it was to Odysseus and perhaps even to the Greek bard so appropriately known as "Homer" (in *Finnegans Wake*, Joyce puns on "home" as "howme," or "how me").[5] Where Stephen and Mr. Deasy differ is in their attitude toward sin. Mr. Deasy associates sin with otherness: specifically, with Jews and women. He assumes for himself and for others like him the divine right of kings, arguing that we are "all kings' sons"; Stephen comments, "Alas" (2.280–81). This is Deasy's vision of race: a contest between the aristocratic favorites, backing king's colors, and the dark horses—literally "nightmares"—of history (2.377), who are quite rightly punished for their misdeeds. (Deasy's self-congratulatory view of race is further emphasized by the pictures of vanished racehorses that Stephen observes on the walls of the headmaster's study [2.300–304]. In the *Odyssey*, Nestor was also a charioteer.) The problem with this view of race is not only its hypocrisy (Deasy accuses women and Jews of sin yet keeps a picture of Albert Edward, Prince of Wales, a notorious libertine, above his mantel, 2.265–67) but also its violence: after remembering scenes at the racetrack when he was led there by Cranly, Stephen associates the hurrying hoofs first with the clack of the hockey sticks outside his window and then with battle: "Time shocked rebounds, shock by shock. Jousts, slush and uproar of battles, the frozen deathspew of the slain, a shout of spearspikes baited with men's bloodied guts" (2.316–18). Deasy enjoys such contests—"I like to break a lance with you," he tells Stephen (2.424–25)—and part of his enjoyment comes from his comfortable assurance that he is always right: "I will fight for the right till the end. *For Ulster will fight / And Ulster will be right*" (2.395–98). Similarly, Deasy can comfortably condemn women because, as he argues, "A woman brought sin into the world" (2.390). Stephen's perspective on women is markedly different. He muses that *amor matris* or mother love might be the only true thing in life, an early protection against the brutal human race. He notes that were it not for Sargent's mother (and his own), "the race of the world would have trampled him underfoot, a squashed boneless snail" (2.141–42).

Deasy's view of the human race is unconsciously defined by rhyme: he associates right not only with might but also with light. Joyce challenges Deasy's simple chain of association by painting him in sunlight only to expose him as wrong (rather than right) and weak instead of mighty. Both Deasy and Mulligan are depicted as "light" characters, in sharp contrast to their darker (and more ethically substantial) counterparts, Stephen and Bloom. Malachi Mulligan, in his yellow dressinggown, describes his name, with its double dactyls, as "Tripping and sunny like the buck himself" (1.42). Deasy is twice pictured through a wash of sunlight; first, "the garish sunshine [bleaches] the honey of his illdyed head" (2.197–98), and later, the sunlight hardens into gold, a sign of Deasy's acquisitiveness: "On his wise shoulders through the checkerwork of leaves the sun flung spangles, dancing coins" (2.448–49). Deasy's obsession with saving links him to the mercantile Jews he would revile. At the same time, it illuminates another motive for his refusal to understand humanity in more nuanced ways: profit. Money is power, as we can see from Buck's exultation over the prospect of the "omnipotent sovereigns" (1.297) that Stephen will get from Deasy. Mulligan directs Stephen to get money from Haines, and Deasy, too, counsels Stephen to hoard money, to "*Put but money in thy purse*" (2.239), ironically echoing the villain Iago in Shakespeare's *Othello*. Mr. Deasy, who so gravely dispenses Iago's advice along with golden coins, "symbols soiled by greed and misery" (2.227–28), is—like Mulligan—materialistic, racist, and optimistic without the sobering check of humility or realism. We later discover Stephen's view that such "sunniness" is sentimental and opportunistic: as Stephen telegrams Mulligan, a sentimentalist as he defines it is an opportunist, he who would "*enjoy without incurring the immense debtorship for a thing done*" (9.550–51).

If both Mulligan and Deasy would brightly discard the "obscure soul of the world" (2.159) as soiled and worthless, Stephen, in sharp contrast, highly values the knowledge of sin. He advocates an awareness—even an acceptance—of individual and collective sin as a mode of access to the "obscure soul of the world.[6] What links sin with obscurity is an awareness of inadequacy: "obscure" means "lacking or inadequately supplied with light . . . withdrawn from the centers of human activity . . . not readily understood or clearly expressed."[7] When an individual admits inadequacy without succumbing to hopelessness or despair, Joyce suggests that the admission opens the way to the divine heart, which, as Joyce wrote in his article on Wilde, cannot be reached "except through that sense of separation and loss called sin."[8] Sin, then, is another word for exile, without which redemption is meaningless. Only a dark horse can win the human race, because only those who have experienced their own sin and loss through the fullness of mourning will, like the Jews Stephen pictures on the steps of the Paris stock exchange, "[know] their years of wandering and, patient, [know] the dishonours of their flesh" (2.371–72). An acceptance of personal fallibility is the bleak but ethically essential countersign to the assertion of self-worth.

Say, then, that this is the situation at the beginning of *Ulysses*: Stephen and Bloom are dark men, men who have sinned—Stephen through insensitivity to his mother, Bloom through insensitivity to his wife—and who are conscious of their strong sense of separation and loss. Although Stephen and Bloom are far from blameless, their sin is depicted as preferable to the glib ease of their aggressively male but sunny counterparts, Mulligan and Deasy (their emphatic maleness is underscored by the animals Joyce links to them: a buck is a male animal and Stephen associates Deasy, who is much older, with a bullock, or castrated bull). Neither extreme is ideal, but the human race is on, and the two sides have been pitted against one another. Both Mulligan and Deasy use more warlike tactics than Stephen and Bloom, the "toothless terrors" (2.429–30). In the first three episodes, Stephen shows that he is not, however, simply the inverse or shadow of his opponents by refusing either to join or revile them. First, he will neither fight his opponents nor abandon his own position. He gives up the key to the tower and agrees to eat the salt bread of exile rather than escalate the warlike competition with Mulligan, although he clearly articulates what he has been holding against Mulligan and does not back down in the face of Mulligan's offensive self-defense. And although Stephen sees through Deasy's self-serving myths of history, he doesn't spurn Deasy completely either, but resolves to "help him in his fight," although he anticipates that Mulligan will make fun of his willingness to do so by dubbing him "the bullockbefriending bard" (2.430–32). Second, unlike Mulligan and Deasy, Stephen is in search of a better balance between darkness and light, one that inclines toward the dark but doesn't exclude light. He thinks of "uncouth" or unknown stars (3.412) as an image of what he yearns for, musing, "Darkly they are there behind this light, darkness shining in the brightness, delta of Cassiopeia, worlds" (3.409–10). Stephen imagines the dark presence of what lies behind the visible world, an obscurity he links not only with sin but also with the soul. As he tells an imagined reader in "Proteus," "You find my words dark. Darkness is in our souls do you not think?" (3.420–21). Stephen is listening for the unconscious, the unspoken, straining for a glimpse of the unbeheld, and he urges his reader to do likewise—not because the darkness is evil, but because it is an image of the hidden beauty of the soul, a darkness shot through with light, or, as the narrator describes it in "Ithaca," a "heaventree of stars hung with humid nightblue fruit" (17.1039). Finally, Stephen differs from Mulligan and Deasy in his determination to resist the promptings of the speaker in Yeats's poem "Who Goes with Fergus?" Mulligan recites the words to him, counseling, "*And no more turn aside and brood / Upon love's bitter mystery / For Fergus rules the brazen cars*" (1.239–41). But the narrator describes Stephen's brain as obstinately "brooding" and "beset" with memories (1.265–66); he is determined to understand those words that caused his mother to cry "in her wretched bed. For those words, Stephen: love's bitter mystery" (1.252–53).

Love's bitter mystery: this is yet another way of describing that balance between opposing forces that Stephen elsewhere calls "the obscure soul of the world" (2.159). Love is a mystery; it is deeply desired and highly prized, but it is also elusive and bitter—or, in the words of my title, it is lonely and bleak. According to the *OED*, the word *mystery* comes from a Greek root meaning "to close (the lips and eyes)." A mystery is inaccessible through the light of reason; it is "a matter unexplained or inexplicable; something beyond human knowledge or comprehension." In religion, it refers to a "truth known only from divine revelation," and it refers more generally to "the condition or property of being secret or obscure" (*OED*). Mystery, then, is a kind of obscurity that is capable of being revealed, but it is not accessible through the light of reason. It is what Stephen imagines as the dark presence existing "behind this light," "darkness shining in brightness which brightness could not comprehend" (3.409, 2.160). It is this mystery that Stephen and Bloom are trying, in their different ways, to apprehend, as when Stephen's heart is fretted by "pain, that was not yet the pain of love" (1.102) as he broods over his mother's tears at love's bitter mystery. A sense of "Love's bitter mystery" is also what *Ulysses* attempts to convey to its readers through its own potentially enlightening obscurity.

So, I am saying (like Richard Ellmann in his preface to the Gabler edition) that *Ulysses* is indeed about love, but (unlike Ellmann) I would specify that love, like darkness, needs to be carefully redefined, because Joyce means something very different by it than do most casual users of the word. As Joyce demonstrates in "Cyclops," love as it is commonly used is childishly narcissistic and sentimental; it is self-satisfied optimism at its most ludicrous, the product of romantic and religious brainwashing aimed at the kindergarten set:

> Love loves to love love. Nurse loves the new chemist. Constable 14A loves Mary Kelly. Gerty MacDowell loves the boy that has the bicycle. M. B. loves a fair gentleman. Li Chi Han lovey up kissy Cha Pu Chow. Jumbo, the elephant, loves Alice, the elephant. Old Mr Verschoyle with the ear trumpet loves old Mrs Verschoyle with the turnedin eye. The man in the brown macintosh loves a lady who is dead. His Majesty the King loves Her Majesty the Queen. Mrs Norman W. Tupper loves officer Taylor. You love a certain person. And this person loves that other person because everybody loves somebody but God loves everybody. (12.1493–1501)

Love, as Joyce redefines the term, offers a more complex challenge. Joyce subjects love in *Ulysses* to a treatment similar to the one he gave passion in "The Dead": he took the popular idea of passion as white-hot desire (which the lover assumes to be reciprocated) and had his protagonist, Gabriel Conroy, act it out. Joyce then pitted Gabriel's model of passion—a frenzy to possess the aestheticized object of desire—against an older model of passion that captures the original meaning of the word: to suffer. Michael Furey's willingness to suffer in order to see Gretta before she left Galway stands in such sharp contrast to Gabriel's self-satisfied assurance of his own desirability that he is pricked to see himself as a fatuous, self-important clown who has experienced lust but has never known love: "he had never felt like that himself towards any woman but he knew that such a feeling must be love."[9]

The problem with the Michael Furey model of love, like that of Christ's passion on which it is based, is that in the act of giving everything for the beloved, the self is destroyed: Furey's gift to Gretta is a ghostly, pyrrhic victory. The question then becomes, is it possible to give love without relinquishing one's life? (As Stephen thinks when he imagines trying to save a drowning man, "I want his life still to be his, mine to be mine" [13.327–28].) Joyce first addresses this question in his only play, *Exiles*: how can love be *given*? is it something that *can* be given or *possessed*? In order to understand Joyce's treatment of love in *Ulysses*, a reader must first come to terms with what Joyce learned in *Exiles*, which he finished as he was beginning the composition of *Ulysses*.

Exiles is a play about homecoming in which Joyce imagines what it might be like for him to return from Italy to Dublin with his lover and their son. The play centers on the interactions of four main characters and two minor ones: Richard Rowan, loosely based on Joyce; Bertha, his partner; Archie, their son; and Brigid, their servant, form one group. The other two characters are cousins who have remained in Dublin while the Rowans were abroad in Italy: Beatrice Justice, who has been an inspiration for Richard's writing and with whom he corresponded while he was away, and Robert Hand, a journalist and friend of Richard's who is trying to help Richard get a professorship at the university. The play consists primarily of conversations between shifting pairs of characters. The dialogue ranges from cliché to melodrama as the audience learns more and more of each character's rather ordinary secrets. Beatrice is a despairing, chilly woman who ventriloquizes her hidden pride and scorn through Richard's writing. Richard is at this point less concerned with Beatrice than with his partner, Bertha: he feels guilty because he has inadvertently fostered Bertha's increasing dependence on him. He had hoped that their evasion of marriage would give them both more freedom, but the shame and uncertainty of their relationship, her greater isolation, and the responsibilities of motherhood have curtailed her freedom and awakened in her a wistful, romantic nostalgia. Robert wants to steal Bertha from Richard, and he is secretly courting her in Richard's own home, but Bertha keeps Richard informed of every move Robert makes. Richard wants everyone to be free to choose his or her own course of action, but he doesn't want anyone to act secretly, "in the dark."[10] Therefore, when Robert is expecting a visit from Bertha, Richard shows up ahead of her and tells Robert that he knows everything. Robert is quite naturally embarrassed, but Richard rather unexpectedly tells him to carry on, that he isn't going to try to stop Robert from seducing Bertha. He just didn't want Robert to think he was putting anything over on him. Richard leaves, Bertha shows up, and Robert is annoyed at her for not having told him that Richard knew. She explains that she is an honest and straightforward person and tells him she would have been honest with him too if he had ever asked her whether Richard suspected what was going on. The act ends while Robert and Bertha are still together in Robert's cottage, and the audience never learns what happened there, or whether anything happened.

The last act opens early the next morning. We see Richard suffering and Bertha sleepless but concerned about Richard. She offers to tell him what happened, but he responds that even if she tells him, he will never know; this is a bleakly truthful understanding of "love's bitter mystery." Beatrice comes in to show them the morning paper, which contains a leading article that Robert has written about Richard called "A Distinguished Irishman" (94). She tells them Robert is leaving town and Bertha sends for him immediately. Bertha chides Robert for planning to leave without talking to Richard, reminding him that such an act would leave Richard with the wrong impression. Robert and Richard speak, and the play ends with Bertha and Richard expressing their feelings of isolation and doubt, respectively.

As this summary might suggest, *Exiles* was not likely to be a box-office success. It's the kind of play that would have driven Artaud wild: if the life of theater is gesture—physical contact and conflict of the sort represented by a Balinese cockfight—*Exiles* has no life. The only way it could possibly succeed as theater is if it were staged as antitheater: an ultraconventional "ghost story" set in the stifling atmosphere of two enclosed rooms, where the only relief comes from opening a window or a door. The unreality of the characters could be emphasized by unchanging, larger-than-life masks—Richard's set in a habitual scowl, Robert's in a knowing smile. Beatrice's mask would give her a thin, pale, bitter expression, and Bertha would have no mask until the beginning of the third act. This is still to visualize what Joyce demanded that we hear: the tinny insincerity of four voices jockeying for advantage under the guise of mutual regard.

Like Gabriel in "The Dead," the four characters in *Exiles* have tried to love, but their efforts seem wasted. More specifically, the characters are unable to reconcile love with either freedom or responsibility. *Exiles*, then, might best be described as a thought experiment in dramatic form. The problems it explores are these: is it possible to give freedom? Can freedom be given or awarded (to a lover, a child, or a reader) as a *gift*? What is the relation between generosity (giving) and forgiveness? What does it feel like for an author, lover, or parent to give this gift? Finally, does the recipient of this gift experience the blended joy and responsibility of genuine freedom, or does he become irresponsible and immoral, lacking any remorse of conscience? (This last change seems to describe what happens to Robert and perhaps even Archie.)

I want to address each of these questions in turn, but first I'd like to draw closer attention to my parenthetical suggestion that freedom may be offered to a lover, a child, or a reader. Part of what differentiates *Exiles* from "The Dead" and ties it to *Ulysses* is that, for the first time, Joyce sets out to explore the connections between generosity, responsibility, and freedom on *three* levels, or in three different kinds of relationships. Most critics focus on the anguished sexual relations in *Exiles*; understandably so, because these relations are the most central. What I want to emphasize, though, is that Joyce is treating all three forms of relation—sexual, textual (or artistic), and parental—as analogous, and that these three kinds of relationships again overlap in significant ways in *Ulysses*.

The problem with mothers and fathers, lovers, and authors and readers is that the tension between generosity and strictness tends to be reenacted between partners in each couple instead of internalized in the individual. I will begin by exploring how this paternal polarization affects their child, which is dramatized in the play through three sets of parent–child relations: Richard's relation to his parents, Beatrice's relation to *her* parents, and Archie's relation to Richard and Bertha. In Act I, Richard introduces the dilemma of how love is related to generosity by contrasting the generosity of his (dead) father with the hard-heartedness of his (also dead) mother. Richard's last memory of his father is of an act of generosity: when Richard was fourteen, his father called him to his bedside to give him both permission and money to do something he knew Richard wanted to do: hear *Carmen*. He died while Richard was gone (24). Richard calls the memory "sweet and noble," referring to his father as "the smiler," whereas he remembers his mother as hard, cold, and begrudging (23). He claims to "pity her cold blighted love" for him, but he confesses that he is still inwardly battling her spirit (23). Her miserly spirit is apparent in two ways—in her obdurate refusal to forgive him, even on her deathbed (forgiveness, as the word suggests, being associated with giving), and in her effect on his life. He says that "On account of her I lived years in exile and poverty too, or near it" (23). Richard clearly prefers the gift of pleasure and music granted him by his dying father to the grim letter of warning sent by his dying mother, but he prays twice not for his father's warmth but for *her* hardness of heart (22, 25). Love is not reducible to mere generosity, then, as much as Richard would like for it to be. And it is not generosity but principle that Richard needs, as we can see in his indulgently permissive relation to his own son, Archie.

Beatrice's parental influences mirror Richard's with the genders reversed. It is her father who epitomizes "gloom, seriousness, [and] righteousness" (30) and Robert's mother (Beatrice's aunt) who gives the gift of music. Joyce adds this information to clarify the point that an affinity for generosity or principle is not linked to gender: men as well as women can be severe, and women as well as men can be joyous and musical. Richard is generous, like his own father, leaving the discipline to Bertha. Bertha perceptively understands that he is repeating the pattern of his own family of origin, projecting onto her the role of "cruel mother" because he never loved his own mother (52). She also intuitively understands the destructiveness of a generosity that lacks restraint, as she denies the implication that her discipline is loveless. (Her solicitude for Archie is particularly apparent in Act III, when she cleans his mouth with her handkerchief, wet with her tongue [92]). Bertha diagnoses the problem with Richard's generosity—he is helpless to be anything other than generous; he cannot say no—to Archie, to Robert, or to her (52, 56). Beatrice, according to Bertha, is Richard's exact opposite—she cannot give; "she is not generous" (55). In fact, Beatrice needs Richard *because* she is unable to give; he expresses the generous sentiments that she has choked off. If love is not reducible to generosity, Beatrice shows that neither is love possible in the *absence* of generosity.

To give a quick recap, then: Robert is greedy, trying to steal (or rob) Bertha from Richard, whom he sees as both generous and—as his name suggests—rich in love. Beatrice is *not* generous, but neither is she acquisitive; she lives vicariously through the expressions of others: Richard's writing, Archie's piano playing. Richard is compulsively generous, and Bertha is simply bewildered by Richard's desire to give her and Robert's desire to take her. What she wants is to keep things as they were when she and Richard first met. The question is, do any of these positions represent a truly loving attitude? At first, it may be tempting to equate Joyce's position with Richard's, because he is the autobiographical character and because he claims to have outgrown Robert's romantic and demonic philosophy of self-assertion. Moreover, Richard tries to justify his compulsive generosity by reframing it as sacrifice. When he asks Archie if he understands what it means to give a thing (46), he is outlining the ethos of sacrifice. He explains that giving is the only guarantee of eternal possession (47). This is clearly a theological idea—he is giving in order to receive, sacrificing in the literal sense of "making sacred" the object of his desire. What is odd—maybe even unique—about this ploy is that Richard is applying it not to food, as the ancients did, but to the realm of sexuality: he is giving away his "wife" in order to forestall losing her, while at the same time sacralizing (or resacralizing) their union. This is such an unconventional idea that it can easily be confused with a radical, even a feminist position: instead of having his Nora walk out on him, as Ibsen's heroine so controversially walked out on her husband and children in *A Doll's House*, Joyce imagines his protagonist *giving* her freely to another man for whom she feels desire.

But Richard's attitude toward love is *not* that of the mature Joyce. The questions Richard never asks are first, whether Bertha is his to give, and second, whether she is a *thing* ("Do you understand what it is to give a thing" [46]). It should be obvious that the answer is "no" to both questions. Despite his predilection for masochistic sacrifice, Richard's motives are as possessive as Robert's. He tries to possess not only by giving but also by remembering; as Richard boasts, he never forgets anything (99). Yet another indirect way Richard tries to possess those he loves is by insisting on telling them everything he knows (to tell one's secrets is also to number or count them, to render them material by putting them into words). He tells Bertha about his infidelities and he tells Robert everything he knows about Robert's attempts to seduce Bertha. Then (and only then) he offers to give them their freedom as a gift from him; he must first possess or master this freedom in order to give it to them—their freedom must pass through his mind and hands.

Robert is just as acquisitive as Richard, although his rationalization is that of a hedonist rather than a saint. Not only does he want to steal Bertha and win over Archie, he also wants to give Richard a reputation for distinction by composing and publishing it, literally authorizing Richard's talent. He recognizes and resents Richard's prodigality when he tells him that the "fatted calf" will be eaten in his honor at the vice chancellor's dinner (45). What Robert resents is the indirectness of Richard's acquisitiveness, its pretensions to being spiritual (and therefore higher) than Robert's carnal appetite. In their youth, they shared a pride of possession, symbolized by the two keys they had to the cottage where they enjoyed a succession of women. Richard boasts that he has given up his key, but Robert senses that it was in order to own one woman more totally. Robert's attitude, however, is not an ethical alternative—he gets not by remembering, but by forgetting, by denying the burdens of consciousness and conscience (he says, "I have no remorse of conscience" [41]). He frames his defense in the language not of God but of Lucifer, arguing that he (like Richard when he was young, and like Stephen Dedalus) will not serve: "I am sure that no law made by man is sacred before the impulse of passion. . . . There is no law before impulse. Laws are for slaves" (87). He tells Richard with Nietzschean fervor, "All life is a conquest, the victory of human passion over the commandments of cowardice. . . . The blinding instant of passion alone—passion, free, unashamed, irresistible—that is the only gate by which we can escape from the misery of what slaves call life. Is not this the language of your own youth . . . ?" (71).

What Robert calls freedom is simply revolt; what Richard calls freedom is false philanthropy. Beatrice feels free by ventriloquizing through Richard's writing, and Bertha reads what the others call freedom as simple loneliness. Although the play is set in Ireland two months after John Redmond had succeeded in getting an Irish Home Rule bill on the docket in Parliament, it is ironically clear that none of the characters (with the possible exception of Archie) has a clue what freedom is. Freedom is neither a thing to be given (as England is considering giving it to Ireland) nor a refusal of law (the Irish rebel position). What, then, does Joyce suggest it might be? Can freedom be a love-offering, something made available to a child, a lover, or a reader without covert implications of anxiety and coercion?

The answer is important politically, ethically, and textually, because freedom is also something Joyce badly wanted to give to those he loved, including his readers. But if he had to discover, like Richard, that freedom is not a thing to be given, and it is not his to give, how then could he encourage freedom of response? Not by doing what Robert does—writing for the common person, using the language of people whose opinions he doesn't share. Although Robert claims to be a patriot, Richard reads Robert's style as lacking independence. In one of the excised fragments of the play, Richard accuses Robert of having "taken the smooth path, accepting ironically everything in which you disbelieved and building for your body and for that function of it which I suppose you call your soul a peace of prudence, irony, and pleasure."[11] Richard boasts that he, in contrast, has "lived without prudence, risking everything, destroying everything in order to create again."[12] Richard's claim rings false, although romantically so, but Robert has sold out too; he is simply more pragmatic about it.

At some point during the composition of *Exiles*, Joyce realized the romantic hypocrisy of Richard's position, seeing that it matched Robert's while seeming to oppose it. What Richard discovers while trying to give freedom is that it can't be given, that it is not always a welcome gift, and that freedom without principle produces nothing more than hedonism or crass materialism, on the one hand, or loneliness, on the other. All the characters glimpse, painfully, restlessly, with brief moments of joy and clarity, how difficult it is to resist (but not defy) temptation, to listen to what is in their hearts, to balance generosity and justice, freedom and principle, in their interactions with others. This is the definition of love that Joyce would take with him when he turned to *Ulysses*: love is the careful creation and preservation of an artful, precarious balance between freedom and limits, generosity and principle, engagement and detachment, openhandedness and justice. Richard is struggling with the difficulty of achieving this balance, however melodramatically, at the end: he refuses to despair, but does not wish to be deceived either. Richard does, however, catch a glimpse of a love so finely calibrated that it rivals great art, but he can only apprehend this idea by first acknowledging a basic limitation of his own: he cannot read the hearts of those he loves.

The most important moment in *Exiles* is Richard's acceptance of the fact that he "cannot read in" Robert's heart, or in Bertha's either (73). When Bertha accuses him of abandoning her when he refuses to tell her what he wants her to do, and he answers, "Your own heart will tell you" (75), he experiences a wild delight. She has become the text and he a reader who sharply registers and attentively enjoys but cannot control that text. He has learned—briefly—to forget his own desires to control her, either by giving her or by interpreting her; instead, he asks, "Who am I that I should call myself master of your heart or of any woman's?" (75). Richard ultimately directs Robert, Bertha, and Beatrice to "free yoursel[ves]" (71)—he cannot free them. But he can try to model the process of self-emancipation, and he does this by acknowledging the difficulty of understanding them without relinquishing his curiosity and wonder at their ability to elude reductive categorization.

The problem with this vision of love, so perfectly poised between self and other, is that it is so difficult, perhaps even impossible, to sustain. *Exiles*, like *Ulysses*, is haunted by the possibility that the experience of freedom, like the gift of virginity, may be unique and unrepeatable. This is Bertha's position. She tells Brigid, "that time comes only once in a lifetime. The rest of life is good for nothing except to remember that time" (91), and she tells Richard, "Not a day passes that I do not see ourselves, you and me, as we were when we met first. Every day of my life I see that" (111). She begs Richard to turn back the clock to that irretrievable moment: "Forget me, Dick. Forget me and love me again as you did the first time" (112). But if freedom of choice is only possible once, the play offers the tenuous possibility that it can live again in children, who signify a temporary renewal of lost innocence. As Robert tells Richard, "Perhaps there, Richard, is the freedom we seek—you in one way, I in another. In him and not in us" (109). For those who decline the presumption of knowing or understanding the hearts of those they love, children, too, may sometimes relieve loneliness. For the most part, however, *Exiles* is peopled by characters who seem helpless to palliate their exile, even when they are most at home.

This insight—that love requires a recognition of but not a resignation to exile—infuses *Ulysses* at every level. It shapes Stephen's understanding of the soul as a dark shape born of sin, which makes him in turn value obscurity over transparency of language (he distrusted "aquacities of thought and language" [7.240]), riddles over journalism, and dark men over their sunnier, more successful counterparts. Parental love in *Ulysses* is haunted by the same insistence on uncertainty: the Blooms had two children, one dead and one living, which leaves them forever pulled between love and grief. The two Bloom children function like the two thieves in St. Augustine's dictum that Beckett's tramps puzzle over in *Waiting for Godot*: Do not despair; one of the thieves was saved. Do not presume; one of the thieves was damned.[13] Erotic love, too, is shadowed by betrayal: Leopold and Molly are united by multiple bonds, but Molly's adultery is a sign of Bloom's abandonment of Molly as well as a counter-abandonment of Bloom by Molly herself. Both Bloom and Molly need a renewed awareness of the bleakness in each other's lives. And Molly echoes Bertha's fear that a free and joyous mutual exchange may be a unique and unrepeatable event in the plot of a relationship. As she thinks in "Penelope," "with all the talk of the world about it people make its only the first time after that its just the ordinary do it and think no more about it" (18.100–102).

What does love have to do with reading? As it turns out, the two are intimately related in the world of *Ulysses*. Reading a text with mastery and ease is like claiming to be able to read the heart of a lover: it may be reassuring, but it is hardly enriching and seldom inspiring. Frustration with reading that resists easy appropriation is a sign of the expectation that most things are easy to penetrate, to assimilate, to conquer. This is what most readers think they want—to *possess* knowledge, as Gabriel desired to *possess* Gretta, but, paradoxically, when a text or a lover is less accessible, it kindles the reader's sense of wonder. In *Exiles*, Richard holds that to take care for the future is to destroy all hope and love in the world. We could paraphrase and extend Richard's comment by saying that to understand a book on a first reading is to destroy all curiosity and wonder in the world. To make understanding difficult but not impossible *is* a gift, but it is not philanthropy. It is a gift of labor that allows the reader the freedom to free herself from self-limiting assumptions. As the narrator cheers in *Finnegans Wake*'s "The Ballad of Pierce O'Reilly," "*Hirp! Hirp! for their Missed Understandings!' chirps the Ballat of Perce-Oreille*" (17.527–28).

Love and reading work in tandem, then, and for Joyce the main gift that a writer can give a reader in a written work, or love letter, is a renewed appreciation for what Yeats in "The Circus Animals' Desertion" calls "Heart-mysteries."[14] The recognition that love depends upon an awareness of the final unknowability of the beloved, although future insight remains both possible and desirable, is to say that love demands an acknowledgment of bleakness, but not a surrender to it. It is Joyce's way of saying what Crazy Jane said so memorably to the Bishop in Yeats's late poem: "But Love has pitched his mansion / In the place of excrement, / And nothing can be sole or whole / That has not been rent" (255). The darkness that Deasy would project outward onto women or Jews, and that a frustrated reader would erase from the pages of *Ulysses*, is actually within us. "Darkness is in our souls, do you not think?" Meaning is an arrangement of that darkness against its bleak background: "signs on a white field" (3.421, 414–15).

Notes

1. Merriam-Webster OnLine Dictionary, available at http://www.m-w.com.

2. According to the *OED*, the history of the word "black" is difficult, because in Old English it was often confused with the word for "white" or "shining," which was essentially the same word when it was spelled, as it sometimes was, with a long vowel. Older forms of the word "bleak" also wavered in meaning between black and white. The *OED* also notes that "bleak" was akin to the Middle English *blecche* (related to "bleach"), which involved placing something in the hot sun. The sun could whiten it, but it could also blacken it.

3. It is important to remember that from the late nineteenth century through the 1940s, Jews were often classified as a race. According to Raul Hilberg, "racism acquired a 'theoretical' basis only in the 1800s ... [when] racists ... stated explicitly that cultural characteristics, good or bad, were the product of physical characteristics. Physical attributes did not change; hence social behavior patterns also had to be immutable. In the eyes of the anti-Semite, the Jews therefore became a 'race.'" Raul Hilberg, *Destruction of the European Jews* (New York: Holmes and Meier, 1985), 19.

4. James Joyce, *Ulysses*, ed. Hans Walter Gabler, with Wolfhard Steppe and Claus Melchior (New York: Random House, 1986), 2.158–60. Hereafter this work will be cited parenthetically in the text by episode and line number.

5. James Joyce, *Finnegans Wake* (New York: Viking, 1939), 173, 1.27. Hereafter this work will be cited parenthetically in the text by page and line number.

6. Joyce seems to have developed this philosophy of the value of sin after reading Yeats's 1896 story "The Tables of the Law," which Joyce describes Stephen repeating to himself (along with "The Adoration of the Magi") in *Stephen Hero*. What attracts Stephen to the story is the figure of Owen Aherne (based on Lionel Johnson), who has transcended human law and discovered the law of his own being. The discovery turns Aherne into a heroic figure like Moses or Jesus, but Yeats unexpectedly emphasizes the loneliness and sadness of that transcendence. Stephen envisions Aherne as a kind of human phantom, leaning "pitifully towards the earth, like vapours, desirous of sin." The story is designed to show the lawless Irish the occult importance of arbitrary law, which is essential in that it alone makes sin, redemption, and community possible. James Joyce, *Stephen Hero* (New York: New Directions, 1963), 178.

7. Merriam-Webster OnLine Dictionary, available at http://www.m-w.com.

8. James Joyce, *The Critical Writings of James Joyce*, ed. Ellsworth Mason and Richard Ellmann (New York: Viking, 1959), 205.

9. James Joyce, *Dubliners*, ed. Robert Scholes (New York: Viking, 1967), 223.

10. James Joyce, *Exiles* (New York: Viking, 1951), 70. Hereafter this work will be cited parenthetically by page number in the text.

11. Robert M. Adams, "New Light on Joyce's *Exiles*? A New MS, a Curious Analogue, and Some Speculations," *Studies in Bibliography* 17 (1964): 86.

12. Ibid.

13. Samuel Beckett, *Waiting for Godot* (New York: Grove Press, 1954), 8–9.

14. William Butler Yeats, *The Collected Poems of William Butler Yeats* (New York: Macmillan, 1972), 336. Hereafter cited parenthetically by page number in the text.

MARGOT NORRIS

Possible Worlds Theory and the Fantasy Universe of Finnegans Wake

In the first chapter of his *Narrative Design in "Finnegans Wake,"* Harry Burrell points to one of the central tensions in the history of *Wake* criticism by heading his discussion with the single word "Narrative?"[1] He writes that "David Hayman, Bernard Benstock, John Bishop, and Margot Norris, for example, have all concluded that there is no underlying narrative and have evolved different systems of dealing with the dilemma" (8). In contrast, he notes, Fritz Senn and Clive Hart continue to yearn for the text's deep structural meaning to be disclosed (8). Burrell's study offers that deep structural meaning by treating the *Wake* as Joyce's rewriting of the Bible and creation of "a new theology" (7)—a claim that, in many respects, harks back to a founding text of *Wake* criticism: Joseph Campbell and Henry Morton Robinson's 1944 *A Skeleton Key to "Finnegans Wake."*[2] But however provocative its argument, Burrell's study does not end the controversy over the "Narrative?" of *Finnegans Wake* nor does it engage the question of the *Wake*'s narrative in a theoretical way. Yet the present moment in the early twenty-first century is particularly opportune for narratological study of avant-garde texts, thanks to a new development in the field that offers tools for more rigorously conceptualizing the nature of fiction itself. Called "Possible Worlds" theory, a branch of narratology that addresses "the fictionality of fictional worlds" has blossomed in the last fifteen years.[3] Gerald

From *James Joyce Quarterly* 44, no. 3 (Spring 2007): 455–474. © 2007 by the University of Tulsa.

Prince gives the following explanation of "possible worlds" in his *Dictionary of Narratology*: "Narratives comprise temporally ordered sequences of states of affairs that are taken to be actual/factual ('what happens') and that are linked to other states of affairs considered non-actual or counterfactual and constituted by the mental activity of various characters (their beliefs, wishes, plans, hallucinations, fantasies, etc.)."[4] The posited separation between what theorist Marie-Laure Ryan calls a "textual actual world" (n.p.) and the nonactual "worlds" that belong to the minds of characters in fiction can be readily recognized in a genre like realism. *Ulysses* is full of events that are assumed to be "factual" and to occur in the "actual" 1904 Dublin world posited within the novel—events like Bloom cooking breakfast at 7 Eccles Street, the funeral of Paddy Dignam, or Stephen's Shakespeare lecture in the National Library, for example. These events are not, in fact, actual or factual in the sense that they historically occurred in the real world, but Joyce's novel *Ulysses* pretends that they did. This pretended textual actual world in *Ulysses* is simultaneously connected to the virtual worlds—or possible worlds—of its characters' ruminations, memories, fantasies, and stories. But how do actual and possible worlds function in the fictional realm of *Finnegans Wake*? Possible Worlds theory offers tools to analyze the *Wake*'s narrative and fictional operation with greater rigor than before. This essay offers an introduction to such an analysis, though it defers exploring the content or significance of the ontological realms that the analysis discloses.

The question of whether *Finnegans Wake* exhibits anything resembling an "actual" or "factual" textual world—analogous to the richly imagined 1904 world of Dublin and its inhabitants in *Ulysses*—has, of course, been an issue in *Wake* criticism from the very beginning. Edmund Wilson's 1939 essay, "The Dream of H. C. Earwicker," posited a model in which the tavern in Book III functions as the site of an actual world in the *Wake*:

> It is a Saturday night in summer, after a disorderly evening in the pub. Somebody—probably Earwicker himself—has been prevailed upon to sing a song: later, when it was closing time, he had to put a man outside, who abused him and threw stones at the window. There has also been a thunderstorm. Earwicker has been drinking off and on all day and has perhaps gone to bed a little drunk. At any rate, his night is troubled. At first he dreams about the day before, with a bad conscience and a sense of humiliation: then, as the night darkens and he sinks more deeply into sleep, he has to labor through a nightmare oppression.[5]

By 1962, however, Hart disputed Wilson's model on the ground that "there is nothing whatever in the text to suggest that Books I and II are a dream of the protagonist whose sleep begins at 403.17."[6] Nonetheless, nearly twenty-five years later, John Gordon's *"Finnegans Wake": A Plot Summary* revived "the hypothesis that the Joyce of *Finnegans Wake* had not turned his back on the aggressive realism of the earlier books," and he offered "to recount the events of Joyce's book in their order of occurrence, and to describe as accurately as possible the place and the people involved in the action."[7] While his study has far more subtlety than these premises suggest, Gordon nonetheless makes good on his promise to recover from the *Wake* a plausible realism. He offers an unequivocal time for its events: "The date of *Finnegans Wake* is Monday, the twenty-first of March, 1938, and the early morning of Tuesday the twenty-second" (37). With equal clarity, he offers a setting for the work: *Finnegans Wake* is set in Chapelizod" in "a building called the Mullingar House" (9, 10). He describes the three-story structure in which the *Wake* family lives, complete with its furnishings, and offers a charming drawing of the parents' bedroom as seen from the vantage of the ceiling, featuring a bearskin rug and patchwork quilt on the bed (34). Because both Burrell and Gordon specifically address themselves to the nature of the *Wake*'s narrative, they will serve as my point of departure for exploring an alternative analysis of the problems it poses.

Gordon's plot summary is as engaging as Burrell's Biblical narrative a decade later, but neither discusses with sufficient clarity how their reductive accounts can actually be derived from the text's troublesome and unconventional semantic structure. "Possible Worlds" theorist Lubomír Doležel suggests a possible explanation. "In literary criticism, two interpretive methods are commonly practiced," he writes: "The first one is intuitive and subjectivistic. A meaning is suggested that the critic feels or believes to be 'hidden' in the text; the text is made to mean what the interpreter wants it to mean" (173). The second common interpretive method is ideological—having one's ideology prompt interpretation—and it does not apply to Gordon or Burrell. But while neither of these *Wake* critics operates purely subjectively and both base their readings on meticulous assemblies of textual evidence, they do appear to share the premise that, because meaning fails to be accessible from the textual surface, it must be semantically "hidden." I will later return to look more closely at the features of the text that appear to invite such readings as Gordon's and Burrell's but wish now to turn to the possibility of a different interpretive procedure for exploring the *Wake*'s fictional worlds.

If one argues that the text semantically represents a mental or a virtual world in its entirety, how can such an argument be justified not merely on intuitive but on logical grounds? This is where "Possible Worlds" theory offers two sets of extremely useful conceptual tools. The first consists of a list of criteria that define the way readers in an actual world are able to achieve mental access to fictional worlds. Ryan calls these criteria accessibility relations, and they include identity of properties, identity of inventory, compatibility of inventory, chronological compatibility, physical compatibility, taxonomic compatibility, logical compatibility, analytical compatibility, and linguistic compatibility (32, 33). These accessibility relations give Ryan a conceptual basis for distinguishing fictional genres—pinpointing with some precision the difference between fairy tales and realistic novels, for example—and they can thereby help us to address more rigorously the generic features of *Finnegans Wake*. Ryan's second set of conceptual tools may be found in her categorization of virtual domains within fiction as private or possible (nonfactual) worlds that she calls "knowledge-worlds" ("K-world"), "obligation-worlds" ("O-world"), and "wish-worlds" ("W-world") (111).[8] When these private worlds lose their connection to an actual world in a work of fiction, the result is a re-centering into different ontological realms that Ryan calls "fantasy-worlds" or "F-universes" (111, 119). Not only does *Finnegans Wake* represent such an "F-universe" but the concept of possible worlds can help us to sort out the ontological realms that conflict and collide in these worlds—collisions that usurp the roles narrative and plot play in more conventional fiction. By confining a demonstration to just one chapter of *Finnegans Wake*—Book I, chapter 1—I will use both Ryan's accessibility relations and her private-world or possible-world modalities to produce a clearer sense of how, precisely, the *Wake* functions as a work of fiction.

Ryan's accessibility relations will reveal little about *Wake* language that the work's readers have not already figured out intuitively. But while little that results from the analysis they produce will be surprising, Ryan's categories nonetheless oblige us to deal more precisely with the surface texture of *Finnegans Wake* and to address its implications for genre and the nature of its fictional worlds. According to Ryan, there are three accessibility relations that all but a very few genres of fiction share, and these are "linguistic compatibility," "logical compatibility," and "analytical compatibility" (34). Linguistic compatibility postulates that fictional domains in a text will be accessible from our actual world if the language of the text can be understood in the actual world. This compatibility can be found not only in realistic fiction but also in science fiction, fairy tales, legends, and works of fantasy. Ryan lists only two genres in which linguistic compatibility fails to pertain: what she calls "Jabberwockism" and "sound poetry" (34). Humpty Dumpty's poem "Jabberwocky" begins, as Ryan observes, "Twas brillig, and the slithy toves / Did gyre and gimble in the wabe" (39).[9] Ryan's example of a sound poem, taken from Hugo Ball, contains such phrases as "gadjiberi bimba glandridi lonni cadori" and so on (39).[10] Lewis Carroll's "Jabberwocky" restricts its incompatibility with English chiefly to nouns and verbs, Ryan notes, and therefore exhibits a compromised but not a total linguistic incompatibility. Ball's poem, in contrast, is seemingly incompatible with any known language. *Finnegans Wake* shares some of the compromised linguistic compatibility of "Jabberwocky" although its unintelligible words are not necessarily restricted to nouns and verbs and may be capable of analysis and interpretation. The syntax of the following line is English—"we hear also through successive ages that shebby choruysh of unkalified muzzlenimiissilehims that would blackguardise the whitestone ever hurtleturtled out of heaven" (*FW* 5.15–18)—and several of the line's unfamiliar words can be interpreted by analogy. Roland McHugh readily glosses "shebby choruysh of unkalified muzzlenimiissilehims" as "shabby chorus of unqualified Moslems,"[11] although the portmanteau structure allows additional meanings to be imputed to the words as well. "Unkalified," for example, could also be glossed as "un-caliph-ied" or "uncalcified." We can thus concede that, in spite of its many portmanteaus and neologisms, the *Wake* exhibits general linguistic compatibility with English.

Analytical compatibility holds that the textual actual world is accessible from our world if "objects designated by the same words have the same essential properties," as Ryan notes (33). The words "hurtle" and "turtle" in "hurtleturtled" presumably have the same general meaning and allude to the same properties in the *Wake* as they do when the words are used in reference to our actual world. It is their conjunction that strains analytical compatibility since turtles do not generally hurtle, except perhaps when they capsize. Logical compatibility becomes even trickier. This accessibility relation stipulates that the textual actual world is accessible from the actual world if both worlds respect the principles of noncontradiction and of the excluded middle.[12] Ryan's example of a work of fiction that violates logical compatibility is Robert Pinget's *Le Libera* in which "a certain character is dead, and thirty pages later . . . he is alive" (38).[13] If, like the man in the song "Tim Finnegan's Wake," a character in the *Wake* text is indeed simultaneously dead and alive, then the principle of noncontradiction and the relation of logical compatibility are violated.

When we consider such accessibility relations as identity of properties, physical compatibility, and taxonomic compatibility, we encounter a world in Book I, chapter 1, whose generic features fail to conform to fictional realism. Identity of properties posits that objects common to the textual actual world and our actual world have the same properties. Physical compatibility assumes that the physical laws of our actual world will pertain in the textual actual world. Taxonomic compatibility makes the textual actual world accessible from our actual world if it contains the same species, and species with the same properties, as our actual world. These categories appear to some degree related in terms of their manifestation (and violation) in the *Wake*, as we can see in the apparent instances of shape-shifting in the text.

In her early appearances in chapter 1, the female figure we later call Anna Livia Plurabelle is indeterminate with respect to her species. "We nowhere she lives," the narration tells us, although it is unclear if her "candlelittle houthse of a month and one windies" is indeed a human habitation on a hill or a down ("Downadown, High Downadown"—*FW* 10.28) or an effigy of a house (*FW* 10.26, 27–28). Her home could be an ornament like a cuckoo clock or a barometric device in which little figures mechanically move in and out of a little house. In this case, ALP's species would be a manufactured bird or human effigy rather than a female person. On the other hand, the description of "that gnarlybird ygathering, a runalittle, doalittle, preealittle . . . helfalittle, pelfalittle gnarlybird" is far too active for a cuckoo-clock bird although its motions are still a little too mechanical to verify that she is here a natural avian species (*FW* 10.31–34). A little later, however, she is more clearly a human woman, however comical, "livving in our midst of debt and laffing through all plores for us" (*FW* 11.32–33). And when the narration returns her to the shore after the deluge, we see her building a peat fire and doing all "a turf-woman can to piff the business on" (*FW* 12.11). If ALP is both a hen and a woman, then her properties do not conform to those of the real world, and physical, taxonomic, and logical compatibility are all violated. This female dual identity is not precisely shape-shifting, however, because we do not actually see her transformed into a hen and back again.[14] But neither can we account for it as purely metaphorical with any certainty. The little hen is too vivid on the one hand, and the woman too caricatured on the other, to clarify which is "real" and which is merely a gloss on the other. According to Ryan, a metaphor does not relocate us into a different fictional world but merely gives us a new perspective on a particular entity (82). So, is ALP *like* a hen as she scavenges and picks up bits of detritus on her scurrying walk, or does she actually appear *as* a hen? Critics generally treat the distinction as an irrelevancy, even when, as in chapter 8, ALP's identity with the river egregiously violates taxonomic compatibility. Gordon, for example, concedes the fluid identity of the female figure but nonetheless privileges the anthropomorphic side of "ALP-as-river" (64).

In the sixth chapter of Book I, the riddles and problems with physical, taxonomic, and logical compatibility continue to intensify the nonrealistic features of the *Wake*'s fiction. The Mookse and the Gripes appear to offer indeterminate species, since the properties of the Gripes, for example, suggest a talking grape or a raisin "parched on a limb. . . . fit to be dried" (*FW* 153.10–11). If so, its taxonomy certainly violates physical laws. This suggests that *Finnegans Wake* generically resembles a fairy tale or the fantasy genre of the Wonderland sections of Lewis Carroll's *Alice* books. The tale of the Mookse and the Gripes, however, is embedded in the lecture of the protean instructor, "Professor Loewy-Brueller," who offers it to his "muddlecrass pupils" as an "easyfree translation of the old fabulist's parable" (*FW* 150.15, 152.08, 12–13). The figures in fables such as Aesop's are patently offered as heuristic devices in the service of illustration and therefore enjoy only a provisional fictional status.[15] Regarding the *Wake* as a generic fairy tale raises a different problem. Ryan points out that traditional fairy tales are genres in which taxonomic and physical compatibility with the actual world has indeed been waived—to produce dragons, fairies, unicorns, and talking frogs. But another accessibility relation—chronological compatibility—generally remains in place. Traditional fairy tales are located, she comments, in a consistent mythical past whose classes of objects are those of "preindustrial societies: cottages rather than condominiums, swords rather than guns, and horses as a primary mode of transportation" (37). But as early as Book I, chapter 1, chronological compatibility appears to be violated in the *Wake*. From the beginning of the chapter, the narrative voice offers both a geographical or spatial survey and a historical or chronological survey. Although the voice appears spatially located in and around Dublin, its moment in time is less clearly defined. We might call its historical indeterminacy a kind of temporal no-man's land, were it not for two notable accounts in which the narrative voice appears to function as a present witness to a scene whose general historical era can be identified. These two scenes—the first in the Wellington Museum or Museyroom and the second on a prehistoric mound—are neither chronologically consistent nor logically consecutive. Although the account of the battle of Waterloo is vivid, its dramatic quality comes chiefly from the description and narrative interpretation of artifacts and representations in the museum display. A guide points to Wellington's dispatch book—"This is the Willingdone's hurold dispitchback"—and proceeds dramatically to relate one of the French messages—"Figtreeyou! Damn fairy ann, Voutre. Willingdone" (*FW* 9.11–12, 13–14). The narrator's presence in such a museum dates the tour as occurring after the eighteenth century. The visit to the primitive cave littered with gnawed bones that follows this some six pages later consequently offers a relocation in time, a kind of time-travel without transition to a distant past. Here the narrative voice approaches a human creature described as a "dragon man" whose language he must establish before he can engage him in conversation—"You tolkatiff scowegian? Nn" (*FW* 15.34, 16.06). A narrator located in two different time frames further contributes to the negation of a textual actual world in the *Wake*.[16]

Since *Finnegans Wake* does not exhibit a textual actual world (as *Ulysses* does), it is most plausibly categorized as a fantasy universe within Ryan's system of fictionality. She writes, "A last type of private sphere involved in narrative semantics is formed by the mind's creations: dreams, hallucinations, fantasies, and fictional stories told to or composed by the characters. These constructs are not simply satellites of TAW [textual actual worlds], but

complete universes, and they are reached by characters through a recentering"
(119). This description is compatible with analyses that treat *Finnegans
Wake* as a fictional dream experience disconnected from a waking figure in a
waking textual reality or waking actual world. Ryan points out, however, that
a fantasy universe may contain its own textual actual worlds surrounded by
private or possible worlds: "By virtue of the inherent recursivity of recentering,
the members of F-worlds [fantasy-worlds] have at their disposal the entire
array of world-creating activities: the characters in a dream may dream, the
heroes of fictional fictions may write fictions" (119). Returning to Book I,
chapter 1, we can now identify its narrative shift from museum to prehistoric
mound as an external recentering from one provisional textual actual world
to another. In other words, the Museyroom feels actual or factual for the
duration of the tour, with the guiding voice warning visitors to "[m]ind your
hats goan in!" and, once inside, pointing to various objects—"This is the
flag. . . . This is the bullet. . . . This is the triplewon hat of Lipoleum" (*FW*
8.09, 12–16). This sense of immediate presence is intensified by reference
to sensation, a complaint about the warmth of the museum's enclosed space
contrasted with the relief of the cool air outside—"What a warm time we
were in there but how keling is here the airabouts!" (*FW* 10.25–26). The same
feeling of a provisional actual world will pertain on the prehistoric mound,
as the narrative voice describes the "carl on the kopje in pelted thongs" who
is "slaking nuncheon out of some thing's brain pan" and takes us on a closer
approach (*FW* 15.29, 33–34). The word "kopje" identifies the place as a small
hill in South Africa occupied by a "kraal" or enclosure for cattle: "Lets we
overstep his fire defences and these kraals of slitsucked marrogbones. (Cave!)"
(*FW* 16.02–03). As in a dream, the narrative consciousness can move (or be
recentered) from one geographical and temporal scene to a totally different
one without being grounded in an external textual actual world. In this sense,
the *Wake* is like Wonderland minus the Victorian setting that precedes
Alice's falling asleep and dreaming and that returns her to a more or less
realistic setting again upon waking. The *Wake* world will therefore be virtual
in its entirety—made up entirely of private or possible worlds marked by the
further recursivity that Ryan has noted.[17] Its narrative consciousness is able
to tell and read stories, to recall memories, to foresee events, and to describe
itself as dreaming. "And as I was jogging along in a dream as dozing I was
dawdling, arrah, methought broadtone was heard . . . Shaun! Shaun! Post
the post!" (*FW* 404.0307), the narrative voice tells us in Book III. The *Wake*
has many such embedded accounts, and Ryan writes, "Embedded narratives,
as we have seen, are mental representations produced by characters. They are
called virtual when they are not verified in the factual domain" (168). The
peculiarity of the *Finnegans Wake* world may be ascribed to its status as an

entirely virtual construction that makes no attempt to present itself as actual but rather flaunts its virtuality.

What then are these possible worlds that comprise the fictional world of *Finnegans Wake*? If we look at the beginning of the first chapter, we may question whether the textual domain is quite as private as a conventional possible world constructed in the mind of a novelistic character. The *Wake*'s initial narrative voice is anonymous and gives itself no distinguishing features that might characterize it as a specific individual. In this respect, it appears to function like a third-person narrator—a position in fiction that carries with it both authority and what Doležel calls an "authenticating" function: "Entities introduced in the discourse of the anonymous third-person narrator are *eo ipso* authenticated as fictional facts, while those introduced in the discourse of the fictional persons are not" (149). Is the opening of the *Wake* a conventional third-person narration after all, describing for the reader an actual or factual world? If not, why not? It is telling that Joyce gives the initial narrative voice of *Finnegans Wake* the rhetorical inflection of a tour guide, because such a discourse carries with it the implied promise of authoritative knowledge grounded in factuality, offering history rather than fiction, promising clarity rather than obfuscation. Yet these premises are effectively violated from the beginning.

If the first paragraph offers us a plausible spatial orientation—a description of the course of the river Liffey winding its way past the church of Adam and Eve to Howth Castle and its environs—the second paragraph offers an unsettled temporal orientation. It alludes to events that have not yet occurred: "nor had topsawyer's rocks by the stream Oconee exaggerated themselse"; "not yet, though venissoon after, had a kidscad buttended a bland old isaac"; and "not yet, though all's fair in vanessy, were sosie sesthers wroth with twone nathandjoe" (*FW* 3.06–07, 10–11, 3.11–12). Without being identified or described, the putative inaugural events of the *Wake*'s narrative are, curiously, postdated. If the narrative voice aims to function like a tour guide, it perversely replaces a historical time frame with an indeterminable temporal relativity. A fundamental condition of narrative is violated at the outset: the condition that offers "temporally ordered sequences of states of affairs that are taken to be actual/factual ('what happens')," to cite Prince again (77). What further intensifies the effect of this initial narrative disorientation, and its displacement of orientation, is the impact of the various violated accessibility relations. For one, tour guides can only be effective if they speak in the language of their audience, and yet this voice speaks English that is simultaneously not-precisely-English. Such partial linguistic incompatibility inserts a pronounced linguistic static into the discourse. From the first page on, the narrative voice is nonauthoritative and speaks not from the ground of an actual world but from the ground of an idiosyncratic knowledge-world.

As the chapter proceeds, it becomes clear that the narrator's knowledge-world is bedeviled by a paradox. On the one hand, the knowledge which preoccupies it concerns public lore—the kind of "social representations" that Doležel finds in "scientific knowledge, ideologies, religions, cultural myths" (126). On the other, this knowledge is both deployed and pursued through epistemic processes that typically characterize subjective knowledge-worlds in fiction. A character's thoughts, like Leopold Bloom's in *Ulysses*, for example, can jump around from one bit of knowledge to another, linked by association rather than causal logic. In the *Wake*, the "fall" off the wall on the first page is described as producing a giant figure sprawled across the landscape "where oranges have been laid to rust upon the green since devlinsfirst loved livvy" (*FW* 3.15, 23–24). The Irish conflicts symbolized by the colors of orange (from the Protestant William of Orange) and green (associated with St. Patrick's shamrock) trigger thoughts of even earlier conflicts, between Ostrogoths and Visigoths or between oyster totems and fish totems—"What clashes here of wills gen wonts, oystrygods gaggin fishygods!" (*FW* 4.01–02). The end of conflict suggests a return to a landscape of fallen and resurgent trees: "The oaks of ald now they lie in peat yet elms leap where askes lay" (*FW* 4.14–15). Thoughts of the fall trigger thoughts of conflict that return back to thoughts of fall and rising again. The Wakean knowledge-world is, therefore, a strange hybrid of public knowledge and private thought-processes that fail to function as epistemic operators generally do in fiction. Doležel writes of fictional characters, "The person's practical reasoning and, consequently, his or her acting and interacting are to a high degree determined by this epistemic perspective, by what the agent knows, is ignorant of, and believes to be the case in the world" (126). But although chapter 1 of the *Wake* appears to harbor an enigma—"What then agentlike brought about that tragoady thundersday this municipal sin business?" (*FW* 5.1314)—the text fails to conform to those kinds of genres, such as the mystery novel, in which the secret becomes the spur to an epistemic narrative. Nor will it produce the kind of inner or outer searching which leads from ignorance or false beliefs to psychological or moral truths in the *Bildungsroman* or some types of Victorian fiction. The problem is partly that the "municipal sin business" is not defined as a factual incident whose unknown causes, agents, or perpetrators can be intellectually pursued and revealed; but it is also that the knowledge-world of the chapter is here yoked to the invocation of an obligation-world, whose criteria of social rules and moral principles are equally impenetrable.

Doležel refers to obligation-worlds as the effect of "deontic" constraints in the form of proscriptive and prescriptive norms operative in fictional worlds: "the norms determine which actions are prohibited, obligatory, or permitted" (120). He goes on to say that "[t]he deontic marking of actions is the richest source of narrativity; it generates the famous triad of the *fall* (violation of a norm—punishment), the *test* (obligation fulfilled—reward), and the *predicament* (conflict of obligations), stories retold again and again, from myths and fairy tales to contemporary fiction" (121). The first page of *Finnegans Wake* virtually predicts this metanarrative description in its announcement of the fall: "The fall . . . of a once wallstrait oldparr is retaled early in bed and later on life down through all christian minstrelsy" (*FW* 3.15.18). For Burrell, this provides the key to the *Wake*: "The search for 'a simple text' as well as a 'germinal deep structure' is revealed in the second and third chapters of Genesis, which tell the Judeo-Christian version of the Fall of Man" (9). There are indeed many allusions to transgressions, guilt, failings, and the like in the first chapter of Joyce's book, but the conflation of knowledge- and obligation-worlds ensures that the deontic norms at issue are placed in question even as they are narrativized. It is as though the narrative voice asks not only what brought about "this municipal sin business" but who sinned, why did they sin, and—most vexingly—what precisely *was* the sin? One of the first narrative stories that supposedly represents the fall tells of "Bygmester Finnegan, of the Stuttering Hand," who appears to live in—or prior to—Burrell's Biblical realm "before joshuan judges had given us numbers or Helviticus committed deuteronomy" (*FW* 4.18, 20–21). But is Finnegan described as building a skyscraper too high and tumbling down, or merely imagining, perhaps in an alcoholic haze ("he seesaw by neatlight of the liquor"—*FW* 4.33–34), "a waalworth of a skyerscape of most eyeful hoyth entowerly, erigenating from next to nothing and celescalating the himals" (*FW* 4.35–5.01). The fall, in this anecdote, if there is one, is described as "larrons o'toolers clittering up and tombles a'buckets clottering down" or tools going up and buckets tumbling down (*FW* 5.03–04)—or is it Lawrence O'Toole, Dublin's patron saint, going up and his contemporary Thomas à Beckett tumbling down? Does Bygmester Finnegan, the character of this anecdote, rise and fall as he does in the ballad or only imagine a rising and falling? And if he does rise and fall, what norm has been transgressed? Multiple possibilities are suggested, from masturbation (the "Stuttering Hand" and the "overalls which he habitacularly fondseed"—*FW* 4.31) to freemasonry, drunkenness ("all the guenneses had met their exodus"—*FW* 4.24), or, like Henrik Ibsen's Masterbuilder, ambition and hubris. The narrative knowledge-world is obstructed in its insight by linguistic static and by the possible virtuality of what is described—that is, fantasy, dream, or imagining rather than the commission of an action.

Neither the tour through the Wellington Museum nor the interview of the figure on the prehistoric mound yields information or knowledge that sketches in the nature of the *Wake*'s obligation-world. In this respect, the

Wake contrasts dramatically with fictions that make their obligation-worlds perfectly clear—for example, Joyce's *A Portrait of the Artist as a Young Man*. The case of Charles Stewart Parnell in this early work exemplifies Doležel's deontic conditions for "the *fall* (violation of a norm—punishment)": adultery is Parnell's violation of the norm, and political disfavor is his punishment. But when the *Wake* alludes to similar infractions, they are muddled and unclear. When we are told that "a gynecure was let on to the scuffold for taking that same fine sum covertly by meddlement with the drawers of his neighbour's safe" (*FW* 14.25–27), are we informed of a theft or of an adulterous molestation? The allusion to the sin of coveting a neighbor's wife gets verbally mixed up with covertly taking a sum from a neighbor's safe.

When the text offers us an embedded tale a little later in the chapter, we might expect that this will shed some light on the deontic constraints at stake in the "municipal sin business." The embedded narrative of the tale of the prankquean appears to allude simultaneously to a transgression (kidnapping and theft) and to Doležel's second deontic narrative construction of "the *test* (obligation fulfilled—reward)." Yet the deontic structures are again, typically, confused. Does Jarl van Hoother fail the test because of his inability to answer the prankquean's riddle—"why do I am alook alike a poss of porterpease?"—or does the prankquean transgress by taking away his child—"[s]o her grace o'malice kidsnapped up the jiminy Tristopher and into the shandy westerness she rain, rain, rain" (*FW* 21.18–19, 21.20–22)? In order for the "Tale of the Prankquean" to serve a didactic narrative purpose as a parable, it would have to offer clarity with respect to the social or ethical norms of its particular world and the consequences of adherence to, or departure from, them. Instead, van Hoother fails to answer the riddle, the prankquean kidnaps the children, and van Hoother, dressed in elaborate and colorful garb, goes abroad, possibly to confront her: "And he clopped his rude hand to his eacy hitch and he ordurd and his thick spch spck for her to shut up shop, dappy. And the duppy shot the shutter clup" (*FW* 23.03–05). He has ordered her to shut up shop, and she complies, and the felicity of the polis has been restored? Is that what happens, and if so, what lesson have we learned? We are given a glimpse in this first chapter of a fictional consciousness whose knowledge- and obligation-worlds operate at cross-purposes, and this collision of possible worlds takes on the role that narrative plot normally plays in fiction.

As the chapter nears its end, a curious shift in person, tone, and modality occurs. The narrative voice moves from third to second person, for a time, and from an impersonal tone to a colloquial and familiar Irish vernacular: "Now be aisy, good Mr Finnimore, sir. And take your laysure like a god on pension and don't be walking abroad" (*FW* 24.16–17). Has the narratorial character shifted or is the initial narrative voice quoting or mimicking the speech of another figure? In either case, the address can be inferred as being made to a corpse who wishes to rise—an inference supported by a distorted reference to a line from the ballad "Tim Finnegan's Wake"— "Anam muck an dhoul! Did ye drink me doornail?" (*FW* 24.15). The shift in modality introduces Ryan's third private possible world—a wish-world— into the chapter, although its function here is most peculiar. Also known as "the *axiological* system" proposed by Ryan (111), the wish-world engages personal values and desires, or what is considered good, bad, indifferent, or desirable by an individual. In an effort to dissuade the dead man from rising, the narrative voice now assures Mr. Finnimore that he is better off where he is: "You're better off, sir, where you are, primesigned in the full of your dress, bloodeagle waistcoat and all" (*FW* 24.28–29). And it promises that his friends will take care of him—or at least his grave: "And we'll be coming here, the ombre players, to rake your gravel and bringing you presents, won't we, fenians?" (*FW* 24.35–25.01). The strategy of imputing what he would value to the dead man requires transferring desires from the domain of the speaker, a maneuver which insures that the transferred values and desires are imagined or made up in a way that doubles their virtuality. Another version of this maneuver can be seen in the way the speaker offers the dead man his own past memories as a compensatory gesture: "If you only were there to explain the meaning, best of men, and talk to her nice of guldenselver. The lips would moisten once again. As when you drove with her to Findrinny Fair. What with reins here and ribbons there all your hands were employed so she never knew was she on land or at sea or swooped through the blue like Airwinger's bride" (*FW* 28.10–15). The erstwhile bride—Earwicker's we presume—is conjured up for the dead man as a figure of his wish-world, but she is quickly interpolated into a scene that would, one might expect, dismay him. This is the news, reported as a rumor ("as it is told me"—*FW* 29.01) of "a big rody ram lad at random on the premises" (*FW* 28.36), presumably to take his place. The wish-worlds in the *Wake* appear frequently to involve domestic relations and domestic scenes and, therefore, generally encompass female figures, while its knowledge—and obligation—worlds extend into the larger community. The *Wake* implicitly offers gender typologies, in this respect.

So what sort of fictional world or worlds have we traversed after reading the first chapter of *Finnegans Wake*? It is one riddled with contradictions, albeit contradictions that can be analyzed. The narrator's hybrid status of a voice fluctuating between anonymous and impersonal third person, yet endowed with a logic resembling stream of consciousness, creates an indeterminate knowledge-world. Its preoccupation with falling, sin, and possible redemption suggests an obligation-world made untenable by its failure to identify norms or the criteria for conforming or violating them.

And insofar as it conjures up wish-worlds, these are imputed to figures rather than expressed directly and are, therefore, also indeterminate with respect to their status as a private possible world. These contradictions can further be ascribed to the text's failure to represent a textual actual world.

Ryan discusses three possible consequences when fictional language fails to produce a representation of a factual domain: the empty center, the unknowable center, and radical lack of authority (39–40). *Finnegans Wake* appears to exhibit all three at various times. A text with an empty fictional center results, Ryan comments, when it "limits its assertions to worlds at the periphery, avoiding the representation of an actual world" (39). This pertains when the *Wake* narrative reports something as rumor or retells a tale or expresses uncertainty about what occurred. Ryan believes that a text has an unknowable center "by leaving it unclear who is speaking, or by preventing the reader from identifying the reference world of sentences" (40). This condition seems to hold pretty consistently throughout *Finnegans Wake*. The frequent use of pronominal constructions, which refer to a "he" or a "she" without a clear antecedent, offers just one example of this problem. "Radical lack of authority" is exhibited by a text when it retracts its own statements or denies its own assertions or otherwise leaves in doubt what is true or untrue—a phenomenon exemplified by the proliferation of versions of various events throughout the work. The following narrative statement from the first chapter exemplifies all three characteristics of undecidable fictional domains: "It may half been a missfired brick, as some say, or it mought have been due to a collupsus of his back promises, as others looked at it. (There extand by now one thousand and one stories, all told, of the same)" (*FW* 5.26–29).[18] What all of this amounts to is a radical experiment with fictionality itself, a maneuver—programmatically, if not systematically—to undo the way fiction operates. It is as though Joyce figured out a way to write a work of anti-fiction which nonetheless remains fictional—a feat that has traditionally been metaphorized as his creation of a dream-world or a dream-work.[19] Insofar as the dream is our model of an alternative world where logic and norms fail to hold sway, where physical laws may be broken and knowledge breaks down, where taxonomies may become confused and identities and properties may shift and merge, the dream is an excellent model for the *Wake*'s fictionality. Possible Worlds theory provides a semantic rather than a psychological analysis of such a world.

To return now to Gordon's *"Finnegans Wake": A Plot Summary* and Burrell's *Narrative Design in "Finnegans Wake,"* we can use the theoretical insights of Possible Worlds theory to analyze better some of their strategies in dealing with the highly unconventional fictional construction of this text. Doležel points out that, because texts are inevitably incomplete, "implicitness is a universal feature of texts" (172). He then goes on to discuss the means by which implicitness is grounded in the explicit texture—the words on the page—of the work. The first is by way of a "felt *absence*," by gaps and lacunae (173). The second is by "the opposite kind of marking: the *presence* in the text of some signals or indexes, particularly hints, insinuations, and allusions, most of them found in co-text or context" (173). Gordon's procedure seems to connect these two kinds of implication to produce his sense of a hidden "realism" in the work. The absence he rightly detects is that of an actual, factual world. But instead of interpreting this absence as an indicator of fantasy or hallucination, Gordon sets out to correct it by weaving the positive indices of disjointed references and sprinkled allusions together in order to reconstruct a more familiar and more coherent semblance of an actual world. In practice, this often requires putting details from various parts of the book together. Here is how he assembles evidence that the Earwicker bedroom contains a washbasin: "The basin is a sink-and-faucet affair, set into the wall. It is mentioned explicitly in I/5, where we hear that HCE 'takes a szumbath for his weekend and a wassarnap [German, "water basin"] for his refreshment' (129.29), a practice recommended on 525.02–3" (21). Gordon's evidence for the time of the action in the *Wake* is assembled in a similar way. A reference to "'a tubtail of mondayne clothes' (333.23–4) reminds us, Monday is washday" (37), he writes. This datum is corroborated by a reference to "'Deemsday,' German *Dienstag*, Tuesday (602.20)" in a quite different part of the book (37). Such a procedure also draws attention to another characteristic of *Wake* language to which I have alluded in passing without pausing to analyze it. What I have earlier described as "linguistic static," the property of words to veer away from standard English in a way that embeds allusions to other words, allows the language frequently to conjure up more than one fictional domain in a single passage or even sentence. Take, for example, the phrase "wolkencap is on him, frowned; audiurient, he would evesdrip, were it mous at hand, were it dinn of bottles in the far ear" (*FW* 23.21–23). If one took the hint of the German "wolken" or cloud as a point of departure, the sentence could refer to a figure under a cloud, perhaps under a dripping eave, hearing the din of battle afar. But Gordon sees in "wolkencap" a "woollen nightcap" and pictures the figure in bed, eavesdropping on a female voice (120). Both fictional scenes—one outdoors and impersonal, one indoors and intimate— are discernable in the sentence as a result of the linguistic overlay. In making the case for realism, Gordon generally privileges the domestic and local domains conjured by the language of the text over other realms that may coexist with them.

    Burrell's procedure depends on another aspect of the role that implicitness plays in fiction, and that is the role of allusion and intertextuality. The latter can, of course, be explicit in fiction—for example, when we learn that Gerty MacDowell has read *The Lamplighter* or that Molly Bloom is familiar with *Moll Flanders*. But the Joycean text also displays significant implicit intertextuality, as the Homeric parallels with the *Odyssey* in *Ulysses* make clear, and as James S. Atherton tracks in his invaluable *The Books at the "Wake."*[20] The function of allusion is to "direct the interpreter from one literary text to other texts," according to Doležel (201), and it therefore supplies the conduit between the words on the page and their hidden textual references. Burrell seizes precisely on this function of allusion to ground his argument: "One of the reasons for postulating that *Finnegans Wake* is the rewritten Bible is that Joyce carefully leaves clues of a parallel structure between them" (15). His overall procedure explicitly acknowledges conformity to the intuitive and subjective method Doležel describes: "[a] meaning is suggested that the critic feels or believes to be 'hidden' in the text: the text is made to mean what the interpreter wants it to mean" (173).[21] Burrell acknowledges that the Bible will work as the key to the *Wake* strictly on condition of this kind of shared faith: "What is required is the proper mind-set. Readers must approach the text with the resolute conviction that Joyce intended his basic level of narration to be his own peculiar transcription of Genesis. If they seek, they will find. The apparent or surface message must be subverted until the underlying association can be made" (13). Part of the justification for Burrell's faith in this master-narrative's function is that it allows him to mobilize two versions of intertextuality simultaneously. Doležel points out that "Riffaterre differentiates two sources of intertextuality: particular texts and universal cultural stock" (200). Burrell relies on Genesis to function as a universal cultural stock whose intertextual presence in *Finnegans Wake* he can then verify by identifying parallels and references to the Bible as a specific text.[22] For Burrell, these parallels reside not only in allusions but also in such structural features as "multiple stories," "digressions," "repetition," and others, including arcane practices such as the use of "masoretic consonants" (18). But Burrell's condition for his reading—that "the apparent or surface message must be subverted until the underlying association can be made"— finally produces reductive paraphrases which violate the *Wake*'s own unique fictional and narrative subversions.

The privileging of one or another "hidden" narrative in *Finnegans Wake* may be the only plausible way to produce a more or less coherent meaning out of the otherwise elusive textual and fictional construction of the work. Other critics like Kimberly J. Devlin, Bishop, and Patrick A. McCarthy have avoided foregrounding a specific "hidden" narrative to replace the surface textual complications and have, therefore, engaged more directly with the virtuality of *Finnegans Wake*'s fictional construction.[23] Devlin resorts to an intertextual reading by considering the *Wake*'s strangeness as an "uncanny" revisitation of Joyce's earlier texts (ix). This strategy preserves both the book's virtual character as a fantasy or dream text while nonetheless giving it reference points in the multiple actual and possible worlds of *Dubliners*, *A Portrait*, and *Ulysses*. Bishop's approach to the *Wake* as a night-book or sleep-book, rather than a dream-book, allows him to dispense with reconstructing an alternative narrative for the text altogether: "No one remembers the experience of sleep, if at all, as a sequence of events linked chronologically in time by cause and effect from the moment his head hit the pillow to the time the alarm clock startled him into rational accountability in the morning" (9). Bishop draws from this insight inferences about the *Wake*'s narrative construction: "If one operates on the premise that *Finnegans Wake* reconstructs the night, the first preconception to abandon wholesale is that it ought to read anything at all like narrative or make sense as a continuous linear whole" (27). McCarthy's exploration of the riddles in the *Wake* is premised on the conviction that "certainty is virtually nonexistent in this book," an insight that implicitly acknowledges the text as the subversion of a possible knowledge-world: "In this respect *Finnegans Wake* reflects the world it describes, a world in which rumor outdistances concrete evidence, in which appearance and reality are inseparable, in which the underlying order of human experience must be reconstructed by each person since the world presents such experience to us haphazardly and arbitrarily" (16). Each of these studies has successfully engaged with the *Wake* as a fantasy universe without the theoretical apparatus of Possible Worlds theory, but while this apparatus may not be essential for exploring the fictional construction of the *Finnegans Wake* text, it nonetheless holds great promise for usefulness in approaching the work in the twenty-first century. Together with contemporary narratology, Possible Worlds theory could abet a more rigorous analysis of the immensely difficult Books II and III, for example. The knowledge-worlds of the Homework chapter (II.2), the recursive narratives in the Tavern chapter (II.3), the obligation-worlds that haunt Shaun in Book III, and the wish-worlds of ALP in Book IV—all exhibit multiple and overlapping possible worlds that invite further theoretical exploration. Now there are new tools and vehicles at hand for just such an intellectual journey into the mind or minds that constitute the fictional domains of *Finnegans Wake*.

NOTES

1. Harry Burrell, *Narrative Design in "Finnegans Wake": The "Wake" Lock Picked* (Gainesville: Univ. Press of Florida, 1996), p. 8. Further references will be cited parenthetically in the text.

2. Joseph Campbell and Henry Morton Robinson, *A Skeleton Key to "Finnegans Wake"* (New York: Viking Press, 1969).

3. See Ruth Ronen, *Possible Worlds in Literary Theory* (Cambridge: Cambridge Univ. Press, 1994), p. 76. Three of the major texts exploring this field came out in the 1990s. Marie-Laure Ryan published *Possible Worlds, Artificial Intelligence, and Narrative Theory*

(Bloomington: Indiana Univ. Press, 1991), followed by Ronen's book, and Lubomír Doležel's *Heterocosmica: Fiction and Possible Worlds* (Baltimore: Johns Hopkins Univ. Press, 1998). Thomas G. Pavel's *Fictional Worlds* (Cambridge: Harvard Univ. Press, 1986) was an earlier text. None of these texts makes any significant mention of Joyce's writing in reference to their theories. Further references to the Ryan and Doležel works will be cited parenthetically in the text.

4. Gerald Prince, *Dictionary of Narratology*, rev. ed. (Lincoln: Univ. of Nebraska Press, 2003), p. 77. Further references will be cited parenthetically in the text.

5. Edmund Wilson, "The Dream of H. C. Earwicker," *The Wound and the Bow: Seven Studies in Literature* (New York: Oxford Univ. Press, 1959), p. 245.

6. Clive Hart, *Structure and Motif in "Finnegans Wake"* (London: Faber and Faber, 1962), p. 79.

7. John Gordon, *"Finnegans Wake": A Plot Summary* (Dublin: Gill and Macmillan, 1986), p. 1. Further references will be cited parenthetically in the text.

8. See Ryan's discussion of K-worlds (pp. 114–16), O-worlds (pp. 116–17), and W-worlds (pp. 117–18).

9. See Lewis Carroll, "Humpty Dumpty," *Through the Looking-Glass and What Alice Found There* (Oxford: Oxford Univ. Press, 1982), p. 191.

10. Hugo Ball's sound poem is quoted in Hans Richter, *Dada: Art and Anti-Art* (New York: McGraw Hill, 1965), p. 42, and also in Susan Stewart, *Nonsense: Aspects of Intertextuality in Folklore and Literature* (Baltimore: Johns Hopkins Univ. Press, 1978), p. 92, and can additionally be found at <http://www.peak.org/~dadaist/English/Graphics/gadjiberi.html>.

11. Roland McHugh, *Annotations to "Finnegans Wake,"* rev. ed. (Baltimore: Johns Hopkins Univ. Press, 1991), p. 5.

12. The principle of noncontradiction would find the statement "John Doe is both bald and not bald" illogical, while the law of the excluded middle would find the statement "John Doe is either bald or not bald" true.

13. Robert Pinget, *Le Libera* (Paris: Éditions de Minuit, 1968).

14. Campbell and Robinson describe the ALP species in this section in this way: "[t]he janitrix herself, in a bird transformation, moves through the twilight, gathering relics" (p. 42).

15. Campbell and Robinson identify the Mookse and the Gripes as echoing figures of Aesop's "The Fox and the Grapes" and Carroll's "The Mock Turtle and the Griffon," but the more serious allegorical object of the Professor's fable, they point out, is the invasion of Ireland by Henry II at the suggestion of Pope Adrian IV's papal bull (p. 114). The Professor's pupils are, therefore, not meant to believe in the fictional reality of the Mookse and the Gripes except instrumentally and provisionally, in order to understand the complex historical story of how Ireland came to be under British rule.

16. If *Finnegans Wake* makes references to events that postdate its writing and publication dates, then its genre would share the features of science fiction, which is marked by a chronologically inconsistent inventory, among other actual world departures. Murray Gell-Mann's 1961 discovery of the atomic particle he called the "quark" does not fall into this category because the *Wake*'s "*quarks*" at 383.01 refer simply to a cheer, perhaps in the form of "quacks." But the description of the "*abnihilisation of the etym*" with its allusion to "*moletons skaping with mulicules*" appears improbably to gesture toward nuclear fission and the splitting of the atom (*FW* 353.22, 26). Yet it is difficult to imagine how Joyce would have learned of the highly secret experiments that were conducted in Berlin and France in 1939 unless there was discussion of their possibility in the 1930s. The references to "television" (*FW* 150.33) are less problematic because the first television broadcasts with levels of

what we would consider modern definition were aired in Britain in 1936, and Joyce could presumably have heard discussion of the possibility of such devices.

17. The frequency of story-telling in the *Wake* may signal a difference from dream narrative, however, since dreams tend to present scenes as lived or experienced rather than as heard.

18. A final possibility raised by Ryan might also be considered for its possible relevance to *Finnegans Wake*: a fictional world that has a "ubiquitous center" because it absorbs "*all* possible worlds within the boundaries of TAW [textual actual world]" (p. 41). Ryan's example of such a text is the virtual Chinese fiction described by Jorge Luis Borges in "The Garden of Forking Paths," *Fictions, Labyrinths: Selected Stories and Other Writings* (New York: Modern Library, 1983), p. 26. In the story, a figure chooses all possibilities when confronted with a choice and therefore creates all possible futures for itself. Such a fiction requires a basic textual actual world, however, which *Finnegans Wake* does not exhibit.

19. Two critical works that explicitly take the dream as their main trope for discussing the experimentalism of *Finnegans Wake* are Margot Norris's *The Decentered Universe of "Finnegans Wake"* (Baltimore: Johns Hopkins Univ. Press, 1976), and Michael H. Begnal's *Dreamscheme: Narrative and Voice in "Finnegans Wake"* (Syracuse: Syracuse Univ. Press, 1988). But while Norris invokes both Freudian theory and structuralist linguistics to argue that Joyce produces his language play on their principles (p. 100), Begnal argues for a less theoretical approach to the *Wake* as a dream work: "Joyce is very much a traditionalist when it comes to the ways in which he will manipulate plot and character" (p. xv).

20. James S. Atherton, *The Books at the "Wake": A Study of Literary Allusions in James Joyce's "Finnegans Wake"* (Carbondale: Southern Illinois Univ. Press, 1959.).

21. Another *Finnegans Wake* study that operates on this principle is Grace Eckley's *The Steadfast "Finnegans Wake"* (Lanham, Md.: Univ. Press of America, 1994). For Eckley, it is the figure of the "crusading [Victorian] journalist" William T. Stead (1849–1912) that provides "the biographical original . . . [of] Humphrey Chimpden Earwicker" (pp. 1, 196). This assertion allows Eckley to read the text chiefly as a historical novel.

22. Burrell calls the Bible "the most published and least read book ever written" (p. 27). He goes on to say that "[i]t is a mistake when approaching *Finnegans Wake* to assume that you know and remember the Bible story unless you reread and consider the exact details and wording, for this is the framework on which the *Wake* is constructed" (p. 27).

23. See Kimberly J. Devlin, *Wandering and Return in "Finnegans Wake"* (Princeton: Princeton Univ. Press, 1991); John Bishop, *Joyce's Book of the Dark: "Finnegans Wake"* (Madison: Univ. of Wisconsin Press, 1986); and Patrick A. McCarthy, *The Riddles of "Finnegans Wake"* (Cranbury, N.J.: Associated Univ. Presses, 1980). Further references to these works will be cited parenthetically in the text.

Chronology

1882	Born in Dublin on February 2 to John Stanislaus Joyce, tax collector, and Mary Jane (May) Murray Joyce. James Joyce is the eldest of ten children who survive infancy.
1888–91	Attends Clongowes Wood College, a Jesuit boarding school. He eventually is forced to leave because of his father's financial troubles. During Joyce's childhood and early adulthood, the family moves many times, from respectable suburbs of Dublin to poorer districts, as its size grows and its finances dwindle.
1892–98	Briefly attends the Christian Brothers School, then attends Belvedere College, another Jesuit school.
1898–1902	Attends University College, another Jesuit school; turns away from Catholicism and Irish nationalist politics. Writes a play, *A Brilliant Career*, and essays, several of which are published. Gradates in 1902 with a degree in modern languages. Leaves Dublin to go to Paris and study medicine.
1903	Works primarily on writing poems and reading Jonson. Learns mother is sick and so he returns home; mother dies of cancer in August, four months after he returns.
1904	Several poems and a few stories are published in various magazines. Takes first walk with Nora Barnacle, the daughter of a Galway baker who is working in a Dublin

boarding house. In October, they leave for the continent, where they will live the remainder of their lives. Joyce works at a Berlitz school.

1905   Couple moves to Trieste, where Joyce teaches at the Berlitz school. Birth of son Giorgio in July. Joyce's brother Stanislaus joins them in Trieste.

1907   After a year in Rome, where Joyce worked in a bank, the family returns to Trieste, where Joyce does private tutoring in English. *Chamber Music*, a collection of his poems, is published. Daughter, Lucia Anna, is born in July. Works on own writing and also begins writing articles for an Italian newspaper.

1909   In August, signs contract for publication of *Dubliners*, a collection of stories. Sister Eva comes to live with Joyce family.

1911   Publication of *Dubliners* is held up, mainly because of what are feared to be offensive references to Edward VII.

1912   Printer destroys the manuscript of *Dubliners*, deciding the book's aims are anti-Irish. Joyce takes the proofs, of which he has gotten a copy from his equally unsympathetic publisher, to London but cannot find a publisher for them there either.

1914   *Dubliners* published. At urging of Ezra Pound, *A Portrait of the Artist as a Young Man* is published serially by the London magazine *The Egoist*. Joyce begins work on *Ulysses*.

1915   Joyce completes his play *Exiles*. After Joyce pledges neutrality to the Austrian authorities in Trieste who threatened to intern him, the family moves to Zurich, with the exception of Stanislaus, who is interned. Joyce awarded a British Royal Literary Fund grant, the first of several grants he will receive.

1916   Publishes *A Portrait of the Artist as a Young Man* in book form in New York.

1917   Undergoes the first of numerous eye operations.

1918   Publishes *Exiles* in London and in the United States. The American magazine *The Little Review* begins serializing *Ulysses*.

1919   *The Egoist* also begins serializing *Ulysses*. The U.S. Post Office confiscates issues of *The Little Review* containing some of Joyce's work.

1920–21	More issues of *The Little Review* confiscated. In September, John S. Sumner, the secretary of the New York Society for the Prevention of Vice, lodges a protest against an issue of *The Little Review* that contains Joyce's work. *The Review* loses in court. Publication ceases in the United States. Joyce and family move to Paris. Joyce finishes *Ulysses*. Sylvia Beach agrees to publish it in Paris.
1922	Shakespeare and Company, Sylvia Beach's press, publishes *Ulysses* in Paris. Nora takes children to Galway for a visit, over Joyce's protests, and their train is fired upon by Irish Civil War combatants.
1923	Joyce begins *Finnegans Wake*, known until its publication as *Work in Progess*.
1924	Part of the *Work* appears in the Paris magazine *Transatlantic Review*.
1926	Pirated edition of *Ulysses* (incomplete) serialized in New York by *Two Worlds Monthly*.
1927	Shakespeare and Company publishes *Pomes Penyeach*. Parts of *Work* published in *Transition* in Paris.
1928	Publishes parts of *Work* in New York to protect copyright.
1929	Assists in French translation of *Ulysses*, which appears in February. Daughter Lucia Joyce operated on unsuccessfully to remove a squint. She gives up her sporadic career as a dancer; her mental stability seems precarious. To his father's delight, Giorgio Joyce makes his debut as a singer, with some success.
1930	At Joyce's instigation, Herbert Gorman begins a biography of Joyce. Joyce supervises a French translation of *Anna Livia Plurabelle*, part of the *Work*, by Samuel Beckett and friends, which appears in the *Nouvelle Revue Française* in 1931. Son marries.
1931	Joyce marries Nora Barnacle at a registry office in London. Death of Joyce's father.
1932	Daughter suffers first mental breakdown; she is diagnosed with a form of schizophrenia. Bennett Cerf of Random House contracts for the American publication of *Ulysses*.
1933	Lucia hospitalized, as she will often be until her permanent hospitalization.
1934	Random House publishes *Ulysses*.

1934	Publishes *Collected Poems* in New York and *A Chaucer A.B.C.* with illuminations by Lucia.
1939	*Finnegans Wake* published in London and New York. The Joyces move to Vichy, France, to be near Lucia in the hospital.
1940	Herbert Gorman's authorized biography of Joyce appears. After the fall of France, the Joyces manage to get to Zurich.
1941	Joyce dies following surgery on a perforated ulcer on January 13. He is buried in Zurich with no religious ceremony, at Nora's request.
1951	Nora dies on April 10. She is buried in the same cemetery as her husband but not next to him, since that space has been taken. In 1966, the two bodies are reburied together.

Contributors

HAROLD BLOOM is Sterling Professor of the Humanities at Yale University. He is the author of 30 books, including *Shelley's Mythmaking, The Visionary Company, Blake's Apocalypse, Yeats, A Map of Misreading, Kabbalah and Criticism, Agon: Toward a Theory of Revisionism, The American Religion, The Western Canon,* and *Omens of Millennium: The Gnosis of Angels, Dreams, and Resurrection. The Anxiety of Influence* sets forth Professor Bloom's provocative theory of the literary relationships between the great writers and their predecessors. His most recent books include *Shakespeare: The Invention of the Human,* a 1998 National Book Award finalist, *How to Read and Why, Genius: A Mosaic of One Hundred Exemplary Creative Minds, Hamlet: Poem Unlimited, Where Shall Wisdom Be Found?,* and *Jesus and Yahweh: The Names Divine.* In 1999, Professor Bloom received the prestigious American Academy of Arts and Letters Gold Medal for Criticism. He has also received the International Prize of Catalonia, the Alfonso Reyes Prize of Mexico, and the Hans Christian Andersen Bicentennial Prize of Denmark.

DEREK ATTRIDGE is a professor at the University of York, England, where he is also head of the Department of English and Related Literature. He is the author and editor of texts on fiction, poetry, and literary theory. He is the author of *How to Read Joyce* and *Joyce Effects: On Language, Theory, and History.* He also edited *The Cambridge Companion to James Joyce* and *James Joyce's Ulysses: A Casebook,* as well as other works on Joyce.

RICHARD POIRIER is a professor emeritus at Rutgers University. Some of his titles include *Trying It Out in America: Literary and Other Performances* and *Poetry and Pragmatism.*

WELDON THORNTON is a professor at the University of North Carolina, Chapel Hill. He is author of *Allusions in "Ulysses": An Annotated List* and coeditor of *Joyce's "Ulysses": The Larger Perspective.*

DAVID LEON HIGDON is a professor emeritus at Texas Tech University. He is the author of *Time and English Fiction* and *Shadows of the Past in Contemporary British Fiction.*

KLAUS REICHERT has been a professor at the Johann Wolfgang Goethe–Universität Frankfurt Am Main. He is an author and editor who has edited many of Virginia Woolf's books in German.

ROY K. GOTTFRIED is professor of English at Vanderbilt University and author of *Joyce's Iritis and the Irritated Text* and *The Art of Joyce's Syntax in "Ulysses."*

MARGARET MCBRIDE has been an associate professor at the University of Texas at San Antonio. She has published essays on *Ulysses* and *Finnegans Wake.*

KERI ELIZABETH AMES has taught at Yale. She has published essays in the *James Joyce Literary Supplement* and the *Joyce Studies Annual.*

JENNIFER MARGARET FRASER has taught in the literary studies program at the University of Toronto. She has published essays in the *James Joyce Quarterly* and *European Joyce Studies.*

NEIL MURPHY is an assistant professor at Nanyang University in Singapore. He is the author of *Irish Fiction and Postmodern Doubt.*

VICKI MAHAFFEY is a professor at the University of York. She has authored *States of Desire: Wilde, Yeats, Joyce and the Irish Experiment* and *Reauthorizing Joyce.*

MARGOT NORRIS is a professor at the University of California at Irvine. Her books on Joyce include *Suspicious Readings of Joyce's* Dubliners and *Joyce's Web: The Social Unraveling of Modernism,* among others. She also is president of the International James Joyce Foundation.

Bibliography

Attridge, Derek. *How to Read Joyce*. London: Granta Books, 2007.

———, ed. *James Joyce's Ulysses: A Casebook*. Oxford; New York: Oxford University Press, 2004.

Balsamo, Gian. *Joyce's Messianism: Dante, Negative Existence, and the Messianic Self*. Columbia: University of South Carolina Press, 2004.

———. "The Necropolitan Journey: Dante's Negative Poetics in James Joyce's *The Dead*." *James Joyce Quarterly* 40, no. 4 (2003): 763–81.

Bates, Robin E. *Shakespeare and the Cultural Colonization of Ireland*. New York: Routledge, 2008.

Beckman, Richard. *Joyce's Rare View: The Nature of Things in Finnegans Wake*. Gainesville: University Press of Florida, 2007.

Begnal, Michael, ed. *Joyce and the City: The Significance of Place*. Syracuse, N.Y.: Syracuse University Press, 2002.

Bertolini, David C. "Bloom's Death in "Ithaca," or the END of Ulysses (Leopold Bloom)." *Journal of Modern Literature* 31, no. 2 (Winter 2008): 39–53.

Bloom, Harold, ed. *Leopold Bloom*. Philadelphia: Chelsea House, 2004.

Boldrini, Lucia. *Joyce, Dante, and the Poetics of Literary Relations: Language and Meaning in Finnegans Wake*. Cambridge, U.K.; New York: Cambridge University Press, 2001.

Boldrini, Lucia, ed. *Medieval Joyce*. Amsterdam; New York, N.Y.: Rodopi, 2002.

Bornstein, George. *Material Modernism: The Politics of the Page*. Cambridge, U.K.; New York: Cambridge University Press, 2001.

Brooker, Joseph. *Joyce's Critics: Transitions in Reading and Culture*. Madison: University of Wisconsin Press, 2004.

Brooks, Peter. "Modernism and Realism: Joyce, Proust, Woolf." *Realist Vision*. New Haven and London: Yale University Press, 2005.

Brown, Richard, ed. *A Companion to James Joyce*. Malden, Mass.: Blackwell, 2008.

———. *Joyce, "Penelope" and the Body*. Amsterdam; New York: Rodopi, 2006.

Burke, Kenneth. "Fact, Inference, and Proof in the Analysis of Literary Symbolism." In A *Portrait of the Artist as a Young Man: Authoritative Text, Backgrounds and Contexts, Criticism*, edited by John Paul Riquelme. Norton Critical Edition. New York: W. W. Norton, 2007.

Castle, Gregory. *Modernism and the Celtic Revival*. Cambridge; New York: Cambridge University Press, 2001.

Conley, Tim. *Joyce's Mistakes: Problems of Intention, Irony and Interpretation*. Toronto; Buffalo: University of Toronto Press, 2003.

Cosgrove, Brian. *James Joyce's Negations: Irony, Indeterminacy and Nihilism in Ulysses and Other Writings*. Dublin, Ireland: University College Dublin Press, 2007.

Cotter, David. *James Joyce & the Perverse Ideal*. New York: Routledge, 2003.

Daniels, Patsy J. *The Voice of the Oppressed in the Language of the Oppressor: A Discussion of Selected Postcolonial Literature from Ireland, Africa, and America*. New York: Routledge, 2001.

Devlin, Kimberly J. *James Joyce's "Fraudstuff."* Gainesville: University Press of Florida, 2002.

Dickson, Jay. "Defining the Sentimentalist in Ulysses." *James Joyce Quarterly* 44, no. 1 (Fall 2006): 19–37.

Doherty, Gerald. *Dubliners' Dozen: The Games Narrators Play*. Madison, N.J.: Fairleigh Dickinson University Press; Cranbury, N.J.: Associated University Presses, 2004.

Eco, Umberto, and Liberato Santoro-Brienza. *Talking of Joyce*, edited by Liberato Santoro-Brienza. Dublin: University College Dublin Press, 1998.

Fogarty, Anne, and Timothy Martin, eds. *Joyce on the Threshold*. Gainesville: University Press of Florida, 2005.

Forbes, Shannon. "Joyce's 'Saucebox': Milly Bloom's Portrait of Modern Feminine Adolescence." In *Women's Transition from Victorian to*

Contemporary Identity as Portrayed in the Modern Novel. Lewiston: Edwin Mellen Press, 2006.

Ford, Jane M. *Patriarchy and Incest from Shakespeare to Joyce.* Gainesville: University Press of Florida, 1998.

Gabler, Hans Walter. *The Rocky Road to Ulysses.* Dublin: National Library of Ireland, 2005.

Gillespie, Gerald. *Proust, Mann, Joyce in the Modernist Context.* Washington, D.C.: Catholic University of America Press, 2003.

Gillespie, Michael Patrick, and A. Nicholas Fargnoli, ed. *Ulysses in Critical Perspective.* Gainesville: University Press of Florida, 2006.

Gordon, John. *Almosting It: Joyce's Realism.* Dublin: The National Library Ireland, 2004.

———. *Joyce and Reality: The Empirical Strikes Back.* Syracuse, N.Y.: Syracuse University Press, 2004.

Hart, Clive. "James Joyce's Sentimentality." *James Joyce Quarterly* 41, nos. 1–2 (Fall 2003–Winter 2004): 26–36.

In-Between: Essays and Studies in Literary Criticism 12, nos. 1–2 (March–September 2003). Special issue on James Joyce.

Johnsen, William A. *Violence and Modernism: Ibsen, Joyce, and Woolf.* Gainesville: University Press of Florida, 2003.

Knowles, Sebastian D. G. *The Dublin Helix: The Life of Language in Joyce's Ulysses.* Gainesville: University Press of Florida, 2001.

Laman, Barbara. *James Joyce and German Theory: The Romantic School and All That.* Madison, N.J.: Fairleigh Dickinson University Press; Cranbury, N.J.: Associated University Presses, 2004.

Latham, Sean. *Joyce's Modernism.* Dublin: National Library of Ireland, 2005.

Levitt, Morton P., ed. *Joyce and the Joyceans.* Syracuse, N.Y.: Syracuse University Press, 2002.

McCarthy, Patrick A. *Joyce, Family, Finnegans Wake.* Dublin: National Library of Ireland, 2005.

McGee, Patrick. *Joyce beyond Marx: History and Desire in Ulysses and Finnegans Wake.*

Murphy, Sean P. *James Joyce and Victims: Reading the Logic of Exclusion.* Madison, N.J.: Fairleigh Dickinson University Press; London; Cranbury, N.J.: Associated University Presses, 2003.

Nolan, Emer. "Joyce, the Celtic Revival and Irish Modernism." *James Joyce Journal* 10, no. 2 (Winter 2004): 51–72.

Pierce, David. *Reading Joyce*. Harlow, England; New York: Pearson Longman, 2008.

Potts, Willard. *Joyce and the Two Irelands*. Austin: University of Texas Press, 2000.

Power, Mary, and Ulrich Schneider, ed. *New Perspectives on Dubliners*. Amsterdam; Atlanta: Rodopi, 1997.

Ruggieri, Franca, ed. *Classic Joyce*. Rome, Italy: Bulzoni, 1999.

Schwarze, Tracey Teets. *Joyce and the Victorians*. Gainesville: University Press of Florida, 2002.

Sicari, Stephen. *Joyce's Modernist Allegory: Ulysses and the History of the Novel*. Columbia: University of South Carolina Press, 2001.

Spurr, David. *Joyce and the Scene of Modernity*. Gainesville: University Press of Florida, 2002.

Sultan, Stanley. *Joyce's Metamorphosis*. Gainesville: University Press of Florida, 2001.

Ungar, Andras. *Joyce's Ulysses as National Epic: Epic Mimesis and the Political History of the Nation State*. Gainesville: University Press of Florida, 2002.

Voyiatzaki, Evi. *The Body in the Text: James Joyce's Ulysses and the Modern Greek Novel*. Lanham, Md.: Lexington Books, 2002.

Acknowledgments

Derek Attridge, "Unpacking the Portmanteau; or, Who's Afraid of *Finnegans Wake?*" From *Peculiar Language: Literature as Difference from the Renaissance to James Joyce.* Copyright © 1988, 2004 by Derek Attridge. Reproduced by permission of Taylor & Francis Books UK.

Richard Poirier, "The Pater of Joyce and Eliot." From *Addressing Frank Kermode: Essays in Criticism and Interpretation,* edited by Margaret Tudeau-Clayton and Martin Warner. © 1991 by Richard Poirier. Reprinted with permission.

Weldon Thornton, "The Structures." From *The Antimodernism of Joyce's* A Portrait of the Artist as a Young Man. © 1994 by Syracuse University Press. Reprinted with permission.

David Leon Higdon, "Gendered Discourse and the Structure of Joyce's 'The Dead.'" From *ReJoycing: New Readings of* Dubliners, edited by Roma M. Bollettieri Bosinelli and Harold F. Mosher, Jr. © 1998 by the University Press of Kentucky. Reprinted with permission.

Klaus Reichert, "Shakespeare and Joyce: Myriadminded Men." From *Shakespeare and the Twentieth Century.* © 1998 by Associated University Presses. Reprinted with permission.

Roy K. Gottfried, "'The Comic Irishman in the Bench Behind': The Portrait with Two Heads." From *Joyce's Comic Portrait.* © 2000 by and reprinted courtesy of the University Press of Florida.

Margaret McBride, "The Ineluctable Modality: Stephen's Quest for Immortality." From Ulysses *and the Metamorphosis of Stephen Dedalus.* © 2001 by Associated University Presses. Reprinted with permission.

Keri Elizabeth Ames, "The Rebirth of Heroism from Homer's *Odyssey* to Joyce's *Ulysses.*" From *Twenty-First Joyce.* © 2004 by Ellen Carol Jones and Morris Beja. Reprinted courtesy of the University Press of Florida.

Jennifer Margaret Fraser, "Intertextual Sirens." From *Rite of Passage in the Narratives of Dante and Joyce.* © 2002 by Jennifer Margaret Fraser. Reprinted courtesy of the University Press of Florida.

Neil Murphy, "James Joyce's *Dubliners* and Modernist Doubt: The Making of a Tradition." From *A New & Complex Sensation: Essays on Joyce's* Dubliners, edited by Oona Frawley. © 2004 by the Lilliput Press and Neil Murphy. Reprinted with permission.

Vicki Mahaffey, "Love, Race, and *Exiles:* The Bleak Side of *Ulysses.*" From *Joyce Studies Annual,* Winter 2007. © 2007 by Fordham University Press. Reprinted with permission.

Margot Norris, "Possible Worlds Theory and the Fantasy Universe of *Finnegans Wake.*" From *James Joyce Quarterly* 44, no. 3, Spring 2007. © 2007 by the University of Tulsa. Reprinted with permission.

Every effort has been made to contact the owners of copyrighted material and secure copyright permission. Articles appearing in this volume generally appear much as they did in their original publication with few or no editorial changes. In some cases, foreign language text has been removed from the original essay. Those interested in locating the original source will find the information cited above.

Index